FREAK OUT!
My Life with Frank Zappa

FREAK OUT!
My Life with Frank Zappa

Pauline Butcher

Plexus, London

All rights reserved including the right of
reproduction in whole or in part in any form
Copyright © 2011 by Pauline Butcher
Published by Plexus Publishing Limited
25 Mallinson Road
London SW11 1BW
www.plexusbooks.com

British Library Cataloguing in Publication Data
A catalogue record for this book is available from the British Library

ISBN-13: 978-0-85965-479-1

Cover photo by Ed Caraeff
Cover and book design by Coco Wake-Porter
Printed in Great Britain by Bell & Bain Ltd.

*This memoir would not have been possible
had my mother not kept my letters for forty years,
and I dedicate this book to her.*

ACKNOWLEDGEMENTS

I would like to thank my agent, Laura Susijn, for believing in me; James Friel, for setting me on the right path; Tom Branton, for his kind and thoughtful edits; my husband, Peter Bird, for making it possible; our son, Damian Bird, for his endless encouragement; and Sandra Wake, for taking a chance.

PART ONE

1

The day I met Frank Zappa began like every other day over the previous five years. Had I realised how momentous it would be, I might have clipped my dangly earrings to my ears with more care, raced into London with greater speed and answered the phone at the office more eagerly. But on that dull, drizzly August afternoon in 1967, I had no idea.

I earned ten shillings an hour at a printer in Dover Street. Not a printer with huge machinery and hordes of men, but a large office space with golf-ball typewriters and twenty girls seated in squares of four. We typed menus, programmes, adverts, film scripts and sometimes novels by hopeful writers. At the end of the room, behind a glass partition, two boys worked enormous photocopiers.

But we girls were not mere typists, not at all. We ran around town with portable typewriters and notebooks to hotels or private homes. Our clients could be very important people indeed. Why, only the week before, I'd worked for the grandson of Haile Selassie, the Emperor of Ethiopia. When he'd fallen down drunk in his toilet I'd called the concierge because I thought he was dead. And Margaret, Duchess of Argyll, who suffered agonies of embarrassment in her divorce case. Nude photographs of her wrapped round a series of aristocrats had been splashed across the tabloids. She said to me, 'Miss Butcher, you don't spell telegram with "mme" on the end,' but I must have been brain-dead that day because I insisted, 'Oh, no, you're thinking of the American version.' Perhaps because she was so traumatised, she believed me.

Noisy, almost deafening, Forum Secretarial Services was owned and run by Miss Bee and her diminutive husband, Dr Lederer, both of whom had fled the Hungarian Revolution in 1956. 'Vee started in a basement in Duke's Yard vith nothing – a paraffin heater and coffee pot. Darling, vee nearly starved to death.

But now look vhere vee live – on Park Lane!'

Miss Bee, short and full-bosomed, wore a fine gold chain round her ankle, so risqué to us English girls. She did care for us but if we stopped typing to gossip, she would rap our knuckles.

On that particular day, 16 August, she was at the hairdressers, so when the telephone rang I answered it. The concierge said, 'Royal Garden Hotel here. We have a client who wants a typist at six-thirty.'

'Hold on.' I cupped the receiver and called out for offers but the other girls shook their heads. Since *I'd* taken the call, *I* would have to go.

'All right,' I said into the receiver. 'Miss Butcher will come.'

'It's for Mr Zappa. Room 412.'

Mr Zappa? How dull that sounded! Sometimes we worked for film stars like Gregory Peck – whose teenage son, strangely, I found more seductive than his famous father. Other illustrious clients included Marcel Marceau, the mime artist, and glamorous politicians from Buenos Aires or Israel, but most of our clients were top executives from global conglomerates and I reckoned that Mr Zappa must be one of those. The name Zappa gave the impression of a foreign man, fat and bald.

In slow motion, I gathered up my portable typewriter, pushed paper, carbons, Tipp-Ex, pens and pencils into my briefcase, stomped down the stairs past the tailor on the ground floor and into the cool summer air, where I half-heartedly hailed a taxi. As we crawled through the traffic of Knightsbridge and on into Kensington, even the stylish windows of Harrods displaying the latest craze for paisley failed to excite my attention.

I was not unhappy, but life was dull. Somewhere along the way, I seemed to have missed my turning, a turning that had pointed to journalism, my dream job. I'd thought of applying to music papers because they were easier to break into than serious ones, but music seemed too narrow for my broad interests. I'd posed the question to Tom Mangold, a journalist I'd met at a party. When I told him I was twenty-one, he said, 'You're too old. Journalists without a degree start on local newspapers at sixteen,' and right there I allowed him to demolish my dream.

Not beautiful enough to make it big in modelling – 'Your face is too long and thin, your eyes turn down, they should turn up,' and I certainly wasn't Jean Shrimpton with her pert little nose – I'd settled for minor catwalk bookings (£25 an hour), teaching modelling (one guinea an hour), and supplementing this with secretarial work. After five years of the same routine with no knight in shining armour having come to my rescue, I'd decided to save hard. The next year, with sufficient money, I would travel. I was not sure where – it was the vaguest of plans.

The taxi driver broke into my reverie. 'Got a hot date?'

'No, working unfortunately.'

'I could give you a good time.'

'Oh, go on, I bet you've got six kids at home.'

'*Seven! And* counting.'

I laughed and when I swung through the circular door and crossed the marbled lobby toward the lifts, I was still smiling.

A tall, handsome black man with features like Sidney Poitier and a small beard on his chin watched me approach. He wore a dark suit and tie and a beige cashmere coat slung casually over his shoulders. We stepped into the lift together: I pressed the fourth-floor button; he pressed the fifth. My hair was cut by Vidal Sassoon in a Faye-Dunaway-*Bonny-and-Clyde* style, and when the stranger appraised me up and down – admiring my flat, white calf-length boots and green dress with its little white collar – and remarked, 'Wow, even in California girls don't wear skirts *that* short,' I was ready to flirt. 'Well this is London. In fashion, we lead the world.'

'And I'm from Hollywood,' he said, 'In entertainment *we* lead the world.'

'You're in films?'

'Music. Rock'n'roll.'

'Oh, well.' I rummaged in my bag and handed him a blue-floral printed card. 'Give me a call if you want typing done. I do shorthand too.' I stepped backwards from the lift.

'I sure will, Par-leen,' he called, waving and peering for a last look as the lift doors closed.

What a pity I wasn't working for him. Still, he'd cheered me up and I trotted along the corridor to Room 412, set my cases on the floor, and knocked.

Nothing prepared me for the figure that opened the door.

Squiggly, ink-black curls fell below his shoulders. He had a long, thin face with a thick, drooping moustache and an extra tuft under his bottom lip. He wore an orange t-shirt and pink trousers over the skinniest of bodies. I blurted out, 'Oh, I'm sorry, I've come to the wrong room.'

'Par-leen Butcher?' he said in a deep, American drawl.

'Yes. Is Mr Zappa here?'

He held out a straight arm and I stood there, astonished. *This* was Mr Zappa? Undeniably, he had a Mediterranean air with his swarthy skin and dark eyes that held mine in a bemused gaze. We shook hands and he said, 'Come on in.' He pressed his back against the door as I picked up my bags and brushed past. He kept nodding confusedly, as if he'd expected a fifty-five-year-old with flat shoes and Lisle stockings.

Inside, male bodies lolled over orange-striped sofas and chairs. Mr Zappa introduced me to Herb Cohen, his manager, an English journalist wearing a jacket and no tie whose name I didn't get, and the rest, in colourful t-shirts and jeans, were a blur. I said 'Hello' to the room in general. They nodded, staring beyond me, uninterested. I looked to Mr Zappa for support but he'd disappeared to the bedroom. I was not dismayed. I normally worked in hotel bedrooms; few businessmen could afford a suite.

On the desk, a reel-to-reel tape recorder waited. As I took my typewriter out of its case, Mr Zappa said, 'What I want you to do is type the lyrics from the tape. I need them by tomorrow.'

He pressed the play button to check the machine worked properly. Strange noises resonated from it. I was in for a long night.

A loud knock at the bedroom door distracted us and in came the good-looking man from the lift. 'I went to the wrong floor,' he said, and then he saw me and exclaimed, 'Par-leen, you're working for Frank, godammit? Frank, how come you get the best-looking secretaries?'

Frank Zappa looked surprised, so I said, 'We met in the lift.'

Hearty greetings and back-slapping followed. Tom Wilson, Mr Zappa's record producer, had just arrived, it seemed, after a delayed flight. Mr Zappa invited him through to the sitting room to meet the others but Tom Wilson hung back and said to me confidentially, 'That guy is a musical genius. Stick by him and you'll go far.'

When Mr Zappa returned, I asked him, 'Should I know who you are? Are you famous?'

I heard chortles from the loll-abouts in the other room. 'A few people in London know who we are,' he said modestly. 'Ever seen this?'

He handed me the sleeve of an LP, *Freak Out*; a fuzzy coloured photograph of five men. The middle one, despite the stylised distortion, was unmistakeably Mr Zappa.

'The Mothers of Invention?' I read aloud. What an odd name for a band.

'That's us,' he said. 'The ugly guys.'

Trying to be nice, I said, 'Oh, I wouldn't say that.'

He dismissed my comment with a wave. 'I choose all the people in my band for their ugliness. Everyone else is doing the pretty thing. We make money from being ugly 'cause that's how society is, *ugly*.'

I caught his eye and he smiled. Yes, he had a beaky nose in a narrow face, but the high forehead, heavy eyebrows and thick moustache made him oddly handsome. And although he looked like no other living creature I'd seen, in peacock colours and with hair like Charles I, I found his quiet manner arresting. It showed in his direct and concentrated gaze and his very low voice, articulating each word distinctly. I couldn't wait to tell the girls at the office. They'd be so cross they didn't take the call.

He handed me a second album, *Absolutely Free*. This time, Mr Zappa's stern expression filled the sleeve while the other Mothers peeped up from the bottom edge. Inside, the blurb asked fans to send one dollar for a copy of the lyrics. Here in London, the *International Times,* an underground newspaper I never read, agreed to print the lyrics for free. Transcribing them was my task.

While Mr Zappa checked I was comfortable and brought me coffee – kindly gestures almost unheard of in clients – I pressed the play button and gobbledygook burst out. As he disappeared through the door, I called out, 'Mr Zappa!'

He stepped backwards. 'A-huh?'

'Is this in English?'

He curled one side of his mouth in a wry smile. Pleased that he understood my humour, I smiled back cheekily. He gave me one last cool appraisal, and then vanished to join the others. I stared after him, wanting him to stay and talk more.

The first track was 'Plastic People'. Plastic people?

The cool, deep tones of Mr Zappa's voice introduced the President of the United States and I started typing. But then what did he say? Was it *'he had sex'* or *'he's been sick'*? Neither made sense. I typed on. More gobbledygook followed and I had to play it repeatedly. Why couldn't this be like the Beatles or the Rolling Stones, easy lyrics with words I recognised? I struggled on.

The next track, 'Duke of Prunes', created more confusion. It had humour and satire, which made me smile, but why the wailing and orchestral instruments changing the beat every which way? The discordant sounds grated on my ears. Then, thankfully, in the middle came a long, jazzy, rhythmic big-band section and, in no time at all, my toes tapped and I leaned back in the chair to let the sounds wash over me. I liked them. This man had talent.

Through the door, I could hear the clink of glasses and subdued chatter. As I strained my ears, the odd phrase pierced through, *'Albert Hall', 'Speakeasy',* *'Suzy Creamcheese'*. How wonderful to be a pop musician, to create your own chaos and pay other people to make sense of it.

The lyrics started up again: stuff about vegetables on a train. I didn't get it.

The clock on the desk said nine o'clock and my neck ached. Making corrections on two carbon copies each time I changed my mind created messy copy and took too long. Better to transcribe everything into shorthand first and type it at the office the next day. Besides, it would give me an excuse to meet this enigmatic man again. I popped my head through the door.

'Mr Zappa?'

He jumped from the sofa to join me and dropped into the easy chair by my desk.

'Let's not be formal here, Pauline, you can call me Frank.'

I told him I would return with the typed copy the next afternoon. 'In the morning, I'm teaching.'

'You're a teacher?'

'Just modelling. I teach modelling.'

'How did Pauline Butcher become a modelling teacher?'

His curiosity amazed me. How often had men I'd worked for over the past five years dismissed me out of hand? Yet this man showed a keen personal interest. 'Oh! I took a modelling course and when I graduated, the owner of the school asked me to help teach the other girls. So, all of a sudden I had three jobs, modelling, teaching modelling and part-time secretarial work. Some days I rush around and do all three.'

I had never met a man who listened so closely and attentively and watched me with steady, enquiring eyes. I liked that.

'I really wanted to go to university, but my parents dragged me to America during my O-level exams. Now I regret not going back to school to re-sit them because it meant I missed out and now it's too late.'

Frank Zappa shook his head. 'Don't fret yourself. Education can fuck you up.'

For someone like me, whose most ferocious swear word was 'schizzle', this use of the f-word made my eyes blink. No one I knew ever used such a word.

And could he be serious? Did he really admonish university education, something that I revered like the Holy Grail? And even if education could mess you up, surely *no* education would mess you up even more? I hurried on, 'Yes, but in England if you're a girl and you don't have a degree, the only job you can get is secretarial work, and I really regret not having a degree.'

'So? Go to the library and teach yourself.'

'Well, I do. I read widely and I watch educational programmes on television.'

He tapped a cigarette from his Winston pack and placed it between his lips. No English person would dream of lighting up without offering one to the other person first. It was almost a crime not to do so. After the earlier courtesies, I found this odd.

He began to tell me about *his* education, how his father had moved from job to job, trailing his family through Maryland, Florida and California. 'I didn't enjoy it,' he said. 'By the time I was fifteen, I'd enrolled in six different high schools. Do you have any idea what effect that had? Not a lot of fun when you're suffering with acne. It makes it kinda hard to make friends.'

No other man I'd worked for had talked so personally. It made me feel valued. I didn't flatter myself that I was special, but he did seem to like me.

Beyond the door in the sitting room, we heard shuffling and repeated goodbyes. I called out, 'Hang on, I'm coming.' Frank called back, 'That's a good title for a song,' and everyone laughed. How good to be the source of his witticism; I grew another two inches with pride. Frank continued the jokey mood when he shook my hand in a mock, formal farewell, a wry smile on his lips. Mirroring his mockery, I bobbed a little curtsey. Despite his weird moustache, the unruly tangle of his hair and mismatched clothes, there was something compelling about him, something different from any man I'd ever met. I was hooked.

2

The next morning, I stroked on layers of mascara, worried that Frank Zappa might find mistakes in my work; I hoped to distract him with my appearance. On my bed lay the Correge-inspired mini, a white knit with one bold red stripe off-centre from shoulder to hem and a black stripe across the bust, but that would mean wearing the white boots again – not imaginative. I decided on the Biba denim suit with low hipster trousers and flared bottoms to enhance my legs, the jacket tight at the waist to emphasise my slimness, and a narrow satin shirt underneath – a business look, yet stylish enough for modelling class.

In the kitchen, I dropped a slice of white bread into the toaster and flicked on the kettle, feeling the need to hurry. My mother appeared in the doorway, clearly annoyed I'd taken over her role. I stepped aside so she could make my tea and butter my toast.

'*You* were late last night.'

'I worked for a pop star. Strange-looking man.'

'Will you stop pushing that toast down your throat? I don't know why you don't get indigestion.'

I was the tenth child, the tenth child of eleven, the only child christened with one first name, Pauline. On the birth certificates of the other ten, including my youngest sister Carole's, there are two Christian names. Carole was the eleventh child, Carole Joyce. Of the eleven children, only three remained: Pat, Carole and me, tied to my mother's apron strings, still conditioned by her strong, moral values. Carole often rebelled; I conceded; she stamped and yelled; I submitted – Miss Goody-Two-Shoes.

The radio droned in the background, something about anti-Vietnam demonstrations.

'Isn't it all right, you know,' my mother said, 'those young boys out there fighting for us? What good do these damned people think they're doing? Sitting on pavements? It's all wrong.'

I murmured agreement, buying my mother's conservative views as I did most of her beliefs. But I was not a lapdog, not entirely. Secretly, I'd considered dying my hair green, pictured gasps on the train, the flutter of attention in discos – but the wrath of my diminutive mother stamping her feet, eyes wide like saucers, held me in check. I was completely fearless when talking to a hall full of students about a career in modelling or travelling alone late at night on the tube in London, but I lived in fear of my mother's rage. Living at home and paying little rent, my laundry and food provided, I felt it my duty to toe the family line.

My mother was five feet tall and when I stood up, I tucked her under my arm. 'What are you doing down there?' I asked, our constant joke, and as usual she pushed me away in mock annoyance. 'Get away with you.'

'How do I look?' I asked twirling in a circle, though I knew the answer before she spoke. 'Oh, go on. Who's going to look at you?'

Who's going to look at you? My mother's lament, an attempt to protect me from disappointment. I usually accepted her remark without comment, but maybe because a record producer *and* a pop star had paid attention the previous night, my confidence grew and I retorted, 'Someone might.' In fact, I relied on Frank Zappa doing just that.

I stooped down and pecked her on the cheek, picked up my modelling bag, dashed out the door and jumped into my brand-new maroon Mini parked in the short drive. That car was my joy, bought from my labours, although how much I earned was a secret I kept from my dear father, a retired carpenter who would bring me cups of tea in bed. I was proud of what he'd accomplished – supporting eleven children against the odds and forced to toil all his life on building sites, high up on planks with no safety net, dangerous work that left him skeletally thin. Now I earned more in a week than he had made in a month simply from prancing up and down a catwalk and bashing a typewriter.

After the slow slog from Twickenham into London, I left the car in Hyde Park in a free-parking zone. Then a taxi whisked me to the London School of Modelling just off Bond Street.

Twenty-five girls in that Wednesday class sat waiting in two lines in front of mirrored walls either side of the raised catwalk. They leaned forward eagerly, ready to learn how to become the next top model, but most of them were short and fat. Gordon Eden-Wheen, the owner, did not care that their chances rated zero. He would take their £70 fee and in return, they learned to apply make-up that would never see a professional camera, and walk with grace that only their families would notice.

I had no conscience about this either, aware I'd become an accomplice in a cynical business, a means of making a living. In any case, occasionally, a knock-out girl would walk through the door, a natural star, someone like Sarah, a Jean Simmons lookalike with doe eyes, perfect cheekbones and a chiselled jaw-line, so beautiful the other girls couldn't help but stare. A quick glance round the room told me she was not among them, maybe staying away in protest after our little debacle.

The previous week, she'd asked me to join her for dinner with Billy Wilder, director of the film *Some Like It Hot*. She was only seventeen and I hardly knew her but, intrigued, I'd agreed to go because although I worked as a model, I never fell in with the smart set and my life was not glamorous. Here was a chance for some glitz.

We joined the famous director and his two overweight friends in a sumptuous suite at the Dorchester Hotel where we sat round a large table and I cut through the most delicious filet steak I'd ever tasted. The movie moguls, all in their sixties, talked about *Blow Up*, the latest sensational film from England, a film none of them seemed to understand, its success bewildering them.

'Those clowns at the beginning, what the hell was that all about?' one of them grumbled.

'They were symbolic,' I suggested, 'of what is real and not real.'

Oh, all right, hardly profound, but you'd have thought I'd told them to stand on their heads judging by the contemptuous looks they gave me. I glanced at Sarah, who sat straight and serene. She had grasped that we two girls were adornments.

After the meal, the moguls withdrew to the bedroom, an exotic room with blue and gold drapes, subdued lighting and a four-poster bed raised on a platform. Two of the men dropped into lavish armchairs while the one with the paunch threw himself onto the bed. He called out, 'Come on in, girls. Make yourselves comfortable.'

Immediately on my guard, I hovered in the doorway. 'Excuse me?'

'Come on in,' he beckoned kindly, 'get your clothes off.'

All three of them gazed at me expectantly and my hackles rose. Obviously, we'd walked into a lair of vultures, though Sarah was now perched prettily on the edge of the bed. I snapped, 'We're not taking our clothes off.'

'What did she say?' he asked, as if I was talking Japanese.

'Sarah, I think we should go.'

She stood up, hesitating while the guy with the bald head got out of his chair and snarled, 'Are you kidding?'

'No, I'm not,' I protested and metamorphosed into my mother, hands on hips.

'Either get undressed – or get out,' he shouted, waving his arms. 'Who is this dumb broad?'

Boiling with indignation, I grabbed a bewildered-looking Sarah and pulled her to the door, convinced she would see me as some kind of saviour. But, in the lift, tears dribbled down her face. 'Oh, Pauline, they promised me a part in their film. Now you've ruined it.'

I stared at her speechless while she blew her nose into a handkerchief. When the lift opened, she stalked across the lobby and vanished through the circular door.

And now, here today, no Sarah.

In the lesson, we twirled coats, jackets and shawls with drama and, because there were twenty-five of them, it took two hours of twisting and folding before they finally got it. 'Next week,' I told them, 'we'll practise the catwalk,' which brought on great titters of relief.

At last, I could speed down Bond Street to Forum to finish Frank Zappa's lyrics. Always careful with the presentation, I found this no easy task as I struggled with the unintelligible words. Still, it was a more exciting job than oil shipments or sugar-cane prices. When it was done, I was so eager I almost threw myself in front of the taxi.

At the hotel Herb Cohen, Frank's manager, opened the door. Inside, Frank, dressed in plain jeans and yellow t-shirt, his hair pulled back in a band that revealed deep, heavy sideburns, was talking to three men in suits. He turned to greet me with a look of appreciation, his eyes sweeping from brow to toe.

Once again, he and I adjourned to the bedroom and once again he brought me coffee. We lit up cigarettes; a Rothman for me, a Winston for him. He plumped up the pillows on the bed and leaned back to read my typescript while I sat on the easy chair by the window, placed my own copy on my knees and anxiously awaited his verdict. Below, in Hyde Park, I watched a teenage girl run from a boy until she turned and fell into his arms.

After a few moments, I heard a quiet wheeze. I looked over. Frank, agape and bouncing on the bed, banged his knees, threw back his head and laughed so loudly the hum of voices in the next room suddenly ceased. 'Oh, man, this is funnier than the original.'

Feeling a little encouraged, I said, 'I didn't understand a lot of it so I made it up.'

'A baby doll makes a filthy poo?'

'What should it be?'

'A case of airplane glue.'

'Oh!' I ruffled through my copy searching for the place and said rather sheepishly, 'I expect there'll be more,' but he was already shaking the pages.

'Based on this, you should be writing your own.'

Startled by his compliment, I said, 'I wish I could,' and then, feeling emboldened, added, 'but if I did, I'd make them less rude.'

'*Rude?*'

'I mean, "Brown Shoes Don't Make It" is pretty strong stuff to put on a record.'

'You think so? That's one of our most popular songs.'

I laughed. 'Probably because it *is* so rude.'

He looked at me indulgently. 'Your perception, Pauline, tells me more about you than it does about the song.'

A little knocked back, I said with as much authority as I could, 'I can't be the only person who's said it. You must admit, these lyrics are hardly edifying. All right, if they're not rude, then at least licentious.'

'Not to our audience, they're not.'

Losing the argument but determined to stand my ground, I leafed through the pages, trying to find the right spot. I read aloud lines about a thirteen-year-old girl and a middle-aged man who wears brown shoes. They make out on the White House lawn and play at 'father and daughter'. I looked up to get Frank's reaction but his face gazed back at me, a blank.

'It's not nice,' I said.

'Not *nice?*'

'No.'

The smile disappeared. 'If you want to hear nice little tunes with empty little words, there are plenty of other people that will write that for ya. I have no inclination to do it. There's no reason to crowd that particular market place.'

Not wanting to lose his good will, I acquiesced. 'I suppose if you sell enough records, you don't need to worry what people think.'

'We sell enough. We have a niche market despite the radio stations refusing to play our music and despite what the record company has tried to do.'

'But surely you're in business to make money, just like everybody else. Why are you deliberately damning your chances writing songs that disc jockeys refuse to play?'

He didn't answer and looked sour, slightly cross, and I suppose I should have stopped there but, fired up, I pressed on. 'Maybe your fans are older than me, more worldly-wise.'

'Not at all.'

'Well, how old are they?'

With a bored tone, he said, 'Anywhere between thirteen and forty-five, somewhere around there.'

'Thirteen! As young as that! Well, if you don't mind my saying so, I don't think thirteen-year-olds should hear this.' I sounded like my mother, but I couldn't help it, the words just tumbled out.

'Oh, I don't know,' he said. 'You really have to argue with a thirteen-year-old about that. If it makes them happy, somebody's gotta take their fancy. As far as

I'm aware, they don't object.'

'Yes, but their parents might.'

He waved his hand in disagreement. 'People who buy our records are not troubled by what their parents think. Generally, we seem to thrive where there's dissent between generations because we tend to – pep things up.' He seemed pleased with this idea and, to my relief, a little smile appeared under his moustache.

His willingness to engage me in debate both surprised and pleased me, his readiness to accept my challenges head on and with such good will astounded me even more. No other man had given my views a moment's heed and I felt a surge of gratitude and warmth. I barged on. 'You are in danger of corrupting a whole generation's mind.'

'You think so?'

'I do.'

He shook his head. 'Think about it. Most of the songs that radios broadcast are songs about love. All we hear on the radio is love, so if the lyrics *were* having an influence what would we have here? Fantasy-land. But we don't.'

'But most people do believe in love, don't they? So you *could* blame the songs, maybe they *do* have an influence.'

He studied me quizzically through wisps of smoke. Well, at least he wasn't throwing me out. Heartened, I hurried on. 'This line.' I pointed to another section of the song about making out on the White House lawn. I read it aloud, '"*Smother my daughter in chocolate syrup and strap her on again.*" Honestly, I think that's immoral.'

'The way you read it, with your accent, it does sound kind of bizarre.'

And so the dogged back and forth continued: the more I scolded, the more he seemed to enjoy the game. I felt heady, each challenge spurring me on to see how far I could go. 'Are you suggesting, metaphorically, that the President of the United States, President Johnson, is having it away with young girls?'

This remark finally impelled him to jump from the bed and pound the stub of his cigarette into the ashtray. 'No. I'm not pointing the finger at any one person in particular, just in general, the assholes who run our governments.'

Oh, phooey, I thought, dismissing his words. Politicians did their best and we should commend them. I changed tack. 'I showed your lyrics to a girl at work. She thinks this song is about incest.'

His eyebrows went up and down. 'Does she have big tits?'

I laughed, 'No-o-o-o.'

He settled on the edge of the bed close to me and I felt flushed and breathless, like I'd run a hundred-yard dash. He nodded to my notebook on the table and said gently, 'Take this down.' He crossed his legs and leaned one elbow on his knee, his cigarette poised while he collected his thoughts. Presumably, because of my puzzlement with some of the lyrics, he felt compelled to dictate an explanation for each of the tracks.

'"Plastic People" are the insincere assholes who run almost everybody's country. "Vegetables" are people who are inactive in a society and who do not live up to their responsibilities. "The Duke of Prunes" is a surrealistic love song and the words, *"prune me, cheese me,"* are transmuted from the basic "fuck me, suck me, till my eyes roll back baby."'

Not having written these swear words in shorthand before, I hesitated over the strokes, quickly adding vowel signs to ensure no misreadings later. He raced on, clearly enjoying himself, hugging one bare foot over his knee. '"Brown Shoes Don't Make It" is a song about the unfortunate people who manufacture inequitable laws and ordinances, perhaps unaware of the fact that the restrictions they place on the young people in a society are the result of their own sexual frustrations. Dirty old men have no business running your country.'

I signalled for him to let me catch up and he waited, his eyes glued to my pen's swirls and circles speeding across the page.

'"Uncle Bernie's Farm" is a song about ugly toys and the people who make them. Implied here is the possibility that the people who buy ugly toys might be as ugly as the toys themselves.'

I threw him a disapproving look – was everyone to be condemned?

'"Son of Suzy Creamcheese" is a stirring saga of a young groupie. Her actions are motivated by a desire to be "in" at all times. Hence the drug abuse – blowing her mind on too much Kool-Aid.' He paused. 'That's acid, Pauline. Okay?'

I nodded.

'And stealing her boyfriend's *stash,* stash is a hidden supply of drugs. Put that in parentheses.'

He'd reached the end and stretched his arms above his head.

Though I disliked his sweeping generalisations, I acknowledged his boldness in raising these issues and was impressed by his businesslike approach, intelligence and lucidity. If not an intellectual, he appeared miles more astute and clever than those pop stars I'd seen on TV. All right, so John Lennon and Paul McCartney rattled off witty and sharp retorts in interviews, but this man spouted knowledge and erudition. Who'd have thought that the clownish apparition who greeted me at the door only yesterday could dictate so fluently, be so deadly serious?

While I prepared to transcribe my notes, Frank began reading through the rest of the lyrics, making corrections. It was ten-thirty when I pulled the last sheet out of the typewriter and handed him the bill.

As he helped me on with my jacket, he said, 'Some of us are going to the Speakeasy real soon. How would you like to be my *date?*' His eyebrows went up and down in a mock expression of a come-on. I tried to arrange my face to hide my keenness, how chuffed I felt. He could choose from a harem of women: London was full of beautiful girls.

In the foyer, we discussed whether to go in my car but decided on a taxi. As we spread out in the spacious seats, I told him about my Mini. 'I bought it brand new. It cost over £500 and the first day, a man walking with a milk cart came round the corner and smashed straight into my passenger door. Walked right into it!'

'A milk cart?'

I laughed. 'Yes. It was not funny.'

A line of people queued along Margaret Street and around the corner to Oxford Circus, but someone ushered us straight down the stairs into the black interior, past the long, wooden bar to our table at the back by the restaurant, a table laid with a red-check tablecloth. Here the music blasted my ears a little less, but we still shouted our orders to the waiter: whisky on the rocks for Frank, and another with water for me.

As my eyes adjusted to the darkness, I scanned the scene and noticed people at the tables in front of us turning and nudging each other, careful not to point directly, 'No, don't look now, but who's that?' I wanted to tell them, 'He may look zany, weird and slightly mad, but in reality, he's stable, erudite.'

On the stage, at the far end, a man unravelled microphone cords while speakers blared out the Rolling Stones' 'Let's Spend the Night Together'. On the small dance-floor, boys with Beatle haircuts gyrated next to Patti Boyd lookalikes. Procol Harum's 'Whiter Shade of Pale' came on and Frank asked me to dance. Strangely, everyone else sat down and we were alone, as if performing some kind of cabaret. Could it be the Charles I hairstyle – unusually long by London standards – or maybe his floor-length coat that made every head turn? I caught words passing down the line, 'That's Frank Zappa.'

He held me close and I was blushing but proud. Then he said in my ear, 'You wanna do something really strange?' and before I could answer he began some peculiar knee bends, hops and skips, like a Russian. I was not the best dancer in the world, but I did know the basic steps. *This* I did not know. Was it the tango? He pressed our cheeks together and stretched my right arm out, pulling it high and low. Did he deliberately want to act the fool, to live up to his reputation for the bizarre? I was used to attention on the catwalk, but under this excruciating spotlight, I became rigid with embarrassment. Giggling and trying to hide my face, I clung on while Frank, a strange little smile on his lips, upped the tempo of jumps and pirouettes for the growing audience. I caught a glimpse of sniggers behind cupped hands, astonished stares. At last, the final chords of the record faded away and with relief, I stumbled back to the table giddy from so many twirls.

Still wearing his coat, Frank dropped beside me. Out of the gloom a figure with a mop of hair and long sideburns appeared. 'Frank, Frank, great to see you, man.'

Whoever this was, he pulled up a chair.

Frank turned to me, 'Pauline, Eric Clapton. Eric, this is Pauline Butcher.'

I shook his hand, and leaning forward like a benevolent music teacher, asked, 'And what do you play?'

His eyes slithered to Frank, then back at me. He came close to my face and said confidentially, 'I play the guitar.'

'That's nice,' I said.

An awkward momentary silence followed while Frank coughed and Eric shifted in his chair. Clearly I'd said the wrong thing. I delved into my patchwork bag on the floor searching for cigarettes, found them and shoved them back to the bottom, keeping my head down. I could hear Eric telling Frank about his forthcoming gig at the Fillmore in San Francisco. Frank warned him about flower-power. 'If people try to put beads round my neck, I tell them to fuck off.'

Eric asked Frank to introduce their band shortly and Frank agreed. Then he disappeared into the murky gloom.

Frank turned to me as I re-surfaced. 'Where have you been hiding, Pauline? Don't you know who that is?'

'No, I don't.'

'Your country's best rock'n'roll guitarist.'

'Well, how would I know?' I retorted, 'I was brought up on "Rustle of Spring". I don't know anything about rock'n'roll.'

'That's for sure,' Frank chided.

To tell the truth, I did know something about it. My friend, Oonagh, worked at the Scene, where I'd watched the Animals perform 'House of the Rising Sun', and another night felt the excitement when Jimi Hendrix played at the Bag O' Nails, although, from my standing position, I'd taken more interest in John Lennon – squashed in among the tables with Paul McCartney – than Hendrix's guitar playing. But for the most part, rock'n'roll meant Herman's Hermits, the Dave Clark Five or any of the others who'd made it to the top of the Hit Parade.

In the Speakeasy, Frank and I gazed our separate ways.

Looking back on it, I think it possible that under the deafening noise, Frank had misheard. Instead of 'Rustle of Spring', he might have thought I said 'Rite of Spring'. Many pianists included 'Rustle of Spring', a solo piano piece by

Christian Sinding, in their concert repertoire, though I had never mastered it. If Frank heard me say 'Rite of Spring' instead, perhaps he deduced I was a fan of Stravinsky, one of his favourite composers. Later I would hear him say, 'No one can understand my music if they've never heard Anton Webern or Stravinsky.'

Frank motioned for the waiter to order another drink, but I declined. Though *he* seemed to have recovered from my gaffe, *I* felt upset and disoriented, furious with myself. Booming guitars blasted my ears, the smell of charred meat and stale smoke caught at my throat, and when other fluffy-haired boys, presumably musicians, showed up at the table wanting to grab Frank's attention, I fell silently into the shadows, unwilling to make another fool of myself. Frank looked relaxed and happy but when I tapped him on the arm and said, 'I have to go home,' he looked disappointed.

'Okay,' he shrugged.

I grabbed my bag and hovered above him, hesitating.

He looked up somewhat icily and quipped, 'See ya,' before turning to his ragbag of friends.

With my stomach somewhere in my shoes, I stumbled out past queues of people still waiting in line. I instructed the taxi driver to find my Mini that waited in Hyde Park. It looked lonely now that all the other cars had gone.

3

September arrived, cloudy and miserable, chilly with lots of rain. Work dragged on and my social life, although I had many friends, felt boring. Nothing compared to the day I'd met Frank Zappa and, despite my determination to cool my interest – because where would it get me? – I scoured the music papers.

Melody Maker's cover showed a full-page photograph of Frank wearing a floral mini-dress, his hairy legs wrapped in fishnet stockings and his thick hair tied in two bunches which flopped on each side of his head like a King Charles spaniel's ears. Frankly, I was disappointed. Did he have to prove his ugliness to the world? When I showed it to the girls at work, they said, 'Ugh, he's revolting.'

In *Record Mirror*, David Griffiths wrote about Frank's concern with 'product' and 'promotion'. 'I'm dealing with businessmen who care nothing about music, or art, or me personally. They want to make money, and I relate to them on that level or they'd regard me as just another rock'n'roll fool.' I could just hear his quiet but scornful tone.

The Mothers of Invention arrived on 18 September. A photograph in the *Evening Standard* showed a hairy bunch with a girl, Suzy Creamcheese, standing among them. The journalist asked Frank, 'Is she your girlfriend or something?' Frank replied, 'Or something.' Hmm.

Every day I hoped for an assignment at the Royal Garden Hotel, if not from Frank, then any other businessman, so that I could accidentally, on purpose, bump into him. Infuriatingly, no one called. Would it be impertinent to phone Frank myself? In the end, I could not summon up the courage, the memory of his rather sour face as I left the Speakeasy disturbed me still. Instead, I bought a ticket for the concert.

Dressed in my royal-blue Biba coat with its wide belt slung low on the hips, I joined the crowds shuffling into the Albert Hall. I felt my hidden hair piece to ensure that it remained safely in place, pinned to my crown and brushing the base of my neck, thick and lustrous.

The house was not full, the tiered boxes mostly empty. Someone near my seat in the raised section at the side pointed to the front stalls and said, 'There's Jimi Hendrix and Jeff Beck,' but all I could see was rows of mop-heads decked out in artificial boas.

When the Mothers of Invention finally ambled onstage dressed in outfits apparently chucked together from a jumble sale, the audience applauded politely. I skipped a beat at seeing Frank again and marvelled at his casual, nonchalant stroll across the stage, as though he was pottering around his back garden. For five minutes, he ignored the audience, adjusted dials, tuned his guitar and tied his shoelaces. He chatted inaudibly with the other Mothers, equally hairy and equally casual, who tuned up their instruments, ran up scales and patted out trills on the drums.

Finally, Frank stole a puff from his cigarette, hooked it on his guitar, fiddled with the strings, swept back his flowing hair, moved into the microphone and said, 'Hello boys and girls.' His soft American drawl, magnified, fascinated me all over again and I could not drag my eyes from him.

Like a ballet dancer, he jumped into the air and all at once the guitars, clarinet, trumpet, electric keyboard and two sets of drums pounded out a series of medleys and songs including 'Call Any Vegetable' and 'Big Leg Emma', which I could proudly join in with. Then he introduced ten musicians from the London Philharmonic Orchestra who wandered on looking embarrassed. As each musician sat down behind their music stands, the Mothers' trombone player made fart-like noises that made everyone laugh, including Frank. It was the prelude to a long comedy sequence. Two of the Mothers, one fat, one grey, aped the Supremes and sang 'Baby Love', followed by renditions of 'Blue Suede Shoes' and 'Hound Dog', all of it parodied and spoofed up. When one of the Mothers climbed the walls to the mighty Albert Hall organ and played the opening strains of 'Louie, Louie', the audience erupted. And that was without the driving instrumentals, pounding rhythms and stunning solos, so much more powerful than listening to the album. Throughout Frank used funny hand signals and conducted with a swinging hand, his head bobbing about like a soft doll's.

Though I knew I'd met someone very unusual at the Royal Garden Hotel, I had no idea he could be so compelling a performer. And yet soon he began to throw quips of mockery at the audience. Before 'America Drinks and Goes Home', he said, 'Americans are ugly; this music is designed for them.' Introducing others, he quipped closely into the microphone, 'You're not gonna like this,' or 'You'll find this song repugnant,' or 'I'll explain the background to these lyrics 'cos I'm not sure you're gonna get it.' Before they played, 'Why Don'tcha Do Me Right?' he said, 'This song is designed to appeal to dumb teenagers.'

I thought it condescending. What was the point? Was he deliberately trying to rile up the audience, turn them against him?

Suzy Creamcheese stood to the side tapping a tambourine. She had straight hair almost to the waist and sported the cowboy look with a check shirt, jacket and brown corduroy trousers. At one point, she spoke out the words to 'Mellow Yellow' and later, when the orchestra played chamber-like music and some people slow handclapped, she said into the microphone, 'Maybe you're not ready for this kind of music yet.'

Could she be Frank's lover? I studied their body language for clues. While she strolled around chatting with the other Mothers, he completely ignored her, but it could be a deliberate ploy to distract journalists.

At the end, the pulsating music seemed to go on even after the Mothers had left the stage. How many other groups had I seen live in the clubs? The Animals, Procol Harum, Jimi Hendrix – but here in this grand hall, the Mothers beat every one of them for sheer diversity and innovation.

As I trudged out with the crowd, some buzzing, some looking baffled, I found myself tracing the circular wall of the Albert Hall until I reached the stage door where a cluster of people waited. I stood behind them, unsure what to do next, when the door opened and a younger, skinnier, more handsome version of Frank Zappa appeared. He had the same flowing locks and little beard, and on his shoulder he carried a large camera. Behind him came Frank. It was a shock to feel so close to him again. He seemed shorter than I remembered, maybe because I was wearing very high-heeled winkle-pickers. I shifted from foot to foot while he signed autographs and answered questions, all in good humour. Then he saw me and with a grin of recognition said, 'Come 'ere, Pauline,' and drew me into his arms. Surprised, but chuffed and aware of the curious crowd looking on, I returned his embrace.

'Do you have your Mini with you?' he asked.

Astonished that he'd remembered the model of my car from a casual remark three weeks before, I stuttered, 'Yes, I do.'

'Well, let's go,' he said, and strode off.

Not foreseeing this turn of events, I scuttled to catch up, to point him in the right direction. As we walked, he introduced me to Calvin Schenkel, his good-looking counterpart. We nodded hello and when we reached the car, I pushed my seat forward so Calvin could climb into the back. Frank slid into the bucket seat beside me. Really, it was no distance at all and they could have walked, but I would not pass up this opportunity, nor would I crank the gears, I felt so puffed up and important. Frank swivelled round to Calvin. 'Did you get some good shots?'

'During the concert? No.'

Frank turned further in his seat to check he'd heard correctly.

'I was hungry. I went out to eat,' Calvin explained.

'You went out to eat?'

'Yeah.'

I expected Frank to explode. Instead, he raised his eyebrows and said quietly, 'I brought you three thousand miles to do one fucking thing – take photographs of the show – and you go out to eat? How long does it take to eat?'

'We couldn't find anywhere. It took a while.'

A quick glance in my rear-view mirror and I saw that Calvin lay sprawled across the back seat, apparently unconcerned. No one spoke for the rest of the journey. I took a sideways glance at Frank. He pushed his index finger into his moustache and twisted his mouth, and that was it. No one spoke again until we reached his room, me least of all, lest I break the bond with this man who half an hour earlier had mesmerised thousands. He might suddenly wake up and wonder who I was.

Within minutes, Frank's suite became jammed with well-wishers all declaring the brilliance of the show. Mostly male and decked out in colourful pants, brocade jackets and satin shirts, they told Frank they'd never seen comedy mixed with rock'n'roll before, let alone jazz and orchestral music too. Frank leaned back in the sofa, placed his feet gently on the coffee table and accepted the accolades.

Feeling lost, I found a space behind a hefty armchair by the deep windowsill. Suzy Creamcheese arrived with Jeff Beck and Ronnie Wood. Smiling and eyes sparkling, she re-introduced them to Frank and then made a beeline for me. Close up, she seemed taller, bigger and broader than she'd looked onstage. She had a natural beauty: oval face devoid of make-up, small, straight nose, perfectly formed lips, smooth white teeth and pale grey eyes that surveyed me with a haughty air.

'Who are you?' she asked, holding her head sideways and brushing her waist-length hair from scalp to tip.

'Pauline Butcher.'

'And?'

'I typed out the lyrics of *Absolutely Free* on Frank's previous visit.'

She stopped brushing and lowered her voice. 'Did you fuck him?'

With involuntary petulance, I snapped back, 'Why? Would you be jealous?'

'Par-leen!' she laughed, holding her arms up in mock surrender. 'I've offended you. I'm sorry.'

What did she mean? Noting my bewilderment, she reverted to a heavy, serious tone. 'Frank and the Mothers are my best friends, okay?'

I felt decidedly uneasy in her presence and was relieved when Herb Cohen intervened. A short man with black, closely cropped hair and a small beard, he was proud to have booked the virtually unknown Mothers of Invention into the prestigious Albert Hall. When I raved about the concert, he soaked up the praise as if I was lauding *his* performance.

Frank, still lounging on the sofa, talked about forthcoming concerts in Denmark, Sweden and Scandinavia and people began shuffling to the door. I started to join them but Frank leapt up and grabbed me. 'Hold on, Pauline.' I hesitated a moment but noticed Calvin still lounging in an armchair. He'd not uttered a word to anyone and looked bored, as if he wished to be somewhere else. I felt a kinship with him – two lonely souls in that busy space. For a flicker of a second, he caught my eye just as Suzy Creamcheese, who everyone addressed as Pam, turned at the door and called out with a cheeky grin, 'Have fun you guys.'

So then there were three, except Frank moved into the bedroom and threw himself on the bed, plumping up the pillows into cushions. He called me to sit beside him. I left the door open and dropped instead into a yellow upholstered chair. It was not Puritanism, not entirely. Rather I wanted him to think I had thick, lustrous hair and I worried that he might lunge at me and my hairpiece would fall off.

I said, 'They were very enthusiastic about the show.'

'And very stoned,' he rejoined. A rather churlish response I thought, given that they'd done nothing but heap praise.

'Do you like to get high, Pauline?' he asked with one raised eyebrow.

'No, I don't.' Indeed, I had even less idea about drugs than I did about rock'n'roll, though I wasn't going to tell Frank that.

'I've smoked marijuana a few times,' he said, his cigarette dangling from his lips, 'but it gave me a sore throat.'

I said, 'It's the sense of losing control that worries me. It's my greatest fear.'

'Well, no one should walk around with a drug-retarded mind. I've never taken LSD.'

Encouraged, I launched into a story. 'I met a journalist once at a party and he invited me to go with him to Heathrow Airport where he was doing an interview about drug smuggling. He said we could pick up some LSD. I had no idea what he meant so I said to him, "What do you mean LSD? Are you offering me money?"'

Frank laughed aloud, a big, hearty rap of a laugh.

Pleased I could bring pleasure to his face, I laughed, too. 'Needless to say, I never saw him again.'

'You really didn't know?'

'I didn't know.'

'Come 'ere,' Frank said kindly, patting the place beside him with both hands. This time I did clamber over, but when he moved to put his arm round my shoulders I told him I'd rather sit separately and shuffled back another few inches, facing him and resting on my knees. This he accepted, distracting himself by seeking out his ashtray on the bedside table.

'When did you start the Mothers of Invention?' I asked.

'About three years ago.'

'And this is your first trip to Europe?'

'Right. We spent most of this year at the Garrick Theatre in New York. Two shows a night, six nights a week, can you imagine how boring that can get?'

No, I couldn't, but I gazed on.

'We tried to liven things up a bit, invited people up onstage. That's when we developed all the weird stuff we do. I worked out that interaction with the crowd is an important part of the performance.'

That explained his chiding of the crowd at the Albert Hall, a failed attempt to rile a response from them.

'One night,' he went on, 'two marines, dressed in full uniform, stopped by. I threw a doll at them. "This is a gook baby. Show us how we treat gooks in Vietnam." The next thing I know is they're tearing the doll apart.'

Frank screwed up his nose as if describing the most disgusting thing he could think of, but I did not understand his horror at all. What else did you expect trained killers to do when urged to perform onstage?

'That's how we started our visual aids, as I call them. It works for us because we're old men compared to rock'n'roll standards, and there's no sex appeal to an old man singing a straight song. So if we do something that makes us bizarre, we've got that happening for us.'

When I made no response, he said, 'How about you, Pauline. Tell about secretarial work and the exciting men you meet in hotels.'

'It's like any job. Sometimes it's boring and sometimes we meet interesting people. I mean, look, I met you.'

With deep, dark eyes resting on mine, he said, 'Do you get any nookie with these clients of yours?'

I laughed. With anyone else, I would have taken offence, but his droll manner led me to believe this was more of a prod, a search into what made me tick.

'No, I've never been propositioned.'

'I find that hard to believe.'

'Well, I have noticed that if their wives phone while I'm there, after they put the phone down they usually *do* ask me to stay for a drink, but I always refuse.'

'You mean these businessmen get *hot* talking to their wives and you reap the benefit? An interesting slant on the situation.'

As I chatted and laughed and cast quick glances across, I felt pleased that I'd attracted such a charismatic man, yet I had an uncomfortable awareness that some of the time I trotted out twaddle. Frank lay back on the pillows. 'You are "it". You are unique,' he said, articulating each word.

A compliment! Could I believe him? My brother Peter had warned me not to believe flattery from men. They use it, he warned, with one aim in mind – to get into your skirt. From that point on, I'd found praise from men difficult to deal with. Now here was Frank telling me I was 'unique'. Could it be conditional? Inspired by Scott Fitzgerald's short story, I told Frank rather grandly, 'No one can be totally unique. We all share *some* characteristics. The only unique person would be a man or woman, born old and gradually through life gets younger and younger, and then dies when they're a baby, when they're born. That person would definitely be unique.'

He said, 'I'd like to meet that person. That would be great.'

Right there, Frank Zappa showed his own uniqueness. I had never known a man listen to me so intently or consider my words with so much respect, no matter what I spewed out. He made me feel I had worth. For two hours, I lapped up his teasing and wry humour until our yawns indicated that the golden time must end. I did not want a repeat of his sour expression at the Speakeasy, so when Calvin, who'd been sitting like a ghost in the other room, got up to leave, I jumped at the opportunity and thankfully, Frank did too. In a few hours' time, the Mothers would leave for Amsterdam and he needed to sleep. He gave me Herb Cohen's number and told me to get in touch if I was ever in New York.

As I put on my coat, he carefully, solemnly lifted my hair, smoothed it over my collar and said, 'I've had a good time.'

I thanked him for a lovely evening and pecked him on the cheek and when I glanced back at the door, he was smiling.

4

Four months later, in January 1968, I flew out to Washington DC for a two-week visit with my three older sisters, who'd moved there one by one with their families. Somewhere in New York, conveniently on the way, lived Frank Zappa. Hardly a day had gone by when I hadn't pictured his amused, admiring eyes or heard the soft lilt of his voice.

From my tiny room at the Belvedere Hotel, I dialled Herb Cohen.

A light voice came on the line, 'Hello-o-o.'

'Herb Cohen? It's Pauline Butcher here.'

'Who?'

'Pauline Butcher. We met at the Royal Garden Hotel last year after the concert at the Albert Hall.'

I could hear his brain ticking over. 'Oh, yeah, yeah, yeah,' he said, slightly bored.

'I'm sorry to trouble you but is it possible to give Frank Zappa a message for me, please?'

'Frank? He's not here.'

'Oh, well, I'm in New York for a couple of days and I wondered if he had any secretarial work.'

'Secretarial work? Like what?'

'Well, you know, like I did before? When I typed the words of *Absolutely Free?* Frank said to call *you*.'

'What did you say your name was again?'

'Pauline Butcher.'

'Okay, well, give me your number. I'll call you back.'

Herb Cohen's manner gave me a sinking feeling. Why hadn't I gone round there instead of phoning? He would have remembered me straight away without explanation.

Ten minutes later, the phone rang. 'Here's what we're gonna do,' Herb said down the line. 'Frank is at Apostolic Studios. He'll be there all evening, so you and I will go out to dinner and then I'll take you over to Frank's apartment. How's that?'

How was *that*? Well, yes please. An invitation to anyone's home in New York was a bonus, let alone a famous person, a guru in the music business. But it wasn't just Frank Zappa's fame that thrilled me. He and I had connected in some way and *that* thrilled me. He found me unique, and *that* thrilled me too.

I suggested the Russian Tea Room, the one place I wanted to go where I knew Woody Allen and a whole host of celebrities dined. Herb agreed and I almost dropped the phone with elation.

I put on my stunning new coat from a recent modelling assignment. It was made from alternate downward strips of blonde rabbit fur and beige leather and had a matching leather belt, four inches wide, which, when I pulled it tight to my waist, lifted the coat above my knees. When I added high heels, it took me no time at all to hail a taxi. At the restaurant, I swept past the doorman as if I were a film star.

Inside, Picasso-like paintings hung on the green walls and in a red-leather booth Herb Cohen waited. I scanned the other white tables for a famous face and found none, but no matter. Soon I would meet my own shining star.

Herb suggested we skip the starter and choose the beef stroganoff in a mushroom-soured cream sauce. While I tucked in, I wondered why he was bothering to whittle away an evening with a stranger and why I couldn't have gone straight to Frank's apartment on my own? Could he be following Frank's orders, to ensure I didn't change my mind? Or maybe Herb fancied his chances with a lone girl in New York? But his eyes failed to rake me over in a lover-like way. In any case, it must have been obvious from my conversation that I had a real eagerness to see Frank Zappa again.

'The thing about Frank is,' Herb said, 'you can't define him.'

I nodded in agreement, not knowing what he meant.

'Is it rock'n'roll? Jazz? Satire? No, it's all of those things. You name me another group who can go from doo-wop to classical.'

He was asking me, a musical philistine?

'There's no one,' Herb went on. 'Frank's in a class of his own. When you listen to *Freak Out!*, that is a fucking brilliant dig at middle-class conformity, but most people don't get it.'

His enthusiasm for Frank's music touched and pleased me.

'Frank produced *Freak Out!* as if it was one piece of music. It inspired *Sergeant Pepper*, no question about it.'

I happily stabbed into my food, looking forward with even more anticipation to my forthcoming meeting with Frank, unaware that a pot-hole was waiting to swallow me up.

Herb said, 'Have you met Gail before?'

'Gail?'

'Frank's wife.'

I attempted not to change the expression on my face.

'They got married last September.'

'*Before* their tour?' I muttered. 'How odd, he never said.'

I searched my mind back to that night at the Royal Garden Hotel, trying to remember any mention, any hint of a wife. We'd talked about the band, the concert, Pam Zarubica, the war in Vietnam, but I would have remembered if he'd mentioned that he was married, news that would have stopped me in my tracks. Married men were just off my radar.

'Gail was nine months pregnant,' Herb went on, 'which explains a *lot*. He did what good Italian boys do – he married her.'

Pregnant? A baby? Things were hurtling downhill fast. Why had none of the music papers mentioned anything about a wedding or that Frank had become a father?

'It helped with his tax situation,' Herb said with a shrug.

Now everything changed. Even the red leather seats seemed to dull under the Victorian lamps. I felt a strong sense of unease. Why would I want to share the early morning hours with a newly married couple, doting and in love? Why had Frank invited me? I felt drained and tired from my journey and surely not looking my best – after all, midnight in New York meant five o'clock in the morning my time.

Things got worse when Herb Cohen told me he had another engagement and could not go with me to Frank's. He grunted an address to the taxi driver and turned on his heel.

As the cab rolled through Manhattan and into Greenwich Village, I wondered about Frank's apartment and, more importantly, about Gail. Would she be weird, like Yoko Ono, or maybe a willowy, glamorous blonde?

The taxi stopped in Charles Street outside a row of red-brick terraced houses. As I ascended the steps to the front door, a girl's voice with a soft accent called from below, 'Pauline?'

I returned to the pavement and opened an iron gate at the top of steep, uneven steps that descended to below ground level. In unsteady heels, I clung on and lowered myself down.

'I'm Gail,' she said and held out her hand.

I took it and said formally, 'How do you do.'

She gave a little smile, almost shy. She was extremely pretty, like Brigitte

Bardot minus the make-up, her light brown hair tousled and uncombed. She wore tight jeans with a roll-neck black jumper, and bare feet.

'Come on in,' she said, and led me along a narrow hallway, past a full-length poster of Frank, then turned right into a dimly-lit room cluttered with guitars and bongos, odd bits of furniture and a faint smell of dirty nappies. And there, from the back of the room, came Frank, a cheeky grin on his face, and the heavy, drooping moustache with the funny little tuft of hair still poised under his lower lip. Although he shook my hand, a more formal greeting than when we'd parted in London four months before, he had a soft gleam in his eyes, affectionate almost. He'd tied his hair back and wore cream, tight-fitting cords and a shirt with a v-neck jumper over it, all mismatched in a throw-it-together sort of way.

Gail offered to take my coat, and while I fumbled to undo the three narrow buckles on the belt, she asked, 'Where's Herb?'

Suddenly embarrassed to have arrived alone, I told them, 'He said he had another engagement.'

Gail shot Frank a look which he seemed not to notice. He said, 'Pauline thinks our lyrics are *indecent,*' which made Gail giggle. Frank gave a hefty chuckle. I smiled, not sure if I enjoyed being the butt of a joke.

'Would you like some tea?' she asked, flinging my coat over her arm, and when I nodded, 'Yes, please,' she blinked her heavily lidded eyes and disappeared somewhere through the back.

Frank invited me to sit by the door in a low, ramshackle chair that made my legs stick out and I struggled to get an elegant pose shifting this way and that, pulling down the skirt of my beige, wool sleeveless dress with a roll neck.

'What would you like to hear?' he asked rifling through a stack of 45s, 78s and LPs in the opposite corner.

With no wish to make a fool of myself, I said, 'Oh, anything. *You* choose.'

He pulled out a 45 and placed it on the turntable, setting the needle on the shiny edge to ensure it didn't start mid-note. A harsh guitar with strong rhythms and a wailing voice filled the room.

'Know who this is?' Frank asked.

I shook my head.

'Muddy Waters,' and to my blank look, he said, 'He's just about the best blues player on the planet.'

'Really?' I said lamely.

'This is the music to listen to, not the Beatles or the Rolling Stones,' which I thought was a bit rich since I listened to neither. If I had to choose, I preferred the Rolling Stones over the Beatles – the success of *Sergeant Pepper*, which everyone raved about, had baffled me.

Frank proceeded with a lecture on the blues and various black musicians, including John Lee Hooker and Buddy Miles. He showed me sleeves of their records and I was flattered by his desire to enlighten me.

Next came Jackie and the Starlites, which Frank said was doo-wop. While we listened, I had a chance to scrutinise the room, its walls pinned with posters, photographs, letters, bits of comic books, cuttings from magazines, advertisements and pop art. In pride of place, there hung a large photograph of Gail at her piquant best. Through the knocked-down wall that made one long room, I could see Calvin quietly working by the far window. So Frank hadn't sacked him for his misdemeanour at the Albert Hall!

He strolled in, bringing a piece of artwork to show Frank. He wore torn jeans, his hair tied in a band, and looked just as handsome as in London. He nodded a quiet 'Hi' and I smiled, reassured by his presence, a sort of balancing act against Frank and Gail.

It gave me a moment to reflect. What was I doing in Frank Zappa's flat? Why had he invited me? What did I have to offer? I was not even a music buff. It would have pleased me to believe I'd made such an impact that he could not pass up the opportunity to see me again, but even my ego, normally flat but now marginally inflated by this invitation, did not allow me to go that far.

Frank suggested changes in colour and wording and Calvin, with a nod, took the work back to his table.

Frank played more doo-wop and I asked, 'If you like this kind of music so much, why don't you play it with the band?'

'I'm working on an album right now. It's called *Cruising with Ruben and the Jets*. In fact, I'm working on several projects.'

Gail arrived with crockery on a tray and from there on Frank fell strangely silent, settling into a rocking chair by the window that creaked every time he moved. After Gail served a perfectly brewed cup of tea with milk and sugar, she pummelled a cushion and sat on the floor at Frank's feet, watching me closely. From behind the lashes that fluttered with slow, even regularity flowed the message, 'This is my husband, so beware; get too close and I'll eat you alive.'

Desperate to show amenability, I pressed my legs under my chair and leaned forward in her direction. 'It's very unusual for an American to drink tea.'

'I picked it up in England. I lived in Chelsea for several years.'

She reminisced about happy times in swinging London. Did I know Terence Donovan, the well-known fashion photographer? Yes, I knew *of* him but no, I didn't know him personally. She rattled off a list of English pop stars she'd met there, which seemed to be just about everyone with a Top Ten hit.

'How did you meet them?'

'You go to clubs and you stand there, and before you know it, Gerry and the Pacemakers or Jimmy Page or Jeff Beck is standing next to you, you know.'

No, I didn't know. Besides her stunning prettiness, Gail had a soft, unthreatening, almost bashful air. I could imagine boys scrambling over themselves to reach her. Tall and angular, I lacked that kind of appeal. If *I* stood around in a club, that's where I would stay for the rest of the evening, alone.

'What sign are you, Pauline?'

'Sagittarius.'

'Frank's Sagittarius, too.'

Sagittarians, I knew, enjoyed each other's company but rarely made lovers. Perhaps that explained Gail's satisfied smile. I glanced Frank's way to gauge his reaction but he'd closed his eyes and lay back in his rocking chair, his right hand hanging over the arm, a cigarette smouldering between his fingers.

Suddenly a baby wailed and Gail jumped up and disappeared towards the sound. I glanced over to Frank, hoping to rekindle our connection, but he was lost in the music. Gail returned almost immediately, swinging an infant in the air and saying, 'Ups-a-daisy.' Frank and Gail's three-and-a-half-month-old daughter, Moon Unit, was gurgling and full of dimples. A nappy hung somewhat precariously around her midriff. I dutifully cooed at her but she stared back, poker-faced. Lovingly, Gail smothered her with kisses and Frank seemed delighted too, smiling and tickling her tummy.

She laid Moon on her back on the floor and I dropped on my knees to join her. I found it easier talking to Gail about the baby than to Frank about music. In any case, he seemed to have withdrawn into himself and for the next hour, I don't think he spoke. While Gail and I tried to chat, he would give a little cough or shift his position, his disapproval slicing through our conversation like a sword, and our sentences petered out. Normally, I would fill silences with chatter, often wincing an hour later at what I'd spilled out, but Frank's heavy silence made it clear that we should not talk.

I could see how Gail's presence changed the dynamic between Frank and me. In London, he'd been warm, casual and light-hearted, unable to get enough of my stories, digging deeper for details, but here, not a single question about what I'd been doing these past four months. As the minutes passed, I considered getting up and looking at the cuttings on the walls, making a joke, falling to the floor even, anything to ruffle things up, but his remote air kept me rooted to my chair. It felt slightly surreal, as if every day I entered this renowned musician's home and sat in silence with him and his wife. How to explain why they'd invited me? Were they wondering that themselves?

I desperately hoped for a few minutes alone with Frank to reassure myself that we could still tease each other. It looked like my only chance would be on leaving, when he would escort me to the taxi, but when I stretched and pleaded jet lag, it was not Frank, but Gail who followed me out.

So, we two girls stood alone on the corner of Charles and Seventeenth Street at three-thirty in the morning, Gail fearless while I shivered in that frightening and dangerous city where roughly four murders occurred every day and two violent crimes each minute. Temperatures had plummeted on that January night and, as much for protection as from cold, I wrapped my fur coat tightly round me. I thanked Gail for inviting me over and as she peered up the empty street, she said, 'It's normal for us. Frank invites *people*, period. Guys, girls, weirdos, you name it.'

Okay, I got the message – their invitation may have excited me, but don't overplay it. I let the information float between us and scanned dark shadows under the trees where robbers might lurk.

'*I* could never invite a guy though,' she added coyly.

'Oh? Why not?'

'Because.'

'He's not jealous!'

She nodded, eyebrows raised, acknowledging my surprise.

'Is that why you talked about your boyfriends, a way of balancing things out?'

She smiled. 'I did?'

We moved to the middle of the crossroads, the streets eerily empty in all directions.

'One time,' she went on, 'we were walking along the street here in New York and I saw this guy I used to know before I knew Frank.'

She shook her hair from her face as if to add drama to the story.

'He was on the other side of the street and I ran over to say hi. I really only talked to him for a couple of minutes, it was not flirtatious or anything, but when I crossed back, Frank's face was like, black with fury. I couldn't believe it. He said, "Don't *ever* do that again. If you do, you're out. Subject closed," and he stormed off leaving me standing there. And I know he means it, so – '

Her words left little wisps of breath floating into the darkness.

I felt a small dart of jealousy, and maybe that was the point of the story. Why else tell a stranger intimate details of her life? Or perhaps she hoped that this girly confidence would spur me on to dish out my own intimacies, in particular those with Frank. Her eyes sought mine but I studied my toes on the icy ground and avoided her gaze.

Out of the gloom, a taxi arrived and Gail hugged me and with a shy smile said, 'Good to meet you, Pauline.' For a moment, I bathed in her warmth. Why be conspiratorial when she just wanted to be my friend? But then I dismissed that thought – more likely a case of, 'Hold your friends close, your enemies closer.'

As the taxi rocked up Sixth Avenue, forcing me to hang onto the strap, I felt both exhilarated and disappointed: exhilarated not only from my close proximity to Frank, the aura that seemed to ooze from his quiet frame, but also the privilege of peeking into his home, the clutter, the artiness, the flair, the pure density of talent compressed in there. But yes, I was disappointed too. Frank was married and that was that. Why pursue daydreams about him further? I would probably never see him again. I could hardly ring him up in two weeks' time and say, 'Oh, by the way, do you need help with secretarial work?', a subject which had never been raised and which I'd forgotten about completely. I looked down. In my hand, I held the piece of paper on which Frank had written his phone number. I placed it carefully in my handbag.

5

The two weeks' holiday in Washington DC in January stretched through to April. My three sisters, generous with hospitality, kept urging me to stay as I moved from one family to the other enjoying a life of leisure.

Letters arrived from home. The Transport Minister, Mrs Castle, had brought in a new motoring rule – the government would fine anyone with worn tyres on their cars up to £50, so Carole, my sister, bought new ones for my Mini. Miss Bee had rung displeased at my prolonged absence and hoped to see me by the beginning of March, and the modelling school had booked me for the 'coloured girls class' starting 12 March. I let both dates slide by. But when my sister Ruth and her husband Harold, who owned a Jaguar car sales business, planned a trip to New York for the Jaguar show, it seemed a perfect way to end my trip – a few days in the Big Apple.

As the train rumbled nearer to New York, I felt a sneaking desire to see Frank Zappa again. I could not say he had never been in my thoughts. When his album *We're Only in It for the Money* had come out in March with a cover showing Frank posing in a black mini-dress, I'd considered buying it, but my sisters had scoffed. They thought he looked deranged, like a drug-crazed hippy, and none of my protests that he was a polite, intelligent human being could persuade them otherwise. No intelligent man, they argued, would want to look like *that*.

In a letter home, I'd described my visit to his flat in New York. It revealed my ambivalence: 'Frank himself is very sane and businesslike and I can't help being surprised every time he speaks that he sounds so normal when it comes out of such a grotesque-looking creature.'

A case of denial? Protection against his married status?

So, how to approach him? 'I'm on my way to England. Ha ha ha. Can you spare a moment to see me?' No. Not good at all. Much too forward. 'I'm just passing through and wanted to say that I hope to see you when you're next in London.' Better. No pressure.

I knew you were supposed to leave other women's husbands severely alone no matter how temptingly attractive they were. But then, if Frank *hadn't* wanted me to phone, why had he given me his phone number? And why, as I left, had he embraced me so warmly and said, 'Keep in touch.'

And what about Gail? She'd been friendly before but what choice had she had? Supposing she answered the phone, what then? She'd find some excuse I was sure. 'Frank is in the studio,' or 'He's at the dentist.'

I was never one to risk rejection, but once I'd hauled my suitcases into my hotel room, somehow the hidden piece of paper in my shoulder bag appeared in my hand. I unfolded it, read out the number and dialled.

Frank answered.

'Frank?'

'That's me.'

'It's Pauline Butcher.'

'Well, hello, Pauline. Where the darn are you?'

'I'm in New York. I'm on my way home.'

'Had enough of this crazy country, huh?'

'Well, not totally. I've been here three months. I can't believe it, it's gone so quickly.'

His deep, very quiet drawl sounded wonderful. 'Have you time to come over?'

'Today?'

'Why not? Gail's in California.'

Alarm bells rang. Protocol banned visits to married men in their apartments when their wives holidayed elsewhere. My mother would stamp her foot if she knew. On my hesitation, he said, 'We could go eat. Are you hungry?'

I'd arranged dinner with Ruth and Harold but no matter, this would be more exciting. 'Yes, I am.'

When the taxi arrived at Charles Street, Frank came out to meet me in a black bearskin coat that reached the ground and a red knitted cap over his ears. He was smiling and gave me a big hug. Then we walked along his street, softly black with overarching trees, and entered a small bistro on the corner. We sat opposite each other in a booth divided by red curtains that hung on brass rails. I ordered a steak with onions, jacket potato and salad. Frank ordered the same but added, 'Hold the onions.'

He opened up on a myriad of subjects and our conversation rolled along as if we were old friends, just like in London. He teased me about my accent and aped it badly. I did better. 'Don't fret yourself, education can "f you up,"' I mimicked, and he laughed uproariously.

He told me Gail was searching in Hollywood for a house to rent. They planned to move back there as soon as possible and I expressed pleasure at having caught him in time.

President Johnson had just announced his withdrawal from re-election, a topic that led Frank into verbal abuse about politicians. 'They'll say and do anything to get votes.'

'Not *all*, surely?' I asked.

'What we have today is not really politics. It's the equivalent of the high-school election. It's a popularity contest. It's got nothing to do with politics – what it is, is mass merchandising.'

I tried to protest but he was off on a tirade. 'The problem with Americans is they have this self-image of we're so fair, we're so honest, we always take the high road. If only it were true, this would be heaven on earth, but it's not true. And when you see 240 million people willingly deluding themselves with this idea that they're somehow God's chosen people, you've got a real problem.'

As he talked on, he sounded so logical, so intelligent that I was partly convinced. 'It's very impressive how much you know about politics,' I said. 'You don't expect it in a musician.'

He visibly preened with my words. 'Yeah, well, it so happens, I've been commissioned to write a book.'

'A book, how wonderful!' I could talk all night about writing. 'What's it about?'

'A political perspective, whatever I want to say about this shitty country of ours. I have more or less carte blanche.'

Thinking fast and half joking, I said, 'Why don't you send me the chapters and I'll type them for you in London.'

'I haven't even started it,' he said somewhat sourly. 'Probably won't for a month or so.'

'Well, when you do, I'd be really happy to help. We have lots of people send us work from abroad.' This actually wasn't true, but it was a long shot, a way of staying in touch.

'I don't see the point in sending it overseas,' he said, and my heart sank, a golden opportunity lost. He fell silent, like a philosopher pondering the verities, or perhaps a theory to be vanquished. I worried that I'd overstepped the mark, sounded pushy. Then he said, 'I've got a better idea, why don't you come out to California and type it there?'

Stunned, my mouth popped open, the simplicity of the proposal making me gasp. Could this be true? Was he really offering me a chance not only to work in America, but on a book, my one real interest and love? It could not get any better. But then a natural caution held me in check. Was he being flippant? 'Ha ha ha, what a great idea! Yes.' Slap on the back, and the next day, 'You didn't really believe me?'

I searched his eyes for a clue. 'Are you serious?'

'I make you a proposition and you doubt me? *Par-leen!* No, this is a genuine offer.'

I stared at him, desperately wanting it to be true. Could I be on the threshold of a new career? I gulped down the wine, but then another thought struck. Was Frank using this as a bizarre seduction routine, a carrot dangled in front of my face, a bargaining tool for sex while his wife searched for a house on the other side of the country?

'I think it's a very good idea,' he said.

'But aren't there regulations? Isn't a working visa required?' This would be a test of his resolve, an acknowledgement of the impossibility of the situation.

'I'm sure there's a way round it,' he said. 'I'll talk to my lawyer. Can you go back to Washington and wait there while I investigate how we can do this?'

Oh, gosh, what would my sisters think? Would they really want me back again after the farewell party, gifts and all of that?

'Maybe we can employ you as a flautist in the band. If we can demonstrate it's some kind of exchange, I don't think you need a visa.'

So right there, he swept the insurmountable barrier aside. The magic of this man, brimming with ideas, knew no bounds. 'Can you play the flute?'

I laughed. 'No, piano, but not very well.' In fact, not true. My teacher had put me forward for the London School of Music to study music for three years but my damaged ears had let me down on the aural tests. I couldn't sing the middle note of a chord.

'Well? What do you think?' he broke in. 'A life in Hollywood?' His eyebrows went up and down with a touch of mockery. The whole thing seemed like a dream, something that happened to other people, never to me – at least, up until now.

My inside bubbled with excitement as the idea began to seep in. Who would say no to Hollywood, the centre of glamour? And a book to boot! And not any old book, oh no, not some trashy novel, but a serious-minded, political tract. I might even help write it. I envisaged all the research work interviewing politicians, checking historical journals, maybe even going to the Capitol in Washington DC – I could not imagine a more perfect job and my mind rushed forward. Surely, this would be an introduction to film stars, directors, producers, the crème de la crème of Hollywood, maybe even a ticket to the Oscars and a chance to work for writers in the film industry, my ultimate goal, but I kept myself in check. I looked at Frank and his eyes danced with excitement while I was beside myself with disbelief that such good fortune should fall my way. It felt as though we'd both been hit by a eureka moment, but no one would have noticed, we were both outwardly calm.

Throughout the rest of the meal, he continued to talk about Hollywood and how much he'd missed its leafy hills after the grime of New York, but again and again he returned to the plan on which he had resolutely settled, for me to help him research and prepare the book ready for Stein and Day's deadline on 1 January 1969, eight months away.

After he paid the bill, we returned to the flat where Calvin and Suzy Creamcheese – or, to use her real name, Pam Zarubica – were bent over the table in the back. I felt puffed up with new importance and called out, 'Hi, Calvin,' and he gave a little wave and half-smile back, but Pam bounded through to greet me as if I were her best buddy, grabbing my shoulders in a semi-hug. 'Pauline, it is *so* great to see you,' she said, smiling her widest smile and revealing perfect teeth.

Frank immediately told her our news and explained the pitfalls. She said, 'I sure hope you can come, Pauline, because you and I are gonna have fun.' But when Frank went through to look at Calvin's work, she lowered her voice conspiratorially.

'Gail and I don't get on too well. Did she tell you that?'

'Well, no.'

She pulled me over to the front window to whisper her story in a slow, pedantic drawl, as if the whole thing was a drag. 'Frank and I lived together for seven months – platonically, okay?'

I nodded.

'And then I introduced him to that bitch and she moved in. What can I say?' She shrugged, throwing her hair behind her shoulders. 'It wasn't a scene I could stick around in, so I split for Europe, y'know? Hitched all over for a year, got pregnant, came back destitute, called up Frank and he said, "Join the band," so here I am, Suzy Creamcheese.' She shrugged at the inevitability of her place by Frank's side, as if he couldn't possibly manage without her.

'I take care of the fan mail, do what I can,' she said with a wearisome tone implying, what else could she do with *Gail* around? She lifted her chin and peered at me through narrowed eyes.

'I'm not a groupie, Pauline.'

'I didn't say – '

'I'm an intellectual.'

When Frank returned, she chose to leave and told me, 'We are going to be great friends.'

Almost immediately, Calvin strolled through pulling on a battered airman's leather jacket. He glanced at me and glanced at Frank. 'See ya,' he said quietly, without revealing his thoughts, and disappeared through the door.

A slight unease set in now that Frank and I were so suddenly alone, but I felt it would be too dramatic for me to charge out the door as well. In any case, I felt our relationship had moved on to a business level.

'Would you like to hear my latest album? There's some artwork over there if you want to look at it.' He pointed to some photographs on a side table.

Lumpy Gravy! What crazy names he thought up and how odd he looked! Pictured from above, his ink-black hair looked like a chimney-sweep's brush, his face distorted and large over his shrunken body and legs. A second photograph of Frank sneering from under a magician's hat was no improvement. 'It's not released yet. I'm having a gigantic fight with the record company.' Not at all impressed, I carefully laid it down again. From the tape recorder, jazz-like sounds merged into weird classical riffs so it sounded like no music at all. Apparently another hour of mute communication and listening to records stretched ahead.

Frank gestured to the sofa under the window. When I peered up through the iron grid, I could see people's high heels and boots passing by. He poured us each a glass of bourbon and we clinked glasses, the burning liquid warming my veins.

Then Frank sank into the cushion to my right, placed his arm along the back of the sofa and began picking up strands of my hair and letting them fall. I thought I must stop this, but I was in a tricky situation. Here was my potential employer making rather intimate gestures, an employer who had offered me a path to a bold new adventure and I thought, If I pull away would that mean he'd no longer take me to California? If I spurned these little touches of intimacy, then what? Was this the embodiment of anxiety I'd felt in the restaurant – that the job offer was, after all, conditional?

I began gabbling about Gail and how pleased I was to have met her and what sort of house was she looking for and would she make the decision all on her own?

He answered politely and I felt somewhat reassured until he pulled me close and pressed my head against his shoulder. We continued talking in a light-hearted, jokey way while a thousand incoherent worries niggled in my mind. He leaned down and brushed the base of my neck with his moustache and I scrunched up my shoulders and giggled. That set him off and he began tickling me all over.

'Are you ticklish, are you?'

In protective mode, I tried to tickle him back but he grabbed my arms to prevent me. There was a bit of tumbling about, teasing and playing. I had not bargained on this and my face was growing hot with embarrassment. Before I knew about Gail, about Frank's marriage, I might have welcomed this bit of horseplay, but now it was different. Within my hazy brain, that old mantra reared up – business and pleasure do not mix, let alone pleasure with someone else's husband. Somehow in the thrashing about, he found my lips and kissed me. His moustache tickled my face and almost on reflex, I pulled back.

'What's wrong?' he said, 'Don't you like being kissed?'

Flustered, I muttered, 'Oh, it's not that. I'm surprised more than anything.'

As if he hadn't heard me, he pressed his lips into my hair and cheeks and finally found my lips once more. He was extremely seductive and this time I responded, the mixture of wine and whisky spinning in my head. How was I going to handle this predicament? I wanted the job but this was no way to go about it. Things were getting steamy and out of control. When his hand moved over my breast, I pushed him away uttering a silly, 'Oh, gosh!'

He jumped up to grab his cigarettes, zapped his Zippo and sank again into the sofa, this time retreating into the corner. I was relieved to see he was still comfortable, still okay. He tipped his head back, inhaled deeply and on the exhale directed the smoke to one side, all the while watching me through half-lidded eyes.

'So, Par-leen,' he said at last, 'what's the next stage?'

I wasn't sure what he meant.

'Do you think if we fucked you could still work for me as my secretary?'

I stared at him in shock. I had never met anyone so direct. Every other man I'd flirted with had at least pretended to have some kind of deep liking, if not love, before attempting the first stages of seduction, and even then after months of carrying on. And yet here was Frank, bold as you please, jumping to final base with no more than a two-minute smooch. I felt I should be insulted but strangely, in that first startled moment, I was not. Rather, I felt irritated that Frank had placed me in this indelicate position or – even worse, I suddenly realised with a jolt – maybe I had brought the whole situation on myself, that I had led Frank to believe that I was an eager and willing sexual partner? Was the very fact that I'd remained in his flat alone in the early hours of the morning sufficient provocation? Could I, in all honesty, plead the moral high ground? Was I to blame?

I shifted slightly along the couch, dizzy and confused, my options not clear: sleep with this man and lose the job in Hollywood? Or, sleep with this man and win the prize? After all, who was to say that one night of sex *would* preclude a dream assignment? Wasn't it more likely that if I rejected his advances, I might risk wounding his ego – a step full of minefields since everyone knows that a man's ego is the most precious commodity he owns. Wouldn't my odds be greater if I jumped into the fire for a one-night stand? And not even one night, maybe lots of nights? Would Frank expect to continue the tryst in California? The thought was inconceivable and I dismissed it out of hand.

Frank watched me keenly. Into my mind came Lady Rhys-Williams, a regular client at Forum and granddaughter of Eleanor Glynn, the original 'It girl'. Lady Rhys-Williams, much more taciturn, had warned me with a wagging finger, 'Remember, once a man's caught the bus, he wants to get off.' I believed her.

I turned to Frank and blurted out the first words that came to my lips. 'I don't think it would make any difference to me, but *you* might think that it would make a difference, and I would think what you might think, and then you would think . . .' I let the words fade away, not knowing what I did think, quite sure my fabulous future was sunk.

He got up from the sofa, picked up the whisky bottle and poured it slowly into the glass as if searching for an answer. I hardly dared breathe but when he turned his soulful eyes on mine, to my great relief, he said, 'I think so, too.'

I almost cried.

'Okay,' he said briskly, 'I'll see what I can do.'

It was so obviously the moment to depart and Frank telephoned for a taxi. 'I'll call you in a week,' he said as I found my way out into the cold darkness.

For the next seven days in Washington, I endured sleepless nights, unsure if I'd made the right decision not to return to England. Had I shown sufficient enthusiasm? Acted too casually? I remembered the time in his flat when he had told Pam Zarubica our news, how they'd joked and parleyed in some private language I hadn't understood. Now I dreaded hearing his voice, and prepared myself for the inevitable let-down. 'Sorry, Pauline, I was a little too hasty. Without a green card, it's really not possible,' and I would have to be at my gayest, most spirited self, 'I understand, some other time maybe.' Or worse, he would not call at all, the whole thing some kind of high jinks, a joke at my expense. I even considered putting a call through early. If my fears were correct, at least it would end the agony of waiting, of not knowing.

I passed the time exploring new parts of Washington, the town I might return to with Frank to interview politicians, visit the Capitol and Congress. I'd already come to love its wide tree-lined avenues, clean white monuments, the museums and the river winding slowly along by Georgetown. Policemen with guns hanging from their holsters no longer shocked me, but had I known how dangerous it could be to meander through its back streets, I would have stayed home.

One afternoon, I drove slowly past the front of the White House and peered across to see if, by chance, I could see President Johnson on the lawn or, more pertinently, any teenage girls rolling around in syrup! Instead, a solitary armed policeman waved me through and two blocks later, wishing to find an alternative route, I took a right turn. Almost immediately, the ambience changed. Rows of crumbling, brown-brick houses lined the streets. Lost newspapers floated in the wind, bits of dirty clothing trodden into the pavement fluttered by empty beer cans and other trash in the kerb. I turned right, hoping to turn right again to reach familiar streets, but the one-way system forced me to turn left and then right and soon I was lost in a black neighbourhood. At a crossroads, I braked at a stop sign. Groups of men in ragged clothing lounged against lampposts or sat on the ground playing what looked like craps. All eyes turned to stare at my sister's brand-new Jaguar. Fear licked through my veins sharp and hot. Images of lynched negroes flashed in my mind and for a ghastly moment I feared retribution, that I'd be dragged out by my hair and trawled along the road till my clothes lay in tatters and my lifeless body was left to rot. Instead, no one moved. I shoved the shift into drive and shot up the road, gripping hard on the steering wheel until at last I found a tree-lined street, just across from the White House. A day later and my story might have been different.

On Thursday, 4 April 1968, James Earl Ray, an escaped white convict, assassinated Martin Luther King while he stood on the balcony outside his motel room in Memphis, Tennessee. Reaction was swift as the cry went out, 'Freedom now,' and 'Black Power.' In cities across America, all hell broke loose, the worst in DC. In the very streets I'd been lost in the day before, they burned down and decimated buildings. Over the next four days, the riots killed twelve people in Washington alone.

The government imposed a curfew and allowed no one out after six o'clock – break it and you faced a fine of $300 or a jail sentence. Troops roamed everywhere. One afternoon, I ventured into town but in the jumpy atmosphere, every time I saw an African-American I thought he would shoot me, a silly notion as the majority decried the violence. All shops were closed except food stores, which the police guarded. By the week's end, we were out of food, ate sandwiches for dinner and watched the funeral on TV. I found the music extremely moving and wished they'd make a record of it that I could buy.

When the curfew ended, parts of DC looked like London during the Blitz, with smoke still rising from the shells of buildings. A sombre mood descended everywhere, which only added to my gloomy state of mind and loss of confidence about Frank's job offer.

When the phone rang, I'd rehearsed my lines to such perfection that it was a disappointment when I found I didn't have to say anything at all.

'Hello, Pauline,' rang his soothing voice. 'All set to get on a plane?'

Was I just?

'I've talked to my lawyer and here's what we're gonna do. You are going to be a songwriter. We'll put you down on the books as a composer. How do you like that idea?'

'Um . . .' How wacky could this get?

'We'll pay you an advance for one of your songs. The song will be a flop, so at the end of the year we'll write the sum off as a loss.'

'Oh, wow, that is so clever,' I gushed.

'In practice,' he continued in a businesslike drawl, 'I'll pay you seventy dollars a week and we'll supply you with a room in our house and food. How does that grab ya?'

'It sounds fantastic.' Violins must've been playing somewhere.

He went on, 'Gail's found a great house in Laurel Canyon. It's in the hills overlooking Hollywood. It has fourteen bedrooms, seven bathrooms and caves underneath which we'll turn into a recording studio.'

I shook my head in wonder, my temperature rising.

'There is also a swimming pool, and get this, it has a tree house.'

'Really?'

'Yep. Built in the tree. Calvin will probably skivvy that up a bit.'

'It sounds wonderful.'

'Can you get yourself there, say May fifth? That will give you a day to settle in before I arrive on the sixth.'

'Yes, I'm sure I can.'

'Gail will meet you at the airport. Give her a call when you've arranged your flight.'

When I put the phone down, I laughed in soft excitement and spun about on my toes. Frank Zappa was taking me to Hollywood! How brilliant to embark on a dream journey, to live in a luxurious Hollywood home! I'd seen enough magazines to know what it would be like: wall-to-wall fluffy white carpet and white furniture, a huge patio with steps leading down to a gigantic pool and luxurious loungers under awnings beside blue water. I would sip iced tea through a straw.

I telephoned my mother in England. 'He's famous. If I work for him, I'll get the glow from his aura.'

My mother's voice flew down the line, 'Oh, you do talk Tommy-rot, Pauline.'

'When you tell your friends I'm working in Hollywood for Frank Zappa, they'll be impressed.'

'Frank Zappa!' she snapped with scorn. 'Now if it was Frank Sinatra, *that* would be different.'

PART TWO

PART TWO

6

On the flight from Washington DC to Los Angeles, I bought a first-class ticket in the hope that I'd meet someone important from the film business, like the head of MGM or Paramount. I wanted to be up there with the big and powerful and make crucial contacts for my future life. Instead, I sat next to an old man from Baltimore who owned a factory that made detergents. Excitedly, I told him about Frank Zappa but he grumbled about the food. Then he suffered a severe coughing attack and they gave him medical attention. I thought, 'Never mind, I'll watch the film,' but even there I was out of luck. While economy and business class enjoyed *How to Succeed in Business Without Really Trying*, in first class, the steward informed us the equipment had broken down.

As I struggled across the concourse in Los Angeles a voice boomed out over the tannoy, 'Would Pauline Butcher make her way to the information desk.' When I got there, a rather bored girl with beehive hair handed me a message from Gail Zappa to phone her.

With the hubbub of the airport drowning her words, I could just about hear she wanted me to grab a taxi. 'I can't get there right now,' she shouted. 'I'll give you the money when you arrive. It's the log cabin, 2401 Laurel Canyon Boulevard.'

'I know. I have it already.'

'Good. Well, I look forward to seeing you.'

'Yes, me too.'

'Oh, and Pauline?'

'Yes?'

'The house is in bad shape, but don't worry, we'll fix it.'

The taxi raced across the valley, broad and flat, toward the distant hills rising out of the smog, smog which I could taste and which furred my throat. What did Gail mean, *bad shape*? Roof tiles fallen off? Outside paint needing a touch up?

The taxi driver pointed out Universal Studios to our left. Oh! Film studios were not even in Hollywood, but stuck out here in the valley? How disappointing.

'The log cabin, you say?' he said, briefly turning round.

'Yes, do you know it?'

'You kidding? Everyone in Hollywood knows the log cabin.'

'Oh, wow! Is it very posh?'

'Posh?'

'Well, you know, like luxurious, rich, that sort of thing.'

'I wouldn't know about that. Let's just say it has a reputation.'

'What sort of reputation?'

'You don't know?' He studied me through his rear-view mirror for a moment. 'Ah, forget it. You'll find out soon enough.'

The road wound steadily up Laurel Canyon and cut through the hills. I tried to catch a glimpse of the houses but they nestled behind trees in steep inclines on either side. We curved over the top and began our descent toward Hollywood. Suddenly, the taxi turned right and slammed to a halt in a wooden carport big enough for four or five cars. I stumbled out to see an outside wooden staircase and, beyond it, a screen door. The house, all in wood, towered to my left, and to my right the hillside rose sharply, covered with a tangle of dried-out foliage. I dragged my suitcases across and pushed at the screen.

Inside I found a square kitchen with one large window by the door. A wooden table filled most of its centre and beyond, by the sink stood a girl who turned and tottered toward me. 'You must be Par-leen. Come on in.'

'Thank you,' I said, dropping my suitcases and bag.

'I'm Christine, I'm the babysitter.' She giggled and offered me her limp wrist. 'Welcome to the log cabin.'

Tall and stick-thin, her hair was a mass of frizz with silver paper and ribbons woven into it. She wore a see-through blouse that shadowed nipples on a flat, bony chest, a white frill for a skirt that she'd tied at the waist with mauve chiffon, and bright pink tights. From her china-doll face, large blue eyes stared as if she were blind.

'Come on through, I'll show you around.'

We passed into an adjoining room where two frizzy-haired boys were dumping boxes on the floor; others lay already spilled open, their papers scattered and trodden on. Rubbish, furniture and litter lay everywhere, the carpet stained and dirty.

'This will be your office.'

'Next to the kitchen?'

'That's what Gail says.'

My desk – what you could see of it under the clutter – stood by a wall of leaded windows. One of the panes of glass had a small, splattered hole. I took a step closer. It looked suspiciously like a bullet hole with its circle shape and splayed edges, but I had no time to ponder. Christine had already turned right into a short, dark hallway, its wallpaper curling and buckling at the edges.

'This is my room,' she said, opening a door on the left to reveal silver walls and a mattress on the floor. 'Carl painted it.'

'Carl?'

'He's king of the freaks.'

'Oh!' I said, none the wiser.

'Yeah. We're called the freaks 'cos of the way we dress and our life style 'n all. We used to live here, we all did, but I'm the only one left now.'

'You mean you come with the house?'

'Well, when Gail stopped by one time, she saw me playing with the baby, and she was like, so impressed, she hired me right there which is great, 'cos I'm expecting a baby too.'

Expecting a baby? Do people who look like children have children? A quick glance at her left hand showed no ring.

Catching my look, she said, 'Oh, I'm not married. I'm too young to be married.'

'How old *are* you?'

'Eighteen. Ha! That sounds so much younger than nineteen.'

The little hall opened up into a large room – the drawing room – where someone had dumped bits of furniture and rows of unopened boxes, head high. French windows peeped through on either side. Paper peeled from what little I could see of the walls.

I said as casually as I could, 'So, has Gail just arrived?'

'No. She's been here three days. She moved in Wednesday.'

We filed next door into the nub of the house, a cavernous room, at least sixty-feet long and thirty-feet wide, its walls made of roughly-hewn wood. The cathedral ceiling was crossed with beams from which hung a huge candle chandelier. To our left, either side of the heavy front door, sunlight poured through fine glass panels creating pools of light on the floorboards. Opposite, a massive stone fireplace, big enough to crouch in, dominated the room. Through small windows set high above cupboards on either side of the fireplace, we could see the hillside rising up.

In the middle of that great space sat one sagging sofa perched on a rug that struggled to cover a portion of the floor. The whole impression was exactly as you would imagine a giant log cabin to be, large and sheltered from the sun. Indeed, it was so cool I was glad my mini-dress had long sleeves. Incongruously, just inside the front door, two men were unwrapping a grand piano.

Confused, I'd failed to catch Christine's last words. 'Now all the girls go, "Oh, Christine!" Ever since they found out I was going to have a baby, they've crossed me off the competition list.'

Her frame was so bony, I felt compelled to ask, 'Have you been pregnant long?'

'A month I've known I'm pregnant. Before that I'd known I was pregnant but I thought I was going to get rid of it, so I don't really count that because I wasn't expecting to have a baby then. It hit me all of a sudden. Instead of finding out that you're two months pregnant, it was like far gone.' She spoke with a delicate, refined accent that overrode the muddle of her logic.

We traipsed along the length of the room towards a wide wooden staircase, its banisters made from branches of trees.

'Frank and Gail sleep up there,' she pointed.

At that moment, Gail sashayed down, one heavy bundle resting on her hip – Moon, a little milk dribbling from the corner of her mouth. Dressed now in a t-shirt and little jeans, she looked so cute I wanted to squeeze her, but instead I reached forward and said, 'Hello, it's me again,' and let her clutch my little finger. She studied me soberly and then looked at Gail as if to ask, 'Who's she?'

Gail beamed her attractive, slightly goofy smile. Barefoot and tousled, she wore white cotton pants and a loose blouse. As if to make amends for not coming to the airport, she offered me tea. I really wanted to see my room but never mind, a cup of tea would be good, too. We trudged back along the length of the living room, weaved through the maze of boxes in the drawing room, past Christine's room in the little hall and into my office before turning left into the kitchen, now seemingly bright and sunny after the gloom of the main part of the house.

I sat at the table where a fly buzzed and settled on crumbs of food still not wiped away. Christine boiled a pan of water while Gail, the baby straddling her hip, wandered around holding court. Strange-looking people, either extremely ugly or very beautiful, breezed in through the back door, stayed ten minutes, grunted ten words and left. No one introduced me but when there were gaps, I tried to start a conversation of my own. With a bit of a strain in my throat, I said to Gail, 'This is an amazing place.'

'It could be if the fucking landlady would get off her butt. We're paying $700 a month and she does fuck-all. She's driving me *nuts*.'

Gail peppered her language with more four-letter words than Frank but then, maybe he'd played the gentleman and Gail performed for her audience. 'Don't worry, Pauline,' she continued, 'Frank will take care of it.'

I was haughty, of course, convinced that had *I* scoured Hollywood for a house worthy of a rock star, *this* would not have been it, with its torn and dirty floor in the kitchen, a cooker that apparently didn't work, and the dishwasher and garbage disposal both broken. 'It's been fumigated,' Gail assured me, as if that put everything right.

Built forty years earlier by some rich man who wanted a place for him and his friends to escape their women folk, the house had once been a grand mansion. The ceiling in my office had an elaborate faded, renaissance-type mural with cherubs puffing on trumpets. They said Tom Mix, the movie cowboy, had lived there for a while, and buried his horse somewhere in the garden, but I found that hard to believe because when I looked later – except for the area round the pond in the front, there was no flat piece of land to be found.

Suddenly, Calvin appeared through the back door looking as gorgeous as when I saw him in London, his scrawny frame dressed in hipster jeans and nothing else. I suppose my face lit up because he gave me a small smile and shook my hand. He turned to Gail, 'Do you have a screwdriver? I broke mine.'

'Calvin, do I look like I have a fucking screwdriver?'

'I helped you pack them.'

'Well, then, it's in one of the boxes.'

'Which one?'

'Which *one*? There's three hundred fucking boxes in there. Do you think I know the fuck which one?'

'Oh, well, whatever,' he said and disappeared again. Throughout my stay at the log cabin, Gail and Calvin bickered; always they bickered. Yet, in his absence, she praised and glorified his artwork, his talent, his aura. People mumbled that she was in love with him, but I didn't buy that – more of a power thing was my hunch.

An hour had gone by and I itched to see my room. At last, Gail offered to help and after she'd delivered a boneless Moon into Christine's thin, white arms, we dragged my suitcases along the length of the house and struggled up the two small steps to one side of the staircase. When Gail opened the door, my heart sank. Copper pipes stared out through two large holes in the walls, twelve inches round. Black, dirty marks smeared the white walls, the doors were filthy, and brown stains marked the ceiling where water had leaked through. A standing lamp with no shade or bulb stood behind a bed. On it lay a lumpy mattress – its history I didn't care to think about. Thankfully, Gail offered to let me have one of hers. The large rug, half-lifted because Gail planned to remove it, revealed floorboards stained and splintered, but I decided I could clean the rug with a good shampoo. A small tacky coffee table and a chest of drawers completed the furniture.

Despite the drawbacks, the room was large, about twenty feet by twelve feet with two picturesque lattice windows overlooking the front on the left, and another window at the far end, all of them shielded with lots of foliage so no one could see me, even with no curtains. Except in Washington, I'd never had a room of my own. In our house with endless children and three bedrooms – well, you can do the maths. If I could abracadabra this room into my taste, it could be beautiful and I would be happy.

In the bathroom, however, things got worse: a mildew ceiling, a split toilet seat, no hot water in the sink or bath, and rust on every surface. I quickly peeped through the door on the other side that led into Pam Zarubica's room, a room I would never stray into: it was too dark, too exotic with its red walls, mattress on the floor and candles creating circles of yellow light. I could also walk through the wardrobe from my bedroom into hers and with no locks anywhere, I saw that, just as I'd done all my life, I would undress under my housecoat.

After the two frizzy-haired boys changed the mattress and then disappeared, I made my bed with the sheets Gail had left me. I couldn't bear to unpack – hanging spiders in the dark and dusty walk-through wardrobe might be anywhere. Perhaps I could straighten my office instead. I traipsed back to the other end of the house only to find Gail changing Moon's nappy on the floor by my desk.

In the kitchen, Pam Zarubica jumped down from the worktop to greet me like I'd known her all my life. I had to admit that despite my disappointment with this shamble of a house, at least the people who lived there were friendly and welcoming. Pam, who from then on I called PamZ (Pam Zee) to distinguish her from another Pamela who was a friend of Christine's, suggested she show me the garden – a chance at last to escape the banal chitchat in the kitchen.

I followed her up the hillside along crumbling steps studded with Arabic tiles. Overgrown shrubs and flowers, yellow and dried from the sun, hindered our progress, while sunlight filtered through lemon trees under which we ducked. I noticed PamZ wore short brown leather boots, a sensible choice despite the warm weather given that snakes might be anywhere in the wild foliage, whereas my high heels and mini-dress suddenly felt out of place. Up we went past damaged statues until my legs started to tire, but then she turned and entered a man-made cave carved into the hillside, its white-washed walls surprisingly fresh and bright despite being more than forty years old.

She turned and faced me, pulling cigarette papers, a small tin box and a cigarette lighter from the pockets of her brown corduroy jeans. Skilfully she tipped a small amount of 'tobacco' into a long thin line on one of the papers, rolled it into an irregular shape, lit one end, inhaled deeply, billowed out blue smoke and said, 'Do you get high, Pauline?'

When I shook my head, she murmured, 'Well now – we have to be honest with each other.'

Honest? In my book, honesty was a given fact, not something you needed to state. In fact, I prided myself on my honesty even though at school it had gotten me into trouble. Whenever I talked in class and the teacher called out, 'Was that you talking in the back, Pauline?' I would reply, 'Yes, I was talking, sir,' which forced him to give me a detention. By the end of term I'd scored thirteen detentions, the highest number for any girl in the school, an event that had led to the threat of expulsion, much to the shock and amazement of my family. Now here was PamZ urging me to be honest as if I were some kind of regular liar. I resented that. One minute earlier, I had not thought to doubt her. Now I watched her closely.

She lifted a piece of stray paper from her lip. 'Frank won't allow anyone to get high in the house so there's nothing for it but to come up here. It'll be our secret, okay?' She handed the cigarette to me for my turn but I brushed it away. She threw back her head and laughed, 'Give it time, you will girl, you will.'

How would she know? Would my stay at the log cabin be the start of a slide into drug addiction? I could not imagine it.

'I'm gonna bring the Mothers up here when they arrive.'

'You'll get caught, you know,' I said, but she swept my objections aside.

'Frank is so fucking naive about drugs. He doesn't know hash from heroin.' She said Frank had a pathological fear that if the police found drugs in his house, they would arrest everyone and we'd all go to jail. This explained his very strict rules, PamZ said, and the reason why, on tour, he stayed in a different hotel from the rest of the Mothers, and why Gail had kicked the habit the day she moved in with him. 'But you, Pauline, you're different.'

Transfixed by her steady gaze and defiant air, I felt awkward, a prude even, for refusing to share marijuana with her. Yet, I felt sure of one thing: Frank liked the fact that I rejected drugs so I had no reason to feel threatened by a girl I hardly knew. But here she was suggesting I collude with her against him. Maybe she was testing my loyalty or maybe, in some perverse way, she sought to ram a wedge between me and Frank by luring me into drugs. Or maybe she genuinely wanted to be my friend and I was being a conspiracy nerd.

I stepped out of the cave into the clear air. Somewhere below, hidden from view by the jungle through which we'd climbed, stood the log cabin. Wild, mauve flowers would make a pretty bouquet, I thought, and on the way down I picked some for the kitchen, which felt hot and steamy after the cool of the hillside. Christine was telling the latest visitors about a party the freaks held at the log cabin when seven hundred people had turned up. No wonder the place was a wreck.

'Carl Franzoni? He organised it. He's insane. He stood in the doorway with pink curlers clamped in his pubic hair.' Her laughter was light, like notes on a xylophone.

The house was ideal for parties, no doubt about that, and they talked excitedly of Frank's plans to throw one of his own and invite every rock star in Hollywood. In this house? Here? How could anyone contemplate inviting *guests* to this dump of a place? They must mean *after* they'd refurbished it to its former glory. Such was my hope.

In the meantime, even though I was fatigued from my journey, I longed to set to and start clearing out the mess in the house – after all, Frank would arrive tomorrow – but despite offering several times, Gail wished only to wander round the kitchen table with Moon, now comatose on her shoulder, and hold court. She expounded on the injustices in America and received plaudits from those odd-bods leaning or sitting on various surfaces around the kitchen.

I was weary of listening so when Calvin wandered back in and told me I might get carpet shampoo at the Country Store about half a mile down the hill, and agreed to drive me, I could have hugged him.

We climbed into his old jalopy in which he'd hobbled across from Philadelphia, breaking down three times on the way. Surprisingly, it started despite the grating roar of resistance from the engine. He hooked one wrist over the steering wheel and glided us down the bends of Laurel Canyon, swinging into the car park of a little shack nestled under a rock face and hidden from the road by plants climbing up trellis work. Inside exotic smells from the food counter stirred my hunger pangs but I assumed a meal would be served at the log cabin so, with shampoo in hand, we returned to the house.

For the next two hours, on my hands and knees, I scrubbed the carpet in my room, managing only to slide grubby suds from one faded flower to another. I inspected one of the cracks in the plaster and tapped gently at it. A huge mound of debris, decaying wood, dirty old rags, rotten leaves and ash fell into a mountainous heap on the clean floor. Clouds of dust rose up and almost choked me. Wearily I tried to clean it up. Then, in a vain attempt to pretty up the vandalised room, I re-arranged the chest of drawers and coffee table before returning to the kitchen, near starving to death. Without pause, Gail continued gossiping with her red-headed friend Janet, the last of the visitors, while I fidgeted and shifted and sighed. Finally, at three o'clock in the morning (six-thirty my time) it dawned on my weary mind that neither of them would magic up any kind of food and so, with my stomach rumbling and grumbling, I limped off to bed. As I wearily pulled the sheet and two blankets to my chin, I wondered if Frank had any idea what he'd brought me to.

7

When I awoke the next morning at eleven-thirty, the first day of my new life, hummingbirds chirruped their mating calls and sunny shadows from the foliage wiped away the grime on the walls. Still, it was not pleasant to wash in cold water and I stood at the sink in high heels, not wishing to touch the yucky floor with my bare feet.

When I entered the kitchen, a smell of burnt toast made my stomach salivate. Gail was bouncing Moon on her shoulder and still chatting to Janet. Had they not gone to bed at all? 'I'd really like you to come to the airport with me,' Gail was saying to Janet. 'We'll get there early. Frank really appreciates it.'

Neither offered me food or drink and I was too shy to ask or search round the kitchen, so I pulled out a wooden chair at the table and suffered the twisting ache in my stomach in silence. Gail took an airmail envelope from the side and held it out. The return address was from my mother.

'How did this get here?' I asked incredulously.

'I flew it over in my own private jet, Pauline. I thought to myself, "If I do nothing else, I'll make sure Pauline gets a letter from her mother." Okay?'

Janet, who was chewing gum, giggled while I, feeling foolish, tucked the envelope under my thighs. Left on the sidelines while they conferred like the closest of pals, I was relieved when Calvin, wearing low-slung jeans and a t-shirt spattered with paint, wandered in and said to Janet and me, 'I'm going into Hollywood. Wanna come along?'

Would I? I could have hugged him. Anything to get out of the tenseness of the kitchen, and what's more, it would give me a chance to see tinsel town, home to glamorous film stars, chauffeur-driven cars, and commissionaires in green and gold uniforms opening limousines in front of boutiques glitzy with jewels. But when Calvin's jalopy reached the bottom of the Canyon, leaving behind the leafy and wooded glen, I found streets, straight and tree-less. Temporary looking one-storey boxes lined either side of Santa Monica Boulevard with hoardings on their roofs, each with a parking lot dotted with cars. Such space and bittiness prevented cohesion and atmosphere – London's King's Road or Carnaby Street had more pizzazz.

Calvin stopped the car on Sunset Strip, the trendy part of town, according to Janet. We clambered out in front of Ben Frank's, a café/restaurant with a flashing sign: 'Open 24 hours a day.' While Calvin roared off to buy paint stripper, Janet and I slid into a huge orange and gold coloured booth and, without looking at the menu, I ordered a cheeseburger with fries, my lips drooling. When it arrived, thick as a doorstep, I ravaged it like a vulture.

Janet made do with a milkshake. She had long, waving red hair, pure brown eyes and a sprinkling of freckles on her straight nose. She knew the Mothers from New York.

'Motorhead isn't really a Mother,' she said. 'He's the roadie, but Frank brought him onstage at the Garrick. He plays the triangle and saxophone sometimes.'

'Motorhead? What a funny name.'

'His real name is Jim Sherwood but they call him Motorhead, I think, because he's always tinkering with motorbikes and stuff. He used to go to school with Frank.'

'Frank's still in touch with school friends?'

'Yeah, well, Frank's very good like that.'

'Do you have a favourite?'

'No, they're all great, except maybe Ian Underwood. He's the newest one. He's a little square,' she said, 'but *you'll* probably like him.'

Back in my room, while I refilled a bucket with warm water in a vain attempt to clean the paintwork, PamZ appeared through my bathroom door and threw herself on my bed.

'We-e-e-ll? What's ha-a-a-ppening?' she demanded.

'I've got red hands from scrubbing. How about you?'

'Why the fuck should I do anything when Gail does fuck all?' she drawled.

I wanted to challenge her, but dared not. She had such a foreboding air, as if to say, 'Don't meddle with me girl, or else.'

Sometime late in the afternoon, I heard the scattering of gravel on the drive, the screech of brakes, car doors slamming and the distant sounds of excited voices. Shrieks of laughter permeated from the kitchen while I ran to the mirror and checked how I looked. Mascara had smudged round my eyes and I hastily wiped it off with toilet paper. I washed my hands, still smelling of detergent, and dried them on my brown mini-skirt, took the pins from my hair and teased it with my fingers. Then I stepped into the living room, annoyed with myself for being unprepared.

Frank, wearing beige jeans, a mauve t-shirt and with his hair tied back, strode toward me with two of the Mothers. I blushed when Frank gave me the warmest, longest hug. It was wonderful to see him again and I could tell by his bright-eyed little smile that he was pleased to see me too. He introduced Ian Underwood who, skipping formalities, kissed my cheek and tickled my nose with his long, bushy sideburns. I smelled aftershave, something spicy. He had a Russian look about him – like Nureyev, with fine chiselled features – and I thought him most handsome. Janet was right; I might like him. Ray Collins was more ramshackle, his fine hair brushed out like a nest. Almost shyly, he shook my hand.

Frank said, 'Got your notebook handy?'

I ran to the office and grabbed a Bic pen and pad, flipped to a clean page and clattered down the wooden staircase to the basement, an area I'd yet to explore.

Frank, Ian and Ray were standing by a fireplace set in the back wall of a large, open space. It was decorated with elaborate ceramic tiles and had presumably been a games room. It ran directly under PamZ's room and mine. 'We can fit our equipment in here,' Frank declared in his quiet voice. 'This is where we'll rehearse.'

We moved on further under the living room, where the lower ceiling trapped a pungent, damp smell. There we found a complete bowling alley. Ray picked up one of the huge balls and rolled it to the end where, with a hollow, muffled sound, it crashed into skittles and knocked down every one. We all clapped. How odd that in this derelict place, the bowling alley was in perfect order. Frank shook his head in disbelief.

But that was the best part. In three smallish rooms along the front, dingy and rancid, we found punctured holes, obscene drawings and graffiti daubed everywhere. I expected Frank to turn tail but instead he became exhilarated and darted back and forth. After a quick inspection, he said, 'We'll take down these walls and build a recording studio.' Could he be serious? Next we found a bathroom long past its glory, many of the beautiful yellow, blue and green Arabic tiles smashed, the toilet broken and the shower head hanging limply from the wall.

Most bizarre of all was a walk-in vault complete with a solid iron door and dial handle, a find that set Frank alight. Cut deeply into the knotted pine walls were etched Elvis Presley, Bob Dylan, and Paul McCartney. Frank hardly seemed to notice. He squatted in the middle, his long hands dangling between his knees. 'What sort of guy would build a vault this size? How many thousands of dollars would you need?' He raised his eyebrows high, his eyes wide with wonder.

'More than we'll ever earn,' Ian laughed, sliding a glance at Ray.

'Well, if we get Herbie off his backside,' Frank added sourly. He turned to me and proceeded to dictate a whole list of repairs and changes he wanted made, his vision clear, his ardour infectious so that as his words filled my page, I began to see that perhaps it could happen. They could restore this dungeon into a state-of-the-art studio.

Eventually, we moved upstairs and by the time we'd inspected every room, I had pages of notes. He wanted the living-room floor completely re-polished, new flooring in the kitchen and replacement of all white goods. He perched on the corner of my desk, laid his Winston in the ashtray, untied his hair, pulled it back and fixed it again while he gathered his thoughts. 'Dear Fania, I note that work at 2401 Laurel Canyon Boulevard has not yet begun. I set out below a list of needed repairs. Unless this work is carried out within three weeks, I will consider our contract null and void.'

I had to admire his decisiveness, solving problems in his quiet, dignified way. If they carried out the work, then I could live in the house. For the first time I felt reassured and optimistic. 'Do you have an address?' I asked.

'I believe she lives next door but Gail will give it to you. And send a copy to my lawyer, Mutt Cohen.'

Though confident that Frank's epistle would do the trick, when I'd finished typing and put the letters in envelopes, I couldn't send them because no one could find any stamps. Frank seemed unconcerned, which annoyed me. 'Ask Gail,' he said, which annoyed me even more because when I did approach her, she muttered vaguely, 'Okay, when I go to the stores.'

'When will that be?'

'I don't know, Pauline. When I get there.'

This I must change. I would not go running to Gail with every request, wait on *her* readiness to act, because from what I'd noticed so far, she had three speeds: slow, very slow and stop. In any case, secretly I hoped they would not carry out the work because then we could break our contract and move to a proper Hollywood home.

In contrast, Frank wasted no time setting up his own work area in the living room. He placed his desk against the wall by the square arch into the drawing room. Behind him, to the right of the front door was his grand piano. In the opposite corner, by the fire-place, he began unpacking the boxes of his huge record collection ready to store in the built-in cupboards. He seemed unconcerned or unaware that people must march through the middle of his work-space to get from one end of the house to the other. With the sofa moved over, everything now clustered in the nine hundred square feet to the right of the front door; the other nine hundred square feet to the left lay empty.

*He opened the door and I said, 'Oh, I'm sorry, I've come
to the wrong room.' He said, 'Come on in, Miss Butcher.'*

Melody Maker

August 26, 1967   9d weekly

MEET A MOTHER!

Above: The Mothers of Invention with Suzy Creamcheese (PamZ) at Heathrow, 18 September 1967. A journalist asked, 'Is she your girlfriend or something?' Frank replied, 'Or something.'
Below: I showed this cover to the girls at the office. They said, 'Ugh, he's revolting.' 26 August 1967.

Opposite above: The log cabin in the 1930s. Opposite centre: My recollection of what the log cabin looked like. On Halloween 1981 it went up in flames. Opposite below: An interior ground floor plan of the log cabin as it was while we lived there.

Schenkel

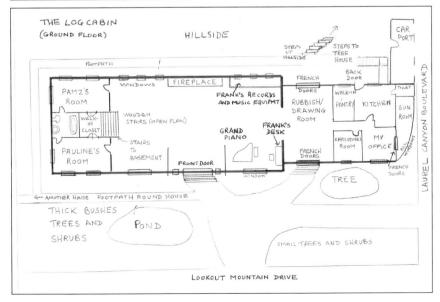

THE LOG CABIN
(GROUND FLOOR)   HILLSIDE   CAR PORT

STEPS UP HILLSIDE   STEPS TO TREE HOUSE

FOOTPATH   BACK DOOR

WINDOWS   FIREPLACE   FRENCH DOORS

PAMZ'S ROOM

FRANK'S RECORDS AND MUSIC EQUIPMT   WALK-IN PANTRY   KITCHEN

WOODEN STAIRS (OPEN PLAN)   RUBBISH/ DRAWING ROOM   SUN ROOM

WALK-IN CLOSET

FRANK'S DESK

STAIRS TO BASEMENT   GRAND PIANO   CHRISTINE'S ROOM   MY OFFICE

PAULINE'S ROOM

FRONT DOOR   FRENCH DOORS

WINDOW   FRENCH DOORS

TREE

← ANOTHER HOUSE   FOOTPATH ROUND HOUSE

LAUREL CANYON BOULEVARD

THICK BUSHES TREES AND SHRUBS   POND

SMALL TREES AND SHRUBS

LOOKOUT MOUNTAIN DRIVE

Clockwise from top left: Ray Collins's song 'Anything' nearly caused a rift between Frank and I; Frank eating at the log cabin – he always ate alone; Frank with the GTOs at the log cabin; Marianne Faithfull, Captain Beefheart and Mick Jagger, all photographed in the log cabin's basement on 11 July 1968.

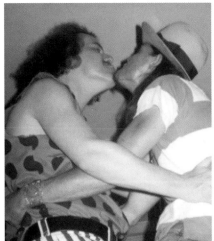

Above left: Art Tripp and Motorhead foolin' around. Above right: Mercy, a member of the GTOs, showing off her assets. Below: The GTOs at the zoo, attracting as many spectators as the animals, 13 August 1968.

Above left: Cynthia Plaster Caster in her pre-casting days. Above right: Cynthia and Dianne, plaster casters ready for work. Below: Cynthia's wonderful drawing of her failed attempt to cast Procol Harum's Gary Brooker.

Opposite above: Frank conducting the Mothers in his inimitable style. Opposite left: Pamela Zarubica and Grant Gibbs. Opposite right: An application form for United Mutations, the Mothers' fan club.

Clockwise from top left: Pauline, Jose Feliciano, Mutt Cohen, Tiny Tim and Gail at Caesars Palace, Las Vegas, 16 August 1968; Pauline and Donna at the new Bizarre offices on Wilshire Boulevard; Gail on tour with Frank and the Mothers, October 1968.

He handled the records as if they were precious jewels, occasionally taking a 78 out of its brown wrapper or, if he wanted to play a 45, replacing the stylus and inserting a central disc. Soon BB King and John Lee Hooker resounded through the house. If Frank seemed happy sorting through his collection, I was thrilled. All right, the house was a dump, but to work beside a man who fascinated me beyond all others – it could not get much better. Oh, if my friends in England could see me now!

We worked in silence, Frank sitting cross-legged on the floor while I, who had an aversion to dirty surfaces, took a not-much-cleaner cushion from the sofa and knelt on it. Within minutes, a visitor arrived and Frank leapt up to greet her. She was Robyn, assistant to Art Kane, the editor of *Life* magazine. *Life* had commissioned Frank to write an article about the influence of the 1950s on the present-day rock scene. They would pay him $2,500 for five thousand words and he must complete it in two weeks. If nothing else, it showed that the media now viewed him very seriously indeed. What other rock star would be invited to write a vital piece by a glossy magazine?

Robyn, in her early twenties, slim with long brown hair, had brought a contract for Frank to sign. He crouched to his knees and read it through with studied attention. Occasionally, he asked her a question and I could see her thinking, 'Why he's nothing like I expected, not a loud-mouthed weirdo at all.'

He turned to me. 'Robyn will be rounding up guys to be interviewed. Your job will be to transcribe the tapes.'

I felt a savage envy well up. How brilliantly *I* could do Robyn's job. I had the necessary gall, tenacity and joie de vivre. Had I obtained a degree, *I* could be a journalist, sauntering around town interviewing celebrities. Instead, for the rest of my life I would be a secretary, a mere flunky, and all because I missed university. For a brief moment, I considered the unfairness of it all until I remembered my brothers' sarcasm, *poor you, poor you,* and swallowed my pride. I was a *good* secretary, as good as you got – settle for that – but if I could, I would swap jobs with Robyn in a flash.

After she'd departed, Gail brought Moon to join us and here we were again, the four of us, but this time I was no longer an outsider. Instead, I could take pride of place beside Frank, second in importance only to Gail.

Soon Frank stopped sorting the records so he could talk. He told stories of people he'd met on the road, stories that I thought may well end up in a song.

'You make life on the road sound so much fun,' I said.

'Most of the time it's not fun at all,' he said. 'Take a peculiar example like last night's concert at Phoenix. The audience was very drunk, and there was one guy who was pressed right up to the stage in front who was vomiting, which is a little tough to watch while you're singing.'

His tone was wry but changed to bitterness when he spoke about the Mothers' performance. As he laced his fingers in front of him and cracked the knuckles one by one, he said, 'I'm thinking of leaving the band.'

'Excuse me?'

'The music I'm writing now is too complex and difficult for the band to play.'

'But they sounded great at the Albert Hall.'

'That was the easy stuff. What I'm writing now I have to teach to the guys in turn. Do you know how much energy that takes? I don't have the time or inclination to do it anymore.'

'But you're just beginning to make a name for yourselves.'

He shook his head and said quietly, 'Who gives a fuck? If the band can't play my material, what am I busting my guts for?'

I was pleased he trusted me with his confidence. Didn't that show high regard, that he valued my counsel? But, whereas in London I could chide and tease him, now that I was on the payroll my position had subtly changed. In London I might have said, 'Aren't you being unfair? How will they make a living? How will they manage?' but I remained silent, my tongue muted by this new closeness.

Still, the Mothers' break-up could mean good things for me. Frank would have more time to write his book, more time for other projects. But what projects? What direction would his career take? I kept these questions to myself and strained to hear his voice, which was quiet and low.

'I've been paying each member of the band $200 a week. Then there's the expense of shipping the equipment. It's costing me a whole lot of money I can't afford and it's pissing me off.'

Throughout our task, Frank had chain-smoked, lighting one Winston with the stub of the other until the ashtray on the floor beside him overflowed. 'The problem is they're my friends and I have no idea how to tell them.'

'How do you think they'll react?'

'Not very well,' he said.

The sombre mood made me feel uncomfortable. Gail, who'd been listening intently, mirrored Frank's moods like a seismograph. To his jokey stories, she'd laughed and grinned broadly; now as he talked seriously, she commiserated, showed concern and support. By reflecting his frame of mind, she brought them together. I felt sidelined, but what should I expect? Who was I but an interloper?

I had hoped that Gail would cook dinner now Frank was here but for the second night in a row, she produced no food. So hunger gnawed at my stomach when at two o'clock I made an excuse, blaming jet lag, and trudged self-consciously across that wide space to my room. When I turned on the light, one bare bulb flickered from the centre of the ceiling, the three windows made black oblongs in the walls and the giant holes stared at me like two watchful eyes.

8

On Monday, I started my first working day at the log cabin, or should I say, 'working night'. Frank called me out of my room at 10:00 pm and said, 'Let's get to work.'

Earlier, when I'd woken up, the smell of eggs and bacon had wafted through the house like an elixir, and drooling, I'd followed the delicious aroma to the kitchen. To my surprise, Gail was by the stove. 'You want breakfast, Pauline?' she'd trilled, all bright and airy, and spooned scrambled eggs and two rashers onto a plate. I sat down and cut off huge chunks of bread and dipped it in the runny yolk, longing to shovel it down, but I forced myself to eat slowly and relished each mouthful. Sunlight streamed through the windows so the kitchen felt warm and cosy despite the torn lino and broken goods. I was happy to take my time.

Frank, I quickly learned, never ate in the kitchen, preferring instead to eat his meals alone, seated at his desk or grand piano. I would walk past and there he would be – one bare foot resting on his knee, his long fingers outstretched to balance the plate close to his face as he stabbed at the food with his fork. He was in good spirits that day, clearly happy to be back in Laurel Canyon. He called a deep, 'Hello, Pauline,' as I passed and I chirped, 'Hi, Frank,' and we both beamed.

When, later, he went out on interviews with Robyn, I took a deep breath and began clearing out the rubbish from my office, happy at last to get to grips with my job. Humming to myself, I heaved the desk and filing cabinet to the fireplace just inside the kitchen door and pushed another long table under the window. I opened one of the file drawers to take a closer look. Cascades of un-mounted photos, press cuttings, menus, advertisements and scribbled pages of scripts spilled out. I found letters from five years ago and suggested to Gail we throw some of it out to which I got the emphatic and uncontrolled angry reply, 'Frank never throws anything away. You do not throw anything of Frank's away.' Heeding the vehemence of this message, I closed the drawer and satisfied myself with hoisting boxes of unopened fan mail on to the long table. I assumed Frank would get to it sometime soon.

Better to do something positive – go out and get stationery. I sought out Calvin in the tree-house to take me into Hollywood. His tree-house was not a house but an apartment and not in a tree at all, although to reach it you did have to climb an outside staircase by the back door, and there was another slatted stairway winding around a huge tree at the front.

I found Calvin kneeling on the floor in his living room. He was sawing a long plank of wood balanced on an old chair. To my request for a ride into Hollywood, he pushed up on his knees and said simply, 'Okay.'

Calvin's dishy looks had not escaped Christine's friends' eagle eyes. As I passed his bedroom door, I caught a glimpse of one of them, Sandra. She pulled the sheet to cover her bare breasts but Calvin seemed happy to leave her sitting there on the mattress.

In the car, he was monosyllabic, preferring to twiddle with the radio rather than talk. In fact, we were out for three hours and exchanged no more than four words. While Calvin stocked up on artwork and tools, I bought stationery, stockings and a white shower curtain which, in the absence of anything else, I hung up with string across the bath.

During the rest of that first Monday, I swept and scrubbed so that by dusk, my office and bedroom were the cleanest, neatest rooms in the house. I stood back and admired my handiwork. Without any instruction from Frank, I carried out this tidying and buying – a pattern that became standard throughout our working relationship. Most of the time he left me alone – I was my own boss.

At ten o'clock that night when Frank knocked on my bedroom door, I was busy writing a letter home, trying to describe as truthfully as I could my first three days in Hollywood; a combination of dismay, disappointment and wonder. I hid the ten pages under my pillow.

In the living room, Frank said, 'Christine is gonna tell us her story. Do you think you can take it down in shorthand?'

Christine, her halo of hair decorated with silver papers, bows and ribbons, wore flower-pink petti-pants, a green sweater decorated with blue artificial flowers and a Vito button. She pulled her thin legs in orange tights onto the sofa and clasped her long white fingers demurely in her lap. Beside her, Frank sank into a wing chair which had part of its seat missing, but someone found a cushion to make it comfortable. I chose the other end of the sofa.

First, Christine described how she had dropped out of high school and how Carl Franzoni had lured her to the freaks at the log cabin.

'Why? Was he trying to ball you?' Frank asked.

'Yeah, but I don't like that.'

'Carl doesn't get along with people who don't fuck him.'

'Actually, this is the truth. I used to keep a hammer next to my bed and he used to come in and I used to jump on the bed and go, "Carl, if you don't get out of here, I'm going to hit you."'

Ian Underwood and Dick Barber (who was Gail's helper and minder) sat together cross-legged on the floor and chuckled. Gail was smiling too as she propped Moon against the base of the sofa and patiently stacked toy bricks one on another.

'Outside of Los Angeles,' Frank said, 'there doesn't seem to be anything that equals this particular scene, not that I can see.'

'It's hard,' Christine said. 'I was riding around the other day and some man asked me to be in the movies about speed freaks, 'cos I used to be skinny in a way, skinny and white and pale, really electrified-looking.'

Used to be skinny and white and pale? Had she not looked in the mirror lately, seen her reflection? Did she not know it wasn't natural for bones to stick out? I took a peep to see what the others were doing. Everyone was hooked except Ian, who caught my eye and raised one eyebrow as if to say, 'I agree, it's nonsense.'

'How long do you think you'll continue to be a freak?'

'I don't know, just as long as my health and stamina keeps up.' Her little Clara Bow lips, painted bright red, hung open for a moment as she collected her thoughts. 'It's a lot of mental energy even if it isn't physical.'

It had taken months to work out her look, she said, and hours each day were spent doing her hair. 'To other people, when they look at us, it all looks really nasty, but when you get right down to it, Pamela and Sparkie are virgins, I'm hardly ever with boys and Miss Lucy doesn't like to fuck. You see only scantily dressed little girls, but it's just not like that.'

Some of my early optimism began to fade. Not only did the triteness of Christine's story rankle, but also the sight of Frank's rapt attention, his total absorption with Christine, as if she was the President of the United States delivering a major speech. Why had I foolishly flattered myself that when Frank had been equally engrossed with *my* stories, I was somehow special? Here was proof, if proof were needed, that listening with one hundred percent focus was Frank's natural way and I must get used to it, get off my high horse and stop thinking I was of primary importance. I felt sulky. The room once again became a vast, dull and gloomy place.

There was a pause and I looked up. To my relief, Frank seemed to have run out of questions. He asked me to read back my transcript and Christine convulsed into giggles hearing her words spoken with an English accent, while the others were surprised I had it word for word.

Frank said, 'Can you type that up tonight?'

'Tonight? It's already after midnight.'

'I'll try to see you don't work more than thirty-six hours a day.'

'Thank you, Frank,' I said, pleased that I could still evoke dry humour from his lips. But frankly, he disappointed me. How could this way-out girl help Frank with his *Life* magazine article? What could she reveal about the 1950s influence on society in general, or the music scene in particular? In my naivety, I had imagined that Frank's interests would be with the upper echelons of society, that he would interview the cream of the music business. Instead, he sought out this drop-out off the streets of LA, the kind of person I would never give a moment's glance. He might as well visit the local doss house; I might as well be a social worker.

I sat amid Moon's clutter on my office floor and pounded at my typewriter. When I'd finished typing, I handed the transcript to Frank, who now chatted to the latest visitors, a pretty blonde dressed in flowing robes, and her partner, sporting a drooping moustache and a cowboy hat. I learned the next day that they were Joni Mitchell and David Crosby, but at the time the names meant nothing to me and, even if they had, it was the third night of retiring after three in the morning and I was too tired to care.

9

News that Frank Zappa had moved into the log cabin spread like a bush fire, and during those first few days as we settled in, the house filled with freaks, hippies, musicians and groupies. They moved slowly through the house. First they hovered in the kitchen, sidled into my office, then past Christine's room, snaked through the boxes in the drawing room and finally found the inner sanctum, Frank's workplace in the living room. I had no idea who these visitors were but since Gail did not halt their progress, how could I? It was impossible to distinguish rock stars from anyone else because they all looked the same; boys with droopy moustaches and shoulder-length hair, the girls covered from head to toe in faded Indian prints, deep fringes and with bandanas tied round their heads.

I noticed it was not the custom to stay longer than half an hour, but that was long enough for me to slowly learn who they were. Graham Nash, whose English accent made me do a double-take; Stephen Stills of Buffalo Springfield, who was thinning on top but who I found most attractive; Peter Tork of the Monkees, whose dark mop I did recognise; Mama Cass of the Mamas and the Papas, who almost filled the doorway; Spencer Dryden and Grace Slick, respectively drummer and singer with Jefferson Airplane, she looking as fragile and delicate as a gossamer fairy. All were much bigger stars than Frank but still they made their homage-like visits.

Apart from pop stars, there grew up around Frank's tolerant and non-judgmental presence a group of weirdos and hangers-on, all poor in purse, all searching for a different life, the drop-outs of society. I didn't hate them but I certainly looked down my nose, superior and lofty. Mostly they were Christine's ragamuffin friends, Sparky, Pamela, Sandra and Lucy. Just as weird-looking as Christine, they each dressed in their own quirky way, wearing cobbled together garments. A noisy, ragged bunch, they carried themselves with casual abandon and took pride in lounging about the kitchen telling wild stories about their adventures in what sounded like a foreign language: 'where it's at, gross, outta sight, groovy, hung up.' Still, Frank obviously thought there was something genuine about them and I knew I should try to be charitable and feel as he did. He never complained, even when he came back from interviews and they were practising their dancing in the living room. Indeed, he positively preened in their presence. 'We're your biggest fans, Mr Zappa,' 'We love you, Mr Zappa,' 'We would die for you, Mr Zappa,' and he would reply, 'Why you little vixens, you.'

Worst of all was the mad Wild Man Fischer, who would stand in our living room and start singing (or should I say, ranting) until someone took notice. He had thick, matted hair like a coiled rug and his ill-fitting clothes, dirty and torn from living on the streets, hung loose on his thin body. Hyperactive, he jerked and twitched and whenever he came near me I feared he would pull out a knife. Frank tried to be kind, refusing to believe he was mad just because he stood on the sidewalk on Sunset Strip and asked people for a dime in return for an impromptu performance of one of his songs. Had Frank known that Wild Man had tried to strangle his mother three times and often lived in mental institutions, he might have revised his opinion. Despite great opposition from Herbie and everyone else, Frank stuck to his guns and welcomed Wild Man.

Some of the visitors stared when they saw me, eyeing my page-boy hair and shift dresses with a look to say, 'What are *you* doing here?' but I didn't care. Frank wanted me in the house and that was what mattered. In any case, I liked being different. I wanted to stay that way.

There were seven of us living at the log cabin: Frank, Gail, PamZ, Calvin, and me, plus Ian Underwood and Dick Barber, both of whom had set their sleeping bags up in the basement. Dick was a friend of Frank's brother, Bobby. His job was to look after the house, help with shopping and errands and guard us while Frank was on tour. Though in his mid-twenties, Dick was heavier than the others and losing his hair in front, but his eyes were soft, grey-brown and gentle as a collie dog's. I warmed to him immediately and he became a rock within the household upon whom almost everyone relied.

Like me, Dick was down in the dumps about the cabin. The more he looked, the more carnage he found. He stood with his thumbs in his belt and shook his strong, handsome face – no words could express what a broken-down wreck we were living in. Why, I even had a bucket in the middle of my room collecting rusty drips that now seeped through the ceiling and threatened to pull it down.

If the house was a wreck, perhaps the food would be good. I had looked forward to communal meals but here, too, I was in for a shock. There were

no guidelines and, because during that first week Gail cooked only twice –
spaghetti bolognese on Wednesday evening, and the one tasty breakfast – I
starved, surviving on grapefruit and toast. People opened frozen pizzas, ate
half and left the rest to go mouldy; packets of cheese and ham lay open on the
table and flies soon descended; bread cut in chunks went stale. Everyone left
plates unwashed anywhere in the house.

By Thursday Frank's face had taken on a stern, hard look. Whereas in
the beginning he'd revelled in the attention of the endless stream of visitors,
moving to his wing chair to whittle away half an hour to exchange tales from
the Canyon and playing Stravinsky or BB King, now unless he had a reason
to stop work he would stay at his desk and the visitors would linger uneasily
while silences followed and very soon, they would leave. Well, how were we
to know who he wanted to see and who he didn't? Those of us who lived at the
house assumed that if they weren't friends of Frank or Gail, then someone else
must be the target, either PamZ or Christine or Calvin or Dick Barber or one
of the Mothers, so it was not pertinent to tap them on the shoulder and say,
'Excuse me, who are you?'

Frankly, I was supercilious. A simple solution was at hand – repair the
door bells and locks on all six external doors, two of them in the basement.
But no one offered to take on the task and Frank, who'd so impressed me with
his business prowess in London and New York, now seemed fixed in a state of
helplessness, unprepared to delegate and issue orders to halt the onslaught.
It seemed he would rather allow the muddle to drift on around him than face
the challenge.

10

Not until Thursday of the first week did the Mothers become a constant presence in the house. Jim Sherwood (Motorhead) drove up in a huge lorry and somehow manoeuvred it up the drive in the front. With Dick Barber and Ian's help, he unloaded the equipment, stumbling through the basement doors with giant speakers and hoards of heavy cases. They unpacked the instruments in the foyer directly under PamZ's and my room, ready for rehearsal that evening.

I had not been particularly interested in the other Mothers until now but they quickly won me over when, throughout the day, they stopped by my desk, friendly and jovial. I liked each and every one – Roy Estrada, the bassist, with his constant refrain, 'I didn't do it'; on drums, Jimmy Carl Black, the Indian of the group; Rae Collins, the vocalist, with his gentle, twinkling eyes; the percussionist, Art Tripp, twenty-four, the youngest of the Mothers, chubby and cuddly; Bunk Gardner on woodwinds, looking like one of Jesus' disciples with flowing grey locks; Don Preston, the keyboard player, always witty and teasing; Jim Sherwood, hard of muscle and teen appeal playing tambourine; and Ian Underwood, formal and sedate on piano and woodwinds. These were the people I got to know and admire.

Early that afternoon, Eric Clapton wandered in. I wasn't sure if he remembered me – it had been dark in the Speakeasy – but just in case I kept in the background. Unassuming, he moved soundlessly around the house and rarely spoke. It was clear he revered Frank; no one else in the business could match Frank's musical genius, he told Dick. 'There are no boundaries with Frank. Who else would think of mixing Johnny Guitar Watson with Edgard Varèse?' If someone of Eric's calibre could think so highly of Frank, surely I should do so too? On a personal level, I did, but some of his ideas I couldn't agree with.

Around eight o'clock, I heard under my floor the twang, twang of instruments tuning up, so I clattered down the wooden stairs to watch. A strong smell of fresh paint – which had covered over the obscene drawings, writings and graffiti – filled the air. I was miffed because the promised redecoration of *my* room had not materialised, yet here in this dank basement, the decorators had been busy at work.

While they waited for Frank, the Mothers gulped down cans of beer, relaxed, strolled around, stretched and meandered among their instruments, tightening or tuning them up. Their talk built up quickly in spurts of wisecracks, jokes and insults that marked them together as a group. Jim kept them entertained with tales about his drive across America in the truck, but soon their good humour turned sour as they unleashed their venom on their manager, Herb Cohen, for whom they seemed to have a pathological hatred, the expletives hitting the air like firecrackers. Jimmy Carl Black, a Cherokee Indian and the most vocal of the group, told me that he would have left the band because of his loathing for Herb and only his respect for Frank's genius had kept him there.

Earlier, I'd overheard Jim and Herb in a heated discussion. They'd faced each other across the head-high boxes in the drawing room as if behind enemy lines, Herb in his standard cream, short-sleeved nylon shirt, standing straight and determined like a soldier; Jim with ringlets hanging like a Cherokee warrior. I kept tripping through pretending to search in the boxes.

'Five fucking gigs so far this year, Herb. What the hell are we rehearsing for, more rehearsals?'

'Don't get prissy with me, Jim, no one's got gigs, it's a bad time.'

Jim countered, 'If you paid us for the European tour that would be something.'

'You'll get your money.'

'*Frank* gets his money, you mean.'

The Mothers still smarted that, after five months in New York, two gigs every night, for which they'd grossed $103,000, Herb had told them, 'The band is broke.' Money had disappeared on rent for the theatre, electricity, publicity and $200-a-week wages during the run.

'Remember, Jim, we're all in this together.'

'Bullshit,' Jim hollered. He pointed a menacing finger into Herb's face, but Herb refused to flinch. 'If we're all in it together, how come we're the last to get paid? Where's this proverbial fortune you keep promising us? Huh? Huh?' Jim raised his eyebrows high so that deep lines formed in his forehead.

'There'll be more than enough money.'

'Maybe, but meantime, we're *starvin'* man.'

It did seem odd. While Frank and Gail appeared to want for nothing, the rest of the band begged for a living wage. Now, as they sweated and fumed in the basement, Jim turned to me. 'How's it going with Frank, Pauline?'

'Well, I haven't done much work yet.'

'He's not an easy guy to get along with. Talented, but not easy.' He ripped out a quick rattle on the drum. 'But you'll find out. You'll learn.' His face wrinkled into a deep grin.

What I had already learned, in dribs and drabs from Frank and from what I'd read in the papers, was that Frank had joined the Soul Giants four years earlier, a group formed by Jimmy Carl Black, Ray Hunt, Roy Estrada, Ray Collins and Davy Coronado. Then Dave, their leader, left because he alone refused to play Frank's music. Then Frank became their leader.

The name Soul Giants sounded too bluesy, so they formally changed it to the Mothers. Their break came in 1966 when Herb Cohen booked them into the Whisky a Go-Go just as Tom Wilson happened by. Tom had offered them a contract with MGM and Frank called the resultant double album *Freak Out*. The record company insisted they be called the Mothers of Invention.

By the end of their five-month season at the Garrick in New York, Frank had hired more Mothers, so then there were nine. Now, here they were in the basement of the log cabin.

Jimmy Carl Black continued to grumble. 'We started this group, did he tell you that? Ray, Roy and me? If Ray Hunt hadn't left the Soul Giants, Frank wouldn't even have a group. We are *the Mothers*, not *Frank Zappa* and the Mothers. You know what he told us? "You play my music and I'll make you rich and famous." Bullshit! It's been four years. Where's the money. Where's the fame?' He peered into my face, his eyes wide and questioning, as if I might have the answer.

'Well, you had lots of publicity in London, I can vouch for that,' I said. 'I was there.'

'*Frank* had lots of publicity in London, you mean.' He leaned forward again, his heavy-bagged eyes wide and challenging. 'When we got there, do you know what he said? "*I'll* talk to the press, not you guys," you dig? Delusions of grandeur. It's bullshit.' He banged on his bass pedal and reverberations bounced off the walls. 'Frank's a brilliant guy, don't get me wrong.' But his praise did not stop the grumbles. 'Something's going down. Come on, Pauline, you can be open with us.'

'I don't know anything,' I lied, bearing his gaze wide-eyed. 'Why would Frank say anything to me?'

Jim grinned, his face folding into deep creases. 'I can read you, Pauline, I can read you,' he said.

Later that evening, while those nine Mothers blasted out 'Why Don'tcha Do Me Right?' and the sound nearly lifted the floor of my room, blue lights from a police car flashed through our windows. Two huge policemen, heavily weighed down with weapons, strolled into the house and generally frightened the lot of us. Gail flew downstairs to warn Frank and the bellowing music stopped immediately. Within seconds Frank bounded up, Gail in nervous pursuit.

Frank had a pet hatred for the police but face to face he appeared guarded and anxious to please. 'What's the problem?'

'We've had a complaint about the music,' the two clean-shaven police officers said politely.

Frank, patting out a Winston from his pack, looked visibly relieved. No doubt, he'd feared they'd found drugs somewhere and were about to throw him in jail. A *music* problem he could deal with. 'It's too loud?'

'Yes, sir. We could hear it half a mile up the street. It *is* a quarter after eleven.'

Continuing his mellow tone, he told Frank that if they wanted to rehearse they must finish before ten o'clock. That, or soundproof the house. 'There's another group, the Monkees, they live right up the street on Lookout Mountain. I suggest you have a word. We have no complaints about them.'

Frank's face was wary but stern. He pledged he would look into it immediately. The policemen, reassured, thanked him for his cooperation and swaggered out. Frank resolved the issue by bringing rehearsals forward to six o'clock, so from then on, every evening until ten, the logs of our enormous cabin vibrated and shook like taut elastic bands.

But there was none of that tonight. While everyone straggled away, Motorhead strolled into my office and lopped one tightly-jeaned leg over the corner of my desk. He wore a white t-shirt that emphasised his broad shoulders and well-honed body. His light brown hair waved down his back under a cowboy hat which he pulled down over his forehead. It shadowed his prominent cheekbones and straight nose. His eyes skimmed over my cream mini-dress. 'So what's *your* trip?' he asked.

Somewhat disarmed, I fluffed, 'I'm fine, thank you.'

He jigged his shoulders with mirth and mimicked my accent, 'I'm fine, thank you. So how would you like a ride into Hollywood? What?'

He made me feel uneasy, but any excuse to escape from the house was welcome so I said, 'Thank you, yes, I'd like to.' He turned on a perfect smile and I smiled back, after all, he was the only Mother who was clean-shaven and, quite frankly, I was not fond of beards.

During the drive, he threw crude comments my way, 'Do you like to get laid? Are you feeling hot? Do you wanna fuck?' He was testing me out, I suppose, but soon my cool response caused him to change tack and he metamorphosed into the perfect gentleman, dropped the swearing and began pointing out the sights as if I was the purest lady. I liked that. Hollywood though was disappointing, no more exciting at night than by day.

On Sunset, cars the length of buildings, many with gull-wing fins, cat-eye tail lights and two-tone paint, crawled bumper-to-bumper in both directions. Their occupants, mostly teenagers, hung out the windows. Perhaps, like me, they were searching for film stars.

Caught in the jam ourselves, we watched the parade go by. Each strolling person was either a freshly laundered movie mogul dressed in pink or lilac satin shirts, brocade jackets and brightly coloured flared pants, or else they were bohemians with straggly hair and beards in shabby clothes – each type seemingly invisible to the other. Then, as we watched, I noticed something else – everyone was young, at least under the age of thirty, as if the middle-aged and old were banished. Where were they all? Jim said he hadn't noticed and quickly returned me to the log cabin.

The next day, Friday, the house buzzed as the Mothers hauled their equipment out to the enormous truck ready for their first concert at the Shrine. I looked forward to it until Frank said, 'I want you to stay home with Christine and Moon.' Feeling dejected and disappointed, I watched him leave. But in the evening, Jeff, a thin, short-haired friend of Calvin's, arrived after hitching across the States from Philadelphia. He looked ready to drop. However, his arrival meant *he* could guard Christine and Moon, and suddenly, just like Cinderella, I was free to go to the ball.

Gail had left cold chicken legs on the table for anyone to enjoy and I gobbled down two before tumbling, partially replenished, into Dick Barber's Volkswagen alongside Gail and Calvin for the five-mile journey to a run-down part of town. I thought we were going to *the* Shrine, the venue where every year they held the Oscars, but disappointingly, the Shrine Expo Hall was a building at the back, a vast empty barn of a place already crammed with fans standing or sitting in groups on the floor.

Proudly I walked to the stage set forward in the arena, past a few stragglers hanging around at the back, and climbed the steps to the high rostrum. Not a mere spectator, I was attached to the show, a small player maybe, but still part of the in-crowd. The band was no longer a bunch of strange-looking bearded men, but famous individuals I could now talk and joke with. Technical assistants busy with wires and cords ambled on and offstage. Herb Cohen tried to look authoritarian checking everything out, and the freaks, dressed in tarted-up rags and remnants, danced around as if they owned the place.

I worried that Frank would be angry that I'd disobeyed his order, but instead he grabbed my arm and propelled me through the crowd to Carl Franzoni.

Carl, wearing bright red ballerina tights and a black cape over his bare, barrel chest, had one fang for a tooth, a long goatee beard, and hair matted in tight corkscrew curls that looked like he'd last washed it an aeon ago. Frank sauntered off while I seethed with embarrassment and indignation. How dare he dump me with this man?

'Frank can be a motherfucker at times,' he said, and I gave him a tolerant smile. 'My philosophy is in the dance. Watch the dance and you'll groove.' Irritated that he assumed I was interested, I said with disdain, 'I've heard a lot about you,' and he said, 'I'm a good fucker.'

By now, I'd grown accustomed to everyone I met using the f-word, mostly as an adjective rather than a verb – Frank, Gail, the Mothers, musicians, even journalists – but I resolved to resist. I would not lower myself to their base level. I realised the word itself caused no physical harm, but then neither did a house painted with psychedelic colours; it was just distasteful.

Incomprehensibly, girls threw their arms round Carl's neck and avowed their love. One of the most renowned freaks, Miss Lucy, who had slanting eyes and a supple, slim Puerto Rican body, wore a topless dress with two narrow straps striving to cover her pert breasts, but as she moved, her dark-red nipples poked out. Another girl with skin like grey tissue paper pitted with sores, jerked, shrieked, snorted and dribbled – my first experience of a completely zonked-out drug addict. I asked Carl, 'Are you not concerned about her?' He merely shrugged and said, 'She's a free agent. She can go fuck a goose for all I care.'

When I rejoined Frank, who chatted to Lucy by the back wall, I said, 'I suppose you thought that was funny.'

'Got yourself a hot date?' he said, and his eyebrows went up and down.

'No, I did not,' I said somewhat primly, 'and I would appreciate it if you would allow me to find my own dates,' but Frank merely whacked the knee of his flowery bell-bottoms and dropped his jaw in silent mirth. Clearly he found the whole thing a thunderous hoot.

Two other groups opened the show, harmonica player Charlie Musselwhite, with his Blues Band, whom Frank and I watched from the side of the stage while everyone behind us chatted and hob-knobbed; and Sweetwater, whose wailing female singer was just too weird for my taste.

Then the Mothers ambled on, endlessly tuning up their instruments, but once they got started I thought they were fantastic, covering every different kind of music from doo-wop to jazz, from rock'n'roll to progressive classical. Add in comedy routines that made me laugh aloud, and you had complete entertainment. Although I'd seen much of it at the Albert Hall, I loved it all over again. How could Frank consider breaking up the band? They were quite simply superb.

Eric Clapton, who'd quietly mingled with everyone on the side of the stage, walked on and played a solo, but little enthusiasm or applause greeted him even after Frank, at the end, announced his name. I felt somewhat vindicated. I was not the only person ignorant of Eric Clapton.

During another number, Carl Franzoni led the freaks onstage. Their flamboyant dancing with its sexual overtones astonished the audience. I turned my nose up but Gail thought they were wonderful.

The next evening, after gulping down two more scrawny chicken legs, I was so tired I fell asleep for three hours. Gail woke me at eleven, just in time to see the second show.

In the kitchen, Gail and Calvin had one of their weekly spats and he stalked back up to the tree-house, refusing to budge, so Christine took his place in the car, bringing Moon with her. I decided to watch from the front of the auditorium, where I could soak up the atmosphere rather than remain at the side of the stage where everyone socialised rather than paying attention to the music.

I was stunned all over again by the performance, but what I noticed this time and had missed before was the way the Mothers' eyes rarely left Frank, keeping a close watch on his signals, which seemed to have grown in number and complexity – a jump, a twirl of his hand, a thumb held aloft or turned down, three or four fingers raised, nods of his head. No one would question who was in charge or who their leader was.

It made me proud and happy to be included in his inner sanctum. He was a big celebrity in Los Angeles and now I could see why. With his nonchalant, yet commanding manner onstage, there was no one else like him.

After the show, the Mothers climbed down and mingled with the fans. Despite their wild and weird appearance, they acted without swank or swagger, just a bunch of happy guys who'd put on a good performance. *When,* I wondered, was Frank going to drop his bombshell and tell them he was packing it in?

On our return drive, Frank sat at the front of Dick's Volkswagen while Gail, Christine, Moon and I squashed in the back, but unlike the previous night when he'd glowed with pleasure, tonight he seemed edgy and his voice had a sharp, biting tone. 'Are you telling me we pay out all this money and there's no one at the house to look after Moon?'

At the log cabin, after Frank, Gail and Moon had gone to bed, everyone congregated in the kitchen for their regular late-night 'family' meeting: PamZ, Dick Barber, Calvin, Christine, Motorhead and Ian. The conversation invariably hovered around three topics – first, who had the clap or crabs and who was balling whom, their claims made without shame or rancour; secondly, the 'fucked up' state of America, for which all parents and politicians were blamed – 'education in this country sucks' – and finally stuff about the Mothers and, more pertinently, groans about Frank.

On previous nights I'd left them to it and gone to bed, but this night, partly because of my earlier sleep, I lingered until the end with Ian Underwood. He moved to join me around the only clean corner of the table, where we spun away two happy hours exchanging stories.

He told me he'd met Frank when he saw the Mothers playing at the Garrick and that he'd walked up to Frank and said, 'How do you do. I like your music and I'd like to join your band,' and Frank had said, 'What can you do that's fantastic?' and Ian had apparently stunned him not only with his saxophone performance, but on the flute and piano as well. Frank had hired him immediately.

While he talked, I observed his brushed cotton, long-sleeved check shirt and jeans belted at the waist, a more conservative style than the other Mothers. He also had shorter hair, just above his shoulders. He told me he'd grown up in a suburb on Long Island and that his father was an executive for a steel company. In childhood, he'd learned to play alto and tenor saxophones, flute and clarinet. A classically-trained concert pianist, he had graduated from Yale University in 1961 with a BA in composition and completed a master's degree in 1966 at the University of California, Berkeley, specialising in Mozart. Then he'd heard the Mothers play in New York. 'I liked their music,' Ian said, 'because they combined different kinds of music, sometimes, all in one composition! I was impressed.'

I found Ian's polite, cultured voice very appealing and felt mildly disappointed when I learned that he had a girlfriend, Ruth, who lived in New York. A classically-trained percussionist, she had also worked with Frank in New York on his album *Uncle Meat*. Ian planned to fly out the following week to see her. Of all the Mothers, I realised, I would miss him the most.

11

A week after my arrival, I wrote in my diary: 'Everyone except Frank watched John Lennon and Paul McCartney on TV. Felt awkward raving about them in front of him.'

Watched TV! The twelve-inch television had lain hidden all this time in the back of a cupboard. Christine and Dick placed it on a tower of boxes in the drawing room and then Calvin, Dick, Gail, Moon, Christine – and her weird friends, Lucy, Sandra and Sparkie – and I perched on boxes to watch the tiny black and white screen as those two English boys brushed off questions in rapid succession.

'What'll you do when the bubble bursts?'

'I'm still looking for the bubble.'

'Who is the spokesman of you two?'

'If he has the spoke, it's him; if I do it's me.'

I loved hearing their English accents and quick-fire routine and I felt proud of their down-to-earth directness. In fact, it was because of the Beatles that I, too, enjoyed a special éclat in the United States. As soon as anyone heard my English accent, they cornered me. Was there the smallest chance, the remotest possibility that I could be friends with, have met, or merely touched the sleeve of one of the Beatles, a touch that would bless me with holiness, so revered were those four boys? Sorry, I would have to tell them, 'No.'

Christine's friends, who screamed adulation at the TV each time John or Paul uttered a word, must have disturbed Frank, who was at work through the square archway. Suddenly, we realised he was standing there, the sternest expression on his face. We glanced at each other, shifting nervously like children caught up in mischief. Was he annoyed because we'd broken his concentration while he composed? Or was it a touch of jealousy over our enthusiasm for two boys whose music he frankly had no time for. To be fair, in

London he had told me, 'The Beatles have shown other teenagers that anyone can achieve success regardless of their start in life.' Their music, however, was something else. He rated it average. Many years later, on a BBC radio show, he listed *Abbey Road* as one of his favourite records but not, he hastened to add, because of its content but because it was the best mastered, best engineered rock'n'roll record he'd heard.

Another explanation for his look of gloom and twitchy moustache could be that he frowned upon anyone watching TV of any kind, which explained its existence, hidden away. Once the Beatles finished their interview, Gail returned it into the deepest recesses of the cupboard and I never saw it again. Not even when Frank appeared on the *Les Crane Show* on 22 May did he show any interest in watching it. Disappointed, I'd hoped to see the news and find out what was going on in the world but I dared not ask. Since I'd arrived, I'd not seen a newspaper, heard the radio or television.

As we splintered through the house, each going our separate ways, Gail to crash with Moon upstairs, some to the kitchen or my office, others to the basement, Frank called me into the living room. Would I like to hear the final mix of *Cruising with Ruben and the Jets*?

Delighted that Frank had singled me out for a special review, I settled sedately on the sofa next to Frank, who sat cross-legged on the floor. I had quickly learned from my visit to his apartment in New York that when Frank invited you to listen to music, you must not speak.

As the album played, I found that each track sounded the same and kept hoping the next one would be different, an instrumental maybe, the kind of instrumental that, as far as I knew, only Frank could write, the part of his music that I liked the most – but I waited in vain. I let my head tip back against the sofa as the album droned on, dull and boring, and I wondered what I would say to be positive. Then, at last, a track came along that I liked – 'Anything', a beautiful love song.

When the tape ended, Frank bent intently over the machine and pressed rewind. Above its whirr, I felt his silence waiting for my verdict.

I blurted out, 'I'm surprised they are all slow numbers.'

Now he looked at me, a flash of pain in his eyes. When I'd rehearsed those words in my head, *I'm surprised they're all slow numbers*, they'd sounded innocuous, harmless, but he heard them as criticism of his months and months of hard work. In a rush and trying to rectify things, I said, 'I really liked "Anything". I think I liked that the best.'

He said quietly, 'That's the only song I didn't write. Ray Collins wrote it.'

If there was such a thing as instant petrifaction, at that moment I should have turned to stone. He placed the tape carefully in its box and the box in its correct and tidy place. He brushed a rag of black hair from his face, gathered up his cigarettes and mug of coffee and said, in a flat monotone, 'I'm going to bed.'

As he trod his way across that vast room to the staircase at the far end, I wanted to call after him, utter some reassuring or flattering words, but it was too late. Rejection wafted back from his heavy steps and I felt gloomy and lost. He would find solace, I knew, with Gail. She would smother him with incontrovertible praise. 'It's brilliant. There's nothing like it.' It would have been so easy for me to do the same, to have waxed lyrical. What would it have cost me to lie?

I struggled to collect myself and, after a few minutes, joined PamZ, Calvin, Ray Collins and Dick, who straddled various surfaces in the kitchen. The conversation concerned Frank: how aloof and unapproachable he'd become to the band. The criticism rambled on until five o'clock in the morning and I felt reassured. Perhaps it was not so wrong to speak my mind to Frank; perhaps I should not feel so rotten. Still, I could not throw off that awful torn feeling in my stomach after saying the wrong thing, and I tossed and turned until dawn.

The next afternoon, when I opened my door about two, I found Frank at the piano doodling on the keys. The light from the windows either side of the front door cast him in shadow and I could not read his face. There was nothing for it; I must pass by. I thought he would express in some way his disappointment from the night before, but instead he looked up through the hoisted lid and called me over. 'Pauline, you know what I think you should do?'

I approached nervously. 'No.'

'I think you should write an article about your life here at the log cabin. You could make yourself some money.'

Astonished, not only by his lack of hard feelings but also because it showed he still had faith in me, still trusted my judgement, I must have stared goggle-eyed.

'You can do it,' he went on, 'because you have a unique perspective.' He nodded his head lightly as if approving his own words.

'Well, yes, I'd love to,' I spluttered, 'but – '

A dozen thoughts flashed across my mind. How could I, a cuckoo in the nest, possibly put down on paper my disappointments about my life at the log cabin, thoughts only revealed in letters to England? What could I say without sounding like a whining whinge about the cat-fights with Gail over the mail and telephone that had recently begun to grow day by day? Or worse, reveal Frank's shortcomings as I saw them. Look at the way he let the house run on in shambolic fashion and allowed the freaks to invade whenever they wished. And what about his ruthlessness? On the cover of *Absolutely Free*, the Mothers' second album, was a full-face photograph of Frank and on the inside, the rest of the band lay on the floor at his feet. The group had been struggling together for four years, so why not produce a democratic album cover, why not a photograph giving them equal space? As far as I knew, no one complained.

He shrugged. 'I don't care what you write about me.'

Really? What if he read my diary, those pages where I'd run down the way he condemned the government, never finding a good word to say about any political party or any part of the establishment, would that not surprise him? Would he still encourage me then? In fact, I did not know for certain what I did think about Frank Zappa. There were so many things I liked and admired. I liked the way his whole life revolved around music, the way he practically ate, drank and slept it. When he was awake, music flowed through the house, Varèse, Stravinsky, Lee Hooker, Buddy Miles. I felt music was the only thing that made him happy, the only thing that he was comfortable with. That month, a magazine in Los Angeles had voted him Pop Musician of the Year, which was something, and although out in the bars someone might shout out that his music was rubbish, almost everyone who came to the log cabin seemed to think he was some kind of genius. But if he was a genius why, mixed in with the good stuff, the fine instrumentals and insightful social songs, did he write so much trivia – lyrics about sexual shenanigans, for example? Although I liked his progressive music very much, I did not share his condemnation of American society, a condemnation that seemed rather juvenile. Indeed, I often felt I'd landed among a bunch of juveniles who hadn't quite grown up, even though most of them had seen and experienced more of life than I had.

Perhaps he had another reason to encourage me. Perhaps he believed I was so enamoured that I could not say anything negative about him. I tried to rearrange my expression, fearful that he might read the treacherous, treason-like thoughts written on my face. I said, 'I can't. I couldn't.'

He banged out a couple of chords and said, 'Give it a try. Who knows what you'll come up with?'

Over the next week, I laboured from one false start to another. Although I wrote screeds of letters home easily describing my true feelings, racking up the irony, trying to make the story funny, rigor mortis set in once the word 'publication' formed in my mind. In any case, I had no idea who the reader would be or who might publish it. Should I write a personal account with me at the centre adding in my own prejudices? Or should I be dispassionate and discount my presence, make it a documentary, a piece of reportage? The fact that Frank had put forward the idea showed his awareness that the log cabin scene, unique in time, *should* be documented.

In the event, after chucking page after page in the wastepaper basket I gave up, finding the task impossible. For the time being, I realised, my journalistic ambitions would have to wait.

12

From the time I arrived at the log cabin, PamZ determined I would be her friend. Each night after I finished work during the first two weeks, she shunted me into Hollywood to the Whisky a Go-Go, to friends' houses, to cafés or bars. Ray Collins, the singer in the band, softly spoken and laidback (like everyone else I met in Laurel Canyon), more often than not acted as chauffeur. Sometimes he just dropped us off at the Whisky, where we bypassed the queue outside and waltzed in without paying because PamZ was Suzy Creamcheese, and I got in free because I was her friend.

Inside, the Whisky was surprisingly swish, not unlike a Parisian nightclub, with a long bar and ornate French-style modern paintings on the panelled walls. People peered from a balcony, but the most startling feature was the cage suspended from the ceiling in which a girl in a fringed mini-skirt and white boots swayed to the music. PamZ shouted that she was the DJ.

Groups played on a small stage, back-draped with red curtains, usually boys like the Nazz from Philadelphia, who looked like the Beatles. People crammed onto a small dance floor, separated from the gold tables and chairs by a low railing. I wouldn't say people danced – aping epileptic fits was more like it, arms jerking, bodies quivering, heads flopping like mops.

PamZ and I would sit in the red leather booths raised at the back where we could socialise with pop stars. PamZ knew everyone and tried to get me a boyfriend, but I was too wrapped up in my work to worry. So when she introduced me to a heavily-built stranger with dark curly hair, mid-thirties, kind of handsome, who chatted and flirted with me, I responded like a wax dummy. Presumably exasperated, he wandered off. Then PamZ told me he was Lou Adler, one of the hottest producers in town, who recorded artists like the Mamas and the Papas, Johnny Rivers and Sam Cooke, and had recently sold his record company for three million dollars. Perhaps that explained why a glazed look came over his eyes when I'd asked him, 'What was your name again?' and another of PamZ's friends, Joe Boyd, who was standing nearby, overheard me and laughed out loud.

Joe, a stunning, Scandinavian-looking American who lived in London and managed the Incredible String Band, turned out to know my friend Oonagh, who worked for Ronan O'Rahilly, the owner of Radio Caroline, a pirate radio station that broadcast from a boat on the River Thames. I felt relief to make a connection with someone from home.

Joe asked how I'd come to work for Frank, a question I faced every time I met someone new. Sometimes I said, 'Frank liked me arguing about "Brown Shoes Don't Make It".' Or, 'He thought I said "Rite of Spring" and that I was a fan of Stravinsky.' But, in reality, I had no idea why Frank had offered me the job – it was the one thing I had never asked him.

When PamZ was not preventing a very drunk Jim Morrison from falling between the tables, she and I and whoever chauffeured us would abandon the Whisky in favour of Barney's Beanery, an extraordinary hub of a place open twenty-four hours a day. We would stand crammed in the crowd at the long, wooden bar, shouting above the cacophony of loud music and TVs blasting out American football.

When we were hungry, we sat in striped leather booths and chomped through cheeseburgers for 95 cents, including fries. Thus, I saved myself from starvation. Under the glass tabletops, photographic collages of Hollywood actors and singers created a diversion if conversation fell flat, which it did when PamZ dragged along American musicians like, for example, two boys from the Doors whose mutterings melted away. Compare that with the exuberant energy dished up by the English boys, usually Cockney-types like David from Them, whose conversation sparkled with witty retorts, none of the soul-searching, verging-on-neurotic self-analysis of the American boys.

PamZ invited everyone that she met during our soirées back to the house and, sure enough, days later, there I would find them, looking lost, wandering through the middle of Frank's workspace, taking the long walk across the living room to knock on PamZ's bedroom door.

I could not fathom her role there. She was no longer touring, no longer Suzy Creamcheese, and served no apparent purpose. With no income, she lived rent-free with food on tap, but how she paid for anything else I never understood. When Gail gave me my first $70 wages, I invited PamZ for a meal, calling on Calvin to chauffeur us to Schwab's, the famous drugstore just off Hollywood Boulevard. After we'd ordered BLT sandwiches and iced tea, PamZ leaned into the corner of our booth and gave me one of her supercilious stares. 'You've been here a week now, Pauline.'

'I know. I can't believe it's gone so quickly.'

'W-e-e-l-l?' she said.

No other person could say so much with one word. The heavy tone of her question suggested she expected some profound insight, and since I wished to show I had as much intuition as she had, and determined not to be outdone, I replied, 'You could say, I suppose, that Gail is more in love with Frank than the other way round.'

'Ex-a-a-a-c-t-l-y,' she said, like a teacher encouraging her pupil. 'You and I are coming from different places but we know, because we're intelligent, we can see what's going down with Frank and Gail.'

Always willing to dazzle me with her insider knowledge and power, she said Frank would *not* be holding a party as everyone hoped and that if I wanted to understand Frank fully, I needed to know certain things. 'See, Frank would like to cut his hair and wear suits and be a regular businessman. The only reason he doesn't do it is because he's too fucking scared it will ruin his image.' She laughed with short intakes of breath that I found quite fetching. 'He never takes Gail anywhere,' which was not strictly true, *rarely* would be more accurate, 'and he hates all those freaks of Christine's dropping by.'

'What do you think of them?'

'Un-fucking-believable. As boring as fuck, as boring and vacuous as is humanly possible to be.'

I found her savage wit so amusing, it was impossible not to like her.

'See Pauline, I love Frank and I want him to be happy, but I'm not in love with him.'

I nodded. In fact, now that I thought about it, it was not a bad description of my own feelings.

Casually she tapped the table with the coaster. 'You know what I think you should do? You should lure him away from her.'

My burger stopped in my throat and I almost choked.

'Make him fall in love with you,' she went on, heavy and serious. 'You can do it. He really likes you. *Really* likes you.'

'How do *you* know?'

'You make him laugh – a lot. In any case, it's my job to know these things. And I'm psychic.' She pushed her plate away, rested her face on her palm, her gaze steady on mine. 'You do know, don't you, that she was seven months pregnant when they got married.'

'So? Lots of people are. And he's not likely to leave her now that she's got the baby, wouldn't you say?'

'Have you ever seen him play with Moon? Take her out?' She began brushing her hair, confident she'd made her point.

It was true. Now that I thought about it, apart from a few tickles on her tummy, Moon received no more attention from Frank than anyone else in the house, at least not in our view.

'Pam, why are you telling me this?'

'I'm telling you this because I'm extremely emotionally bound in this stuff.'

'I see that.'

'See, Frank is spiritually guided. He believes he isn't human and – in a way – he isn't.' Her voice was flat and heavy. It made her words even more incongruous. 'He seeks to connect with humanity in a certain way, and he seeks the intellect and the intellect comes, but sometimes he forgets the humanity.'

I stared at her not knowing how to arrange my face – incredulous, believing, sceptical? 'You know what you should do?' she said, suddenly bombing down to earth.

'No?'

'Grab his balls.'

Despite myself, I laughed.

Throughout the following week, PamZ never let up. What she explained, time after time, in my bedroom, in bars and cafés, in the dim red lights of the Whisky a Go-Go, and often under the influence of alcohol, cannabis and maybe much more, was that during the seven months she lived with Frank before the fateful day Gail arrived, *she* had been his closest confidante. With her help, he had not only found his way round the Laurel Canyon community, he had also worked through his political views. She was his social agent, gleaning information from high and low and bringing it to him like a dog with a bone. More importantly, what she was doing now without reservation, I finally understood, was waiting to reclaim her rightful place by Frank's side.

Most nights we ended up in my bedroom, sitting on my bed hugging our knees, giggling and gossiping and revealing everything about each other, very often until dawn. She told me without bitterness about her father. 'He is this horrible murdering guy on the level of Hitler, a truly, truly, bad person. When I was sixteen, he murdered my mother, okay?'

My mouth hung open, but PamZ was used to that.

'I've barely found my feet, y'know? The drink and the drugs and the craziness, it's my way of surviving. This is where my delicate psyche is coming from, are you with me?'

'Yes, yes, yes.'

To escape from her father, she'd undergone a marriage of convenience with a man who needed to stay in the States. They'd parted immediately. 'I was a reject when I was sixteen, and Frank was a reject and when you're a reject at school, the only fucking friends you have are other rejects. I think that's something that Frank and I really understand about each other, being rejected, and then suddenly I'm attractive and the same with Frank, suddenly Frank's attractive.'

'But what I don't understand, Pam, is how you could have lived with a man like Frank for so long and not had sex. How could that have happened?'

She surveyed me with lowered lids. 'Because he's in love with me, okay? That's the deal.'

'Right, right,' I said, still bewildered.

I enjoyed and looked forward to our nightly sessions. They soothed my fraught nerves if I'd had clashes during the day with Gail. But there was more to it. I knew that if I did not keep PamZ as a friend, she would very swiftly become an enemy – and I did not want PamZ as an enemy.

As a 'thank-you' gesture for her friendship, I bought her a present, but when I handed it over, she said, 'What is it?'

'What do you mean, what is it? It's a tissue box. You put your box of tissues in it.'

She looked at the box and looked at me.

'Is it all right?'

'Well, I dunno, Pauline,' she said with a shake of her head, 'you blow me away.'

I felt the blood drain from my face. Obviously, I'd made an error, the sort of error that would become the butt of jokes between PamZ and Gail, and now that I glanced again at the plastic, lacy box, it did look rather lame. With a feathery laugh, I said, 'Oh, don't worry. I wasn't thinking straight,' and made to fold the corners of my bed, already tight as a drum-skin.

Meanwhile friends from England wrote to ask if PamZ was a lesbian, suspicious because she always wore trousers, shirts and waistcoats and did not possess a dress or skirt. I reassured them with a definite no. One day, she did borrow one of my dresses. The courts had summoned Ray Collins about a missing tail-light on his car and, because PamZ wanted to accompany him and women were not allowed in court in trousers, she chose my green mini-dress with yellow sleeves and yellow trim round the bottom. To finish the effect, she squashed her feet into my court shoes. The outfit did not suit her at all. In fact, she looked ridiculous because she walked as if she still wore her heavy boots. I never saw her in a dress or skirt again.

Despite PamZ's declaration of intimacy with Frank, they rarely spoke to each other. Then one night about three in the morning, she rolled into the log cabin completely drunk and stoned out of her mind. She stood in my office and yelled at the top of her voice, loud enough for Frank, who was working in the living room, to hear, 'I don't want to be in this house, there's no love in this house, no one kisses, no one hugs, it's cold, it's miserable.' She screamed on and on in this vein until she stumbled through to her room, still muttering to herself.

The next afternoon, while Gail and Christine were out shopping and I sat at the kitchen table feasting on my only food for the day – apple pie, cherries and toast – PamZ, now recovered and perfectly sane, perched on the counter banging her heels against the cupboard doors. She was telling me about Nick Venet, with whom she'd got drunk the night before. 'He's fucking brilliant. Produces the Beach Boys, Bobby Darin and zillions of others,' she declared, languid and bored. I'd met him one night when he'd extravagantly bought a drink for everyone at the bar at the Troubadour while the James Cotton Blues Band played in the background. I loved Nick's quiet voice. In fact, all the men I met at the log cabin spoke this way – Frank, Calvin, Ian, Motorhead, Dick – as though their voices had been flattened and softened through a sound machine.

Frank came in and opened the refrigerator, searching for something to eat.

'Frank,' PamZ called, 'guess who's staying up the Canyon in Johnny Smothers's pad.'

'Ronald Reagan?'

'Paul and John.'

'So?'

'We could invite them over.'

Frank began pulling out leftover food from the shelves. 'How old are these frankfurters, do you know?' He held one up and sniffed it.

'So what do you think?' Pam went on.

The refrigerator door slammed with a dull clunk. 'About what?'

'The Beatles. Shall I invite the fuckers over?'

Frank slapped the frankfurter between two slices of bread, already lying cut on the breadboard and probably stale. He found some mustard in the cupboard and squirted it all over. 'First of all, I have a stack of work to get through, and second, if you girls need to wet your underpants, they can come by any time. They know where we live.'

Disappointed, but clearly not beaten, PamZ shrugged. 'Okay.'

This was frustrating for me since John Lennon was the only pop star I had any interest in, the only singer whose voice could send tingles under my skin.

After taking a bite out of his snack, Frank stopped at the door and added tersely, 'If you're planning on calling them, would you please install your own phone line.'

PamZ's face went white at this sudden command.

'And while you're at it,' he went on, 'Isn't it about time you went out and got a job?' He raised his eyebrows, waiting for her to object. She stared back, dumbstruck.

'Get to it,' he said, and disappeared.

PamZ threw me a desperate look and chased after him.

Later, she paced my room, picking apart his words for underlying meanings and groaning. Was she losing her touch? Was he planning her demise? She strode back and forth, brushing her waist-length hair, flicking, brushing, flicking. 'Tell me what the fuck I should do, Pauline?'

But I would not be drawn, knew not to offer advice.

13

By this stage, my daily regime had fallen into a pattern. I would get up about eleven, grab half a grapefruit, toast and coffee and walk down the path to Laurel Canyon to collect the mail from the mailbox. The house would usually be quiet at that time and if there were letters from home, I would happily sit at my desk for an hour reading. Then I would set aside envelopes addressed to Gail and make a separate pile for Frank, opened and smoothed flat, ready for him to look at.

That was on good days. But if Gail was around, she took over and snatched the envelopes from my hand, literally snatched them away and whisked them off to Frank. I never got used to it and each time it happened, I sat at my desk in shock, unable to move. Other times, like a guard on duty, she would watch me from the kitchen doorway, Moon hitched on her hip. Under her gaze I felt inept and self-conscious. I would pull open the files too briskly, skim through the papers too rapidly and slam the drawers too loudly until, thankfully, a visitor would turn up and she'd point Moon toward them and return to the kitchen.

Of course, I should have gone right up to her the first time it happened. 'Look here,' I should have said, 'why are you doing this? Why don't you leave me alone and get on with your own job?' But she had already summed me up, knew I would not retaliate or go to Frank and complain.

Some respite came in the form of a new man on the scene, Herbie's brother, Mutt Cohen, mid-thirties, a divorce lawyer who also advised Frank on business deals. PamZ introduced me to him one night at Barnie's. Tall, slightly overweight with sharp, darting eyes, full lips and a small moustache, he covered a thinning patch by brushing his black, collar-length hair to one side. PamZ told me he was divorced and rich and that I should 'get in there'. She said this so often, I began to wonder why, if all these men were so wonderful, she didn't 'get in there' herself? Was it a sign of true friendship, a real concern to find me a boyfriend? Or, could it be that they were not suitable for *her* choosy taste but *I* could not be so fussy?

Mutt telephoned the next evening and invited me and PamZ out to dinner and, as an afterthought, invited Gail too. She leapt at the chance because Frank and the Mothers had left for Fresno that morning and, as PamZ had pointed out; he never wined and dined her. I was not too pleased because Gail and I had had another scrap earlier which had left me fuming. But all that was forgotten as we sat next to each other in Scandia on Sunset Boulevard and sparred jokingly as if we were the best of friends.

Scandia was not a twenty-four-hour bagel and cheeseburger joint, but a place with a doorman and male waiters and walls decorated with coats of arms, the first proper meal I'd eaten since leaving Washington DC. We ordered smoked salmon starters with dill sauce, followed by veal with béarnaise sauce, asparagus and mashed potatoes and then a delicious custard rice pudding. We even drank wine. I savoured every delicious mouthful while PamZ and Gail competed with each other, teasing Mutt mercilessly about his endless girlfriends.

After we dropped Gail at the log cabin and PamZ had taken off for the airport to fly south, Mutt drove me to see his house further up the hills on winding Woodrow Wilson Drive. There he proudly showed me his four dogs, two cats, a goat, a dozen aquariums full of fish and tortoises and a prize collection of plants and cacti. So, despite his legendary womanising, I reviewed my opinion of him upwards. Anyone devoted to animals had to be kind.

We lounged on a black leather sofa in the kitchen/family room where Dusty, one of the cats, jumped on my lap, warming it like a fat hot-water bottle. Opposite, set into the wall, prize fish swam goggle-eyed in the aquariums.

Mutt's job as a divorce lawyer presented him with a harem of women desperate for a man. 'You can always tell when a woman's going through a divorce,' he said, 'the first thing they do is cut their hair. Never fails. Look around, every time you see a woman in her thirties with short hair, she's either going through a divorce or recently signed the papers.'

He brought more wine and as he filled our glasses I sensed he saw me as a conquest, but I'd decided he was too old, at least in his late thirties, so I steered the conversation on to neutral ground and found myself babbling about my job. 'Even though I work long hours, when Frank is on tour I have so much free time I can't possibly complain: on average I only work about two days out of seven.

Without explaining further, Mutt said, 'Soon you'll have more work than you can handle.'

I took that to mean that I had a secure future and felt relief. I'd been worrying that if Frank stalled on the book, then what would happen? Would he give me the sack, send me back to England?

Dusty shifted her position against my tummy and Mutt leaned over to stroke her. Hastily, I threw her off, drew my legs under me and began gabbling again, this time about Gail and before I knew it, all my pent-up feelings about her flooded out. 'I'm having a lot of trouble with Gail,' I began.

'That doesn't surprise me,' Mutt said.

'It's the telephone; we've only got one in the house and it's in the kitchen and Gail always snatches it up, so I never get to know who Frank's visitors are or why they're there. And it's not only the telephone,' I moaned, 'we fight over the mail as well.'

Even as I wailed about these tribulations, I could also hear how petty my voice sounded because despite these daily spats, Gail and I lived our lives on two parallel lines. On one line, we fought at loggerheads, and on the other, we were good friends, the two different relationships zigzagging along, side by side. I did not devise this pattern, Gail did. A skilled manipulator, she never allowed ill feelings to trip her up. After any of our disagreements that left me grinding my teeth, two minutes later she would bounce in to see if I wanted to go shopping for a bikini or jeans or sandals. Her ability to smile and be friendly two seconds after an argument stumped me so I could hardly believe we'd had any differences at all. And despite the fact that I thought her a total scallywag, strangely I found her warm and easy to live with – a much more relaxing girl than PamZ, whose heaviness often dragged me down.

'When we first moved into the log cabin, Gail and Christine were best friends,' I told Mutt, 'but now they've fallen out and suddenly *I'm* Gail's best friend.'

Mutt went to the fridge and brought back cheese and crackers with two plates and knives but I was too busy talking to eat. Now that I'd started, I couldn't stop. 'In the first week, Christine frizzed Gail's hair. She spent hours winding it on the tiniest of curlers and then took nearly as long to undo it. I think it helped them to bond. Anyway, it came out like an Arab head-dress.'

'I'd like to have seen it,' Mutt said.

'Frank took one look and said, "Wash it out, now," and she did. She never retaliates, never stamps her foot or protests, and the next day she had it back to her shaggy, all-over-the-place best.'

'You call that "the best"?'

'You've seen the log cabin, haven't you? You know what a mess it always is? Well, one afternoon, Gail cleaned the lounge. I couldn't believe it. She piled three single mattresses on top of each other and turned it into a couch, set a long wooden stool behind and decorated it with flowers, and placed two old leather trunks for coffee tables in front, and when Frank came back from a weekend on the road, he said, "It's the first time the house has looked like a home," so he really does like the house to be tidy! I don't know why he doesn't make his wishes more clear and issue orders for people to clean up, but he never does. I just accept now that interference is not his way.'

Mutt shook his head while busily pouring more wine. He didn't smoke but tolerated my need and I lit up.

'Sometimes when Frank's on tour, Gail comes out with us for a drink, like with Pam and Ian and Dick and me. You can tell she loves coming because Frank never takes her out, or at least that's what Pam says. And when we get there, usually at Barney's, she gets surrounded by men because she's got that kind of pretty, sexual allure y'know?'

Mutt raised his eyebrows and shook his head sceptically.

'She always acts coy and guarded and makes it clear she's out of bounds, but you can tell she loves it because she flutters her eyelashes and gets all flushed. But what's so strange about Gail is that two minutes after we've been out on these trips, all friendly and chatting, she's on my back again. When I go to my desk and start typing a letter she wants to know who I'm writing to and what it says. She says, "Show it to me before you show it to Frank." And what is so ridiculous, like a little lamb, I do.'

I waited a moment for Mutt to offer some condolence, but he kept his eyes down, cutting more cheese.

'I don't know why she's doing it. Am I a threat to her position? Look at the way she always makes sure I'm never alone with Frank, always intervenes somehow or other. But what can I do? She's Frank's wife. And *he* doesn't object, which makes me a little cross. And then she gets all friendly again. It makes me so mad.'

'You know what I think,' Mutt said, 'I think you worry too much.'

'I do because I have a recurring nightmare about executions. I stand in line for the gallows but while everyone else seems to accept their fate, shuffling toward the noose, I search around for an escape. Sometimes I get out in time and sometimes I wake up just before it's my turn. Do you think it has any meaning?'

'I'll ask my psychiatrist.'

'Maybe it's a warning to take firm action and confront Frank? But then, what could I possibly say? "I find your wife an interfering busy-body," or "Don't you think she could spend her time more profitably cooking for the family or preventing the eternal riff-raff from wafting in every day?"'

Mutt gave a wry shrug. 'Might work.'

'No, it wouldn't because it sounds weak, I realise that. Deep down, I know that if Gail treats me as putty in her hands, it's because I'm not positive enough, don't exude enough confidence. If I acted more of a stalwart, I think she'd back off.'

'Okay, so why don't you?'

'I can't. Do you think Frank really wants to hear us squabbling? What good would it do to force him to take sides? It's unthinkable. Anyway, I doubt if he could be bothered. I think he trusts me to get on with my job unsupervised precisely so I can sort these problems out myself.'

Mutt kept pouring wine, the level in the glass never seeming to go down.

'In fact, I often wonder if Frank actually does know what Gail's doing. Maybe he approves, encourages her even? For all I know, they lie in bed together passing witticisms about me, enjoying the joke.'

I looked to Mutt again for reassurance. Instead, with a little smile, he said, 'I'm trying to imagine Frank and Gail in bed.'

'What if he said to me, "I know Gail is usurping your space, but tough, *deal with it*," what would I do then?'

'I see your point.'

'I think I need to suss things out a bit more. I need more evidence of where he stands.'

In other words, I needed osmosis; I needed an ally. And here was Mutt, who might do it.

I'd been ranting on for hours and when we drove back to the log cabin while the first grey of dawn rose over the hills, I felt sure he would support me in my battle. If he would have a word with Frank about my complaints, that would be ideal, that would be osmosis working. In fact, it would take just two weeks.

14

s part of the research for his *Life* magazine article, Frank invited a
succession of black musicians and singers to the house; musicians
who'd been successful in the 1950s, some of them spruced-up in ill-
fitting clothes for the occasion. From dusty, time-worn eyes, they threw guarded
glances at Frank as if to say, 'Who *is* this freaky-looking guy?' But soon, after
Frank had expressed admiration for their music, the frowns would lift and
you would hear them talking freely and loudly, so that by the time they left
it was an all-round hearty, hand-shaking, back-slapping and joking farewell.
Afterwards he would grumble. 'See how tragic this business is? These guys
are forced to work at the local car wash because no one wants to listen to real
music.' There was no mistaking the bitterness in his voice.

If there was nothing else to do while I waited each day for Frank to give
me the tapes, I would type endless letters home, so that into the third week,
I wrote:

> *Nobody thinks of going to bed before three-thirty to four in the*
> *morning. Everyone just sits around and talks in various parts*
> *of the house, mostly in the kitchen, living room or in my office.*
> *And because there are so many people living here, now ten in all,*
> *even when we have no visitors, I am completely entertained and*
> *kept busy with all the dramas, fun and life inside the log cabin. I*
> *like it very much and can't think of anywhere I would rather be.*
> *I have no interest in going out on dates or finding a boyfriend*
> *because I am too involved sorting my job and decorating my room.*
> *When Frank and the Mothers played in Miami last weekend, Gail*
> *dumped tins of white paint on the floor with the clear message, 'If*

you're so upset then get on and do it yourself,' and I did. I patched up the holes with stiff white paper and taped round the edges. To paint the ceiling I had to use a chair and nearly broke my back craning upwards. Still, my spirits rose as the clean white surfaces crept round the walls like a tide of fresh water. Who would believe that I, a girl who had never raised my hand to make more than a cup of tea, should knuckle down to scrubbing, cleaning, painting, decorating? I'm really proud of what I've achieved.

Otherwise, my life is relaxed and easy and I choose my work hours. If I go shopping all day (and it takes all day to get two or three things), then that is all right, too.

I was so engrossed in my words that I jumped when I saw Frank leaning by the window watching me. How long had he been there?

'We're going out to eat with Robyn. Would you like to join us?'

I could hardly believe my ears. Since I'd arrived, I'd survived on grapefruit, toast or cheese sandwiches. Well, what else was I supposed to do? If you'd grown up with five older sisters who banished you from the kitchen, you too would be an ignoramus cook. And if, during the first week at the log cabin you learned there was no such thing as a mealtime and if you wanted to eat you must help yourself, then finally you, like me, would have plucked up courage and made a sandwich, three slices of processed cheese between two pieces of cut white bread, no salad, no tomatoes, no dressing – and that's what I'd been living on for nearly three weeks. Bland as it was, I would rather suffer than demonstrate to everyone in the house what a hopeless cook I was.

Ian, though, had cottoned on to my shameful secret and one morning had shown pity: he cooked porridge, which just about staved off my collapse. Another time, he demonstrated how to fry eggs without burning the whites or ending up with a soggy mess. The trick, he said, was to use the lowest heat with a small amount of butter and olive oil, and be patient.

As sod's law would have it, that very afternoon, when Frank was out with Robyn from *Life* magazine, Gail had retreated upstairs with Moon, and Calvin went out shopping with Dick and Christine, I had finally plucked up courage to follow Ian's recipe and it worked: two circular, yellow yolks in the centre of perfectly-shaped egg whites, each on a piece of lightly grilled toast. Brilliant. I'd also cut some ham from a big leg that was in the fridge. So even though I was not suffering my usual pangs of hunger because I'd already stuffed myself with a mini-feast, I jumped at the chance to have an early dinner with Frank.

We climbed in to their hired Buick and, with Gail at the wheel, drove in silence to Denny's Restaurant on West Sunset Boulevard.

If Frank wanted to avoid recognition, it was a weak attempt. He had tied his hair back, but his long tweed coat to the floor with shoulders that hung over the edge, combined with his black moustache like an upside-down anchor and rumpled fringe, could not be missed. People nudged each other, who is that strange, freaky-looking creature? I wanted to tell them he was not a weirdo and that underneath the strange beard, hair and clothes lurked a very straight, intelligent person, conservative even.

Once we'd settled in a booth, I ordered a steak, assuming it a safe option, medium rare, with chips and a side salad. But then Frank and Gail and Robyn ordered a hamburger each and I felt embarrassed that I had not known the protocol, an awkward moment made worse when they swallowed their food in five minutes and sat patiently watching while I cut small portions of meat and balanced the onions, English-style, on the back of my fork. We had no starters, no puddings and no light-hearted repartee, the whole meal rushed through in twenty minutes. Frank hardly spoke. Robyn valiantly tried to pep up the conversation about New York but Gail, in a dutifully wifely way, remained silent, so the whole meal felt edgy and tense. Frank did tell us a story in boring detail about how vibrations influenced living things, vibrations being the basis of all existence, he said. The rest of the time, we sat in silence, the only sound being my knife and fork scraping the plate.

I could not understand why Frank was as dry as toast. Compare how much fun we'd had in London and New York, how charming, ebullient and ready to chat for hours he'd been. Could he be worrying about the article on which he'd laboured for days? Lyrics poured out of him with ease; he could rattle off album cover notes and be eloquent in interviews, but prose proved more difficult. True, he'd already penned a history of the Mothers for *Hit Parader* magazine, but his article for *Life* required that he express his ideas and for several days he'd struggled, handing me draft after draft as he tried to bash it into shape.

The deadline was the next day so, with less than half of it written, Frank prepared to start work after rehearsal at ten o'clock, determined to stay up all night if that's what it would take. He sat on a kitchen chair next to my desk, placed cigarettes and a coffee flask on the corner and readied for a marathon session.

For whatever reason, Gail chose that moment to rope in Dick – our guardian and willing aid – to help decorate the walls of my office. So for the next several hours, Frank and I breathed in the fumes from the paint, but while he showed no sign of pique, I glared at Gail. Since Frank had arrived at the log cabin, except to listen to *Cruising with Ruben and the Jets*, I had not spent a moment alone with him. Whenever I'd attempted it, Gail had waltzed in, Moon on her hip, keeping an eye. And here she was again. Petulantly, I said, 'You mean you're not washing the walls first? You're painting over the grime?'

She replied blithely, 'This is not the Hilton Hotel, Pauline,' and slapped the roller any which way, pale blue above the dado rail and a muggy green for the area below. Both colours clashed with the mural on the ceiling – delicate, cream cherubs and flowers. What with the brown wood of the dado rail, four different colours now graced my office. Ugh. Frank didn't like it either. I told them it looked like a scullery but no one knew what a scullery was.

All this while, Christine sat on the floor joining pieces of mismatched fabric together, fabric that would soon metamorphose into a unique outfit to wrap around her emaciated body. Moon played beside her, chucking one wooden brick after another out of reach so Christine had to stretch out a thin white arm to retrieve them.

'Family nights' like these – rare occasions when no visitors dribbled in – were intimate and calm and in that respect, I was happy. Apart from Moon's constant babbling and shrieks, we worked in silence, Frank hunched over the page before handing me rewrites.

He had given the piece a clever title, 'The Oracle Has It All Psyched Out', but it lacked an overall theme. In the first part, Frank argued that, but for the emergence of rock'n'roll in the 1950s, the Swinging Sixties would not have happened. He wrote about his favoured black music, rhythm and blues. He gave special mention to high-school heroes, Johnny Otis, Howlin' Wolf and Willie Mae Thornton. But then, in 1955, the landmark film *Blackboard Jungle* came out with its world-stopping soundtrack, Bill Haley's 'Rock Around the Clock', and teenagers everywhere had soaked it up. Parents, though, were appalled. Rock'n'roll was bad because it contained a sexually provocative beat based on black music. In response to the outcry, the music business tried to tame down its acts and sanitise their records. Simple love songs by Pat Boone and Elvis Presley won the day, preparing for the early 1960s and innocent lyrics like 'I Wanna Hold Your Hand'. Gradually though, more adventurous rhymes crept in and by then there was no going back.

It was a good essay. The trouble was it filled only half the article, so he went on to talk about sexual repression in the 1950s, which he argued had not only caused teenage vandalism and gang warfare, but also brought about many misguided laws.

Was this true? As far as I could see, Frank never read a book, newspaper or magazine, never watched TV or listened to the radio. How he formulated his views I did not know, since he rarely went out into the world except for TV interviews or awards shows. I gathered he'd read widely in his teen years and had a formidable memory, but nowadays he seemed to devise his ideas from bits of information people brought to him. Although one could never accuse Frank of being narrow-minded, I felt that the data on which he based his views was scanty. When I'd raised this point with PamZ, she'd told me, 'He always said he went to the library and learned everything in the library.'

'Before he met you?'

'Yes. He spent all his time in the library.'

'And he learned about Freud – '

'Library, library, library.'

By three o'clock in the morning, Christine had retired, Gail and Dick lay down their paint brushes, and Gail whisked Moon, who had dropped into a slumbering heap on the floor, off to bed.

At last, Frank and I were alone and I hoped we might stop for a break and a chat, but I should have realised that when Frank undertook any task, be it composing, writing, performing or even socialising, he concentrated on it one hundred percent. And so, for the next six hours, we worked in comfortable, familiar silence save for a night bird's mating call.

Still two thousand words short, he added a section on groupies and then sidled into the progress of recording techniques from single track to the present eight track and the future twenty-four or even seventy-two tracks. Other sections covered a long analysis of Jimi Hendrix's appeal, and a moan about radio stations' continual refusal to play progressive music. He finished with a grand finale about throbbing rhythms and their sexual ramifications.

Before we realised it, the Californian sunshine had slanted across my office and at eight-thirty I typed in the last edit. We'd guzzled innumerable cups of coffee and smoked enough cigarettes to choke a chimney. We'd toiled for more than ten hours and, though my back ached and I longed to rest, my psyched-up state would not allow me to sleep.

After Frank had thanked me and taken himself off to bed, I wandered outside into the car port, round into the front garden and paused by the pond, over-laden with plants and big enough to be a small lake. Where the algae separated, I could see my reflection, gaunt after my night's labour, but I was not sad. How could I be? I had a job, a high-status job, more than a mere secretary. I had attained my first goal: escape from the concrete of London for a leafy, picturesque canyon, a haven not only in the heart of Hollywood but for one of the most charismatic figures in the music business, an association that might, one day, help me become somebody of relevance myself. I would use this foothold as a propeller into the movie industry, an industry that boasted mature, glamorous men and women, men and women who, according to magazines, lounged in luxurious homes and lived sophisticated lifestyles. In contrast, the music business was filled with boys and girls bent on self-destruction, smashing up hotel rooms, killing themselves with drugs and swapping sex partners like fleas. Apart from Frank, I had no interest in them at all.

I walked on through the open gate to wait on Laurel Canyon for the mail to arrive. I was not homesick but I cherished letters from home. They gave me an anchor from the strange world in which I was sinking.

Unfamiliar birdsong and the whirr of insects chorused around as cars crawled down the hill. I saw one of the Monkees whose name I did not know and at one point, a boy leaned out of a car and shouted, 'Hey, man, that's the Zappa pad.' I laughed and waved back.

In my zombie-like state, I failed to notice one and a half hours slip by before the postman arrived with a letter from my mother. A reward indeed. She wrote: 'I am glad to know that Frank is against drugs. We think of you a lot and wonder how you are getting on, but we know you are wise and know all about life now.'

I placed my mother's letter on my recently scrubbed chest of drawers, and with daylight streaming through the shrubs outside my window, I crawled into bed at eleven o'clock and passed out.

At dusk, Gail roused me, shaking my shoulders. Dick had covered the pale blue walls in my office with muggy green paint to match the lower part, making the room look stark and drab. To cheer it up, I placed photographs of Frank around the wooden dado rail. Gail giggled as if to say, 'Okay, Pauline, we know you're in love but let's keep a little perspective here.'

In the article, Frank had found one typing mistake and we posted the finished copy off to New York. The next task, I hoped, would be the political book. I could not wait to start work on the book.

15

Now the pattern was set: I worked all night and slept through the day.
Four days later, Gail ruffled my covers late afternoon. 'Pauline,
wake up.'

Still groggy, I struggled onto an elbow. 'What time is it?'

'Four o'clock. Listen, can you arrange your sleep time to match Frank's?
He's been up for hours.'

Puzzled, I muttered, 'Frank didn't say.'

'Yeah, well, I'm telling you now,' a cursory remark which made me feel
wretched, not only because I'd displeased Frank but also because I'd given
Gail another reason to issue orders.

Normally, Gail preferred the 'just stepped-out-of-bed look', so I was
surprised to see she'd run a brush through her hair, stroked on mascara and
smoothed a layer of pink on her lips – the first time I'd seen her groomed.
When I descended the two steps into the living room, I found out why.

Seated on the edge of a wicker chair was Frank's mother, a pretty, neatly
dressed woman who shook my hand warmly. Candy, Frank's seventeen-year-
old sister, her hair cut in a bob, perched on the sofa playing guitar and, with
a surprisingly deep voice, was singing possibly one of her own compositions.
Brother Carl, although twenty years old, hovered in the background as timid
as Frank was bold, while Mr Zappa, Sr circled the room with the rigid posture
of a military man as if to add to his height. He'd actually been a maths
teacher and numerous other things in science and research. Frank told me
he'd written a book called *How to Bet and Win Money*, which was odd since
Frank had paid for their family to return to California from Florida. Clearly
proud of Frank, Mr Zappa gestured in Frank's direction, nodding and smiling
at Frank's every word.

Yet it was not always so. Gail later told me that when Frank had first grown his hair and beard, his father had banned him from their home. And when Frank lived 'in sin' with Kay Sherman, Mr Zappa cut off all contact, relenting only when Frank married Kay. And now that Frank had a second wife, Gail, I noticed a definite coolness towards her.

Watching these two sober Catholic parents, I wondered how they had produced such an unorthodox offspring and successful musician like Frank Zappa. They must have done something right, yet he'd rebelled against them. Why? What had made him turn heel?

Years later in 1988, when I visited Frank in his hotel in London and he was a father of his own four children, I asked him that question. 'What was it about your parents that made you the way you are?'

'Not very much,' he replied, 'because basically you get to a point and you see that your parents are behaving in a way that is either illogical or irrelevant, and you may not wish to argue with them because they have been nice to you, so you just ignore them and find your own way, because I think that if I had followed every rule that was in the house when I grew up, I would be like them and I wouldn't have had a very good time.' This thought amused him highly and he'd chuckled at his own words.

With his own children, he said, he showed more tolerance. 'One of the things that I do that's different from the way my parents raised me is that if my parents said no, it meant no, even if it didn't make any sense at all, but in our house if I say "no" and any one of the kids disagrees with it and they can logically prove that I'm wrong, they win. I think that's a good way to teach kids to use logic and make them learn to negotiate. I think that's something that ought to be developed in homes.'

But in 1968, Frank politely entertained his parents, brother and sister like any other dutiful son while Gail offered glazed smiles and idle chitchat. Noticeably, neither Frank nor Gail used any swear words during the hour-long visit, a change of behaviour which showed that no matter how avant garde their lifestyle, beneath it all, they still honoured basic traditional values.

Maybe their visit put Frank in an ebullient mood, because after rehearsal Frank made one of his rare social appearances in the kitchen, pulling out a chair and joining Christine and me at the table. Everyone else was out and Gail had crashed upstairs with Moon. Christine had made a chocolate cake which had been scoffed without decorum, but a spattered piece lay in the centre. Frank jumped up to search for a plate but Christine quickly pulled one from the dirty stack in the sink, washed and dried it and presented it to Frank with a fork. He scraped over the scrappy portion and gobbled it down in a trice.

He told us a story about Richard Berry, who he seemed to think was one of the most important sources of rhythm and blues from the 1940s. 'He told me he was working with a Latin band at a place called the Harmony Park Ballroom and the band had an instrumental that went so, and he scribbled out the lyrics for "Louie Louie" on a paper napkin in the dressing room. Then he sold the rights for five thousand dollars. Can you imagine how much money that song's made?' Frank asked incredulously. 'Now he's walking around trying to get a contract.'

Frank was wide-eyed with wonder but I kept my mouth shut, still none the wiser about a song that seemed to spring from Frank's lips every time there was a story to tell.

'I'm planning on inviting Eric Clapton and a few other guys to stay at the house when they're in LA.'

'It seems to me you don't have to invite anyone,' I said, 'they just roll up anyhow, pure entertainment right here. I worked it out. We have eight people living in the house, then six Mothers roll in for rehearsal, which makes fourteen, and that's without the visitors. I reckon there are at least twenty people wandering around in here at sometime or another each day. Did you see that boy and girl sitting on the floor in my office today, cracking open cans of beer, about fourteen years old? Who were they? Nobody seems to know.'

'Well, maybe we can be a little more – *selective*,' he said with a wry look.

Well, okay, that would be good, but how? He made no suggestion and for a moment the room went quiet.

Then began what would become a constant repartee between us, like a game of ping-pong: Frank throwing caustic remarks about my sex-life and me batting him off.

'When are you going to jump on one of the guys, Pauline?'

Somewhat huffily, I muttered, 'Thank you for your concern, Frank, but my work is sufficient for now.'

'Ah, go for it. Don't you want to get laid?'

'No.'

'Think of the delight you're missing.'

'My life is already delightful. In any case, I like to be at least wrapped in the realms of love before sex will enter my head.'

'You mean you believe in all those "love" lyrics, that if you say, "let's make love", that somehow purifies your actions more than if you say, "let's go fuck"? Come on now, what kind of wazzy believes shit like that?'

'Apparently, I do,' I said with my nose in the air.

Christine, who stood at the sink scraping a pan, an apron tied round her waist, said, 'I think deep down guys like girls to be virgins.'

'Why?' Frank asked. He hooked a chair with his bare foot and hoisted his feet up. 'It doesn't matter to me how many guys a girl has fucked. What difference does it make?'

Christine returned to scrubbing and thankfully Frank returned to the subject he liked talking about most – his music – a subject that required no words from me, just nods and admiration.

Had I realised how rare an occasion this social visit to the kitchen would be, I might have treated it with less casualness, written it down in my diary in more detail. I assumed there would be many more to come. How wrong I was.

16

Frank's love of music did not extend to a love of the Mothers of Invention. He tolerated them merely to hear his music played, music that was increasingly beyond their reach, music that he composed in happy isolation in his corner, stroking those little notes onto music sheets.

Outside of rehearsals, dictation or socialising, he worked every night until six or seven in the morning, slept most of the day and started again late afternoon. Gradually, his hours slipped around until the routine reversed and he'd get up at six in the morning, compose all day and retire after rehearsal.

You would find him hunched at his desk, or he'd shift across to the piano bench, contort one bare foot on his knee, a cup of coffee by his side, a cigarette burning in the ashtray, and start tinkling the keys. Something compelling emanated from that quiet corner while he worked, his presence so intense and concentrated that, like iron filings, he seemed to draw people to him yet, at the same time, repel any advance. Wherever Frank was in the house was the centre of gravity.

No one lingered in the living room to listen – it would have been an intrusion – but sometimes I sat on the two steps outside my room and experienced a stirring hour as Frank produced music before my exalted eyes. He could see me, motionless, some fifty feet away, too far away to interrupt his flow but near enough to convey my admiration. Repeatedly, with one thorny finger, he picked out the melody and occasionally added in a chord. From time to time, he changed the tempo or emphasis of one of the notes, repeating the changed version many times until, satisfied, he would stop, dip his pen into a pot of India ink and, with the help of a ruler, transfer the passage in neat, feathery tendrils onto the page. Sometimes he would pick up his guitar and pluck out the melody on the strings. At this stage, it sounded disjointed, like no tune at all. Then Ian would join him on the piano bench and play the piece with both hands, something that Frank could not do. Suddenly this fabulous melody would ring out and, as Frank turned the page, his face would soften and become serene, while sometimes tears of exultation I did not understand would trickle down my cheeks.

If Frank's beautiful melodies astonished me, the perfection of his manuscripts surprised me also. You would think he would scribble the crochets, minims and quavers onto the page in a hurry to get them down, but when I occasionally got a chance to inspect those A3 sheets, there would be no smudges, no alterations, just perfectly formed notes, which themselves made shapes like works of art.

Late afternoon, before rehearsal, Frank would dictate letters and I would rattle them off ready for him to sign when the band finished about ten in the evening. Then Frank and several of the Mothers would congregate in my office for ten or fifteen minutes to chill out. On this particular evening everyone had taken off, Gail had settled Moon on the floor, and Frank had checked through my work. I hoped he would start work on the book; after all, we had a deadline less than seven months away. But no, he laced his fingers, cracked his knuckles and began another profound moan about the Mothers' lack of musical expertise. 'The music I'm writing now is too complex and difficult for the band to play. I need to find new musicians, a different group of people who can read what I've written. I want to leave the band and I'll have to find some way to tell them.'

Since arriving in California, the Mothers had played two concerts in twenty days and, although Herb had booked a few gigs up the West Coast in June, he'd arranged only five for the whole of July. Hauling masses of equipment around the country for so few dates was clearly not economic. 'That's another thing,' Frank complained, his eyes seeming to sink deeper into their sockets, 'They've got things ass backwards, demanding more money.'

Once again, I felt chuffed that Frank was confiding in me and valued my counsel, but inside I felt unworthy of his trust, not the wise person he seemed to assume I was.

'Do you not worry about the Mothers' own future?' I asked.

'No, I don't,' he said emphatically. 'Their future is not my responsibility. They'll do what other members of bands do when they break up, they'll join other groups. They're good enough musicians for a rock'n'roll band. It won't be a problem.'

Yet the next day, Frank did not divulge his plans to the Mothers during their trip to Salt Lake City on 29 May. Instead, he came back positively glowing and told Jerry Hopkins, who'd arrived with his Uher tape recorder to interview

Frank, that for the first time he felt the audience wanted to listen and had understood their music. How, I wondered, could he even conceive of breaking up the band when it was going from strength to strength?

Seated by Frank to take down the interview in shorthand, I gave Jerry a quick glance to see if he could read my thoughts. No one seemed to realise what a wealth of information secretaries tucked away in their heads. Secretaries remain soulless creatures, forever invisible, and so Jerry picked up no clue as to the upheavals rumbling beneath the surface. Had he probed a bit more he might have sussed Frank's underlying disquiet, but his questions moved toward Frank's marketing skills and control of the album-cover designs and his use of the underground press for publicity, actions that made Frank so unusual. Such acute business acumen and grasp of complex matters impressed not only Jerry but all journalists who interviewed Frank.

While I typed up the interview, Ian Underwood, his handsome face lost in a book, waited in my office to go out to eat. Until he found somewhere to live, he'd been hanging out at the log cabin every day and throwing his sleeping bag on the floor in the basement. I liked him because, like Frank and Motorhead, he did not take drugs, and we sought each other out, driving into Hollywood each day for breakfast and dinner (so I no longer starved). One time, we'd driven along Sunset Boulevard to Malibu for a stroll along the beach. I found his company refreshing because he alone at the log cabin failed to pick fault with American society and he was, by any standards, a brilliant musician, very attractive and intelligent. There was no one else like him. A lover of music, he stood apart from the other Mothers with his interest in foreign films, literature and the arts. But now I had some gossip to divulge over our meal.

We ate at the Country Store where Ian picked up the bill, a real treat, but once I'd related Frank's groans about the Mothers, he became surprisingly exasperated and angry. He rattled off a tirade of his own. Did Frank not realise he was not the only dissatisfied Mother? Did he not know they were all tired and fed up with his sour face each day at rehearsal? Who was he to make them feel worthless after they'd put in hours of hard work practising new material? And how could they play their best when he spouted nothing but criticism and never offered praise? When would Frank begin to show some appreciation for *their* hard work and contribution to the band's success? Had he forgotten the sacrifices Ray, Jim and Roy had made during their years in the wilderness? Wasn't it time for just rewards now that the band was about to take off in a big way?

I tried to reassure him. 'Oh, I don't know, Ian. Perhaps I've overstated the case. He'll probably change his mind at the weekend. He's done it before.' But it was too late. More fired up and angry than I'd ever seen him, Ian raced back to the house to confront Frank, but unusually, Frank was already in bed, so alone in the kitchen, Gail became his victim.

'I hear Frank's planning on leaving the band.'

'Really!' she said, in a tone of denial.

'Give him a message for me, will you? Tell him that with his attitude and the way he's been expressing himself lately, this band's going down the tube anyway and if there's going to be anybody leaving, I'll see to it personally that he won't have any band left to leave. *Personally*.'

Gail stood in the kitchen, gently rocking Moon in her arms, her lashes beating a steady defence, her benign expression gradually fading to a frown, as Ian ploughed on with his barrage of complaints. By the time he'd spat out his last tirade, she looked pale and shell-shocked.

'Ian, are you sure about this?

'Dead sure.'

At rehearsal the next day, Ian learned that his onslaught would not bring about the hoped-for truce but, instead, had backfired spectacularly. Frank informed the Mothers that he'd made his decision, his future with the band would end as soon as they agreed a suitable date and, he added emphatically, this decision was final.

Not privy to the meeting, I heard it third-hand. Apparently, they were devastated. Motorhead, who had more to lose than the others since he was not a musician and not likely to find a livelihood with any other group, woke me the next morning. 'Come with me to the beach. I gotta try to sort out this fucking trash before I go mad.'

So unexpectedly I found myself enjoying a second splash along the gentle shore of the Pacific, the horizon lost in haze and smog, while Motorhead convinced himself that because he'd known Frank since school days, longer than any of the others in the group, he could appeal to his human side. He vowed that on Saturday, during their gig in San Bernadino, he and the other guys would force a showdown. 'Our backs are to the wall,' he said. 'We're not going to let this die without one hell of a fight.'

And so when the band returned on Sunday morning and Frank and Ian entered the house together, laughing and joking, a rare occurrence in recent days, I stopped and stared. And – even more of a rarity – cheerful and bright-eyed, Frank accompanied Gail and Moon to a birthday party for Groovy, the little daughter of Vito, the sixty-year-old king of the freaks. Frank was not a hands-on father, so I wished I could have seen him play 'daddy' along with the other dads.

Ian kept me in suspense, refusing to relay his news until everyone had gone to bed. He appeared in the doorway with an armload of firewood tucked under his chin and, with Motorhead's help, they both hunkered down, layering the logs in the enormous grate. I brought in coffee and we lounged on the floor in the fire's flickering light while they told me the news.

'We all agreed,' Motorhead began, 'that the Mothers could not exist without Frank. That was our starting point, but then it got mighty heated and Frank put up a real dogged resistance to all our complaints.'

'Frank made the point,' Ian said, 'that he could not compose effectively when he had to waste his time teaching the guys their parts, so I suggested, "How about *I* take over rehearsals, *I* teach the guys the arrangements and you join us when the guys are ready?" And, finally, he agreed.'

He turned and slapped Motorhead's hand in a congratulatory gesture.

'Well, if it was that simple,' I asked, 'why didn't you think of it before?'

'Because Frank doesn't communicate, that's why,' Motorhead said. 'Frank didn't let us know what was bugging him. Sometimes he's not the best communicator.' There was a palpable sense of relief from both of them as they took it in turns to stoke the flames.

I wondered at what stage in the Mothers' evolution they had accepted Frank as their absolute leader, their boss. In the beginning, they were just a bunch of guys trying to put a group together. Why was it necessary, just because they played Frank's music, for him to be totally in charge, the drover, the autocrat, the captain? Why had the other Mothers allowed that to happen? Motorhead did not question it. For him, Frank had always been the guru, the one with the creative drive, whilst Ian had joined the group after Frank's rigid control had become complete.

The next day, after rehearsal, Frank dictated a long letter to each of the Mothers. He reiterated that Ian would, in future, rehearse the band. He thanked them for their hard work and dedication over the past four years and affirmed how much he looked forward to working with them in future. It was, word for word, an answer to Ian's accusations days before.

17

That was Monday. As I put the last of the eight conciliatory letters in their envelopes at about three-thirty on Tuesday morning, it occurred to me that if the Mothers could resolve their differences so amicably with Frank, perhaps I could too. Perhaps I could put my differences and problems with Gail to Frank, and we three could work out some resolution. My chance came unexpectedly, courtesy of Ian.

After everyone drifted off to bed, I remained wide awake and decided to wash my hair. Then I heated some porridge with milk (as Ian had shown me), made myself look good and, without a wink of sleep, prepared for a day's work.

Late afternoon, Frank, in full creative mode, was composing the prettiest piece of music, 'Would You Like a Snack', especially for Grace Slick, the lead singer of Jefferson Airplane. He asked for a recording session to be set up starting at midnight and, as I hurried through to the kitchen to make the call on the only telephone in the house, Gail raced past me, grabbed the phone and began searching through the Rolodex for studio numbers.

'I can do it, Gail,' I said, jostling for position.

'It's okay, Pauline. I have the number right here.'

'Look, how can I do my job . . . ?'

My words faded away and I felt as useless as the broken locks on the doors. I needed to talk to Frank. I wanted him to define the parameters of my job. But always when he composed at his desk, his hunched shoulders signalled the message 'do not disturb', and even if I did dare to interrupt, Gail would inexplicably appear and I would become tongue-tied. There was nothing for it but to wait, like a hawk, for my moment and pounce.

My moment came unexpectedly. Just after Grace Slick and Frank left for the studio, some mad person shot Robert Kennedy in downtown LA. I learned about it at the house of PamZ's friend when a reporter broke into a television programme. Desperate to be the first to tell Frank, PamZ dragged Ray Collins and me to the recording session, where we found him seated at the control panel with Grace.

'Have you heard, Frank?' PamZ burst in. 'Did you hear?'

He stopped and signalled through the partition for Ian at the piano and Art on drums, who were reading from their music sheets, to stop. But once Frank had grasped the basic facts of PamZ's story – that Robert Kennedy had just given a victory speech after winning the Democratic Californian Primary, that a man in the pantry of the Ambassador Hotel in downtown Los Angeles had shot him in the head, he was conscious and talking, had been taken to the Good Samaritan Hospital for brain surgery, his condition remained critical and they had arrested the attacker – Frank turned back to the task in hand with a cryptic comment, 'Who are these assholes?'

PamZ had more. 'You know the most amazing part, Frank?'

'Nope,' he said, pushing levers.

'They shot Martin Luther *exactly* two months ago today! Uncanny, huh?' She shook her head marvelling at the profundity of her words. 'Is there a conspiracy, or what?'

'I see a trend,' he added.

'Who's next?' PamZ asked conspiratorially.

Their eyes met with a lingering look not explained to me until later.

In a flash, Frank was back talking through the microphone to Ian, and for the next four and a half hours no one mentioned Robert Kennedy.

Seeing Frank in the studio was a new experience. I watched spellbound while the beautiful piece he'd written that afternoon gradually metamorphosed into something else. After Ian and Art had laid down piano, vibes and drum tracks, Spence Dryden, drummer with Jefferson Airplane, added extra drum rolls and then Grace Slick wailed and half-spoke her part with a clarinet accompaniment. Then, naturally, Frank had to add his weird noises, making us all laugh with his funny hand signals conducting a chorus of grunts, snorts, burps and snarls. I felt privileged to see the complete creative process, even though what had started as a very pretty piece that afternoon ended up sounding like no music at all.

When Spence had finished putting down his drum track and Ian had finished his part, we three snuck outside for a bite to eat. For weeks, Spence had made a point of dallying in my office teasing me about my English accent, pulling up a chair, propping his feet on the corner of my desk and tipping his cowboy hat to shadow his drooping, soulful eyes. And there he would stay until his band-mates dragged him away.

In the all-night coffee shop, Spence flicked at the miniature juke-box on our table. 'This is for you, Pauline,' he said and pressed the button for Janis Joplin's 'Piece of My Heart'. Flattered that, without even trying, I had attracted the leader of a group voted the top rock'n'roll band, I was rueful too. What was the use? Grace Slick was Spence's girlfriend. Would I never attract an unattached boy? I glanced at Ian. He studiously studied the menu.

Just as dawn broke, Ian brought Frank, Gail and me home but I was unable to go to bed because in the kitchen, Frank looked me straight in the eye and said, 'Telephone extensions are coming at eight o'clock. Make sure you see them in.'

The subtext was clear: 'I'm paying you good money, so damn well earn it.' Could Mutt have relayed to Frank what I had told him? 'On average, I only work about two days out of seven.' Had this fact been news to Frank? Had I made a mistake to be so open? Having had no sleep the previous night, I dared not lie down. Better to tackle the second coat of high-gloss on the windows in my room. And that's where I was, hours later, when Ian flung open my door and blurted out, 'How would you like to drive to San Francisco with me?'

I could have hugged him. His words were nirvana to my socially-starved soul. Out of pure boredom, I had stopped going to the Whisky with PamZ, but a trip to the Bay Area I could not resist. Plus, I realised in a flash, Frank would be in that great city *without* Gail. Here was my chance to tackle him head on about my job. Without considering details, I threw clothes and toiletries into a bag just as PamZ poked her head round the door. She waved Ian's air ticket at me and gestured a thumbs-up sign. She, too, was going to the ball.

Within half an hour, Ian and I were flying along Route 10, leaving others in the dust. He flicked on the radio but every station carried minute-by-minute bulletins of Robert Kennedy's condition. I was now in a zombie-like state, punch-drunk, so utterly exhausted from two nights in a row without sleep that I drifted off mid-sentence, my head rolling over, but Ian kept nudging my ribs. 'Stay awake, listen, there's more news about Kennedy, he's in a coma, come on, stay awake, talk to me. Let's talk about Europe, talk about France.'

Ian was the only person I'd met in LA who liked to discuss Europe. When I'd said to Calvin, 'Did you see they're having terrible riots in Paris?' he'd merely replied, 'Yeah?'

'My mother wrote me, the students have gone on strike, they've barricaded the streets, most of the workers have joined in, and the country's paralysed.'

'Uh-huh.'

'The government is about to fall. De Gaulle is in hiding. It could mean civil war.'

'It's happening all over, I guess.'

End of conversation. For those living at the log cabin, Europe might as well be on the moon. Even the Vietnam War barely got a look in. But Ian and I discussed everything, everything except our sleeping arrangements in San Francisco.

We arrived at the flat, the second floor of a very large Victorian terrace, at one o'clock in the morning. Ian's friend, Bob, was a composer and, according to Ian, the best classical pianist in America. Tall and slim, he wore a paisley cravat in his pink shirt, slacks and grey suede slip-ons. His short, sleek hair, parted on one side, framed his thin face, and as he talked he balanced a cigarette holder between his teeth. They played a classical record recently released by some other pianist and savagely criticised it, though to my untutored and weary ears, it sounded brilliant.

Finally, at four-thirty, Bob showed us to a spare bedroom, tall and narrow and stacked with books and records. I sighed a secret sigh when Ian quietly placed his sleeping bag on the floor while I, comatose, struggled into my nightdress in the bathroom. I could have slept standing up but inexplicably, once under the sheets, I found myself wide awake listening to Ian on the floor pumping his pillow.

Why had he invited me? Was it simply that he needed a companion for the drive? He found me attractive, I knew that, but as he told me so many times, he was madly, besottedly in love with Ruth. Because of Ruth, we were free to be friends, to open our hearts to each other without complication. Because of Ruth, Ian could not fall in love with me, nor I with him.

Still I wondered. Did he hope I would climb in beside him? If *I* seduced *him*, would that absolve his guilt if any guilt he felt? Would he tell Ruth, 'She fancied me, so what could I do?' I wondered if he also pondered his moves? If he did this, then I might do that – if I showed willing, would he . . . ? But it was out of the question. As Frank had told me, I was just too darned cerebral. I leaned toward Ian's bare shoulder showing up blurred and grey.

'Thank you for bringing me, Ian.'

'Thank you for coming.'

'I wish I had my licence, I could do some of the driving.'

'No, no, no. That's all right.'

His comforting voice sent me, at last, hurtling into unconsciousness, trustful and protected.

Late the next morning, after a drive around Berkeley campus and a walk through Ian's old music department, we sailed over Bay Bridge and I caught my first glimpse of the majestic skyline of San Francisco.

In contrast, the Fillmore West stood in the grottiest, dustiest part of the city and we arrived just as the Mothers were testing the sound system. Frank had on a white, long-sleeved shirt outside his cream jeans that stopped short of his ankles. He sent me a wave and I crossed the huge stage. 'Frank, I was wondering, do you have any spare time? I have a few things I'd like to discuss.'

He stopped twanging the strings and thought for a moment. 'How about after rehearsal, come over to the hotel.' Goodness, it was so easy.

Later, in the taxi, neither of us spoke and the silence did nothing to quell my nerves. How to complain to Frank about Gail without sounding like the school tittle-tattle? Besides, what to protest about now? That morning telephone technicians had delivered three extensions. They'd placed one on Frank's desk in the living room, another in Frank and Gail's bedroom, and a third, a nice bright red one, by my bed so I could answer the phone first thing without even getting up. But, best of all, the original phone, the one in the kitchen, the one that Gail cosseted, they'd taken *out* of the kitchen and placed it on my desk in my office. Ho, ho, ho! What was Gail going to make of *that*?

In Frank's hotel room, the first thing I noticed was its tidiness, its contrast with the log cabin, stark. Even the music sheets on his desk, which he moved aside to make way for a tray of coffee he ordered, lay stacked in a perfect pile. I sank into the soft chair next to the desk where Frank poured the coffee. When he bent to light my cigarette, an intimate gesture that brought our faces close together, I could smell the shampoo in his freshly washed hair.

'What's on your mind, Pauline?'

Not knowing how to get on to Gail, I steered off course, gabbling about how much I enjoyed working with him and living at the log cabin and how a university education could not be a better preparation for life than this and now I was in San Francisco and really looking forward to sightseeing and the concert tonight and wasn't it terrible about Robert Kennedy and I didn't know he'd died till we came out this lunchtime because no one had turned on the TV.

While I talked, he focused his soft, enquiring eyes on mine as if I was the centre of his world. Occasionally, he inhaled and pointed the smoke skywards or flicked the ash into the ashtray with his thumb; from time to time, he might wiggle his shoe that rested on his knee, but the whole aura of the man radiated calm, quiet, stillness.

'Makes you worry about the sanity of the people in this country, doesn't it,' he said. 'It's just so phooey.'

'They're talking about Teddy Kennedy carrying on for the family, but I can't see why anyone would want to run in these circumstances.'

Without moving a whisker and still holding my gaze, he said, '*I'm* thinking of running for president.'

I stopped mid-inhalation and almost choked. He must be joking. With a strangled voice, I said, 'Really? When?'

'In eight years time,' and, seeing my mind doing the maths, he added, 'in 1976.'

I should have known. Frank did not deal in trivial talk. He accepted my surprised expression with no surprise of his own and said, 'Well, what do you think?'

What did I think? Though flattered that he even sought my opinion, I thought it was a crazy idea. How could this man who shrank from issuing orders in his own home ever expect to hold the office of Commander in Chief? Who in Washington would back him and, given his image, who other than freaks and drop-outs would vote for him? What would he do to woo red-necks in Middle America and those in the Bible Belt, the people he despised? In fact, he despised so many groups of Americans that he'd already lost the election right there. And if he could not win, why go into it in the first place?

As if reading my thoughts, he explained, 'In every small town there's this little outcast or weirdo that buys our records. And this little guy has a best friend who isn't quite so creepy and they manage to communicate to a few more people and those people buy our records and gradually you go up and up the social scale until even the loftiest people in town are listening to what we have to say. Multiply that throughout the States and you've got your base.'

Not totally convinced, I struggled to think of something to add without revealing my misgivings. 'You'll need to raise lots of money first.'

'That would be a very good first step,' he said with his heart-warming personal charm. No one else listened to my words with such consideration and respect. I could have applauded him right there.

'I'll raise enough money to get on the ballot in every state and I won't campaign. So what I expect to happen is that the news media will call up and ask me, "What do you think about this?" and I'll tell them and let the others guys spend the money and argue about it. I think if I could get enough information into the marketplace of ideas and let them know what I think about various things, the day they get to the poll, they'll have an alternative. Imagine the entertainment value of a guy who refuses to campaign, sitting at home just saying, "Look, you wanna find out what I think, come and see me." It's one possible strategy and I think it could work.'

Like so much of what Frank said, it sounded convincing, but what puzzled me most was this question: where did Frank get his enormous ego, his unabashed belief in himself? Even with his broad range of talents, surely he suffered self-delusion to believe people would elect him President of the United States? Although he had a considerable reputation with the underground press, his fan base was small by comparison with the Beatles or Rolling Stones, and if the mainstream press were anything to go by, they saw him as a drug-crazed, one-off loony, good only for a moment's entertainment, not to be taken seriously. But then in a meritocracy like the United States, everyone grew up with the belief that regardless of your start in life, if you worked hard it *was* possible to become president. And supposing it *were* to come true? Then I wanted to stick around. I would love to work in politics. I'd lived in Washington DC. I liked the town. I could do that.

Being flippant, I threw in one last pitch. 'Are you willing to risk the chance of being assassinated?'

He laced his fingers together, bent them back so the knuckles cracked and said with deadly seriousness, 'I have a feeling I will be assassinated anyway, even if I don't run for president.'

Again, I gaped. Did he imagine himself on the same level as John F. Kennedy, Robert Kennedy and Martin Luther King? I paused, trying to gather my thoughts, to find the appropriate thing to say. 'Well, I hope to goodness,' I said at last, 'for my sake that never happens. I would hate to lose you.'

'Ah, Pauline,' he said with a gratified smile, and I blushed.

The perfect moment to change tack and get on to what I'd come for. I cleared my throat and asked, 'Do you have any idea when we might get started on the book?'

He pushed back a mop of hair from his forehead. 'As soon as I can. When I get back from the next tour, maybe.'

'The book could be a useful political arena for you, an opportunity to set out your beliefs.'

'It could do that, but I plan on using United Mutations as my recruiting ground. It's the basis on which I will build.'

Here was my opportunity. I'd watched with dismay as more and more fan mail had piled up in my office. Apart from that, hundreds of others remained unopened from the previous year and no one seemed concerned, including Frank. 'There's a mass of letters in boxes. Is there a reason why it's not being answered?'

'I think,' he said, suddenly absorbed in inspecting the sole of his shoe, 'Gail's waiting for the stationery.'

'Yes, but when it comes, should I start answering them?'

'That'll be okay but if you have any questions, ask Gail. She's been taking care of it for the past year.'

Taking care of it? Procrastinating, you mean. I gave him a blank stare. Did he not realise, could he not see from my expression how dismayed I was by his response, by the idea of having to ask Gail for anything? This was not good enough: pandering to his wife was not right. I should push further, but how? His answer made it clear he expected Gail to be involved. For me to protest would irritate him. With a sinking heart I realised I would have to find another way, that to stand up and shout at this moment would not do. So instead of going for the jugular and demanding he clarify the boundaries of my job vis-à-vis me and Gail and explain where my duties were supposed to start and Gail's to end, I veered off in another direction completely.

'I have a chronic ear infection. I've had it since a bout of measles when I was little. It's got worse since I've been here and sometimes I find it difficult to hear you. I hope you don't think I'm being rude if I don't answer on occasion. It's because my ears are blocked up.'

He listened, as he always did, as if I'd said something of world-shattering importance. I wondered why other men hadn't worked out how beguiling it was to have a man hang on your every word. Clearing his throat, he said loudly, 'I'll try to ensure I speak up in future.' He mouthed the words with such precise emphasis, I wanted to laugh.

He talked for a while about his revised optimism for the band and his forthcoming records, particularly *Hot Rats*. When the topic got on to music, I always found it best to nod and smile, adding a 'really?' or 'that sounds good', and he would expound on and on.

We'd been talking for nearly two hours when he stood up and gave me a big hug. He said, 'That's to tell ya I like ya and I like working with ya.' He emphasised the 'ya' rather than 'you', chummy, not sentimental.

Flushed with pleasure, I spluttered how much I enjoyed working for him, too. But his simple hug was sufficient to hold my spirits high for several weeks.

Still, I was cross with myself. I'd let the moment go, had not confronted the very issue I'd come here for, my altercations with Gail. I'd failed in exactly the same way I criticised Frank's failure in confronting issues at the house. From now on, because of my own timidity, Gail and I would continue on a collision course.

Frank had talked about BB King and Booker T, the warm-up acts for the evening, and I looked forward to meeting them, but there were so many black musicians backstage, I could not distinguish who was who. When BB King began his set, Frank called me over to stand with him and Ian by the side of the stage. 'These are the people you should be watching. If you want to hear real music, listen to these guys. They should be topping the bill. We're diddly-shit by comparison.'

There was no mistaking the bitterness in his voice. I had to admit BB King's band played instinctive, swirling, throbbing, emotional music that prickled under my skin. So when the Mothers finally took to the stage, they sounded awful. Their numbers droned through one and a half hours that felt like three. Was it because two superior bands, BB King and Booker T, had played before them and the Mothers, by comparison, sounded inferior? Had Frank's depressed mood affected the band? Possibly Ian's efforts at rehearsals hadn't worked out. Whatever it was, their performance sounded disjointed and lacked brilliance.

The following two nights when Christine's friends, the freaks – who'd hitch-hiked from LA and hung around Frank all afternoon – joined the Mothers onstage, the Mothers' set continued to lack the lustre, fun, dynamism and sheer virtuosity I'd heard before. I felt they'd cheated the fans but in the car afterwards, Ian said, 'That's why live performances are more exciting than records. You never know what's going to happen.'

I did manage a lonely walk through Chinatown, but the rest of the three days, I hung out with PamZ and the Mothers. I'd grown to love their unassuming manner and easy charm, their lack of arrogance or self-importance. They had a wacky sense of humour and chided me about not smoking marijuana. Jimmy came close to my face and said with his deep gravelly voice, 'You wanna snatch?' For one split second, I imagined myself onstage with the Mothers, stunning Frank with my fantastic piano playing and making him laugh with silly play-acting.

On the last afternoon, when Ian and I drove to Frank's hotel to collect him, I was surprised to see a young girl on his arm. 'This is Gemma,' he said.

'Oh,' I said. 'Hello Gemma.'

There was something about her I didn't like, possibly the way she wrapped her legs round Frank in the back seat. He kept whispering into her ear, sending her into gales of giggles, and I could feel my anger build. Despite our differences, I felt indignant on Gail's behalf if not a little jealous for myself.

We arrived at a shabby-chic abode on the outskirts somewhere and met two more friends of Ian's, classical pianists, short but thin. We lounged on squishy sofas and chairs in a large room with picture windows to the floor while the pair played duets on their grand piano, a performance lasting about an hour. We applauded after each number but throughout I kept an eye on Frank. It didn't matter what we thought, they played for him and, thank goodness, he kept nodding with approval.

Our entertainers complained that, as a double act, they could not fill an auditorium and therefore work was scarce.

'You know what you should do,' Frank said with a straight face, 'after you've finished each piece, you should take off one item of clothing. Arrange it so that by the last piece, you're completely naked. That would be a very effective way to get publicity and bring in the crowds.' Everyone laughed thinking it was a joke, but I knew better and Ian probably did too.

With an evangelist's zeal, Frank drove home the point. 'Strip off onstage and you'll fill twenty, thirty auditoriums. It'll be great.'

The two pianists sent looks to Ian as if to say, 'Is he for real?'

We drove Frank and his woman to the airport and left them there, still locked in each other's arms, while Ian and I drove south, talking non-stop. It was almost as if we'd grown up together.

When we reached the log cabin at four-thirty, the house brimmed over: Motorhead, Dick, Calvin, Christine, Gail, Moon, Sandra, Sparkie, Pamela and Lucy. With the screen on a flimsy tripod, Frank was showing a film. Too tired to pay attention, I sneaked off to bed. Just as I slipped into the twilight zone, Ian knocked on my door. 'Pauline? Are you awake?'

'Not really.'

'Listen, er, Gail's ranting.'

'Again? What about?' I grumbled, annoyed to be woken.

'Oh, you know, "This is not a doss-house, this is not a hotel." She wants Motorhead and me to fuck off out of it and find somewhere else to crash.'

'At this time of night?'

'Do you think I could put my sleeping bag in your room?'

'Oh well, what will Gail say?'

'I don't see how she can say anything.'

'I don't know.'

'One night?'

I flopped back on the pillow. 'Okay.'

I lay on my side and listened as he unravelled the bag in the corner under the window, a few feet from my bed. And that's where he stayed for the next two months.

18

If I feared retribution from Gail for allowing Ian to crash in my room, I
should not have worried. She had troubles of her own, though I would not
learn of them until later in the day.

In the morning, she appeared in good spirits. Scraping banana off Moon's
chin and stuffing it back into her mouth, she keenly told me that while we'd
been spinning round San Francisco, she'd been searching for a new home.

It had all begun weeks earlier when Gail was slapping cerise paint on the
stairwell and the stairs had ripped from the wall, tipping her upside down. 'Is
there no part of this fucking house that is not falling to bits?' she'd declared.
She'd also worried about the fire hazard of a house made completely of wood
and with unusual efficiency had bought six fire extinguishers. But when she
telephoned Frank, who was on tour, he had issued the order down the line:
'Start house-hunting.' And so, for the past few weeks, Gail had been doing just
that, and here today, she happily told me about her latest search.

'One had three bedrooms. Do you know how much it cost? $120,000!'

'We're definitely moving then?'

'Who knows?'

The phone rang on my desk and I grabbed it. At last, I could name the log
cabin's visitors. Hal Zeiger, an important entertainment promoter, came first
and lounged on the sofa with Frank for a while and, later, Don Cerveris. Don,
Frank's English teacher in high school, had made a film called *Run Home Slow*.
Frank, at just twenty-two years of age, had written and recorded the score.
Despite the film being labelled 'the worst western ever made', their friendship
had survived and they whiled away almost three hours, an unusually long
time for Frank to stop work. In fact, Frank spent more time relaxing with film
people than musicians. I could hear them chuckling together and Frank's loud

guffaw rang out, 'ha-ha-ha' like three notes down a chord.

At around ten that night, while I perched on my bed shortening my blue mini-dress, painstakingly sewing the hem by hand and enjoying the peaceful moment, the door swung open and there stood Gail with Moon hitched on her hip.

'I'm going to Hawaii.'

'What, *now*?'

'Listen, Pauline, can you lend me a hundred dollars?'

Like everyone else in the house, Gail borrowed money from me. Except for meals out, I had very little to spend my weekly wages on, so Calvin, Gail, Christine, Dick, Jeff, and sometimes Frank borrowed money and then paid me back at the end of the week. Gail shifted Moon to the other hip while I retrieved the notes from their hiding place, under the mattress. I counted them into her palm. Without explanation, she tucked the money into her purse, gave me an apologetic smile, strode past Frank and Don without a word and left for the airport, chauffeured by Dick. Frank didn't even look round.

Gail's sudden departure caused great conjecture in the house. What was going on? Was she upset about the new telephones? Had she learned about Gemma in San Francisco? Had Frank left a telltale token in his luggage – an earring, a strand of blonde hair? In various corners of the house, we whispered our conspiratorial theories and shook our heads, not knowing the answers. PamZ went up to their room to check things out.

'Go look in their bathroom,' she ordered.

'Why?'

'Just go look, okay?'

In Gail's bedroom, I stepped over her clothes, ankle-deep, to cross to the bathroom. On the mirror, a message scrawled in smudgy lipstick said, 'The socio-sexologist is not dead yet.' Could it be a pun on Edgard Varèse's epigram, 'The present-day composer refuses to die,' an epigram that Frank often quoted? I assumed Gail's version meant that she'd sussed out his affair in San Francisco.

A veil of gloom seemed to spread over the house and I decided on an early night at the unheard hour of eleven-thirty, but no sooner had I laid down on my bed to pour ear-drops into my ears to remedy an infection, moving my chin in circular motions to help drain the liquid far down inside, than Frank knocked on my door. 'Come and watch some films we took of the Mothers in London.'

Feeling ambivalent – slightly cross at losing my early night, but chuffed that Frank would seek out my company – I put on my long, gold, velvet housecoat and trundled into my office where, on the flimsy screen, a crowd of us watched the whole concert at the Albert Hall, the one I'd already seen live and would have missed in favour of sleep. Frank seemed determined that Gail's sudden and dramatic departure would not disturb him.

At twelve-thirty, for the second time, I wished everyone goodnight, determined to catch up on sleep, an essential move to prevent myself falling apart, but within half an hour, PamZ telephoned.

'What's *happening*?' she drawled, and when I told her Frank had a film on, she said, 'Fuck it,' and slammed the phone down. At five-thirty she rang again, even more stoned. 'What's h-a-a-p-ening?'

'As far as I know,' I sleepily grumped, 'Gail's not returned, if that's what you mean.' Immediately the line went dead.

In order to wake Frank at nine-thirty as he requested, I arranged an alarm call. I felt refreshed from sufficient sleep, despite the interruptions. PamZ rushed in through the kitchen screen door desperate to prepare Frank's breakfast, but Christine already held aloft a tray filled with eggs, bacon, toast and coffee. She hoisted it up to Frank's bedroom, something I'd never seen Gail do. Furious, PamZ scowled and complained for the rest of the morning.

On a mission, too, I cleared out the piles of boxes from the drawing room which had been there since I'd arrived, heaving one by one to the basement. Then I scrubbed the windows, vacuumed the patterned carpet, hung up the curtains, covered the single bed to make it look like a sofa, re-positioned a red, velvet chair and other furniture and hung pictures on the walls. Although the walkway went through the middle, I thought it the lightest and nicest room in the house with French windows on both sides giving the sun a chance to stream in most of the day.

Even PamZ joined in for the first time. She filled a bucket in the kitchen sink and added a shot of ammonia. 'Got to tackle that chandelier,' she told me. 'I noticed it last week. A *disgrace*.' She never failed to amaze me.

When we'd finished, I hoped I would get praise from Frank, but I waited in vain. He passed through as if none of us existed – a normal behaviour, but that day his solitariness had a chilly feel. Was he beginning to miss Gail? Did he see my endeavours as a trespass on her space?

Later, after a family shop, PamZ, Dick, Ian, Motorhead, Calvin, Christine and me, full of high jinks like kids having fun when mom was away, gathered round the square, chipped wooden table and scoffed down Christine's feast of chicken with potato salad, followed by her delicious chocolate cake. She hoped Frank might join us but he refused, so she carried his plate to his desk where he ate in happy isolation.

Ian was particularly excited, jumping around the kitchen because the elusive Ruth was at last coming to Los Angeles. He said they would marry at once. Intrigued, I looked forward to meeting her: who was this woman who held Ian in such thrall? I supposed she would sleep at the log cabin. What would Gail make of *that*?

And then before we could even clear up, four newcomers arrived: Don Vliet, alias Captain Beefheart, and his band. His huge frame, stuffed in a velvet-collared coat and top hat, seemed to fill the kitchen. I liked his large, heavy face that gazed out calm and kindly. In contrast, his colleagues appeared shrivelled up, grey, colourless: they hung in the background hardly muttering a word.

The Captain leaned one shoulder against the fridge door and in his deep, gravelly Californian drawl chatted in the most amusing and guileless manner. PamZ pulled me into the walk-in pantry off the kitchen and whispered, 'Okay, he's not rich, in fact he's downright destitute, but he *is* a big rock star . . .'

'I know what you're going to say,' I said. 'You think I should *get in there*.'

'Why not? He's got the hots for you, I can tell.'

Well, I did find him fascinating. On the other hand, he was also a little strange. I asked him why he chose the name Captain Beefheart. He said, 'Who's Captain Beefheart? Who's Captain Cook? Who's cooking tonight, who's tight?' He continued this teasing and playing with words while the others dumped dishes in the sink and wiped surfaces, but I could tell they surreptitiously cocked their ears, waiting for me to goof up. 'Who's loosened the noose, know what I mean?' 'No, I don't. You're talking Double Dutch is what you're doing,' I said, and he went on, 'Double Dutch, double edge, double cross.' It was most odd; *he* was most odd. The others exchanged giggles at my bewilderment. Then he confused me even more when he switched from talking nonsense to normal language, sometimes in the same sentence. I played along because as the evening wore on, Calvin told me, 'He really digs you,' and guffawed as if he'd made up a great joke. 'He thinks you're super intelligent.' Well, you couldn't knock a person with insight like that.

Sometime later, Gail and I would visit the Captain, driving twelve miles to his home in Woodland Hills. It was hidden down a dirt-track road in a dark area, so heavily wooded I half expected Hansel and Gretel to wander out of their cage. Our car bounced to a halt on furrowed earth in front of his shack, a dried-out, lopsided wooden dwelling. He lived in that habitat among aromatic plants with three members of his band, starving, surviving on bread and water, as he'd told us so many times. Gail took goodies: fruit, cereal, milk, chocolate bars and a few beers which they clicked open.

Don led us into his small bathroom with one high window. He climbed into the bath fully clothed and lay down, still wearing his sombrero and holding his beer can aloft. We shuffled where we could in that tiny space while Don rattled on in his gobbledygook, of which I understood not one word, though to my amazement Gail managed some kind of jokey conversation. Oh, if my friends in England could've seen me then.

On the third day of Gail's absence, Frank came down the stairs wearing her mauve, opaque tights and bright red t-shirt stretched and threadbare across his shoulders. Over these, he'd put on grey-suede Bermuda shorts, held up by wide straps and hanging baggily below his knees.

PamZ and I gossiped about Frank's queer outfits and I challenged her view that inside his bizarre look, a straight man struggled to get out. 'Tell me why, when he went to an award dinner, he put on a black evening jacket, bow tie but *no* shirt?' I had wanted to laugh when I saw him but dared not.

'He's playing to his image, that's all.'

On another occasion when he left the house for a business meeting, he wore his great leather coat, long to the floor, which in itself looked okay, but then he plonked on top of his Charles I hairstyle an old lady's maroon-coloured hat, swathed in net with one long feather waving out the side. *That* was the worst. Why did he do it? Even Gail, normally tolerant of all Frank's idiosyncrasies, had looked embarrassed.

But now, with Gail in Hawaii, the house fell further into shadow and as Frank withdrew even more into himself, we walked on tip-toe so as not to disturb him.

Frank's poor humour must have affected rehearsals because everyone bypassed their usual chill-out in my office at ten o'clock and I was suddenly alone. Frank returned to his desk, Calvin was locked in his tree-house, Dick and PamZ were out and so when Christine's freak friends – Lucy, Sandra, Pamela and Sparkie – bowled in with shrieks of laughter, I almost welcomed them in. Frank came through and welcomed them too, his mood visibly lifting.

They were dressed in 1930s gear; white complexions, eyebrows painted like Marlene Dietrich, dark red lipstick, slinky, pink satin gowns and smooth hair rolled at the ends. They looked so stunning, I just did not recognise them. Calvin dived around taking photographs and they fell into poses like professional models. Frank even went so far as to invite them to dance again at the Mothers' concert in Anaheim on Saturday. Grudgingly, I had to admit that they had a certain panache, an infectious joie-de-vivre.

In the meantime, Ian's euphoria over Ruth took a dive. Once again, she'd found an excuse to stay in New York, and Ian felt compelled to fly there immediately. PamZ drove him to the airport, and I tagged along.

When she and I returned to the house at nearly midnight, we found Gail in the kitchen bouncing Moon on her shoulder, talking to Christine and another girl, Gail's sister Sherry. Still with her coat on, Gail looked fresh and happy. She smiled her shy smile, passed a whimpering Moon to Sherry and said, 'Goodnight, you guys.' Without flicking an eyelid at my transformed drawing room, she made her way upstairs to find Frank.

19

Frank and Gail were concerned that my social life was taking a wrong turn and tried to find me a boyfriend.

It had happened two weeks earlier when Andy Wickham, an English producer who scouted talent like Joni Mitchell, the Everly Brothers and the Grateful Dead for Reprise, had taken me and PamZ to his friend's house. We had joined a group of A&R men sporting thin, droopy moustaches and mandarin collars on their jackets – like the Beatles on the cover of *Sergeant Pepper* – and had sat cross-legged in a circle on the floor of the tiny living room, the blinds drawn, the candles in the centre throwing shadows on our faces. I had refused to share the two joints but no one minded. Each person inhaled deeply until all that was left was a tiny fragment pinched between the ends of their nails. Their voices lowered to a murmur, mumbling I knew not what. I could not get out of there quickly enough; it was so boring.

On the drive back, things brightened up when PamZ, totally zonked out of her mind, told me and Andy that she'd never had an orgasm, although she'd also told me on many occasions that I should smoke marijuana because it lit up sex, the two pieces of information not quite squaring up. In any case, what sex?

She and Andy dropped me off and I found the kitchen unusually empty and tidy. Voices floated through from within and I tracked them into the living room where, to my surprise, Frank lounged on the sofa with Gail and Moon playing at his feet, a rare sight indeed. They greeted me with unabashed exuberance and I laughingly related my story. 'I was terrified they'd start talking in tongues, run up the walls or strip their clothes off. The smell of marijuana was so strong, I didn't dare open my mouth. I was terrified one gulp and I'd keel over.'

Deep, dark eyes that never wavered. When he turned them on me, I was spellbound.

Above: Pauline smoking with Frank Zappa,
backstage in Anaheim, 15 June 1968.

Above: Pauline with Frank Zappa and the Mothers of Invention on the front lawn, February 1969. Below: Gail at her house, Christmas 1969.

*Above: Pauline with Zal Yanovsky,
late of Lovin' Spoonful, February
1969. He offered me more beer. I
said, 'Just a touch.' He said,
'Where do you want the touch?'
Below: Hippy days with Calvin.*

*Opposite, clockwise from top left:
Moon Unit Zappa, Frank and
Gail's daughter; Mutt Cohen at one
of his parties; Fred Wolf, my first
boyfriend in Hollywood, was an
Oscar winner. He's pictured here
with his business partner Jimmy
Murakami. Together they produced
the phenomenally successful*
Teenage Mutant Ninja Turtles
*series; Herb Cohen, Frank
Zappa's manager.*

Vent-Axia
Best value
in unit ventilation.

London
Monday
February 1, 1971
No. 27,896 5d

Evening News

Eleventh hour shock for 4,400 fans

ALBERT HALL BANS POP GROUP CONCERT

By JAMES GREEN

TONIGHT'S pop concert at the Royal Albert Hall starring one of the world's top groups, the Mothers Of Invention, and the Royal Philharmonic Orchestra has been cancelled.

Albert Hall officials learned the present because of the contents of the musical programme and *lexxxxxxx* audiences were worried about audience behaviour.

Drugs and groupies

THE
SPECIAL PREVIEW
of

FRANK ZAPPA'S

200 MOTELS

at the London Pavilion, Piccadilly Circus, W.1.
on Wednesday, 17th November, 1971 at 8.30 p.m. (Doors 8.00 p.m.).

United Artists

ADMIT ONE   *(Please bring this ticket with you)*   Persons under
                                                              18 not admitted

*Clockwise from top left:
Cancellation of the Albert
Hall concert the day before it
was scheduled; Invitation to
the London premiere of* 200
Motels; *The second incarnation
of the Mothers of Invention with
Howard Kaylan and Mark
Volman from the Turtles,
summer 1971.*

*Opposite: Frank and Gail at
the Oval cricket ground,
14 September 1972.*

*Above: Hippy days in Calvin's
back yard. Below: Pauline.
Goodbye to all that.*

As I ran on, Frank's smile disappeared. I wouldn't say he was *very* angry, but he was definitely rattled. 'Do you have any idea what would have happened if you'd been busted?'

'No.'

'Even if you never touched the stuff, they'd still arrest you. Even if you were in a different room or just standing outside, you'd go to jail. And some jerk would have to bail you out.'

'Oh, I didn't realise,' I said feebly.

Gail, too, was frowning and even Moon peered solemnly from under her brow. It was like having another set of parents, although another set of parents was the last thing I needed, what with mum and dad at home and the rest of my sibling clan always ready with criticism or advice. But then again, I was somewhat pleased Frank was taking such a keen personal interest in my life.

'You should be out sightseeing. Have you been to the film studios, picnicked in the mountains? How about Disneyland, have you been there?'

'Well, no. How could I? I have no transport.'

His dark eyes had softened as he'd surveyed me for a moment. He turned to Gail. 'Al would be the perfect guy. What do you think? Al?'

'Perfect,' she said, grinning.

'Al and I were at school together,' Frank told me. '*He'll* take you to Disneyland.'

While Frank got on the phone to Al, I allowed my mind to wander. Would Al prove to be the destined one? Would we fall madly in love, perhaps even get married? I could set up home in California and become a real friend to Frank, a proper Hollywood person in my own right, not a mere appendage to a famous musician.

But I was in for a shock. Al showed up two days later, a handsome man with even features and a dashing smile – but he wore slacks, a white shirt, v-neck jumper, tie and blazer, his fair hair cut short to the nape of his neck and parted neatly on one side. He could have stepped out of the 1950s. When I'd arrived in Hollywood I might not have raised an eyebrow but after three weeks surrounded by long hair, scruffy jeans and t-shirts, I balked at his straightness. Indeed, I felt strangely superior, as if I had progressed into something else, though exactly what I was not sure.

During the introductions, I tried to hide my dismay, while Frank and Gail stood on the driveway and waved goodbye, pleased as Punch. But then, when we got to Disneyland, we found it was closed. Northrop Aviation, the biggest aircraft company in America, had hired the whole caboose for a private party. How incredible was that?

Though disappointed, I was not about to whimper – after all, the tenth child of eleven often missed out on treats and I'd learned to hide my feelings. I shrugged and told Al, 'Another time, maybe.' We turned eastward and passed a lazy evening eating pizzas and drinking beer in some place by the sea.

Now today, Saturday 14 June, Al and I were due our second date. He had arranged to take me to Anaheim for the Mothers' concert, but things had already begun to go wrong.

Rumours had spread that in the early hours of Saturday morning, a quake with a magnitude of 10.5 on the Richter scale would crack open California, massive holes would swallow up entire towns and a huge tidal wave would destroy the rest. Though dismissed in the press, it was not too far-fetched. Temperatures had reached ninety-five degrees Fahrenheit, shimmering heat rose ominously from Laurel Canyon Boulevard and the grass verge took on an ashy, washed-out look.

The Mothers of Invention were booked to play in Tucson, Arizona on Friday, the night of the feared quake, and would escape the danger, so lucky them. When Mutt telephoned and said, 'Anyone who believes these doomsday idiots is a nutter,' I felt some relief.

He invited me over for an evening swim and I dragged along PamZ, sunburned and sore after a day at the beach, to be my chaperone. While the three of us splashed around in Mutt's heart-shaped pool, Gail telephoned from the log cabin four times. Back from Hawaii only the day before, she planned to drive five hundred miles across the desert to escape the hour of doom. She, Calvin, Christine, Moon, Sherry and Jeff were to travel in Calvin's old wreck of a car for at least twelve hours and meet the Mothers in Tucson. She urged us to follow. 'It's fucking gonna happen, Pauline. Get your butt over here.'

Mutt, full of disdain, drove PamZ and me into Hollywood. 'You think this restaurant would be full if the end of the world was nigh?' We took bets that Gail would not risk it. Calvin's car, which had no back seats, had broken down twice on local runs in the past week and if it broke down in the middle of the night in the desert it could be extremely dangerous, without the added complication of an eight-month-old baby in tow. So, imagine our surprise when we arrived at the log cabin to find padlocked doors and lights blazing from every room – I suppose to make it look occupied.

Mutt offered us bedrooms in his house and loped off to his own. PamZ and I, both secretly terrified, watched the evil hour of three-thirty approach, crying, giggling and snorting hysterically. To our relief, dawn broke, the sun rose through the hazy sky and the larks sang. How could we have been so foolish, and come to that, what about Gail and Calvin scampering across the desert? Even more ridiculous. We calmed down, congratulated each other on being so brave and crawled off to bed.

All through Saturday, I hung around Mutt's house waiting for Al to take me to Anaheim, playing with the dogs and checking out the goats, ducks and rabbits. I was still wearing my dress from the night before.

At the concert, there was the usual milieu backstage and soon I realised I was neglecting Al. He was so quiet and unassuming; he orbited the Mothers as if transparent, and made no demands. I would like to have been nicer to him, to have responded to his keenness with a keenness of my own, but our conversation petered out and the silences became an awkward barrier. And yet strangely, with Frank I experienced silences too, but those silences always felt subsumed with meaning and drew me in like a comforting embrace.

I joined Frank leaning against the far wall, away from the rest of the band. I thought he'd never looked more handsome, his beautiful eyes, arched nose and mouth perfectly balanced by his hair pulled into the nape of his neck. As we puffed in unison, I asked, 'Did you see Gail in Tucson?'

'No, they got there after we left. We spoke on the phone.'

'Gail really fell for the hype.'

Frank made no reply.

'They actually thought California was going to *fall into the ocean!*'

I assumed that Frank, a rationalist, would agree with my scorn but instead he threw a rather contemptuous look my way and said in his sternest voice, 'This is California. The Big One could happen any time, and if it *had* happened last night you wouldn't be talking to me now, you'd be floating some place in the Pacific Ocean.'

That shut me up and to my relief, they called him to start the set. But my hurt feelings could not last long, not when I watched a stunning show from the side of the stage, humming along with 'Who Needs the Peace Corps?' and 'Concentration Moon'. I now understood and admired Frank's hand signals. If he held up five fingers, it meant for the rhythm section to play a 5/8 rhythm; seven fingers to play a 7/8 rhythm; his index and little finger meant vocalize with a 'blahhh'. This method of conducting added to Frank's magnetic presence onstage. I'd watched the Who when they'd played at the Kaleidoscope and found Roger Daltry's sloppy talk on microphone amateurish. By comparison, Frank never spoke unless he had something salient to say. At one concert, someone in the crowd had shouted out that he objected to uniformed security staff in the auditorium. Almost on reflex, Frank had retorted, 'Everyone in this audience is wearing a uniform,' and when the guy continued to scream inaudibly, Frank had said quietly, 'Stop it, you'll hurt your throat,' a response that brought laughter and applause from the crowd. The concert at Anaheim was no different. The lead guitar centre-right, the guy making funny hand signals was the one you were looking at.

During the ride home in Al's car, I perched in the back behind Frank while he ran through who'd played well, who'd 'fucked up' and the audience response. He pointedly gossiped with Al about old friends and families they knew back in Cucamonga and I felt sidelined – unable to tell Frank my own little anecdotes, to make him laugh as I usually could. Slumped in the back, I sensed a gradual slipping on my part, a falling back into the ranks. No longer the brazen girl who'd tripped so lightly into his hotel room eight months before, I was now part of the team. Paradoxically, I realised, if I did not occasionally surprise him, evoke delight, become bold from time to time, he would soon lose interest. On the other hand, he was my livelihood and, in return, he deserved a certain respect.

Midnight, tired and bedraggled, Gail, Christine and Moon returned by air from their flit to Arizona. Frank came through to the kitchen and welcomed Gail into his arms.

Not surprisingly, Al made no offer to see me again.

20

L iving in the house with Frank, I'd learned many new things. He could delight in ribald tales of travels with the band, but complain with the coldest cynicism about their performance. He welcomed people into the house, and then groused when they hung around. He could be a sympathetic listener, or a mocking tease who ripped at your beliefs and enjoyed the flap. He collected people and then behaved like they were not around. He voiced libertarianism but ruled his band with an iron rod. He feted the disenfranchised and outcasts, yet coveted a capitalist's lifestyle for himself. He scorned the American people for their ignorance while criticising the establishment for treating them like children. He stood in judgement on almost everyone in the outside world – and yet I knew no other man more unassuming, humble or compassionate.

He abhorred physical sports.

'What's wrong with soccer?'

'Watching grown men kick a ball round a field? Are you kidding me?'

Perhaps this attitude had something to do with his inability to do two things at once, like playing the guitar and singing. He either played or sang. It was one or the other.

'After music, my great interest in life is lust,' he told me. 'If I didn't spend my life composing and playing music, I'd be into lust at every opportunity. I think it's one of the healthiest activities. Why do people hide it? Why can't people fuck anywhere? In trains? In the lift? In the street?' He asked the question with a challenging raised eyebrow.

'Well, they'd get in the way for one thing,' I suggested. 'And just think of the smell! It wouldn't smell very nice, would it?'

His head bounced about considering the point. 'That's true. It wouldn't smell too good.'

My heart melted when I managed to influence Frank's point of view.

Once when Gail was in the kitchen making coffee, he told me, 'I haven't done it yet, but I met a girl Midwest. I'm thinking of writing a song about her.'

Expecting something bizarre, I asked, 'What does she do?'

'She claims,' he said, 'she can reach orgasm just from stimulation of her nipples!' His eyes filled with wonder: scepticism crossed mine. I told him, 'I don't think that's possible.'

There was a momentary pause while he digested my retort and his smile faded. I hurried on. 'I mean there's no direct connection between nipples and – well – that part of the body which brings on an orgasm. I think the girl's faking it. Girls do.'

Through the uneasy silence, he swallowed a few times, flicked his ash with his thumb, thought some more, looked me in the eye and said, 'Are you sure about that?'

Well, no, I was not sure. In truth, I had no idea whether women could reach orgasm simply from stimulation of their nipples. I had read Masters and Johnson's sensational report on female sexuality that maintained women responded in the same way whether from clitoral or vaginal stimulation. They made no mention of nipples, but who was I to say Frank's girl had made it up? I could see I'd placed doubt in his mind as his face grew long and hurt. Why did he believe me over the other girl? Ian, Calvin and Dick also listened to me on any number of subjects but I never felt the same ability to persuade as I did with Frank. It was quite astonishing.

Sometimes my forthrightness got me in trouble, as when the Mothers appeared on *The Steve Allen Show*. They'd played two numbers, 'America Drinks and Goes Home' and 'Hungry Freaks, Daddy'. Then Steve Allen interviewed Frank and asked him what he thought young people wanted.

Frank replied, 'I'll tell you what they *need*. They need representation in government.' I thought, 'Gosh, he's going to announce his run for the presidency,' but Steve Allen threw questions open to the audience and the moment was lost.

When PamZ drove us back, Frank sat in the front seat, sullen and annoyed. Steve Allen had not taken him or his music seriously, had treated him like any old hippy in fact. He'd made fun of Moon's name and asked Frank if he'd really eaten shit onstage. They'd shown a clip from an earlier show, before Frank was famous, before the Mothers of Invention had ever existed. It demonstrated Frank's talent for publicity. The film, *The World's Greatest Sinner*, for which he'd written the score, needed publicity and he'd wheedled his way onto *The Steve Allen Show* by offering to play a bicycle wheel. At twenty-two years of age, we saw Frank's seemingly inborn ability to command, not only the audience but the orchestra and Steve Allen himself.

'When I make a signal like this,' Frank had said, pointing five fingers into the air, 'I want you to make the worst noise you can think of,' and he instructed the orchestra to do the same with their instruments. Very soon, the studio erupted into a cacophony of screeches, wails and grunts while Frank and Steve Allen created scratches on the bicycle wheels with a drum stick and violin bow. Even then, Frank had shown total confidence and all-round dominance.

But this was the strangest part, he'd looked so *straight* with his pompadour hairstyle, beardless and dressed in a suit, shirt and tie, smart enough for the school prom. Now I could see why Frank had developed his present weird image. If I had met him looking like that, with his large nose protruding from a narrow face and heavily greased hair, would I have given him a second glance? Would his quiet, charismatic manner have won me over nonetheless?

I called from the back of the car, 'I see why you've grown your moustache, Frank. You looked so funny without it. In fact, I don't think I would have recognised you.'

A stunned silence followed. PamZ threw me a guarded look in the rear-view mirror. No doubt Frank, hidden from me, tweaked his top lip and twitched his nose.

Back at the house, PamZ almost throttled me. 'You do not speak to Frank in that way.'

'Well, that's not fair,' I retorted. 'He says what he damn well likes to me.'

Softening her tone, she said, 'All I'm saying is, be careful. If you fuck with Frank, you won't like it.'

'Why? What will he do?'

'I'm just warning you, Pauline. You can't cross Frank and get away with it.'

'Oh, bother it,' I said, and stalked off to bed feeling chilled from wearing the wet tights I'd hastily put on to go to the show. Still, when Captain Beefheart arrived at two in the morning and Frank knocked on my door to ask me to join them, I heeded PamZ's words and with feelings of guilt, dragged myself up, put on my long robe and lounged in the living room with Frank and the rest of the family. They played records until nearly dawn and in between we listened to Frank and Beefheart spinning tales from their youth.

It was not unusual for Frank to invite those of us who lived at the house to join him and his visitors, even though the visitors may not have welcomed an audience. He liked to mix and match people and watch things happen, as if the mix added to his entertainment. If anyone stayed silent for long, he would draw them into the conversation, always courteous and interested.

On one occasion when a group of us sat around, a good-looking boy, dressed in a jacket and jeans with a lock of brown hair flopping into his eyes, asked Frank, 'Does "Brown Shoes Don't Make It" turn you on?'

One might have supposed that Frank would treat such a question with derision but he simply replied with a little shake of his head, 'No.'

'So what does turn you on, Frank?'

He got up from his chair, padded over to his desk, opened the drawer and pulled out a blank sheet of music paper. He brought it over to the guy, tapped it with the back of his fingers and said, '*That* is what turns me on.'

'A blank sheet of music paper?'

'That's about it.'

'Okay,' said the guy, 'so what you're saying is, when you've filled in your page with all those concentrated dots, that's your climax?'

'Pretty much,' Frank said, acknowledging the joke with a twist of his lips.

A discussion followed about what Frank heard in his head when he composed. He said, 'Most of the time I haven't the faintest idea what it's going to be like when it's played. I just don't know. I want to get it down there as fast as I can before I forget what I'm doing, so I'm just as surprised as anybody else when it's done. There are other times when I know exactly what two notes together are going to sound like.'

There was talk about classical music and he said, 'I have no time for Beethoven, I can tell you that. There are a couple of Wagnerian items that I can identify with, but most of the music prior to the twentieth century, with the exception of Gregorian chants and certain types of medieval music, just doesn't click with me. I don't know what it is. I've taken the time, I've bought the records. It just isn't dissonant enough, that's one thing; and the resolutions get predictable – you have a sequence of eight chords, for example, you know for sure where the ninth one's headed. I'm just not that neat and tidy.'

I asked him, 'When did you first realise that music would be the dominant force in your life?'

'About the time I was eighteen.'

Surprised, I said, 'As late as that? Mozart started when he was four.'

Unflummoxed, Frank retorted, 'Yeah, but he lived in Austria, didn't he? Living in the United States and living in a household like I had, there wasn't even a record player in the house until I was fifteen, so I couldn't even hear any music unless it was on the radio, and what they were playing on the radio in those days was things like "How Much Is That Doggie in the Window", so that's not really a rich musical heritage upon which to draw.'

Another time, we'd discussed religion. I was very religious; Frank was not religious at all. 'It's not until you banish Christianity from your life you realise what a burden it is,' he said quietly. 'All the mindless morbidity, bleeding this, painful that, and no meat on Friday, what is this shit? No good ever came out of religion. How many people died from the Kama Sutra as opposed to the Bible? Who wins?'

'What about the music?' I'd suggested. 'Surely, some of the most beautiful music has been inspired by religion.' He'd thought for a moment before finally agreeing. 'Yes, some good music has come out of religion,' but not to be outdone, added, 'but I've always maintained that most of the problems in the world today could be cured if we nuked the clergy.'

Apart from music, Frank had three other addictions: cigarettes, coffee and lust. I once asked him, 'Which is more important, music, lust, coffee or cigarettes?' and he'd replied as if there were no contest, 'Music.' But I wasn't sure if, marooned on a desert island, he would crave music the most. I believed he would relinquish lust and music rather than suffer withdrawal from cigarettes or coffee. He was never without them.

Years later, I posed a similar hypothetical question to him. I'd always found his songs wanting because they criticised everyone: middle-class conformity, sixties counterculture, disco, the music industry, politicians and religious leaders to name a few. Hardly anyone escaped his acidic tongue. It bothered me.

I said, 'Supposing you were locked in a jail and the warden offered to let you out if you would write a new song in *praise* of something, what would you praise?'

'Only Pauline Butcher would think of a question like this,' he said fondly and pondered for a moment. 'It depends how bad the jail was.'

I told him it was hell, so after a little consideration, he said, 'Every rock'n'roll band and every rock'n'roll crew knows that there is a species of crew slut lurking out there who live for the privilege of doing the laundry and performing other services for men who put up the PA system and focus the lights onstage, and "Crew Slut" is in praise of them, Pauline. In *praise* of the crew sluts.'

Afterwards, I was cross that I hadn't pushed for a new subject, that I'd let him get away with quoting a song he'd already written, a song that had lyrics which, in anybody's book, were horribly derisory toward girls, however much he protested, 'I'm a reporter, the messenger.' He seemed to have shifted position from his *Life* magazine article when he'd written about groupies: 'Girls who devote their lives to pop music are one of the most beautiful products of the sexual revolution.'

I had challenged him further and read out lyrics from another song, 'The Jazz Discharge Party Hats', from the album *The Man from Utopia*. 'She passed me her underpants and in the bottom it was like a squashed éclair.'

'Well, that's not an exact quote,' he said. 'I think probably what's on the song is even worse than that, but that's true – what it was.'

'Yes, but that sort of thing upsets people, doesn't it?'

He paused for a moment as if the idea had never occurred to him before. 'No-o-o,' he said with quiet emphasis.

'It does.'

'It doesn't upset Americans.'

'Well, that's why they won't play it, will they? They won't play the record if it's got those sorts of words on it.'

'Squashed éclair?'

I gurgled. 'Yes, er, we won't go into it, Frank'

'I'm a reporter. I saw a squashed éclair in the bottom of the girl's underpants, so I should tell people about that and perhaps warn them of the dangers of wearing such things, you know? I mean, what if it festered?' He let out a deep chuckle and I laughed with him, not sure what I *was* laughing at. It was pretty disgusting really. 'I mean, I don't *eat* them,' he went on, 'I don't *play* with them, but I do *observe* them, so I'm just the messenger here.'

'Yes, but you obviously put it into your song because you *know* it will have a provocative effect.'

'No, I put it into the song because people need to know these things.'

'Who needs to know about a squashed éclair at the bottom of someone's underpants?'

'Well, let me put it to you this way. Perhaps there are young people out there; young men that have the idea that women are something different from what they actually are. Believe it or not, there are girls in this world who walk around with underpants that *do* have a squashed éclair in the bottom. We should be blunt about it.'

He was so serious and practical, his voice so deep, you would think he was discussing the latest stock prices instead of female underwear.

'Are you speaking literally, or metaphorically?'

'No, that's all just literally.'

'I see,' I said, not understanding at all.

'I mean, not a real squashed éclair and you sit in it, but material that would resemble the components of an éclair, that is the custard, the chocolate and perhaps some of the flaky crust material.'

Was there no end to Frank's art of dealing with the most intimate matters in such a prosaic way? Frankly, I was lost for words and blurted out, 'Well, now I'm shocked.'

'Why? You may be one of the fortunate people who doesn't know anyone who wears underpants like that,' he said parodying someone on a soap box, rising to a pitch at the end of each little phrase, 'but let me just *say*, that in travelling around the world playing rock'n'*roll*, you can meet people who – have – this – going – for – them.' He chuckled, delighted at his own words.

When journalists questioned Frank about his lyrics, he explained that he would rather not write lyrics at all but he did so out of necessity. In his mind, he had no choice but to choose subjects that no one else would touch.

'If you don't enjoy it, blow it out your ass. If somebody else likes it that's a bonus. I do it because I have to.'

If I already admired Frank's magnetic presence onstage, it was not until I witnessed several jam sessions at the house that I learned what a unique guitarist he could be. It came to light during the longest and best session, when Sugar Cane Harris made a surprise visit. He joined Captain Beefheart with two of his band, Jack and Arthur, and Frank and three of the Mothers – Ian, Artie and Don Preston. They played seven hours of throbbing, vibrating blues, rock'n'roll, doo-wop and jazz.

Frank, in one of the best moods I'd ever seen him, let rip on his guitar while the Captain played rousing solos on harmonica, his baritone voice growling and hollering. The rest of the guys must have felt his enthusiasm too and, in turn, whipped up their own stunning solos so that I never wanted it to stop, the pounding rhythms sending little tingles under my skin. Don, on keyboard, thumped out electrifying jazz runs, his head waving from side to side like he was watching a speeded-up tennis match; Ian switched back and forth from saxophone to clarinet to piano with thrilling, screeching, sweet music of his own; while Art's drum sticks pounded to invisibility. The surprise turn was Sugarcane, whose stunning runs on his violin soared through the basement with almost religious intensity – feverish, passionate, frenzied.

The big thrill was to be close to Frank while he spun through sparkling solos ten times longer than he played onstage. Forget Eric Clapton. Sitting just yards away, I watched Frank's fingers fly up and down the neck of his guitar, vibrating the strings, his body bending and swaying to the rhythms, eyes closed, lost in the intoxicating sounds. Occasionally, a smile would cross his face and he would nod to the others in approval. Although, by definition, a jam session had no leader, still Frank managed to lead, to control.

In quieter moments, he reverted to strumming accompaniments. Motorhead arrived and added tambourine and blasts on the saxophone, and even Dick got involved, snorting and grunting on Frank's hand signals, the whole cacophony captured on Frank's Uher tape recorder balanced on a chair.

From time to time Gail and Moon and Christine and some of her friends ran down to sit on the floor and watch in wonderment, just as hypnotised as I was. By the time the curfew hour of ten o'clock arrived, they ground to a halt, burned out and exhausted, the air thick with sweat and smoke, the floor littered with stubbed-out cigarette ends and empty beer cans. All had taken their t-shirts off except the Captain, who still wore his long-sleeved shirt and top hat and used a grubby handkerchief to wipe his dripping-wet brow. They stood among their instruments, reluctant to leave, slapped each other on the back and shook hands avidly. Something special had happened that day.

If Frank enjoyed the camaraderie of the band and relished their bawdy high-jinks when on the road, back in LA, outside of rehearsals, he rarely saw them. Still, when the percussionist in the Mothers, Art Tripp and his wife, Adrienne, threw a party to celebrate Independence Day at their house in Canoga Park, they invited Frank and Gail.

Everyone except Ian was there: Loretta, Jimmy Carl Black's wife; Mary, Roy Estrada's wife; Dick Kunc, Frank's engineer, and his wife Patricia; all crammed into Art's small living room decked out with balloons and a giant American flag on one wall. In high spirits and carefree, most of the girls wore flowing paisley or flowered garments, and on the record player, Tiny Tim and Spike Jones blasted out.

The guys had been smoking pot and the air was thick and arid – the party in full swing when Frank and Gail arrived. They sat straight-backed in the corner while the Mothers scurried like naughty teenagers into the kitchen, even though it was Art's house and Art was in charge. Gaiety faded into sombre seriousness, conversation became stilted, polite and formal, voices dropped to murmurs. It served to highlight, once again, the camaraderie between the Mothers and Frank's isolation from it, his weighty presence casting a shadow through the house. Poor Art and Adrienne; despite their hard work to prepare a table full of food, the Mothers rose up in unison. They stood in knots for a moment as they shrugged on coats, made their goodbyes and moved out into the night. It was not yet eleven-thirty. Dick, Art, Adrienne and I were forced to exchange pleasantries with Frank and Gail across the empty room.

And so it was that I learned something else about Frank that day. Though I knew he could be the most scintillating company, with a devilish sense of humour and caustic wit, he could also be a real party pooper.

21

Frank announced that he wanted Christine, Moon's nanny, to be a GTO, the new name attached to Christine's group of dancing friends – Pamela, Sparkie, Sandra, and Lucy. It happened during the concert with the Mothers in Anaheim. The girls had arrived decked out as babies, with plastic bibs and oversized nappies held together by yellow-duck safety pins, sucking on giant lollipops, their hair in pigtails. Frank had applauded: I had snorted. Imaginative and cute maybe, but so was Bugs Bunny. Yet I had to admit their joyful raillery was infectious. Perhaps I was judging them too harshly. Perhaps I should break out of my English straitjacket and be more tolerant.

They had called themselves the Laurel Canyon Ballet Company but during their chatter backstage, Lucy suggested they change their name to Girls Together Outrageously or, for short, GTOs, an abbreviation which could mean many other things: Girls Together Only, Often, Outlandishly. I'd quietly suggested to Ian, Girls Together Off-Puttingly, but in the end, they decided on Lucy's choice and the GTOs were born, a much more professional-sounding name if the girls were to continue to perform with the Mothers onstage.

Soon their mode of dress – Pamela's nipple poking out from under her bib – had attracted the wrath of the Anaheim officials who, almost spitting with indignation, linked arms to form a chain round the girls to prevent them from performing with the Mothers. I felt some sympathy. To please Frank, and despite their outrageous outfits, they'd managed to hitch across county lines only to end up prisoners in a human cage.

And now Christine would be one of them and the other girls, all good friends of hers, were thrilled.

I found Christine to be the sweetest of girls, though she seemed not to know it. Ladylike, she never swore and would gossip without rancour or spite.

'Sandra is trying to attract boys through the sex scene,' she'd say. 'Lucy is the wild one, but I can't compete. I'm trying for my own thing.'

Her 'thing', she said, was 'homely'. She would spend hours washing dishes and baking cookies hoping that boys who wandered through would fall instantly in love. Several times a week she made a creamy gateau and offered it up like a piece of herself. 'I'm ready, I'm available,' she would say, but the strategy failed hopelessly. 'You know what my friend, Richard, said to me yesterday? "You remind me of my grandmother, Christine!"' She gave a tinkling little laugh. 'I'm just a frigid housekeeper, I guess.' Disarmingly honest, she would say things like, 'I'm the cold and cruel one in the group,' and about her one sexual experience, 'I laid under him for a while and then I asked him if he was finished.'

While I delved into a piece of chocolate cake with ice cream, we talked about her baby. 'I'm going to call it Richard if it's a boy and if it's a girl, I think Chrysalis would be pretty. And I don't know if I'm going to keep it, but I'm going to name it just in case.'

Christine's parents were Yugoslavian and lived in San Pedro. 'What do they think?' I asked.

'Oh, they think it's wonderful,' and seeing my look, she added, 'You're surprised at that, I can tell. You think they'd kind of like disown me. My mom says, "It'll be the making of you," that's what she said, so . . . I hope it *will* be a girl 'cos then I can make dresses and she'll be friends with Moon. I want to be a mom like Gail because Gail's a great mom.'

We'd all assumed that Christine's skinny body would soon begin to fill out, but early one afternoon while she broke eggs into a bowl and dumped unmeasured amounts of salt to make a sponge cake, she stopped beating and looked straight at me. 'I'm not pregnant.'

'What?'

She shrugged, her white, doll-like face stoical. 'A phantom of my imagination, apparently.' She scraped the gooey mixture into a cake tin and turned to drop the dirty bowl and spatula into the sink. She was wearing a 1940s pink satin slip that left her back exposed. I was shocked to see her spine. It was twisted into an 'S' shape that forced one of her shoulder-blades to stick out several inches into space. Until now, her clothes had cleverly hidden her deformity but suddenly, here she was flaunting it with unabashed casualness. Could it be to detract attention away from the phantom thing: a misshapen body versus a lost foetus?

For a moment, I gaped. Should I comment on her back or ignore it? I took a deep breath and said, 'Christine, what happened?'

She turned, leaned against the sink and placed her hands on the edge as if to demonstrate how erect she could stand. *'This old ruin!'*

'Can't they do anything?' I asked.

'They tried. When I was a little girl, my auntie told my mom, "You put her in the hospital and she'll soon straighten up." Next thing I know, I'm dumped, just dumped in a cot in a freezing cold ward, just me and my rag doll.' A flush went over her white face and her mouth hardened. 'When mommy and daddy walked out, I screamed so loud, screamed and cried till my insides almost choked up. They came back after about three days, but I turned away, refused to raise my eyes. And I never cried again, never ever. Next time I went in hospital they were real sad, but I made out I was happy to see them go. I just waved and smiled. Turns out I was born to live in a hospital bed.'

She told this story with a light, airy tone totally lacking in self-pity.

'The dumb head doctors, they go, "Christine, we'll just stretch and tie weights," but every time, it stayed this way, all bent and crooked and sticking out. They told me to try again. Can you believe that? This one in particular, he goes, "Christine, we have a new operation," but I went, "I'm not going through another bunch of iron braces."'

'That's a shame.'

She turned on the tap and added soap powder. 'When I was in school, boys invited me to drive-in movies and things, but they acted so uptight, never once holding my hand like you're supposed to. Not one boy tried to kiss me or asked me to go steady. So, one day I just plum walked out. I said, "No more."'

The screen door slammed shut and with a nod, Ian walked through the kitchen and on into the bowels of the house. Christine said, 'Is he your boyfriend, Pauline?'

'No, he's not. He's got Ruth.'

'We all think you're secretly married.'

'Pardon? I don't even have a boyfriend.'

'That's why we think you're married. It's the way you just flick guys off.'

'What guys?'

'Ian. Spence. Mutt.'

She exaggerated, but it made me think, perhaps I was being too standoffish. Perhaps I ought to make myself more available.

The next day, Christine and I hitchhiked to the laundrette. Hitching rides in and out of Hollywood was fun. On every corner, folk stood with their thumbs stuck out and within seconds, someone would stop. It was a way of life, a continuous, free-taxi conveyor belt, and although it was not something I would have done alone, with Christine I happily jumped into any stranger's car. We lived in pre-Manson days, before the Sharon Tate murders, when Hollywood was a trusting community. I loved it, a lifestyle so different from anything I'd ever known.

Christine wore her 1940s slip tucked in pink satin knickers worn over her jeans. Her hair, tightly frizzed from the roots to the ends, stood out a foot from her head. She adorned it with a multitude of bric-a-brac, the envy of any magpie. With her spindly frame and coloured ribbons round her wrist, she looked like a giant stick of candy floss. As we lugged our loaded pillowcases from Dick's car, a man walking by with his dog called out, 'I thought I'd seen everything till I saw her,' but she merely giggled. 'This is so my life.'

'Her life' centred on her many freak friends. 'We talk about groups a lot,' she mused. 'If you have a rave in a band, it's like having a soldier in the war, you write him letters and you worry about him. Mercy [her friend] and I sent the Velvet Underground a dozen roses with our pictures on the back. You can't be subtle.'

She fell in love with Arthur Brown. Gail introduced them at the Kaleidoscope, where he was the warm-up act for the Who. She danced with him and he brought her home in a taxi and she almost floated in, lit-up and excited. Then Gail, Christine and I hitched to the Kaleidoscope so she could meet him again. He looked like a Satanic Jesus Christ, screeching much of his verse surrounded by 'hellfire'. Gail sagely said, 'Frank pioneered rock theatre, now everyone's cashing in.' One of the numbers, 'Nightmare', indicated that he would eat celibate Christine alive. *'You can only come in if you pay the price. The price to come in is sin.'*

Backstage during the interval, Arthur Brown joined us, but to Christine's dismay, no matter how much she fluttered her eyelashes, splayed her thin legs in pink tights, struck out her hips or twisted her pose, he ignored her and bent low into Gail's face. Repeatedly Christine tried to intervene, giggling and making little jokes, but Gail and Arthur Brown seemed oblivious to Christine's suffering.

For a week, she trailed after Arthur and one afternoon hung around his building, sheltered from the sun under an umbrella. When he loped up the drive, he was so brusque and off-hand, refusing to invite her in, that she was forced, finally, to accept he was not in love with her. Heartbroken, she fell into despair and refused to eat. Attempting to comfort her, I said, 'Just think, Christine, very soon you'll be performing live onstage with the GTOs. How good is that?' But her face just became sharper, more pointed, and she got lost in the middle of her sentence. 'Do you believe . . . I'm back to . . . back to . . . ?' Moon pulled on her bony knees, but Christine brushed her away like an irksome fly. I worried that she would cut her wrists and confided in Gail, but Gail airily dismissed my qualms. 'Spare me the melodrama. Why does she play Ophelia just because some guy's fucked her over? She hasn't even kissed him.'

'I know, but that doesn't stop how you feel.'

'Well, you should tell her to stop this moping. It's not as if she's dying.'

Oh! So as long as you're not going to die then everything's hunky-dory. I must have looked unconvinced. She glanced up from changing Moon's nappy on my office floor and added, 'Mark my words: in no time at all she'll be flashing her eyes at an army of men.' In fact, Christine remained true to Arthur Brown for months after he left the country.

If Frank had a favourite among the GTOs, I would say it was Christine. He had plans to promote her as a model and chose her for the cover of *Hot Rats,* the album he would release the following year. There she is immortalised, peeping out of a concrete pit, her long, white fingers pulling her upwards like she's rising from a grave.

Sadly, Christine would never find out who she really was – her rebellious outward image masking the innocent, conservative girl inside. Later, she suffered two more years of painful treatment, including ten months in hospital in a full body cast. A few weeks after the hospital discharged her, she booked into a Philadelphia hotel, locked the door and pumped heroin into her veins. At the age of twenty-two, she died a lonely death. No one knows for sure if it was an accident or something she'd planned.

22

Mutt and Herbie came over to see Frank. They wandered through like patrolmen, checking everything out, and I took the opportunity to show them the boxes of fan mail gathering dust on my side table. 'What are you gonna do about it?' they asked, which got me thinking, what *was* I going to do about it? Why did I leave these boxes of mail untouched? Wasn't I supposed to be Frank's secretary? Wasn't that my job? Should I chance an argument not only with Gail but perhaps even with Frank?

After they'd driven away in Mutt's Mercedes, I took courage into my hands and opened the top box, took out one envelope after another, slit them open, straightened out the creases and began to read. Frank had already told me, 'A typical Mothers' fan is a boy, eighteen years old, has acne, is Jewish, comes from Long Island or its equivalent, and is extremely lonely. He is alienated from his parents, worried about his glands, the war and the draft. Insecure, he needs a friendly big brother image to emulate.'

They wrote with veneration for Frank, a man who understood their dismay at the 'fucked-up' state of America. 'I feel funny because people think I'm strange,' or 'Say that you like me, please, Mothers of Invention, so that I'll keep being strange and I'll stay alive in my small town.' They told him about school, their parents, their friends, all the things Frank talked about in his songs. As I read these messages of woe, I realised how much I had underestimated him. He really did seem to reflect their views – these 'disenfranchised' teenagers, as Gail called them – teenagers who didn't feel represented by their government, by the education system or by the music currently available in America.

From the filing cabinet, I fished out the standard reply that Frank had prepared. It was a form with a list of questions to be answered, questions like 'Who is God?' and 'How will you change your social environment?' There was also a request to enclose three dollars to join United Mutations. To each one I included a short note saying that photographs and a membership card would be sent after we received their reply. I rolled a top copy and two carbons into my golf-ball typewriter, ready to show the first one to Frank.

Within minutes, Gail appeared by my shoulder. 'What are you doing, Pauline? You can't answer fan mail.'

'Why not? Frank's fans deserve better than to be left stuffed in shoeboxes.'

'Did Frank say so?'

'Yes, sort of. The other Mothers think it's important.' Not true. I'd made it up. Only Ian had urged me on. 'It's the Mothers' fan mail, too, don't forget.'

'What insert are you putting in?'

'The questionnaire I found in the file.'

'Well, don't.'

Finally, I snapped. 'If Frank doesn't like what I'm doing, Gail, he'll tell me himself. Would you please stop bitching and get off my back?'

We stared at each other, the pair of us like two boxers waiting to see who would throw the next punch. She softened her tone. 'You're making two sets of files. You don't need two sets.'

'Yes I do. One for name, one for date. Cross-filed.'

'We'll see what Frank says.' She scooped up one of the boxes and marched through to the living room. Together she and Frank sat on the sofa for more than an hour marvelling at the ingenious drawings and inserts, his riotous laugh ricocheting off the wooden walls. Well, at least I'd forced him to look at them.

To some of the letters Frank dictated personal replies. Sometimes he gave them his phone number and asked them to call. When they did so, he would remember, just from the mention of their name, which one he was dealing with and what they'd said in their letter. His memory was astonishing. Several weeks after speaking to one of the fans on the phone, he reminded me almost word for word what the boy had said. He gave them the same dedicated attention that he gave to everyone else. And I sensed he was pleased that finally the job was getting done.

Still, although I seemed to have won this little battle, I could not shake off a sense of unease, especially when I found Gail and PamZ constantly huddled together, either in the sun-porch beyond my office, an area spun with dusty orange light and rarely used, or they'd be whispering, hidden in the pantry off the kitchen, musty and smelling of rancid cheese. When I came near, they would jump apart guiltily as if I'd caught them smoking pot. Perhaps they were not talking about me. Perhaps I should not be so paranoid. But much as I tried to steel myself against emotional malarkey, I let it get me down and my stomach churned.

The next day, Calvin decided to stir up a battle of his own. It happened while I was out shopping with Ian and I would have loved to witness it.

Until a proper accountant was set up, Gail had been distributing everyone's wages, and although it was a wonder I received mine without fail every Friday, more often than not she forgot Calvin, so he was forced to regularly borrow from me. This particular week, he'd blown his top.

Christine, secluded in her silvery room, reported to me that Calvin had shouted, 'How come you pay Pauline and Dick *their* wages, yet every Friday I'm left to beg? I'm fucking sick of it.' That had made Gail angry. 'Quit bellyaching,' she'd yelled, 'learn to budget like everyone else,' and Calvin had laughed in her face. 'You're the last person to lecture me. You can't even balance Moon's money box.' They'd argued about his artwork and Gail pointed out it was time he stopped banging and sawing and got on with the *Cruising with Ruben and the Jets* album cover. 'You should not keep Frank waiting,' she'd snapped and Calvin had shouted back, 'Frank knows where I live, he can come see me himself.' Gail had countered, 'Yeah, well, you may not live there much longer,' and Calvin had yelled, 'Right, fuck it,' and had dramatically chucked clothes into his car. From the carport, he'd bellowed, 'I'm not coming back,' and with Jeff clambering in after him, they screeched off into the night. Gail had bellowed, 'Go peddle your ass with the Monkees.'

Somnolent Calvin, shouting, yelling? Oh, to have missed it! Frank heard the news in the kitchen, his face more stern and angry than I'd ever seen. He told Dick, 'Padlock the tree-house. Hide the key and don't let them back in!'

Like everyone else, I scuttled to my room, unused to temper and tantrums. And because Frank and Gail seemed to treat Calvin like their beloved son, such a major fallout created dark clouds through the house. Without Calvin, Gail seemed adrift. Although they constantly bickered, he remained her strongest ally, her closest stalwart. Now that he'd gone, her position vis-à-vis the politics in the house had weakened. The next day I decided to go for the jugular.

For weeks, I'd silently fumed about the trashy state of my office. Every morning before I started work I cleaned it, grumbling and muttering under my breath as I vacuumed, 'This is not a nursery, this is not a dump.'

On this particular afternoon, Ian and I arrived back at the house after picking up sheet music for Frank. Gail, Christine, Moon and Dick were nowhere in sight but the debris on the floor in my office was worse than ever. Along with the usual discarded clothes, folded but stench-filled nappies, grimy bibs, broken toys, and plates smeared with congealed egg, there were also spilled ashtrays, pieces of soggy bread, broken biscuits and squashed pieces of fruit and currants, all trodden into the carpet, and no one but me to clear it up. Unable to contain my deep-seated anger any longer I grabbed the lucky moment that Frank was home alone doodling on his guitar and not totally absorbed. I marched through heaving with righteous indignation and demanded, 'Frank, something *really* must be done about my office. Would you please come and look?'

He strummed out a loud chord, placed his guitar carefully against the piano, picked up his burning Winston and followed me through to survey the scene, a quick flick of his eyes taking in the wreckage.

'It's like this every single day until I clear up. Every day I spend at least half an hour vacuuming the floor before I can even begin to start work.'

'So what do you want to do about it?'

I thought that was rich. What was *he* going to do about it, more to the point? Should he not issue an order to Gail? 'Keep Moon out of Pauline's office. Honour Pauline's space.' But no, here he was throwing the whole thing back to me. What *could* I do about it?

'This room is really a nursery and a meeting place for Christine's friends. It's not an office at all,' I fumed.

'Do you want to move into the other room?' He pointed to the drawing room.

With its floor-to-ceiling French windows on either side and the boxes now cleared out, it had become a very pleasant room, a desirable choice. Beyond the short hallway between Christine's bedroom and the walk-in pantry, it would effectively cut me off from the kitchen.

At that moment, Ian came up from the basement and joined in. 'That's no solution at all. They'll just move along with you and bring the action closer to Frank.'

'Well, there's nothing else,' I protested.

'Why not transfer your desk into your room?' he suggested. 'That way you'll get total privacy.'

While I stood there twittering, Ian engaged Motorhead's help and before I could say Timothy Two, they hoisted my desk into the air as if it was one of their speakers, sprinted through the house, up the two steps and dropped it against the wall just inside my door.

Without comment, Frank went back to his desk while Ian and Motorhead slapped each other's hands as if they'd won a trophy. Then they, too, disappeared into the basement.

I stood in my room, alone, unsure what I thought of the claustrophobic arrangement, working and sleeping in the same space. What about my privacy? I had no lock on the door – people could walk in willy-nilly. Suppose I was getting dressed? Not only that, the filing cabinet and all the boxes for United Mutations still sat in the office, so I would be forever tramping backwards and forwards through the house. When Gail returned, she was beside herself with anger. She said, 'Everybody else works in a muddle, Pauline. You should, too.'

While I sorted through what papers to take to my room, Calvin's car pulled up in the carport. It was a joy to see him and Jeff again. They ambled in, not sheepish at all. Instead, Calvin grandly waved a handwritten letter at me before bearing it through to Frank. Soon afterwards, as he began unloading his stuff into the tree-house, I called to him on his way up the wooden stairs, his arms loaded with artwork. 'So what was in the letter, Calvin?'

He turned, 'I said I want *you* to pay my wages every Friday, not Gail.'

'My goodness, what did Frank say?'

'He didn't say anything. He just folded the letter and put it away.'

'Which means,' I called with assurance, 'nothing will change. Nothing will be done.'

Calvin stopped at the top of the stairs and peered down at me. 'Someone's gotta be mother round here!'

Mother!

I ploughed on with United Mutations, a continuous slog until three or four each morning. Two weeks later, I stared in disbelief at the last pile of stamped envelopes, over a thousand, and felt that curious state of exhaustion that occurs after exams are over, anxious to catch up with all the fun I'd missed but, now with free time ahead, too deflated to even try.

23

My friendship with Ian had begun to get tangled up and raise eyebrows in the house. *That,* and the fact that he was sleeping in my bedroom. But he was not a happy man. Once again, Ruth had promised to come to LA for their wedding and once again, she'd cancelled. But this time, instead of chasing off to New York, Ian had remained resolute and for three hours he thumped out Mozart in the basement, trying to relieve his frustration while every perfect note filtered up into my room and I floated off into exultant dreams.

'I love the way he plays the piano,' I told Gail. 'I just love the piano.'

She'd giggled. 'It's not the piano you love, honey, it's the guy who's playing it. Come on, now, own up.'

When Mutt telephoned and invited me out to dinner, I turned him down in favour of a visit with Ian to Art and Adrienne's house. We took pizzas and played general knowledge games. I was hopeless with facts and figures but best at charades. I wore my mauve dress with tie, my hair piled on top and, because it was cold despite being the middle of June, I donned my glamorous rabbit-fur coat. In my diary I wrote: 'I know I looked good because Ian teased me affectionately and I'm beginning to wonder how much longer we can go on seeing each other and remain platonic. His complete involvement with Ruth is the key but if he doesn't see her for a month, how long can it last? We keep a purposeful distance.'

That evening, I watched a brilliant concert by the Mothers at the Cheetah, two sets of doo-wop, comedy, rock'n'roll and driving jazzy/classical instrumentals, all of it written and directed by Frank, and rehearsed to every exact note. The audience's tumultuous applause said it all. They'd really caught on to the Mothers' unique brand of entertainment and Ian's rehearsals were clearly paying off.

During the break, I skipped out for a snack with Art and Ian and did something I'd never done before – I leaned affectionately on his shoulder – a major breakthrough because all this time, we'd studiously avoided the slightest brush. After the show, I went so far as to give him a big hug. Now we could touch without embarrassment and it felt so natural. Never mind the fact that Ruth was in New York. Clearly she was not uneasy about our friendship or she would jump on the next plane, push him out of my room and insist he find his own place. Better still, she could relocate to LA herself and end these forced separations which sometimes lasted several weeks. The fact that she did neither of these things suggested she felt no threat from me. It made me wonder what Ian had told her. 'I really like Pauline as a friend, but I don't fancy her.' Hmm.

PamZ, in her inimical style said, 'Just jump on him for fuck's sake.' But how successful would that be? If Ian had come to treat me more as a confidante than a lover, then it proved I was not fiery enough, not the volcanic explosion that everyone said Ruth was.

When I'd worked at Forum Secretarial Services, one of the girls asked me, 'Do you ever get angry? Do you ever get sad? You are always the same. Every day, you are happy.' True. Black thoughts, tears and misery I avoided at all costs – driving a wedge between Ian and Ruth might take me to those dark places. I'd written to England bemoaning how moody I'd become, lapsing into sulky silences or stamping my feet, behaviours my family just would not recognise. Friends in England wrote back with consoling words: 'It's probably because your life has changed so suddenly and that crazy house you live in.'

And certainly my mornings could be chaotic. Now that my desk had been moved to my room, all and sundry would march in, often without knocking. There I'd be still in bed, my hair dishevelled, no make-up on, and Ian curled in his sleeping bag with an open book dropped by his side, lips parted, so at ease with himself he could sleep anytime, anywhere, and I'd be forced to throw on my floor-length robe and deal with people's problems before I'd had a chance to get showered and dressed.

One afternoon, a girl with big saucer eyes and hair cut on the diagonal like Twiggy's came in. She wore a shift dress similar to one of mine. I'd met her the night before at Peter Tork's party, which Ian had taken me to. It had been late and a few stragglers lounged on white leather armchairs or the deep, red carpet. Others gathered by the flood-lit pool. We'd talked with Peter Tork, who – because the press were so derisory about the Monkees, going on about what artificial trash they were – surprised me with his gentlemanly and dignified manner, not loutish like so many English pop stars. He was also taller than me. On film, he'd looked small enough to pop in my pocket.

I hadn't taken my coat off because we'd only stayed five minutes and I'd hardly spoken to this boyish girl, so to find her sitting on the floor in my room was a surprise. Thin and winsome, she told me she was getting married to her boyfriend of three years. 'We've been having sex since the first night we met, but now we're not sleeping together for a whole year. We want to make like we're virgins again.' At last an ally! There I was thinking I was the only person in Laurel Canyon not living out the sexual revolution.

Life magazine published Frank's article and I took it to bed with me to read. As I rested on the pillows, Ian dropped by my side in a bundle and fell asleep, his head pillowed comfortably on my lap. I pushed him across to his sleeping bag in the corner, worried he might think he was in his own bed and climb under the covers.

I knew that everyone in the house had been watching my friendship with Ian deepen and it had become a rich source of gossip, even with Frank. PamZ told me that everyone said I was in love with Ian. It made me smile – all part of the log cabin intrigue.

And so June strolled into July. Frank and Ian went to New York and Frank telephoned that not only had he received a cheque for $2,500 from *Life* magazine for his article, he'd also collected a $27,500 cheque from MGM for part royalties. 'Now we can get things moving,' he said. Then he added, 'Ian is bringing Ruth back to LA at the end of the week. Thought you might like to know that, Par-leen.' Yes, I'd heard that before.

Two days later when, groggy with sleep, I stumbled along to the kitchen, I found Gail giggling and joking with two people seated close together at the table. They looked up and beamed. Ian said, 'Hi, Pauline, I want you to meet my fiancée.'

24

I was cross at my dishevelled state, no make-up and hair awry. I hadn't even showered. When Ruth leant across to shake my hand, I worried a whiff of something unpleasant might waft her way. She had a tumbling waterfall of dark, tightly-waved hair, parted in the middle, not electrified like Christine's, but more natural and relaxed. Her eyes darted here and there, suggesting her brain fired at double speed, too.

'I've heard lots about you, Pauline,' she said.

'And me – about *you*, I mean.'

An undercurrent of amusement rippled around, Christine, Gail and Dick enjoying my discomfort. I fumbled among the chipped mugs to make a cup of coffee, anything to avoid further conversation. So you got here at last, I thought, just when I really didn't want you to, just when I thought something might develop between Ian and me. I heard Ruth's voice say, 'We're going out to eat, Pauline. Would you like to join us?'

It felt like everyone froze, Gail with Moon saddled on her hip, Christine with her hands in soap-suds, and Dick holding the fridge door open. Ian and Ruth stared eagerly as if I was some kind of prize. 'Because you'd be so welcome to join us,' she added.

'Thank you,' I said with as much enthusiasm as a non-believer about to be dipped in holy waters, 'that would be nice.'

While Ian drove, Ruth turned to look at me, smiling and eager. Her dark eyebrows balanced the prow of her nose, expressive, shining eyes and full lips. She wore no make-up, her skin clear and fresh.

In the restaurant, Ruth and Ian slid into a booth next to each other, leaving me the choice: opposite Ian or opposite Ruth? I sat between the two.

She reached across the table and touched my hand. 'When we go back, I'd like you and me to have a private talk.'

Oh, God! The third degree! I glanced at Ian. What did he think? He kept his face blank.

After we'd ordered hamburgers and coffee, Ian turned to Ruth, 'I'm sleeping in Pauline's room just as a temporary measure. Just until you decide to move to Hollywood.'

Ruth gazed at him, wide-eyed, and then with a womanly purr turned to me and murmured, 'Do you like living in Hollywood, Pauline?'

'I love it. Absolutely, love it. At least, what I've seen. It's very hard to get out of the log cabin.'

'And Frank? How do you like working for Frank?'

Why did everybody want to talk about Frank? 'It's great. *He's* great.'

'Have you ever been to bed with him?'

I almost spluttered my coffee all over her. 'No, of course not. I could not work for him otherwise.'

'Would you like to?'

What was this? A confrontation about a subject that Ian and I had never discussed? Did she reason that if something was going on between me and Frank, then I would be less likely to want a relationship with Ian?

'The first time I saw Frank I wanted to go to bed with him,' she said, matter-of-factly. 'He was onstage at the Garrick.'

Was this a joke? Again I glanced at Ian. He stared straight ahead with no reaction, as if he'd heard it all before. 'I suppose that's his appeal,' I replied lamely.

'But not for you?'

'No. Pam says she loves Frank but she's not in love with him. That about sums up my feelings, too.'

'You're not in love with him?'

I felt so clotted with disapproval I could hardly breathe. I wanted to say, I don't want to talk about my emotions with you, Ruth, so please don't challenge me, but instead, I said, 'Why would I be?'

'Could you be?'

With a touch of annoyance I said, 'I don't know what being in love is.'

Ian unwound his arm from behind Ruth's back. 'How about you, Ruth? Could you fall in love with Frank?'

'No-o-o-o, I'm in love with you,' she crooned and curled herself into his arm.

Gail and PamZ's words rushed into my mind: 'Ruth will never marry Ian because she's in love with Frank.' I'd thought they were being facetious but now I began to wonder. When Ruth had telephoned Frank several times about possible work, people gossiped. A little too eager, a little too keen everyone said, but I'd given her the benefit of the doubt. The chance to play xylophone in a funky band must beat staid conservatory music any day.

Back at the house, I led Ruth into my room gesturing for her to take the armchair, a faded affair I'd yanked up from the basement recently. I sat down on the edge of the bed.

'May I close the door?' she asked.

I nodded. No point in broadcasting our conversation to a house already rife with speculation. Well, let them conjecture.

She pushed the door shut and sank cross-legged on the floor by my feet, reached for my hands and searched my face. This was getting too earnest.

I pointed to Ian's sleeping bag in the corner and said, 'It's really rather hilarious because Ian and I are always talking about going to bed and I suppose all the people in the house think we're having it away, but then they open the door in the morning and there's Ian on the floor. It's so-o-o-o funny.' I forced myself into hiccupy laughter.

Her eyes danced over mine, I suppose to check the truthfulness of my words. Somehow, her probing eyes made me feel guilty, as if I'd just spewed out a pack of lies.

She pulled herself up and sat next to me on the bed, still clasping my hands. 'He gets so miserable when we're apart, but I can't leave New York. It's impossible.' Then she added, 'I know he talks to you and you're a great support for him.'

'Yes, but I'm no substitute for you.' Oh lord! So weak.

'It's the other girls I'm worried about,' she said.

'*Other* girls? What other girls?' A queer dart of jealousy entered me when I thought of Ian flirting with other girls. 'There are no other girls.'

'Are you sure?'

'Well, now you mention it, no, I'm not sure.' *Good,* I thought. Keep her anxious.

'Really?'

'Well, how would I know?'

'Whatever, you're the one he cares about and I'm pleased, truly,' she said. Once again, just as I did with Gail, I felt buffeted, tossed about like a plaything. She went on, 'Because when I get back to New York, we're breaking up.'

'Oh, Ian will never accept that,' I said tartly.

She lowered her eyelashes and said, 'Take good care of him.'

I wanted to retort, Ruth, I do not need your permission; I will resolve to take care of Ian when *I* choose, but I stayed silent.

At the end of the house, voices rose up amid shouts and laughter. The Mothers had arrived for rehearsal. There was a knock on the door and Ian appeared with an armload of music sheets. His eyes looked vacant, as if he dismissed any thoughts of our conversation. 'We're about to start. Would you like to come and watch?'

As we all clattered down, two of the Mothers, Bunk Gardner and Roy Estrada, made jokes about the swaying staircase, which now gaped evermore precariously away from the wall. I held on to the gnarled branch that functioned as a banister.

In the basement, Ruth and I sat on a couple of wooden chairs, one with its back broken off, and watched the Mothers clamber behind their instruments, tuning their saxophone and flute, bass guitar and clarinet. Jim and Art adjusted the position of their cymbals and drums. Cigarette smoke quickly gathered in veils beneath the ceiling.

When Frank arrived, Ruth rose from her chair and smiled shyly. He nodded and sent her a cursory smile back. Then the Mothers broke into the first few bars of 'King Kong', one of my favourite numbers and one that required close concentration. They stood like robots for a while until Ian broke into the first solo break on his saxophone, all discordant blasts, screeching and bellowing. Suddenly Ruth threw herself on the floor, her arms above her head, her body snaking in rapture. In encouragement, Frank signalled to up the tempo and I stared in amazement at Ruth, in what looked like an ecstatic spasm. I had never seen anyone so affected by music. No wonder she'd captivated Ian. How could I, with my anal-retentive whatever-it-is, compete?

After a few numbers, Ruth asked if she could take over from Art and she astonished me with her virtuoso playing – arms dashing wildly from cymbal to drum, big breasts swaying. Frank, a wicked little smile on his face, nodded his head and rocked his body back and forth, his guitar zinging off into vigorous chords and runs. If ever I felt like an outcast, this was it. Ruth's dynamic presence riveted the whole band. I slipped upstairs.

PamZ, who up until now had complained bitterly because I allowed Motorhead to share our bathroom and closet, and railed about Ian living in my room – 'Dammit, Pauline, I can't walk around naked. I don't want Ian ogling my tits.' And yet, here, in a surprisingly benevolent gesture, she offered Ian and Ruth her bedroom for the night. In view of Ruth's inflamed ardour during rehearsal, it was a relief that the bathroom and walk-through closet acted as a sound barrier between our two rooms. I felt no qualms of jealousy, which proved, I informed Gail with a toss of my hair, that I was not at all in love with Ian.

Throughout the next day, in between periods of socialising in the kitchen and practice sessions, Ian and Ruth sought me out, lounging in my room, chatting idly. They, too, were careful not to intrude into Frank's space while he composed at his desk. In the evening, we ate out again, and again I placed myself opposite the space between them.

Ian said they had talked everything through (for the zillionth time): 'I know that when Ruth returns to New York, she plans to finish it. She says it's over.'

Ruth was looking at Ian with something not short of adoration. It was most odd.

'Therefore,' Ian went on in his precise and cultured voice, 'I am prepared to move east. As soon as the tour in September is finished, I plan to leave the Mothers and settle on the East Coast with Ruth.'

When we returned to the log cabin, Ian told Frank his dramatic news, a sure sign that this time he meant it. Without rancour or revealing his true thoughts, Frank simply nodded. Indeed, he hardly skipped a beat. We watched them saunter across to PamZ's room for the night, all smiles and arms entwined.

I asked Frank, 'Do you believe him?'

He coughed, 'No, I don't.' Then he stated in a flat voice, 'She's gonna be trouble.'

'I think they're mismatched,' I said smugly. 'I don't think they're suited at all.'

The next day, Ruth went back to New York, but not before Ian announced with glowing happiness, 'We're getting married, Pauline.'

We were sipping coffee and seated in layers on the steps going up the hill just outside the kitchen. Ruth shielded her eyes from the sun. 'Ian's not going to leave the Mothers. He's going to stay in LA and I'll be coming over to join him in a few months.'

By this stage, I flipped my wrist. Theirs was a rollercoaster ride that I could stomach no more, its peaks and troughs too steep, its reversals too frequent. I wanted to bang their heads together and shout, 'Wake up the pair of you, stop being nincompoops.'

On the way to the airport, I slumped in the back seat. Ian said I should go with them because he and I could stop for something to eat on the way back. Ruth seemed okay with this arrangement but in the car she sat immobile and quiet. I sealed my lips too. When they kissed their goodbyes, I looked on sullenly. Why was I drawn into everybody else's game of play? When would I have a game of my own?

25

In general, I paid no more attention to the rock stars that came to the house than I did to the GTOs. Even so, when news filtered in that Mick Jagger might visit on Tuesday night, I have to admit I sat up and took notice. But then I got cross because everyone rushed around spring cleaning. It annoyed me because when I'd worked in my old office and cleaned it every day, very often continuing from room to room, toiling sometimes for hours, no one offered to help. Now the day of the Jagger visit had arrived and all hands slogged on deck.

In any case, I was not in the mood for celebrities, even one as famous as Mick Jagger, because the day before, Frank had dropped a bombshell in my lap.

I had been looking forward to moving into their new house. Frank and Gail had viewed several and from Gail's descriptions they sounded fabulous, but she repeatedly said they were too small: just three or four bedrooms. This news made me uneasy: why did Frank persist in looking at inadequate houses? Finally, I got my answer.

Frank called Calvin and me into the drawing room where, with Gail and Dick looking on, he stood before us and said, 'Okay, here's the deal.' He held up his index and little finger. 'Two things. First of all, when we move out of the log cabin, both of you will have to find your own accommodation.'

For a tense moment, I could not adjust to his words, and then with a jolt I absorbed this horrible news. I glanced at Calvin. His Adam's apple chugged up and down while Dick, looking embarrassed, shifted from foot to foot. Gail threw me a bewildered glance as if she, too, was hearing it for the first time.

'Second,' Frank went on, 'your salaries will be revised to compensate for any increased expenditure, and one other thing, you will both work in Mutt Cohen's building where the offices of Bizarre will be set up.'

I stood there, immobile. Indeed, the very fact we were standing up for the meeting suggested Frank did not intend to prolong it.

He raised his eyebrows and said quietly, 'Okay?'

Like mutes, we all nodded and Frank padded to his desk doing his funny little hesitant bob. The rest of us shot furtive looks at each other, too perturbed to speak. When Calvin made the first move, I followed him like a zombie up the wooden stairs to his house. We needed to confer further.

Planks of wood, pots of paint and parts from cars that he used as sculptures littered his living room. We sat on the floor and knocked back the best part of a bottle of bourbon, grumbling about the grotty news Frank had just unloaded. I say 'we', but mostly it was me and *my* complaints. Oh, I could moan for hours. Calvin's contribution, beside the odd 'hmph', was, 'I am not putting a foot inside a skyscraper. I will *never* set up a studio in a high-rise.'

Calvin and I belonged to the inner sanctum of Frank and Gail's family and we felt as if our parents had thrown us out. 'We've been banished to the streets,' I groaned.

In truth, I did not know which problem to think about first: how would I find somewhere to live without a car? Public transport was non-existent. And what about the problem with my work permit? How would they hide me on their books? Was I still a songwriter receiving royalties for a loss-making flop? Why had I not followed the advice of the official in Washington DC the day I'd extended my visitor's visa? He'd looked at my papers and said, 'What's wrong with you? You have three sisters working in this country, one an American citizen, you can apply for a work permit, no problem. You'll go straight to the top of the pile.' Sensible advice, which I'd ignored. Well, how was I to know Frank Zappa would offer me a job?

But what job now? What was the point of coming all the way to California to be trapped behind a typewriter from nine till five like thousands of other girls? Without closeness to Frank, I felt like nothing at all.

My mind was so splintered that I found myself taking a second shower, forgetting I'd taken the first only three hours earlier.

Ian, to soothe my jangled nerves, took me to see *Hour of the Wolf* by Ingmar Bergman, a grotesque tale of a man on a deserted island facing his demons, a collection of weird and grotesque characters that would not have looked out of place in the log cabin. Not a film to distract me from possible homelessness and unemployment. When we returned, we found the house invaded. News had travelled all around Hollywood that Mick Jagger would visit Frank, and freaks from everywhere had besieged the house. Apparently, when Mick and Marianne Faithfull walked in, twenty people lazed casually in the living room, and although it was not unusual for the house to be over-run, it *was* unusual for visitors to collect together in one place. Frank had made no protest.

Now though, they had adjourned to the basement. Mick Jagger, wearing a white shirt with a deep frill down the front, his brown hair parted in the middle and waving to his shoulders, shook hands with Ian while Marianne kissed him on the cheek and spoke with a bewitching, gravelly voice. '*Or*fully good to meet you,' she cooed. She had short, blonde floppy hair and wore a green mini-dress. Mick, shorter than I'd expected, or at least I looked down at him, shook my hand.

Frank crouched around his guitar to play a new piece he'd written, and Ian sat at the piano to accompany him. Marianne grabbed a tambourine and with eyes closed began swaying and gyrating to her rattling, swishing rhythm. What was it with girls and music? I just did not get it.

When they finished, Mick, with his slightly cockney accent, asked Frank, 'How long did it take you to write that?'

'A few hours.'

'I can do that too, but never when I'm happy. It's strange, when things are peaceful, I can't get anything down.'

'Makes no difference to me what mood I'm in. I can work all day, every day.'

Mick shook his head. 'If there's a deadline, or I'm in the middle of an argument, or there's some kind of really weird scene going on, it pours out. It's like a shot of adrenaline.' He grinned and his cheeks creased into deep lines.

Everyone in the house was agog that Mick Jagger, the biggest superstar of the moment, squatted in our basement, but no one wished to appear 'uncool' or sycophantic, so surreptitiously they drifted in and out. Frank, in his usual manner, made no protest, but Mick and Marianne glanced at the flow of intruders in confused wonder.

Later on, Frank and Gail, Mick and Marianne retired to the kitchen, where they finished off the full bottle of scotch they'd brought with them and generously offered it around. When I walked in, Mick Jagger had already hit his stride, barking on about the ineptitude of Harold Wilson's government. 'They said they would never devalue. Said it repeatedly, then what did they do? Devalue!' He shrugged. 'Politicians! Can't trust any of 'em.'

This was more like it and, wanting to hear more, I pulled out a wooden chair. Christine busied herself wiping the already clean windowsills. Mercy, Christine's friend, slouched against the stove while Ian hoisted himself onto the counter.

Marianne did a pirouette on the torn lino before flopping into Mick's lap and announcing, 'Now the country's *really* going down the drain.'

Frank and Gail, not the least bit embarrassed about the dilapidated state of their kitchen, sent sidelong glances to each other, somewhat bemused.

'The difference is,' Mick went on, 'the English take it lying down. Not like the bloody French. They want civil war.' He grinned again. He seemed to find most of what he said amusing.

'It's always been that way,' Marianne said. 'I favour the Germans. They support women's rights.'

Throughout their visit, Marianne interspersed with Mick. Like a double act, he spoke, she spoke, he spoke, she spoke, excited and passionate, vocal and opinionated about things everyone at the log cabin ignored: the music scene, fashion, art. They reminded me of what I missed from England, the lively chatter and dynamic arguments about issues of the day. Impressively, Mick demonstrated a firm grasp of European history, a knowledge far greater than Frank's, who covered up with droll remarks.

Mick touched on the arrest at Heathrow Airport of Martin Luther King's assassin James Earl Ray the previous month, a subject that no one at the log cabin had mentioned or shown the slightest interest in and even now met with total silence. 'I mean you've got your assassinations and your university riots. What have we got? The Welsh Nationalists! You can go and join them. What a joke.'

'The Welsh Nationalists,' Marianne cooed in her froggy voice.

'So what do you think, Frank?' Mick said, holding his arms tightly round Marianne and speaking over her shoulder. 'I mean, do you think we should be out there riling up the police, demanding a revolution?'

Just like Eric Clapton, Mick Jagger deferred to Frank, and I didn't know why. Was it simply the power of his music and lyrics?

'Revolution is this year's flower power,' Frank said sourly. 'I disagree with revolution.'

'Yeah, well, you'll never get a revolution in England, no mistake. We don't have it in us. We're just too bloody passive.'

'Well, wait just a minute. I was reading a newspaper in London,' Frank interrupted, 'nearly every page had stories of violence.'

'That's true, but, compare the barricades in Paris and Prague with our pathetic turnout. It was a joke, really. If the police hadn't turned up, it would have gone off like a teddy bears' picnic.'

'Why did you march?' Frank asked.

'Well, everyone was calling me up and I felt I wanted to do *something*, so it seemed like a good idea – at the time.'

Marianne said, 'The police should never have used horses. They were scary.'

'Did you march too?' Frank asked.

'Darling, I can't stand crowds. No. It was all over the TV.'

'We should have had ten thousand people on horses,' Mick added. 'A cavalry charge by the protestors. That's what it should have been.'

By this time, Mick's words had begun to slur and Marianne kept getting up and posing, then throwing herself back into Mick's lap.

Frank said, 'You really think walking around the street with a peace sign is going to get us out of Vietnam?'

'It might. Things are moving in Washington.'

'You know when they'll bring the troops home?' Frank told him with authority. 'When it's no longer economically feasible to continue, it'll have nothing to do with how many people hate the war.'

'I don't know,' Mick said, looking doubtful.

'If people want change, I think they should use the ballot box. I think the ballot box is the best way to make things happen.'

'Yeah, well,' Mick said, tipping his chair back too far. He let go of Marianne to grab the worktop behind him while the motion threw her off balance and she slid from his lap, grabbing at air, until all that was left of her was two pairs of wedge-sandals with straps running up her ankles poking over the top of the table. Both of them convulsed into giggles as Mick bent down and tried to pull her up off the floor, their heads and noses snorting together.

I found their laughter infectious and giggled too, but Frank stared his slightly cross-eyed look while Gail, who had not uttered a word throughout, shifted in her chair. Frank said, 'Why don't you come back another time when you're a little less inebriated?' He spoke quietly but with emphasis on 'inebriated' and made his displeasure clear.

Marianne's face, streaming with tears of mirth, peeped above the table as she tried to heave herself up. 'I'd like that. I'd like to come back,' then disappeared again.

They just could not stop laughing, peal on peal of merriment. Mick got to his feet and tried for some dignity, pulling Marianne up with both hands to get her upright, though they were still coughing and spluttering. It was a bit of a sorry departure after such a good beginning, but they danced out happy as larks, unaware that Frank had dismissed them.

The next day, everyone had sore heads. Gail and Christine exchanged cross words in the kitchen. Christine stood on the opposite side of the table, her normally white face flushed as she shrieked at Gail, 'I'm not washing up ever again. Look at this mess! Two hours ago I cleaned it but who would know? Why doesn't anyone wash their own stuff?'

I felt sorry for her. Eleven people now lived in the house without visitors helping themselves. Who would want her job, clearing up after the herds that Frank collected as easily as others collected stamps or coins?

'And Moon – I can't handle her anymore. I want to go. *I want to go!*'

Somehow, Gail calmed her, but once she'd closed that little argument, she directed her venom toward the rest of us by sticking a big notice on the kitchen wall: *'If you can't keep the kitchen tidy, keep the fuck out.'*

Thankfully, by the evening, things had calmed down and while the Mothers readied for their rehearsal, the house gradually filled up with the usual myriad of visitors. Christine introduced Frank to a fresh-faced twenty-year-old called Alice Cooper. They stood holding hands and looked like twins from a comic strip, all stretched-out with skinny arms and legs. Frank agreed to audition Alice's band the next day at seven o'clock.

Captain Beefheart and some of his band arrived, as did the usual motley crew of GTOs. Even Herbie and Mutt made an appearance. Then, in amongst all of this, PamZ nearly flipped when Mick Jagger and Marianne Faithfull snaked back in. From what I learned later, an evening of pulsating, throbbing, thunderous music followed, with Mick Jagger and Captain Beefheart competing for supremacy on vocals. I missed it all because Lee Magid – an old-time record producer whom Oonagh, my friend from London, had asked me to hustle – had invited me out to dinner. By the time I got back at eleven o'clock after a dreary meal, everyone had disbanded except Motorhead, Bunk Gardner, Roy Preston and Art, who still lay around the living room talking to Frank.

There had been speculation about my 'date' that evening and when I walked in alone, Motorhead called, 'Did he get it wet?' a jibe which made Frank go into one of his knee-slapping, mouth-hung-open, silent laughs.

Playing to my audience, I said, 'Jim, one-night stands are not my scene and, quite frankly, I'm a little hurt that you even suggest it.'

'We've been discussing it, Pauline,' Frank said, 'and we think that's exactly what you do need.'

'Well, that's for you. For me, sex is too important to piffle away with some stranger.'

'Okay, how about some of the guys you do know?'

'If any of you are offering your services, you can think again. If you must know, I'm looking for someone who's kind. My father was a kind man. It seems to me it's quite rare among men.'

'Kind? I can do kind' they chuckled while I hovered above them, enjoying my moment in the spotlight, but also a little anxious. Then, throwing caution to the wind, I continued the game in my most precise English accent, as if I were addressing a group of schoolchildren. Half jokingly, half seriously, I said, 'When I was at school, I made a pledge with myself I would have two serious relationships, probably a year or two each, and then marry the third.'

'What number are you on now?' they all chorused.

'We might even live together, though that might be too drastic for my parents to swallow. So I hope it's clear that I think it's important to kindle romance before you climb into bed.'

Their teasing grew relentless and I realised I'd revealed too much about myself. 'Look, can we talk about your sex lives and stop discussing mine like some old piece of laundry?'

Frank squinted up at me. 'You intellectualise too much, Pauline. Knock off thinking about it. Just get it on. Don't take sex so seriously. It's just lust – that's all.'

'Maybe for you,' I retorted, and with my nose in the air, I pranced off to my room.

To my back, Frank called out, 'Ahhh, Par-leen!'

Was it true, I wondered? Was I too *hung up*, the American term that explained so much with so little? Hung up or not, it made no difference. There was no one around to 'light my fire'. Then I changed my thought to 'no one around I fancied'. It would not do to become Americanised.

The next evening, while the GTOs excitedly told me about their interview with *Playboy* magazine, which I'd missed while at Canter's Deli with Ian, Marianne Faithfull waltzed through the kitchen door. Dressed in a brown mini-dress with long flared sleeves, she invited us, with her usual flurry of arm-waving and over-the-top gestures, to Sunset Sound Studios to watch Mick Jagger mix the Stones' latest album, *Beggars Banquet*. A clamour of activity to organise transport followed. Christine woke Frank and Gail, who had gone to bed unusually early, albeit one-thirty in the morning, and they too decided it was a worthwhile adventure, sufficient to don clothes and join the rest of us. As we clambered into various cars Frank, his eyes still sleepy and rumpled, threw me a somewhat contemptuous look when he realised I would be going too, but I was just as excited as everyone else.

Frank and Gail joined Mick, Keith Richards, their producer Jimmy Miller and sound engineer Glyn Johns at the mixing board. Politely, Frank watched Mick at work, although very soon he was pitching in with suggestions and ideas. Maybe that's why Keith Richards seemed to lose interest halfway through and withdrew with his girlfriend Anita Pallenberg. Anita, very pretty, full-fringed, tall and waif-like, seemed more serious than Marianne and sat at the desk adding her own ideas on many of the run-throughs. At other times, she and Marianne chatted to the GTOs, Pamela, Sparkie and Lucy, or they hob-knobbed together like close friends, whispering and giggling.

We heard versions of 'Jigsaw Puzzle', 'Salt of the Earth' and 'Street Fighting Man'. Unfamiliar with the Stones' albums, I accepted everybody's word that these new songs sounded excellent, even better than earlier recordings.

There were too many people vying for Mick's attention, so I stayed studiously in the background talking to Ian. Mick, dressed in a sleeveless t-shirt with low-slung jeans and paisley scarf, focused on Gail and flirted with her until her eyes sparkled but, with Frank by her side, she smiled sweetly, always demure, never provocative. I had to admit, after three viewings of Mick Jagger, I found him extremely attractive and sexy. His intense high spirits and vivacity were infectious; I could see why girls went gaga for him.

Marianne, completely zonked out, rarely sat still. She pranced and posed and flirted with Frank, but if she thought she might attract his interest, she was mistaken because, from what I saw, Frank ignored women attached to other men or, at least, certainly in the man's presence. Why meddle in complicated situations?

To be honest, though, watching a group of people push and pull levers becomes boring very quickly, and it was not particularly pleasant when the studio filled up with leftover burgers in open cartons and flattened cigarette butts on the floor, the air not smelling too sweet. So I was relieved when, at six-thirty and in broad daylight, Ian trundled Frank, Gail and me through the empty streets and home. Little did I dream, as we drove up into the hills, that one day Mick Jagger himself would invite me, Pauline Butcher, to the South of France for an interview.

26

Through the following days I tried to get a private meeting with Frank about my future, even for a few minutes, but his head rarely lifted from those music sheets, on which he tirelessly stroked those dense dots. It felt like a membrane surrounded his private corner and you needed the skill of potassium to seep through it. No opportunity arose and anxiety intensified in my stomach like a gnawing rodent.

I hoped some answers would come my way when, out of the blue, Frank asked if he could hold a business meeting with Mutt and Herbie in my room. His request endorsed the fact that *my* office/bedroom was the tidiest, most comfortable part of the house. I had worked very hard every day to refurbish it. I'd hired an electric carpet cleaner and watched the prettiest pattern of pink and blue roses unfold, like those magic pictures when you scrape them with a coin. I'd bought a brown bedspread to tone with the pink and brown in the carpet, covered my desk and chair with black paint and then streaked gold paint on top for an antique effect. I'd also antiqued the standard lamp, bought a new lampshade, added voile curtains and coordinating cushions on the bed, completing the scheme with a Tretchikoff print on canvas of a man's blue face. I'd bought a long mirror for $16 to hook on the back of my door, but then PamZ told me it was bad luck to put mirrors on doors and, when I asked her how she knew that, she grumbled, 'I don't know, I read it somewhere.'

Surprised, I said, 'But, Pam, I've never seen you read anything.'

'Fuck it, Pauline, you're not my housemaid,' she said.

Neil Reshen, Frank and Herbie's new business manager, a whiz-kid from New York, had flown over especially for the meeting and I felt gratified when they dragged in extra chairs and made themselves comfortable. During the next hour, I scribbled their words of wisdom in my notebook. Mutt, Herbie and Frank listened while Neil Reshen, the financial genius behind it all, blasted out the results of his negotiations. A bull of a man, thirtyish but acting like he'd been in business for decades, he had strong, even features and thick dark hair shaved around his ears. He told us about the deal he had struck for Bizarre Incorporated, a company that would oversee Bizarre Records, Bizarre Advertising and Bizarre Films. The Mothers would release one more album for MGM and then transfer to Bizarre. Frank and Herbie would be fifty-fifty partners with Frank acting as president, Herbie as vice-president and, for his efforts as their business adviser, Neil Reshen would handle all the finances and cream five percent off the top.

Frank personally stood to receive hundreds of thousands of dollars and the general euphoria and bright plans for the future ought to have pleased me, but no one mentioned my position, so the relief I'd felt at the start of the meeting turned to further anxiety as they stood up and heartily congratulated each other.

Some respite came when Gail invited me to go with her to collect their new car because – and here is the strange part – Frank never drove. How could a man, a control freak with his band, sit passively in the passenger seat, as subservient and trusting as a foetus in a womb? In one of his interviews, he told a journalist, 'I don't drive because I can't bring myself to stand in line at the motor insurance office to renew my licence,' the only explanation I heard him give.

Gail's friendly gesture was not a surprise, because only the day before she had asked me to have lunch with her, just the two of us. We had sat intimately round the corner of the table lain with two placemats, knives and forks, even glasses for wine and, over steak and salad, chatted like the oldest of chums. What was going on? Never before had Gail cooked especially for me, so why now? I deduced it was because Dick was with Frank and the Mothers at rehearsal for their concert that evening; PamZ was off the map with her boyfriend; Sherry, Gail's sister, lay cocooned in the tree-house snuggling up to Calvin, and since things had cooled between Gail and Christine, by deduction, there was only me left. This was a game and I was the pawn, I knew that much, but if Gail wished to adopt me as her 'best friend', so be it. It was her great strength.

There was one other possible explanation for Gail's sudden amity. Now that my desk had been moved to my bedroom, initially so that I could work in peace and quiet, it had resulted in something else. It had set me and Gail in competition because my room, now so cosy and warm, had become a place not only for business meetings but somewhere to sit and relax, a quiet retreat for everyone. So gradually two hubs had developed in the house, two courts; Gail's in the kitchen, mine at the other end, in my bedroom. Could it be that, aware of my growing influence, Gail had decided to rein me in?

Whatever the explanation, the next day found us in her new limousine zooming across the Valley which, after the closed-in feel of the Canyon and Hollywood, gave me a sense of agoraphobia. On these streets, so straight and disappearing into the smoggy horizon, a car could steer itself, particularly this huge Buick with the latest technology, beige leather seats and wide, pristine interior. Its maroon bonnet gleamed and the shiny glass windows reflected the low buildings we glided past. I felt that the Zappas were at last moving into exalted realms: the question was, would I be moving with them? Though Frank had appeared unconcerned about my future homelessness, Gail tried to reassure me. 'Stop worrying, Pauline. We're not going to throw you on the streets.'

Only slightly reassured, I still needed to tackle Frank about my job, but how would I ever achieve that?

I turned on the radio and the Beatles' 'Hey Jude' blasted out. 'I suppose there won't be any Mothers' music on here, Gail?'

Without replying, she flicked it off, preferring instead to indulge her favourite subject – Frank. 'It makes no difference to his popularity. You've seen his fan mail; you know what an inspiration he is. Frank is one of the few people in the universe to set the standards. That's why he's so great.'

What standards? Gail's infinite ardour for her husband somewhat dampened my own. He was not *that* great. The man was human. He had faults, but you wouldn't know that to hear Gail speak. She turned the wheel with the palm of her left hand and pulled into the slow lane.

'I notice you never wear a wedding ring, Gail.'

'Does it bother you, Pauline?'

'No, I just wondered.'

'We found out you can't get on the ward to have a baby unless you're married. I was nine months' pregnant for fuck's sake. We didn't have a ring, so Frank picked up a pen and pinned it to my lapel.'

'Isn't it compulsory to have a ring?'

'No. That's sentimental baloney,' she said.

'Not many girls would have stood for that,' I suggested. 'Perhaps that's why you and Frank get on so well?'

'We have a lot in common, both raised as Catholics, childhoods on the move, and we both love music. And I'm his best-est fan.'

Obviously.

The next morning, while I eyed the living room hoping for a moment to catch Frank, PamZ stomped into my room keen to demonstrate that *her* relationship with Gail was much more intimate than mine. It was eight-thirty in the morning. For six hours, worrying about my future and unable to sleep, I'd typed non-stop, screeds of letters home, some of them more than twenty pages of single-space, a cathartic attempt to make sense of my perilous situation. PamZ dropped into my chair and announced with her heavy, low drawl, 'You know what's going down now?'

'No?' I murmured, still typing.

'The bitch is gonna leave him.'

My fingers stopped mid-word. 'She told you that?'

'Yeah, and a whole lot more. Gail tells me everything.' She shrugged. 'I don't need to spell it out, Pauline. You've seen it.'

'Well, not enough to leave.'

'She says Frank has respect for everyone else in the house except her. And when you get right down to it, he fucking does.'

'I'm surprised. Gail didn't say a word to me.'

'What can I say?' she said, examining the split ends of her hair, turning them over with focused attention.

Could it be true? Certainly Frank did not behave towards Gail as if he was in love, but as she had already told me, 'Frank doesn't do love.' And they assuredly had plenty of off-days, barely exchanging words, and when they did, Frank was offhand, dismissive, very often irritated. Gail never reacted. Well, she did sometimes. Only two days earlier, she'd taken off to the beach with Christine, Moon and Janet, her friend. It was an unusual move for Gail, and Frank had scowled all day. But so what if they had marital rifts, what business was it of mine? PamZ's bitching and back-biting was giving me a headache. I was fully aware that I too could be a victim of her lascivious tongue when she gossiped behind *my* back, and so I let her stew into a vapour on that particular issue.

I'd finished my letter and stretched my arms above my head. Only then did I realise how stiff my body had become. I got up and went through to the bathroom to clean my teeth. PamZ followed and leaned against the doorpost. 'There's more,' she said casually. 'United Mutations will be moved to the new house. Gail and I will be running it.'

That stopped me in my tracks. Several hundred fan letters arrived every week and I'd made a real effort to keep up-to-date. If Gail and PamZ's idle hands got to them, a backlog would build up again as surely as Moon's dirty nappies littered the floor. Without the fan club and with Frank showing no inclination to write his political book, what would be left of my job? Again, Gail had said nothing during our two days of bonhomie.

PamZ eyed me through lowered lids while I tried to rearrange my face in placid lines to hide my rising panic. Clearly, I needed to talk to Frank. I needed to hear directly from him how he saw my future. I spread the toothpaste along the brush and began vigorously brushing.

'Where did you slide off to yesterday?' PamZ asked.

'Gail asked me to go and pick up their new car.'

'Well, that makes sense since you're usually fighting like wild cats.'

'I know. If she interferes in my job one more time I think I'll hit her.'

PamZ laughed.

'It's strange. She couldn't have been sweeter,' I said, spitting into the bowl and rinsing my mouth.

'Well, before you get all rosy-eyed, perhaps you should know that Gail is planning on getting you fired.'

I dropped the brush and caught at the sink for support. '*P-a-a-m!* Stop it.'

'Okay, but don't say I didn't warn you.'

I squeezed past her, not wanting to be in the same room with a girl who seemed to gain so much pleasure from bringing bad news.

'You know, Pam,' I said, turning to face her superior expression, 'sometimes I would prefer it if you would not tell me everything that you and Gail discuss.'

'Why not, Pauline? I'm your friend. I really dig you.'

I yanked at my bedcovers, straightening, smoothing. Were PamZ's revelations true or could this be another of her treacherous games? Canny as Gail could be, I found it hard to believe that even she, who had been so warm and friendly in the last two days, could at the same time have been scheming my demise. And anyway, how much influence did Gail have with Frank? Did she have the power to turn him against me?

At that moment, there was a knock on the door. It was Gail and I gave her a glazed stare.

'We're off to look at a house,' she purred, rattling her keys. 'Want to wish us luck?'

What she really meant was, 'What are you two up to?'

'Make it a good one,' PamZ drawled as Gail gave a little wave and closed the door.

'How much did she hear?' I whispered.

PamZ shrugged and passed through the bathroom and into her room. Now that she'd got me all hot and bothered, it seemed she'd lost interest in talking about Gail.

The temperature rose to ninety degrees Fahrenheit, too hot to work, so I climbed the wooden stairs to Calvin's door, stepped across to the roof of the carport, laid out a blanket and sat down, hugging my knees. Across the canyon, I could see Houdini's old mansion, and below a clear view of Laurel

Canyon. When Frank and Gail's car turned into the carport, I would race down and demand a private meeting with Frank. I could not let another day pass without confronting him: my nerves would not allow it.

In England, now distant and vague, life had been hectic but emotionally flat, never exultant nor sad. Now my days were stretched out and unhurried, so it was all the more surprising that I found my moods topsy-turvy, giddy with shock at the bitchiness beneath the friendly surface, the backbiting and underhand hostilities, and yet, on other days, knocked sideways with delightful sessions of mad fun and joy. It was this emotional rollercoaster that left me exhausted and my nerves so on edge that I could never sleep. Night after night I lay twisting and turning, worrying this way and that about who was grinding the knife into whose back next.

At that moment, John Mayall stuck his head over the parapet and climbed up too. Relaxed in our shared Englishness, he often sought me out. Like everyone else, he seemed to believe I came from upper-class English stock and I never corrected this misguided view. Instead, I went out of my way to clip my English accent to a crisp BBC sound, wore dresses instead of jeans and combed my hair into a sleek, shiny page-boy. A total misfit at the log cabin, I secretly enjoyed my out-of-keel status.

'How did you end up with all these weirdos?' John asked.

I'd told the story so many times; it was easy to arrange it in a well-ordered way. Usually I gave short, cryptic answers to the question, but here in the lazy afternoon balminess, I took my time and laid out the whole story, although for discretion I left out the tickling scene in New York, and when we discussed life at the log cabin I omitted all the squabbles with Gail. It would sound like sour grapes to complain about a girl who most men salivated over – or, at any rate, they moved closer to her than they did to me.

When I came to the end, John asked, 'Are you in love with Frank?'

Why did everyone ask that? Was there something in the way I described our meeting? Did my pupils dilate and my eyes shine? I heard the question so often I began to question myself. Undoubtedly, I liked Frank a lot: I liked him because he liked me, and that made me feel good about myself. And by association, his growing acclaim made me feel that I was an important person too. More and more articles appeared that recognised the unique appeal of the Mothers, but always they identified Frank's leadership and musical brilliance.

'No, of course I'm not in love with Frank,' I told John. The next part I varied depending on who was listening. Sometimes I went on the defensive. 'All my boyfriends have been good-looking!' or, 'Oh, gosh no, he's far too way out.' Other times, in more confident moods, I might say something like, 'If he hadn't been married, things might have been different.'

While we chatted, Frank and Gail pulled into the carport and I almost fell down the steps hurrying to greet them by the back door.

'We've found our new home,' they declared, smiling and chuckling, more upbeat than I'd ever seen them.

The house on Woodrow Wilson Drive would, they said, cost seventy-four thousand dollars. A fortune. Set into the hillside, it had a living room, dining room, kitchen, two bedrooms and bathrooms and a third bedroom and bathroom in a cottage in the grounds. There was also a large swimming pool. But, most importantly, the basement ran under the full length of the house and would be Frank's studio, tucked away from the main thrust of the house, and private.

I was forced to abandon my plans to accost Frank when, in high spirits and completely out of character, he organised an afternoon trip to Malibu with John Mayall, Ian and me. We climbed into the spacious back seats of their gleaming new limousine, and with Frank and Gail in the front, and Moon left to sleep on Christine's bed, we glided down Sunset Boulevard and crossed the many mirages of water that streaked its surface.

On the beach, we chose a less crowded part where we spread our blankets at civilised intervals: Frank and Gail on one, John, Ian and me on another. My mother had sent my summer clothes, which included a very pretty, sleeveless, pink beach dress in light towelling that reached just below the thighs. It tied around the waist with pink satin and, after I'd pulled off my hipster jeans, I let it drape around me as I sat side-saddle on my patch of blanket. It gave me time to analyse Gail and Frank's behaviour: did it show any signs of impending divorce? I found none. Neither could I detect any show of enmity or malice toward me. Gail smiled and chatted breezily – if she wanted me sacked, she must be the cleverest actress.

In fact, both were more relaxed and jauntier than I'd seen them in ages. Gail began shedding her vintage dress. Underneath she wore a one-piece swimsuit with a forties halter-neck, a swimsuit that showed off her slightly chubby but sexy body, whilst Frank, with a certain skill, smoothed suntan lotion over her back. Then he pulled off his t-shirt, revealing a lithe, hairy chest and called out, 'Where's your bikini, Pauline?'

'My mother's sent it but it hasn't arrived yet.' And on his continued gaze, I added, 'I only came to America for a two-week holiday, remember? And here I am six months later . . .'

'Then you'll have to go topless.'

'No, I will not.'

'Come on, now, don't you want to get your titties tanned?'

I pulled my prim, haughty face of 'no thank you', continuing the game we seemed to play whenever we had an audience, Frank chiding my prudery and me cranking it up for entertainment.

If a rift existed between Frank and Gail, surely this exchange would raise Gail's hackles, but she giggled freely and caught my eye, sympathetic and genial, though she remained silent. Noticeably, Frank did not urge *Gail* to take off her top, but then he always boxed her off, never allowed her the sexual freedom he extolled in all other women. I concluded that even if Gail had suggested to PamZ that she wanted to leave Frank, it must have been in a moment of pique after one of their spats. Now they appeared happy and content, like new lovers.

Bright heat waves shimmered on the sea, while the washed-out sand blew a little in the breeze. Gail handed round cups of coffee poured from a thermos flask while John Mayall entertained us with stories from England, acrobatics and trying to bury me in the sand.

Frank leaned back on his elbows and called to me once more. 'Pauline, I have a suggestion for ya.'

'Oh, yes?'

'I think you should frizz your hair.'

'I keep getting letters from England begging me *not* to frizz my hair. What is it about me and frizzing hair?'

'Try it and find out?'

'When Gail frizzed hers, you hated it?'

'I didn't *hate* it. It doesn't look right on her, but you should do it.'

'No,' I said petulantly.

'I'll make you a deal. If you frizz your hair for the concert at the Whisky on Saturday, I'll frizz mine, too.'

'I don't believe you.'

'I will.'

'Okay, done.' We shook hands, everything jolly, everyone having a good time, but such pleasantness and fun only served to increase my paranoia. Were they frolicking with me in order to prepare me gently for the boot? The only way to find out was to ask him. But how? When?

We continued our lazy day into the evening when Dick drove us to the Whisky to see John Mayall and his band, a rare outing for Frank, who seldom showed interest in watching English groups, or any groups for that matter.

Frank's good humour at the beach spilled over the next day, Tuesday 23 July, a magical day at the Whisky a Go-Go, a gala performance. Not only were the Mothers on top form again, whipping everyone into a frenzy with 'God Bless America' (a portion of which later appeared on the *Uncle Meat* album); the GTOs sang 'Getting to Know You' and 'Doo Wah Diddy' to half-hearted applause; Wild Man Fischer wailed out his number to a stunned crowd; while Joseph Peresonti, an Elvis Presley imitator, belted out 'Jail House Rock' and brought the house down. Altogether, it was a stunning collective performance and I swelled with pride to be part of it.

I sort of kept my bet with Frank; not totally frizzing my hair, but setting it on small rollers and back-combing each curl separately so it spread into one mass of ringlets. I felt ridiculous but everyone else, truthfully or not, eulogised on how great it looked. Frank didn't keep his part of the bet at all, letting his hair hang out like an Old Testament prophet's.

The next day, while my nerves still jangled, Frank invited me to another meeting. Neil Reshen, Frank, Mutt, Herbie and Herbie's wife, Suzie – a Hollywood-style red-head, glamorous and groomed, whom I'd seen at the log cabin only once – sat round a table at Perino's, a posh oval room on Wilshire Boulevard elaborately decorated in shades of pink. Over the crisp salad starters, Neil Reshen, speaking quickly and putting pressure on my shorthand skills, said, 'We've acquired offices for Bizarre Records on the seventeenth floor at 5545 Wilshire Boulevard, three rooms and a reception area. We take over the lease in two weeks' time but expect to begin business on August nineteenth. We've employed Rick Shaw to set up the office, order the furniture etcetera, and Pauline will help him in this task. Two secretaries will be employed. Herb Cohen will occupy the first office, I will visit two or three days a month and occupy the second, and Grant Gibbs, in charge of publicity and promotions, will use the third.'

Frank seemed happy to let Neil take centre stage, although I noticed that Neil acted deferentially toward Frank, taking his cigar out of his mouth to address him, listening intently when Frank offered an opinion, and not interrupting as he did whenever I dared to speak. Very much in charge of the evening, Neil picked up the tab when the bill came.

With a sinking feeling, I realised that no one had mentioned my role and when I glanced around the table, everyone seemed to avoid my gaze. On the way out, Herbie held my arm. 'I'd like a word,' he said, and waited while the others passed under the sparkling chandelier to the lobby beyond. He said, 'You will be one of the secretaries in the new office, okay? And I'd like you to work for me.' He probably thought it was a compliment, but I stared at him in shock. This was definitely not part of my plan. 'Oh!' I muttered, 'Who will do Frank's work?'

He shrugged. 'What work? He's a composer, a musician. If he's not on tour, he's in the fucking studio.'

'But what about his book? He still has to write his book.'

'It's not gonna happen.'

'Did Frank say so?'

'He doesn't have to.'

Clutching at straws, I said, 'United Mutations. Gail says she'll run it by the pool. I don't think she can.'

'We'll move it to the office,' he said.

I stared at him, horrified. Much as I liked Herbie and always found him pleasant and courteous, I had not travelled to Los Angeles to work for a record company executive: I had come because of Frank. But now my fate seemed to be sealed. Noting my lack of enthusiasm, Herb added, 'Well, you think about it and let me know.'

While the others took taxis to their hotels and Mutt drove Frank and me home, I realised, on reflection, that PamZ's warnings about Gail's plans for me had indeed come true. Without my noticing, Frank *had* sacked me! Alarmed, I ran over the evidence in my mind.

First I had been told I would no longer live and work in Frank's house but must find my own place to live; second, I must work in the office; and third, I would no longer be Frank's assistant but would work for Herbie, which, in effect, meant that Frank *had* given me the boot by proxy. My head went into a spin thinking about how Frank had hidden behind Herbie's stout frame and I determined to hear it from his own lips – even if I had to force myself on him.

I always typed minutes immediately after meetings while the words rang fresh in my mind, but Mutt escorted me to my room. On the steps outside the door lay the little kitten Gail had bought for Moon. Two wild cats that I'd adopted, rangy and gnarled, curled up beside it. I had been feeding them ever since Gail lost interest and, although I'd never owned a pet before, I found I enjoyed the novelty and liked their dependence and neediness. Picking up the kitten, Mutt said, 'I have a spare bedroom in my house. You can stay there, temporarily, till you get yourself straight.' Mutt's Spanish-style house was less than a mile from Frank and Gail's new house along Woodrow Wilson. 'I'm prepared to let you have the room rent-free,' he said, 'but in return I want you to clean house and look after the animals while I'm away.' The animals, by this time, included four cats, three dogs, six rabbits, tortoises, endless aquariums of fish, special breeds of birds and a goat.

A little uneasy, I ventured, 'This would be platonic, right?'

'Absolutely.'

Still, things could get tricky. He was, after all, Herbie's brother, and if I refused to work for Herbie, how would that make Mutt feel? Would he still want me living in his house? Might he kick me out before I'd even moved in?

The next day, the heat wave continued and Frank, buoyed up by the success of the previous outing, arranged another trip to the beach, this time with Gail and PamZ, Moon once again relegated to stay at home with Christine. No one spoke when we started the half-hour journey and, with each passing mile along Sunset Boulevard, the silence thickened like a heavy fog. Occasionally, someone would cough; a dull, clotted sound.

When we got to the beach, we spread out separately, each on our own little towel, our own little island. PamZ lay on her stomach in her jeans and halter top, her hair tied up in a bunch, her head turned away. Frank and Gail lounged together but separately, while I, miserable and burned up with anxiety, sat upright on my blue towel (originally white, but which I'd mistakenly put in the dryer with my jeans). The glorious sunshine and miles of sand and blue sea did nothing to lift my spirits.

A few children splashed at the edge of the waves and I could easily count the heads that bobbed further out. I wandered down to paddle, kicking and jumping the surf and scrambling away from the incoming tide. I hoped that Frank or Gail or PamZ might call out and laugh. They did shade their eyes with their hands to watch me but nothing more. No reaction. Zilch.

The journey back felt like a death sentence, and I sighed with relief when we reached the log cabin. In the kitchen, Christine handed an unusually crying Moon to Gail who cooed, 'Ah, did you miss me, Moonie?' and swept her into her arms.

I grabbed my chance. 'Frank, do you have a minute? I have a few things I'd like to discuss.'

'Sure,' he said. Just like that. Just as if we'd been chatting all afternoon.

The only place for a private discussion was my room. We carried our mugs through and closed the door. Apart from our long talk in San Francisco, this would be the first time I had spoken to Frank alone. It had taken three months. And now he was in a miserable mood.

How would I find the right words to ask, 'Why have you sacked me? Why didn't you tell me directly?' I distracted myself lighting up, collecting ashtrays, straightening my desk and fussing far too much. Frank settled in the armchair, one bare foot on his knee, while I perched by my desk, using it for moral support. When I dared to look up, Frank's calm, unwavering eyes held mine.

'What I wanted to talk to you about was – well, things have been changing so quickly around here – I don't know – I'm confused about what I'm going to be doing.'

'What I want you to do is work at the office for Neil and Herbie and report back to me on what Herbie's up to.'

I was puzzled. Report back to him? Why did Frank need *me* to tell him what Herbie was doing when Herbie could do so himself? As if to answer my question, Frank added, 'I need you to keep an eye on Herbie because a lot of the time I can't trust him to do what I tell him to do.'

His words stirred a new thought in my mind. Had he said the same thing to

Gail? 'Keep an eye on Pauline and report back to me?' Could that explain why she interfered every day in my work? Had Frank, all along, been the cause of our squabbles? Since my arrival at the log cabin, I had thought that Frank left me alone to organise my job as I wished because he trusted my judgement. As a result, I worked harder and longer hours, sometimes toiling all day and late into the night because I wanted to please him. Now it seemed his laissez-faire attitude could have been conditional upon Gail policing my every move. Would he run his political campaign this way? Give someone a job and then allocate someone else to watch over them, wasting human resources?

Still, reporting to Frank about Herbie did have its good side. It not only gave me an excuse to see Frank, it also suggested that he, too, wished to stay in contact.

'There's still your book,' I spluttered. 'I mean, that's the reason I came out here, to help you with your book.'

He grabbed his bare foot and pulled it higher on his knee. 'Yeah, well, it seemed like a good idea at the time, but since then too many other interesting projects have materialised. For one thing, Bizarre Records and the new artists we're signing are going to keep me busy for a while.'

Aware that Frank still had a contract with the publishers, I realised any mention of it might appear critical. He had not only failed to finish the book, he had not even started it. He'd experienced great difficulty writing his article for *Life* magazine and it had no doubt warned him of the mountain of work a book would involve. Still, it was my last throw of the dice.

'What will you do about your contract?'

He flopped back in the chair and scrunched the top of his hair with his fingers. Suddenly very serious and stern, he said, 'I've heard rumours that a guy at the publishers is a cover agent for the FBI.'

I shook my head, more from surprise at the absurdity of his statement than the commiseration he assumed it to mean.

'Can't you just picture him salivating over my manuscript?' His eyebrows were high in his forehead. This was more like him – very wry, quizzical, a touch of humour creeping round the edges. 'So what I'm gonna do is offer them Pamela's diaries. She has a whole stack of 'em. I've seen a couple and they're pretty racy. I'd like you to type them up.'

At this news, I brightened immediately. 'I presume I'll do them at the office,' I said, 'but my problem is I don't want to work "nine to five" or "ten to six". I haven't worked that way for five years. I've always worked freelance.'

'You'll have to talk to Herbie, but I don't think it will make best use of your talents if you sit behind a desk all day. I think as time goes on, we can use you more in an executive capacity.'

I was thrilled. Frank had never given me one iota of a clue that he liked what I was doing; whether he thought it good, bad or indeed, if he even noticed. But what, in reality, did it mean? Was Frank condoning my wish to keep irregular hours? If so, then Herbie would have to accept it too. Although only vaguely stated, under these conditions, I would be prepared to work in the office.

'And I'll tell you something else,' he said, dangling one arm over the back of the chair, 'I think you should develop your article into a book. If you can do that, I think I can get you a publisher.'

He referred, no doubt, to the article he'd encouraged me to write about my experiences at the log cabin, the one I'd abandoned. He not only believed his own horizons were infinite; he ascribed this attitude to those around him. Work hard, believe in yourself, use failure as a positive force, and you will succeed.

He was smiling now, his mood visibly lifted. 'So, you're going to live with Mutt, huh?'

'It's purely platonic I'll have you know. I'm an expert at platonic relationships.'

'Ah, Pauline,' he crooned with that slow, drowsy smile that I loved.

There was a knock at the door. It was Gail. Did Frank want more coffee? The meeting was over and Frank stood up. For the first time ever, Gail's interruption could not dampen my spirits. After all, I could now inform her with some triumphalism that my job with Frank was, after all, secure.

27

'I think there's something missing in the group,' Frank told the GTOs during one of their visits. Perhaps he had in mind that Sparkie was too pretty and sweet, Pamela ardent and keen, Sandra sexy but unassuming, and Lucy a most reluctant GTO. Only Christine was truly bizarre. 'I think Cinderella and Mercy should join. They would add much needed oomph.'

Cinderella and Mercy were both friends of Christine, but not of the original GTOs, and I could see Sandra, Pamela, Lucy and Sparkie disguising their misgivings well. If Mr Zappa thought Mercy and Cinderella should join, well, okay.

Looking like the original fortune teller, Mercy had a bent-up chin and hooked nose emphasised by a permanent headscarf and huge, hooped earrings. She dressed her considerable bulk in layers of dark, flowing cloth and circled her eyes with black charcoal apparently applied with a paddle.

Cinderella, at seventeen years old, would be the youngest GTO. Streetwise, she'd arrived in LA from an upper-middle-class family in Manhattan Beach and could have been the original punk, with her short, streaky hair and safety pins that pinched together her costumes of chains, bits of fur, brightly coloured tights and antique shoes. Her face, smudged with make-up too harsh for her blonde colouring, had hardened from living off her wits. She would sit brazenly, revealing her crotch, a posture that caused David Gilmour of Pink Floyd to snap, 'Will you please close your legs, you're offending me.'

So here they sat at Frank's feet, those seven GTOs, their bodies clothed in various levels of dishabille, picturesque and vaudeville, their eyes widening at Frank's words. 'I think you guys have real rock'n'roll potential. You have great ideas, and maybe even some hidden talent that we can tap. So why don't we capitalise on it? If you can come up with twelve original songs, I'll take you into the studio and record an album.'

A momentary stunned silence followed, and then an explosion of squeals and shrieks as the girls threw their arms around each other and jumped up and down. Frank raised his hand to quieten them. 'I'm serious about this,' he said. 'Base the lyrics on your own experiences and I think we'll have a marketable product.'

For heaven's sake, what would Frank think of next? How could these girls, none of whom could sing in tune, ever produce an album that people in their right mind would want to buy? 'We're going to be pop stars!' 'We're going to be famous!' 'We'll be on TV!' They squealed so loudly that even with my poor hearing, I covered my ears.

Noticeably, PamZ's face turned to granite and she stamped across to her room, though no one noticed but me. For the next few days, she barely stopped crying, emptying tissues from my tissue box (the one she'd refused as a present), the tip of her nose growing red and sore. She feared that the GTOs would replace her role as Suzy Creamcheese.

I tried reassurance. 'If those girls manage to write twelve songs, I'll take you out to eat every day for a week. There's no way they'll do it. You're crying for nothing.'

She waved at me dismissively. 'It's a sign,' she wailed. 'I'm off the page.'

Meantime, Cinderella had fallen in love with Tiny Tim. He was quite the new rage that summer. Tall and stooped, his long crinkly hair falling over one eye, he sometimes spoke in a deep baritone but more often than not in his falsetto, eunuch voice. Extremely religious, he would cite on and on from the Bible while Cinderella mooned around, star-struck, and accepted his strict rule of no sex before marriage. A more unlikely pair would be hard to find.

During one of their visits to Tiny's motel room, the GTOs sang 'Getting to Know You', a performance that set into motion a bizarre sequence of events.

First, Tiny Tim telephoned for Cinderella but, in her absence, warbled to me for half an hour. He wanted his manager to represent the GTOs and to sign them up for a record deal and trilled in his high-pitched, falsetto voice, 'I think they're worth a fortune. *Millions!*' The word 'millions' almost hit High C.

When Cinderella arrived, she phoned Tiny Tim's manager in New York, who brainwashed her with dreams of overnight stardom, insisting that the GTOs move fast while they were hot. He gave her the phone number of *The Smothers Brothers Show*, the top TV programme. She should contact the producer to set up an audition, he said. Over the next two hours, the phone rang thick and fast: more calls from New York, from journalists in LA, and from Digby Wolfe, the writer of *Laugh-In*, the show that had turned the young Goldie Hawn into a star. Their executive producer, George Slater, also rang: he wanted to see the girls now! Amazing! And all on Tiny Tim's say so. Perhaps I had been wrong. Perhaps, after all, these girls could be stars.

Their wildest dreams about to come true, the girls danced round the living room, ecstatic, while I became increasingly on edge. Not only had I allowed total strangers to solicit the girls while Frank lay asleep upstairs, I had positively encouraged it, becoming equally wound up with the euphoria. And although Frank had not yet signed them up, I knew that he looked on them as his product and it was a relief when he trotted down the stairs and I could brief him. Almost immediately, things moved at double speed. Frank summoned Herbie and Mutt to an urgent meeting in the living room and within an hour, the girls were gathered in a semi-circle on the floor, arms linked, while Herbie, swirling his key-ring around his finger, strolled up and down. He spoke softly in a concerned, fatherly way. 'I want you to listen very carefully,' he told them. 'I know you're excited about that crowd around Tiny Tim and what they want to do, but see, Frank and I don't think you're ready to go on TV, not right now.'

The girls' faces dropped and they shot glances at Frank for reassurance. He was sitting with one leg lopped over the edge of his wing chair and remained motionless. Mutt and I were perched expectantly on the sofa, while Gail lay on the floor enticing Moon across her blanket with a wavy toy snake.

'Okay,' Herbie said, 'Tiny Tim and his crew could put you on *The Smothers Brothers Show* and you could sing, "Getting to Know You" or whatever fucking song you want, and you could have a wonderful time, but it would be doing you a dis-favour because you're not ready. They may even take you into the recording studio to record a single. And let's suppose it's a hit.' He raised his eyebrows with the question. 'Now, is that what you want? *One* diddly hit? 'Cos let me tell you, that's what's gonna happen if you sign with those guys.'

The girls pulled up their knees and peered at Herbie's stout, short body. What damper would he bring next? He stopped walking and wagged his key-ring at them in turn to contain their attention. 'Frank wants you to write your own songs because he believes you'll be real stars that last and endure, make an album, not just a shitty single. Those people are not interested in you. Fuck it; they've never even met you.'

Frank nodded in agreement.

'Okay, so here's what I want you to do,' Herbie went on, 'tomorrow, to make sure you're properly looked after, Mutt will bring contracts for you to sign.'

The girls nodded with as much fervour as a child expecting ten swats on the back of her knees. I felt a tug of sympathy for them.

Then Herbie added, 'I don't want you talking to those fuckers again, okay? Frank and I will deal with them.' In other words, enter this cage and watch me throw away the key.

Dejected and confused, the girls began to whisper behind their hands, enough for Frank to intervene. He said, 'We've given this a lot of thought,' which was surely a joke given the rushed circumstances of the meeting. 'As a group, you are unique, the GTOs are unique.' (That word again.) 'There is no one out there remotely like you,' he said.

The girls' faces brightened. Trust Frank to say the right thing.

'If you can write the songs we've talked about and you can put together a snazzy routine, we think you could be the first all-girl rock'n'roll band. *And* –'

Excited murmurs interrupted his words as the girls turned to each other, their eyes full of expectation once again. Frank, no doubt pleased to bring colour back to their cheeks, grinned. '*And* – we'll take you on tour. Not just in the United States but to Europe.'

And why not? In Frank's world, anything was possible. I was even beginning to believe it myself. There were gasps all round.

The girls' rapture returned and they danced and squealed and hugged, their dream to become pop stars unfolding before their eyes. Why, they might even acquire their own groupies! And with the tour to start at the end of September which, good lord, was only two months away, they hardly had time to prepare! Any disappointment they felt at missing *The Smothers Brothers Show* or the *Laugh-In* programme was forgotten. Only Christine remained unmoved, her face a white mask.

'You can use the vault downstairs to write your songs and rehearse,' Frank said. 'I expect you to be professional and work hard. Write and rehearse every day.'

The official meeting over, Mutt and Herbie shook hands with each of the girls and, with a wave of geniality, like two benevolent uncles, departed through the front door. The rest of us, including Frank, moved to the kitchen, the girls tumbling over each with excited babble.

In the midst of this, PamZ returned and the girls told her their fantastic news. A tour in England, the Mecca of rock'n'roll, wasn't that just about the best thing? She murmured her surprise but stood like granite, hands pushed deep into her cords. Though no one else noticed, I could see her fury, her face strained and taut.

'Here's what I think,' Frank said. 'You girls need someone to look after you. My idea is that Pauline is perfect for the job.'

As much a surprise to me as to the girls, they screwed up their noses as if I was a horrible smell.

Lucy said, 'I want Suzy Creamcheese,' and several of them piped agreement.

Oh! The irony of it all! A shrewd operator, PamZ could hide her true feelings and to their faces act like their best friend. They had no idea how she detested them or what sour words of contempt she uttered behind their backs.

'Pammie, will you be our roadie?' they chirruped, and PamZ threw them an engaging smile. I squinted my eyes.

'Here's something you should know,' Frank went on, 'Pauline used to teach modelling. Did she tell you that?'

Well, no. I'd hardly passed two words with any of them.

'Show them how you strut your stuff,' Frank added, chuffed and pleased.

I laughed and shook my head, refusing to play along. Besides, I felt uncomfortable: PamZ and me in competition! Too awful for words.

'Okay, think carefully now and let me know your choice by tomorrow,' Frank said.

After nearly three hours of excitement and conjecture about the future of the GTOs, we'd exhausted the subject and Frank said he was going to bed.

PamZ, who'd hung silently in the background, lunged forward and snapped at Frank, 'Meet me in my room. We need to talk.' With total confidence, she swept past him in a gesture so strong it felt like she'd sucked the air along with her. To my surprise, Frank picked up his flask of coffee and, like a zombie, followed her shadow across the living room into her dark-red, candle-lit bedroom.

Baffled, I scrambled to my feet to watch the door close behind him. Frank and PamZ had barely spoken to each other in three months. Sometimes she'd thrown extremely sarcastic comments his way when she'd passed his desk, comments he'd ignored, never lifting his head from filling in those dots.

One day, when a *Newsweek* reporter rang wanting information about groupies, Frank had called PamZ to the phone but she'd charged past. 'You are fucked, Frank,' she'd bellowed, her boots clumping on the wooden floor as she escaped down the hall. 'I am not a groupie and you are fucked to even suggest I am.'

One hour passed and the door to PamZ's boudoir remained firmly shut. I became nervous. Surely Frank would not be swayed by PamZ? He had been just as animated and fired up as everyone else. Why, he'd almost drooled at the bait, imagining the horror-struck reaction to the girls at the Festival Hall in London.

While I waited, I wolfed down some cold, leftover ravioli lying on the side unit. With Ian away, I'd barely eaten for days, surviving on toast, ice cream and milk drinks. Such a meagre diet was taking its toll. My skirts had begun sliding past my hips and my legs, always slender, now edged toward thin, the calves taking on a stretched-out look. Still, I wore my skirts skimming the top of my smooth thighs. Mercy said, 'Pauline, you're all legs.'

I wandered through to my room passing Christine's open door and looked in to say goodnight. She rested on her mattress, surrounded by silvery candles, her pink slip now adorned with white feathers giving her the air of a fairy.

'I am so angry, Pauline,' she said, stirring a Kool-Aid drink. 'Tiny Tim *is* our best shot. Who knows if we'll still be together next month? We *should* go on *The Smothers Show*. What right has Herbie to stop us?'

'I don't know, Christine.'

'I've been telling the girls but they won't listen.'

Undoubtedly, of the seven GTOs, Christine was the most astute.

It was four-thirty in the morning when PamZ appeared through our adjoining bathroom door and threw herself on my bed beside me.

'I've been talking to Frank.'

'I know.'

'He can't take the GTOs to Europe because, y'know, it would kill him.'

'Really? Why?'

'Because they're a disaster waiting to happen. They're thieves, they're lesbians and they have no manners.'

'So? Frank's always known that. It makes no difference to him.'

She counted out on her fingers. 'Mercy is a junkie – for one, Lucy is a junky – for one, Christine's a speed-freak injecting, and dabbles in heroin, Cinderella's a speed-freak, injecting. Four hard-drug users. And then there's Frank looking the way he does and we're going to go through customs in foreign countries? One bust and it's . . .' she drew a finger like a knife across her throat. 'And not only that,' she added, with the flattest of monotones, which always gave her words extra weight, 'they will ruin his political career.'

'What did Frank say?'

'He's not taking them.'

'I don't believe it.'

She rolled onto her back so that her hair trailed over the edge of the bed to the floor, relishing her moment of victory. 'See, Pauline, I'm Frank's emissary. He still needs me to protect him. I tell him the way it is. That's the way it's always been and always will be.'

Could it be true? Did Frank keep PamZ in the house because as a last resort he valued her counsel, trusted her judgement? She turned over and rested on her elbow. 'I tell him the way it is, that's all. Gail fucking can't, that's for sure.'

With a final flourish, she got up to go back to her room. 'And *I'm* the one he'll call on when the marriage breaks up.'

Oh, so that was it! Still harping after her place next to Frank.

Undoubtedly, I felt a pang of jealousy that PamZ could influence Frank, but this jealousy was tempered the next day when PamZ indirectly did me a favour. Christine overheard her in the kitchen trying to persuade Gail to give Christine the sack. 'Why the fuck do you keep Christine? Who looks after Moon? *You* do. Who cleans the kitchen? *You* do? I mean, what the fuck *does* she do?' So Christine was not fooled when, less than an hour later, PamZ stood at her door and said, 'I'm gonna hitch into Hollywood. You wanna come?'

Later, she barked at Lucy, with whom she competed over Jeff Beck, 'Jeff doesn't want you at his pad, okay? I go 'cos I speak his language and I'm queen of the GTOs.'

When I tackled her, 'Why be so heavy? Why can't things be light-hearted?' she replied blithely, 'I can't be anything other than what I am, Pauline. I am not British. I am how it is.'

Not surprisingly, when Frank questioned the GTOs later that day, they invited me, not PamZ, to be their road manager. Brilliant! Now I could expand my job with exactly the kind of work I enjoyed – odd hours out of the office and with quirky people.

When Frank told the girls that he'd cancelled their trip to Europe, they put on a brave face. Clustered like urchins at his feet, their worship untainted, they promised to write songs and work on their dance routine. *Then* Frank would take them into the studio to make an album. I hoped they would succeed, because now that my job was closely bound up with theirs, our fates were tied – selfish, I know.

Frank appointed a professional photographer, Ed Caraeff, to take pictures of the girls at the zoo. Feeling unwell, with a muzzy head and drained of all energy after days of excruciating pains in my abdomen despite taking painkillers, I trailed around the lion and monkey cages while the girls, dressed in their most wacky outfits, struck attitudes that drew as many spectators as the animals. They piled all their bags and paraphernalia onto me, the dogsbody and, in the kerfuffle, I mislaid my wallet and Mercy's hold-all. But to my utter surprise, when I checked at the post office the next day, they handed me my wallet, still containing fifty-one dollars, with Mercy's bag also intact. What an honest society we lived in!

A letter arrived from my mother. 'It sounds as if you are living an upside-down sort of life, staying up so many nights and spending days in bed. And those strange girls! For goodness sakes don't change yourself too much. We would hate to think of you looking like them. At least stay a bit different.'

I folded the letter and placed it in the drawer now almost full with correspondence from family and friends, and pondered my mother's words, '. . . we would hate to see you looking like them.' What was wrong with looking like them?

28

Because the log cabin had been a squatter's paradise, parents or guardians of lost children often made soft, urgent tappings on our door. And here was another pair; short, overweight, middle-aged, they clutched one another and asked imploringly, 'Could we please come in and search around?' Much as I felt sympathy for their distressed, forlorn faces, I assured them they could not. 'This house is no longer a hotel for people to find a piece of floor to sleep on. It's inhabited by a family.' Of course, had they walked in any of the other five outside doors without asking, no one would have stopped them, so accustomed were we to greeting new and strange faces who loitered and then disappeared. I no longer worried that danger might one day walk in uninvited: I was too preoccupied with United Mutations.

Replies had arrived to my original mailing, all stuffed with the three dollars Frank had requested. A moral obligation now loomed to send something worth the money. Frank's standard reply and enclosures were ready but I wanted to include a summary of the Mothers' story and, at my request, Calvin had already designed a flyer on which I could overlay my précised account, a flyer that I intended to show to Frank for approval. But as Calvin and I huddled over the artwork in my room, Gail walked in. Within seconds, she'd snatched the copy from my hand. 'Did Frank tell you to do this?'

'No, not yet.'

'Well, then?'

'I'll show it to him when it's ready.'

'If it's not Frank's idea, no. Stop right now.'

Incensed at Gail's interference yet again, I started out the door to protest to Frank but stopped in my tracks. Perhaps Gail was right. Perhaps he would not sanction an idea that wasn't his own. Calvin and I glanced significantly at each other. The constant conflicts with Gail were drawing us together. More and more these days I climbed the stairs to his tree-house, or he would find his way down to my room, shovel up the cats and rest them on his lap while he let rip (in Calvin's way) with his own bitter complaints about Gail. Her interference defeated us both.

The first of the evening's visitors arrived: David Gilmour and Roger Waters of Pink Floyd. They had intelligent faces and spoke with more cultured accents than most English groups. Frank invited them to the studio to hear tapes of the Whisky a Go-Go concert and, since Ian played chauffeur, I went along too.

Just as much in awe of Frank as every other English rock star I'd met, David and Roger murmured flattering words of appreciation when Frank played the astonishingly flat GTOs and screaming Wild Man Fischer tapes. What Pink Floyd's true opinions were, one couldn't say, but I supposed that, because David and Roger were also composers, they could appreciate just what musical frontiers Frank was forging and how innovative his albums were. Still, you had to admire Frank's enthusiasm and confidence to showcase such dire material.

Back at the house, an explosion of food seemed to have filled the kitchen, its surfaces splattered with bits of bread, milk and cheese. Too drunk to feel guilty, Jeff Beck and Rod Stewart, a virtual unknown in LA, slouched aside so Frank and Gail could pass through without a word. Cinderella and Mercy, their faces and clothes splashed with as much gunge as the walls, slapped hands over their mouths in shock horror. I'd met Jeff and Rod a few days earlier during a civilised, friendly meeting with Frank, but now I demanded, 'I hope you're going to clear this up.'

'We're up the spout now, lad,' Rod slurred, and Jeff, swinging between the worktop and table like a monkey, ordered, 'Yeah, right, come on girls, don't hang about, get your backs into it.'

Cinderella and Mercy dutifully began to scrape together the bits of coagulated food with their bare hands. I narrowed my eyes and glared. I had as much disdain for those two rock stars as they had for the girls.

The next morning when Frank came down the stairs, I summoned up courage and thrust Calvin's prototype in front of his face. He took the sheet to his desk, wrapped one knee over the other and bent closely over the copy. 'Interesting,' he said at last (so one up on Gail). 'I think it could work if you made the story more detailed, not simply a synopsis. Write the whole story and we'll send it to the fans in future mailings.'

So there it was: Frank's idea, Frank's instruction. But I felt chuffed because, desperate to stretch my job, I'd managed to manufacture another task.

The next two days, I slogged from morning till night writing a light-hearted piece. I cadged humorous anecdotes from each of the Mothers, laughing as I scribbled down their jokes. Pleased with the result, I showed it to Frank. He frowned, not at all impressed. 'Rewrite the whole thing,' he said, 'and make it straight and serious.'

Disappointed but happy to have another chance, I started again from scratch. At three o'clock the next afternoon, I settled at my typewriter determined to finish before Frank left on tour the following morning. I should have known better.

Frank brought Grant Gibbs to meet me. Hired as the publicity and promotions manager for Bizarre Incorporated, I would be working with him to set up the new offices. Tall, slim and handsome, mid-forties, he had the air of an old movie star like Henry Fonda or Jimmy Stewart. Compared with the dynamic, awe-inspiring Neil Reshen, life with Grant would be a gem.

Howard Kaylan and Mark Volman rolled in amid shouts and great bluster, their chirpy voices stirring me to step into the living room. The house steamed from ninety degree temperatures and despite my shortest skirt and halter top, I still bathed in a layer of sweat. Even Frank had peeled off his t-shirt and scraped back his hair and, in an attempt to create a breeze, had thrown open the heavy wooden front door. Not a bush moved or a leaf fluttered.

Howard and Mark of the Turtles had produced more hits, experienced more fame, known more popularity than Frank, but that did not prevent him from hoisting his elbows onto the back of the sofa and suggesting, 'Why don't you two join the Mothers?' They appeared embarrassed and sidestepped the offer, yanking down their t-shirts over their fulsome stomachs, and strutted around telling stories about the Turtles. Their swashbuckling manner seemed to spur Frank on. When talk turned to Robert Kennedy's assassination, Frank nestled further back into the cushions and announced, 'I'm thinking of running for president in 1976.'

If surprised, Mark and Howard recovered quickly. 'Great idea, man.' 'Right on.' They even acted out Frank's inauguration scene on the steps of the Capitol building. Mark stood solemnly to attention, raised his right hand and spoofed the lines with deep gravity, saluted the invisible American flag and then collapsed in peals of laughter. I felt slight unease. Was he laughing at the constitutional ceremony or, more troublingly, at Frank?

I glanced Frank's way, but he remained unmoved, his quiet self-assurance in marked contrast to Mark and Howard's nervous roaming, and he began to reveal what he hoped to achieve when he became president. Mark and Howard finally sat down.

'The first thing I plan to do,' Frank said, 'is cut out corruption in Washington.'

The two rock stars nodded appreciatively.

'The second thing I plan to do is abolish income tax.'

'Income tax! Doesn't that pay for the roads, the military?' Howard asked.

'It does. But I plan to raise taxes on goods people buy. That way they have a couple of thousand extra dollars in their pockets and they choose what to buy. Obviously some items like food will have low taxation because that wouldn't be fair to the poor.'

Mark said, 'I don't pay income tax myself but it sounds good.'

'President Zappa,' said Howard, shaking his head, unsure if he was hearing gobbledygook or the first throw of the towel from the next President of the United States.

I wondered why no one challenged Frank. His experience of command was limited to nine musicians in a band, yet he confidently planned to run a government that employed thousands upon thousands? Was there no one anywhere who would have the gall to say, 'That's a crazy idea, Frank. Mickey Mouse has a better chance, forget it.' But no one ever did, least of all Howard and Mark. Never mind, rather astutely, Frank had drawn the focus of attention away from the flamboyant stars and back onto himself.

I wandered through to my old office where Gail and PamZ, heads together, discussed the very topic. Already they'd booked their place in the White House, Gail as First Lady with her court including PamZ and Calvin but not Herbie, definitely not Herbie. Always the villain, the sooner they annihilated him, the better. The feeling was mutual. Whenever Herbie saw PamZ, he would mutter, 'Here comes trouble.' I never got involved in these feuds. I thought Gail and PamZ lived in cuckoo-land. But I remained uneasy whenever I saw them together. What scheme were they cooking up now?

I left them to it and passed on to the kitchen for a crumb to eat, and while I scoured the empty refrigerator, basking in its cold blast, Wild Man Fischer burst in, rangy and unpredictable. He moved in jerks and smelt like rotten eggs. I skirted round him, avoiding eye contact, my interest in food dissipated.

'When is Frank gonna start recording my album?' he demanded. 'Why are things taking so long?' Agitated in his presence, and having no answers, I led him through to the living room, where our arrival proved the perfect cue for Howard and Mark to depart. Frank somehow always calmed Wild Man and motioned for him to sit on the sofa just as Cinderella, Sandra and Lucy barrelled in and threw themselves at Frank's feet, ready for a short follow-up meeting on their plans. I perched on the corner of the sofa, away from Wild Man. Suddenly, someone said, 'Look!'

A tall, thin figure, silhouetted against the sun in the front doorway, looked in wistfully. Overdressed for August, he wore a neat suit and tie.

'Would Frank Zappa be here?' His voice, light and frail, sounded breakable.

'That's me,' Frank said, jumping up.

The man approached. He had short, oily black hair and a narrow moustache. 'My name is Raven. I brought you a present.'

He handed Frank a see-through bag of red liquid. It could have been blood. I jumped from my seat, alarmed.

Frank took it from him, held the bag aloft and pointed to it as if he was onstage and we were his audience. At that moment, Raven, standing behind Frank, pulled out a steel revolver and I suppose our squawks and horrified expressions made Frank turn. All but two feet away, Raven, his right arm fully outstretched, pointed the weapon at Frank's heart. It felt like everyone shrank back, though no one moved.

Raven said, 'So, hello Frank Zappa.'

The blue of the steel was lethal-looking and Frank had no way of knowing if it was loaded. With the quietest, calmest voice, Frank said, 'Put that thing down.'

'Why?'

'Put it down and I'll tell you.'

Raven hesitated, lowering the gun only slightly.

'You fire that thing, the police will be here and you'll be in big trouble.'

'I'm already in big trouble,' Raven spat and swung around flapping the gun across our path, his face taut and fierce.

I went rigid. Could this be the end? Why hadn't I seen the signs: all these weirdos free to wander willy-nilly through our door? I wanted to call out but my mouth went dry, yet here was Frank, cool as you like, talking to this lunatic.

'They'll lock you up,' Frank said.

'Oh, yeah?'

'Yeah.'

He pointed the pistol back at Frank. 'Can't abide it. Can't abide being locked up.'

He set his feet apart like someone in a western and squinted along the barrel of the gun as if taking aim.

Frank's quiet voice said, 'Best thing you can do is hide it.'

'I just got it.'

'Get rid of it before the cops find out.'

Frank, still holding the bag of blood and apparently calm but for a pulse ticking in his forehead, said, 'And you know what?'

'What?'

'I know just the place.' He gestured towards the sunlight. 'Wanna see?'

We waited. Raven adjusted his stance and tried to whirl the handle but failed. The weapon dropped on the floorboards and everyone gasped, expecting it to explode. Nothing happened. Frank should've grabbed it but Raven pounced first, dropping to his knees and spreading his hands across the gun.

'I'll show you,' Frank said again.

Raven looked up at him, a look of dejection sweeping over his face. He picked up the weapon, this time holding it by the barrel and, as if to keep it safe, pushed it into the pocket of his trousers, where it bulged through the cloth. He nodded to Frank and together they started through the open front door. Frank turned and signalled for us to follow, widening his eyes as if to say, 'Can you believe this?'

He marched alongside Raven, swinging his arms straight like a soldier, even now spoofing it up. Was he the bravest person alive or the stupidest? Too afraid to break ranks behind Sandra, Lucy and Cinderella, I glanced at Wild Man, whose ashen face told me he was more afraid than I was. His fear seemed to eat up some of mine and all at once I could breathe freely again.

With the afternoon sun beating down, Frank directed Raven towards the pond's murky waters and we shuffled where we could around its edges, squeezing between the dense, tangled foliage. A silence fell on us, a silence so deep we could hear the quiet rumble of engines idling in a traffic jam on Lookout Mountain, the other side of the fence. I pictured them drumming on their steering wheels. 'Hey,' I wanted to shout, 'help us, there's a man with a gun here,' but I dared not risk it.

Frank didn't look hot at all; he looked chilly and pale, his eyes blinking more than usual. He picked up a stone and, holding his arm out over the water's edge, dropped it straight down into the water. It sank immediately, causing circular ripples in the green algae. 'Put it in there and they'll never find it,' he told Raven. 'It'll be our secret.' Then he sent us a look that Cinderella immediately understood. She grabbed an apple-like fruit from one of the bushes and tossed it into the water with abandon. Frank gestured for us to follow suit and we scrambled among the dense shrubs and twisted branches. Sandra found a piece of ceramic tile and flipped it into the far reaches of the pond. I broke off a dead twig and thrust it forth but it floated on the algae. I looked round apologetically. Wild Man took off one of his torn shoes and chucked it in. I dared not look at the others for fear of collapsing into giggles.

When we were done, Frank nodded to Raven, whose shoulders sagged, his bravado spent. He had the look of a hurt child forced to give up his favourite toy, the corners of his mouth turned down and I thought he might cry. Then he stiffened and I had another terrifying moment when he pulled the gun from his pocket. He seemed hypnotised and aped Frank's grand gesture, raising his arm straight and lobbing the gun into the water. It landed with a big 'plop' and sank immediately. A collective sigh of relief wafted through as we stared downwards as if looking into the deepest well.

Frank congratulated Raven. 'Neat,' he said and shoved the bag of 'blood' into the Raven's hand. 'You must leave now,' he said, and placed his arm firmly round Raven's shoulders, almost propelling him down the path into Lookout Mountain. They disappeared behind the shrubbery toward Laurel Canyon Boulevard. Only then did I realise I was grinding my teeth.

Once back in the house, Frank pulled the heavy front door shut, but the sudden gloom intensified our fear: was it safe to be alone? We crowded into the kitchen, which rippled with heat as everyone spewed over the dramatic event. 'I've never been so frightened.' 'Do you think it was loaded?' 'I nearly shat myself.'

Frank leaned against the sink and said he acted on reflex, but perhaps the gravity of the situation was finally sinking in. He ordered Gail to fix the locks on all the doors. How differently things might have turned out. The gun, he said, was an army .45.

I said, 'Frank, why don't you call the police?'

His eyes flickered over my face. 'Because if I call the police, the police will arrest him and he'll go to jail and no one deserves to go to jail.'

I thought *no one?* Not even murderers, child abductors? So taken aback by his cryptic, almost sour answer, I opened my mouth to question him further but no words came out.

Frank's aversion to jail, everyone said, stemmed from his own experience when he was twenty-three years old. His first marriage had ended and he lived with Lorraine Belcher in a three-room, makeshift recording studio in Cucamonga, California where he'd scratched together a living, learning the trade and writing and recording the Mexican number-one instrumental hit 'Tijuana Surf'. He also produced cover versions of songs and placed his own material on the B-sides. Unaware that the police had set up a sting operation, Frank agreed to make an audio tape for a $100 for a businessman's stag night. He and Lorraine and her friend had fun huffing and puffing, snorting and sighing to evoke a passionate scene. When, the next day, Frank handed over the tape, a posse of police descended on him and threw him in jail for ten days on a felony charge: suspicion of conspiracy to manufacture pornographic materials and suspicion of sex perversion. Frank described it as the worst experience of his life, squashed in a tiny space with forty-four other prisoners in temperatures over one hundred degrees Fahrenheit, and one filthy shower so over-run with cockroaches that Frank refused to use it.

This incident, everyone believed, had soured Frank's attitude toward the police. When, early on at the log cabin, I had complained about the GTOs' non-stop swearing and said it was obscene, Frank had said, 'You think the word "fuck" is obscene?'

'Yes.'

'I don't think any words are obscene.'

'But that's absurd,' I'd protested. 'There must be *some* obscene words, even to you.' He shook his head, but I'd insisted, 'Give me one. What would you consider to be an obscene word?'

He'd thought for a moment. '*Policeman*,' he'd said quietly. 'I consider "policeman" an obscene word.'

Many years later, he would soften his view of the police, even giving a sympathetic interview about drugs to an ardent fan, Trooper Charles Ash of the Pennsylvania State Police, for a telecast program for schools.

The next day, Friday 2 August, I was unable to show my finished piece to Frank because he left in haste with the Mothers at five-thirty in the morning for a two-week tour of the States. I had hoped for a long sleep-in, but they made so much noise banging and slamming doors they kept me awake for half an hour. I was woken again at eight-thirty when the phone rang. It was Motorhead. His truck carrying the equipment had broken down. Would I phone the emergency services? At nine o'clock, a new fridge arrived to replace the disgusting broken-down one we'd trusted with our food all this time. Again, I trudged back to bed but at ten-thirty, Motorhead phoned once more, yelling down the line, 'We're on the Golden State Highway. Call the emergency services, we're holding up the traffic.' Grumpy and cross, I sorted it out. Couldn't they afford a decent truck?

After three days of non-stop labour on the Mothers' story, perpetual lack of sleep and a poor diet that left me constantly starved, I felt exhausted. When I rolled a sheet of paper into my typewriter, my heart suddenly began to beat so fast I could barely breathe. I gasped one deep lungful of air and the frantic thumping slowed. It happened so quickly that I was terrified of collapsing alone in my room, so I scurried to the other end of the house and sat in the kitchen for twelve hours, from two-thirty in the afternoon until two-thirty the next morning, just sat there like a burned-out wreck, used up and sapped of energy. The tensions that had built up, not only from Raven's visit but also from intrigues between Gail and PamZ, had drained my strength. Was this why I'd come to Hollywood, a life of constant conflict and divided loyalties? What was the point of settling in California if I were to suffer a heart attack and die among virtual strangers?

And then Raven returned. Gail and I saw his shadow pass outside the kitchen window, a moonbeam tracing the top of his cropped head and shoulders. When he stopped behind the screen doorway, taller than I'd remembered, I rose abruptly, clattering a knife to the floor. I grabbed it and hid it behind the toaster. He entered without a word, pulled out a chair and sat down, his back straight like a soldier's. He wore a jacket and white shirt, the collar pressed open in a flat, neat style. His face pale with eyes circled by thick black lashes, he stared and blinked, stared and blinked. Every irrelevant sound and scent seemed magnified, the hum from the fridge, a screech of far-off brakes, and the rancid reek from Moon's nappy not yet picked up from the floor. Gail lit the gas with a match under a saucepan of water and made casual, easy conversation as if he dropped by every day. 'So, how are you, Raven?'

Did she genuinely wish to reach the tormented soul within, or did she believe that if she upset him he might go mad and attack us? I admired her calm bravery. He told us he'd hitch-hiked up from San Diego, that he'd seen Frank in concert and that his voices told him to come. Every so often, he would shout over his shoulder, 'Shut up. Come back later,' or 'I'm busy now, I've got guests.'

A fearful half-hour dragged by in that hot, steamy kitchen as Raven stared straight ahead and twisted and folded his hands on the table. To my relief, PamZ walked in, caught sight of our unwelcome visitor, saw our alarmed faces and immediately knew. She wagged her finger into his face and he stared back, cold and tense. 'Raven, you do not live here, okay? You have to go now.' He appeared to ignore her, but then slowly he scraped back his chair, pushed it neatly under the table and, with a little bow to each one of us in turn, walked backwards into the yard, his right hand, like a five-pronged board, making little circular motions of farewell. Even though it was dark, PamZ was brave enough to escort him through the door of the carport and waited until he disappeared down Laurel Canyon. I had to give it to PamZ. Her forceful style was handy at times. We never saw Raven again.

29

Frank's two-week tour with the Mothers would be his longest absence from the log cabin so far. Those of us left behind remained jittery because Raven's spirit seemed to hang around the house for days and it was a relief when the new bodyguard, Kansas, whom Frank had hastily arranged to come over from New York to guard us, arrived. Kansas would replace Dick Barber, who moved on to become the band's road manager.

Tall, lean and muscular, Kansas turned out to be an easygoing, nothing-would-bother-him sort of guy. He wore Levis and a denim jacket over a bare chest and threaded his dark, straight hair in two braids. I found his presence in the house reassuring, but best of all, I liked his impressive influence on Gail's culinary skills. With Frank gone, she cooked every night for two weeks, often working with PamZ to prepare tasty meals for the rest of us; Kansas, me, Calvin, Christine and John Mayall, a constant visitor. Chicken with baked potato and corn on the cob one night, liver or spaghetti or hamburgers on others. After each meal, Kansas would tip back his chair, pull open his jacket and, like lord of the manor, slap his bare stomach and belch with satisfaction. Because of Kansas I lived better than I had since arriving in Hollywood and my stomach pains gradually subsided.

To my mother, I wrote: 'It is good to have so many people living at the house: Frank, Gail, Moon, PamZ, me, Christine, Dick, Calvin, Jeff, Ian, Jim and now Kansas, twelve in all. One can never really feel lonely. When there are no visitors, the family – those that live here – end up congregating in one room or another and sit around chatting for hours, joking and laughing and it is so much fun.'

We piled onto Christine's mattress, squashed together like a litter of puppies as Calvin threaded up the 8mm projector and pointed the tiny square of light at Christine's silver wall. There was my sister's party in Washington DC, the squishy sofas and plush decor making me realise how, in just two months, my life had radically changed from a sedate, middle-class Republican existence in the nation's capital to this bohemian lair which, with a pull like gravity, drew me in.

If Kansas went out, we girls indulged in 'ladies' nights' when Gail, PamZ, Christine and one or more of the GTOs would gather in the living room gossiping for hours. Frank was away so we could make as much noise as we wanted and one night, smitten by a mad attack, I pranced around aping the Mothers and the GTOs. Hitherto, I had always reined myself in, but now my female audience peered up at me, flabbergasted. Whatever happened to staid Miss Pauline Butcher, the prim and serious secretary? They concluded that my experience at the log cabin had brought on this buffoonery, but how to explain that I'd always had quirky ways? And only that week a friend from England had written: 'I was surprised to find you are in the States, but not surprised at the show. You were always way out.' In England maybe, but never in Los Angeles.

Miss Bee from Forum Secretarial Service in London also wrote: 'Even America had to bow to the nicest cuckoo on earth . . . I am so glad that you have found, at last, the place where you want to be and do the things you want to do. All that is left now, and even not in such a hurry, is that you find your life.' Did she not realise – had I not made it clear in my letters – that I *had* found my life? Why, I even went star-gazing.

Kansas had begun talking in such poetical terms about the new moon that when he said, 'Let's go look at the stars,' Gail and I rushed through the door before he could even hoist Moon onto his shoulders. On the drive, he told us that in the state of Kansas, the sky was black for hundreds of miles so you could see galaxies, millions of them, and several shooting stars every hour.

Soon, we found our own desolate hilltop and scrambled about in the murky darkness, finding boulders large enough to lie on. It was cooler here and, while Moon slept cradled in Gail's arms, Kansas identified the twinkly shapes, and I experienced the quietest two hours I'd known since arriving in California, a quiet so like Kansas's calm influence on our jittery lives. When finally, a shooting star zoomed across the sky, the first and last I ever saw, Kansas explained it was not a star at all but tiny bits of dust and rock called meteoroids. It was thrilling. Was there no end to this university of life I found myself living through?

That was Wednesday. On Thursday, Mutt invited me and Gail to Las Vegas to see Tiny Tim. Gail jumped at the chance, hastily arranging for Christine to take Moon to her parents' house for two nights, and all at once, Gail and

I were sharing a bedroom at Caesars Palace Hotel, an intimacy at odds with the formality of our relationship. But Gail was unfazed and emptied her toilet bag on her bed, threw off her clothes with aplomb and donned a full-length purple velvet gown which hugged her figure. In line with my prudishness, I changed in the bathroom and put on my cerise taffeta mini-dress. We joined Mutt for an early dinner of chicken-fried steaks and nearly froze in the ice-cold air conditioning.

Our excitement grew as we took our table at the front of the stage in the lavish theatre. For so long had I been surrounded by 'scruff', it was a shock to see real glamour, the women jewelled and coiffed as if we were at the Oscars. Even the men wore evening dress. When Tiny Tim appeared from within a bevy of beautiful girls with huge feathers on their heads and sequins sparkling on their heavily made-up eyes, rapturous applause greeted him. He looked grotesque, his face smeared with white make-up and his eyebrows painted black. He sang most of his songs with his ukulele in his high-pitched eunuch-voice that saved the night, but too many of the numbers droned on with his baritone voice, the orchestra drowning him out – maybe deliberately.

After the show at the press party in a smallish room grandly decorated with Roman statues, I was pleased at last to meet this strange man who had almost stolen the GTOs from under Frank's nose. Congratulations flew hard and fast despite his lacklustre performance. I gave him Cinderella's letter and in his high-pitched voice he trilled, 'Thank you, Miss Butcher.' He kept flicking his hand and rolling his eyes as if in a state of fright and ready to faint.

Then Gail and I watched Mutt throw ten dollars a go at the croupier on the pontoon table but frankly, it was as boring as watching Tim Buckley perform. She and I withdrew, supposedly to sleep, but instead we gossiped about Mutt like we were the best of friends. 'For fuck's sake, Pauline, just strap him on, and get it over with. It'll do you good. I'm sure you'll be very happy. I can see you with ten kids. We'll be neighbours, it'll be fun.' So easy and warm were we, I could not imagine Gail and I having cross words ever again.

The taxi carried us straight out across the shrub, leaving me with the impression that lasted for years, that Las Vegas consisted merely of Caesars Palace.

Thick fog delayed our descent in LA for half an hour. Who would believe it was August? Kansas appeared through the haze to drive us home, the sky two feet above our heads. At the log cabin, we lit a log fire and sprawled in front of its flickering light. It was very peaceful without Moon's all pervading presence, constant mess and need for attention.

On Saturday, Frank phoned and, although he'd only been gone a week, it was wonderful to hear his deep, sultry voice. He gave me – noticeably not Gail – instructions to take the master tape of *Cruising with Ruben and the Jets* to the airport and express it to New York. Kansas drove me there and I got a kick out of insuring the package, no bigger than a box of chocolates, for fifty thousand dollars.

A gentle, pattering of rain began – the first rain in three months, an event so rare we ran into the back yard. I raised my face to the sky and felt the drops softly caressing my nose and eyes. Later, I stood in the living room and listened with pleasure to the rat-a-tat-tat on the roof. I had forgotten the drumbeat of rain. How could I, an English person, forget about rain?

I showed my new version of the Mothers' story to Gail. She offered ideas which I said I would adopt. 'I can offer help but I couldn't write it,' she said, which made me feel chuffed, the first time she'd praised me. She was still sweet as sweet, but how long would it last? For five heady days now, she'd managed her job and I'd managed mine. It was like being home again, as if Gail was my mother and she was looking after me. It was three o'clock in the morning and she knocked on my door.

'I've made chocolate cake. Would you like some?'

So there I was in the kitchen stuffing myself with gateau and ice-cream and drinking coffee specially brewed, enjoying Gail's breezy, easygoing company. Janet, her friend, joined us and for the next two hours, they gossiped, incredibly incomprehensible stuff about orgies, past affairs and relationships in marriage. Gail had no inhibitions when talking about her groupie days and the various people she'd had flings with. She thrilled us with stories about Terence Donovan, the famous English fashion photographer. He made love, she said, like a sergeant major. 'He issues orders with a loud voice ringing out, "Right leg up, left arm down, turn to the right, belly-side over."' Very amusing, as Gail could be. I liked her delight in the comic and absurd; even her shambolic lifestyle was beginning to grow on me.

Ian had lent me his car rather than PamZ because my licence had at last arrived. I could see her frowning through the kitchen window so I made a big show of checking the doors and studying the keys before I slid behind the wheel and, with a little smile, waved goodbye.

Independence at last! I took off to Beverly Hills, a couple of miles along Sunset Boulevard. There I found tall, stone buildings with no parking lots between them and buses on the streets. It felt more solid and real than Hollywood. I parked the car behind Saks Fifth Avenue and walked down Rodeo Drive. This was the life I wanted, beautiful clothes and furniture behind expensively fronted boutiques, smartly-clad women tripping by in high-heeled shoes. I'd thought tinsel town would be over-run with actors and actresses but so far all I'd met were rock'n'roll druggies locked in a music scene from which I found it hard to escape. The passing faces I searched, but could find

no Warren Beatty or Paul Newman, no Audrey Hepburn, Mia Farrow or Faye
Dunaway. Where were they all?

I bought the *LA Times* and settled down to read in an upmarket coffee shop
with cream leather seats and granite tables on polished wood floors. I sat
alongside svelte women in black mini-dresses with gold metal belts. News
about the Vietnam War and Governor Ronald Reagan's challenge to Richard
Nixon in the Republican presidential race failed to grab my attention. I
flicked to the film section, all about *2001: A Space Odyssey*, the hit film of the
summer. I tried to find the European news section among the sixty-eight pages
of Monday's edition, but lost patience. I left it on the table, paid the exorbitant
two dollars fifty for cake and coffee and, feeling replenished after my little
jaunt, returned to the log cabin. Gail greeted me with the brightest of smiles
and an offer of a cup of tea.

Rick Shaw, a new employee, slight but handsome, early twenties, took me to
the pristine offices to see in the new furniture. While we arranged desks, filing
cabinets, electric typewriters, copying machine and stationery, I wondered
if Rick could possibly be a future boyfriend. Certainly I enjoyed his warm,
funny, unassuming manner and the day flew by in a flash. After he left, I
stayed on until midnight, typing the first of Pamela's fourteen diaries. Mutt
joined me for a while. 'You've come in at the right time,' he said. 'Possibly
you won't be a secretary for long.' Not *definitely*, but *possibly*, he said. What
was this, a bribe to work at the office? Did I have the gumption to deal on a
par with Neil Reshen, or even Herbie? I sensed they would tear me to shreds
within a week.

At around this time Kansas and Gail took off for the airport to collect Frank
and by 4:00am the kitchen filled with insomniacs; PamZ, Christine, Calvin,
Sandra and me, slouching at the kitchen table, lingering, chitchatting, casting
sidelong glances at the windows overlooking the carport. Only Moon slept,
curled like a cashew nut in her blanket on the floor. And then came the slam
of car doors and Frank, wearing a leather jacket, purple pants and yellow
shirt, pushed open the screen. Suddenly the kitchen was a hive of activity.
Coffee cups were reached for, cheese and bread snatched from the fridge, a
diversion from the ragged welcome queue that formed. First in line was Moon.
'Moony,' Frank said. Christine passed her so carelessly that Frank almost
dropped her. 'Say Fwank,' Frank said to Moon, who could barely open her
eyes. Her head flopped.

Oh, couldn't absence warm the heart. When it came to my turn, he was still
grinning, and said, 'I liked your straight version of the Mothers' story. Get it
copied and include it in the mailings.'

It felt like fireworks had been set off. My first piece of writing would reach readers! Nothing could top it, so I wished them goodnight and walked away while their voices bounced and murmured behind me until they smoothed into one low level. As I climbed into bed, I heard a quiet knock. I pulled the covers to my throat and called, 'Come in.'

The door opened and there stood Frank, looking almost shy. Surprised and flushed, I scrambled onto an elbow.

'It's real nice to see you again,' he said.

'Oh, and you, too.'

His dark eyes regarded me for a moment. 'Good night,' he said and gently closed the door.

That's what got to me, small gestures of appreciation. I flopped back on the pillow and stared at the white paint on the ceiling, my perfect handiwork.

30

While in Chicago, Eric Clapton had introduced Frank to Cynthia Plaster Caster, a girl who not only made plaster-casts of rock stars' penises, but also kept detailed diaries of the proceedings. Frank brought three of the treasured books for me to transcribe as well as a tape of his interview with her. But disclosing details about living rock stars' private parts was, to say the least, indelicate, possibly libellous. To find out, Frank, Gail, Kansas and I drove to Mutt's house for legal advice. Could Cynthia's diaries be published? We flipped through the pages, aghast. They were too intimate to read aloud.

In time, I would learn Cynthia's bizarre story. Originally, she had been a super-square teenager with a huge collection of Broadway musical albums. Then one eventful day, a friend brought a photograph of George Harrison to school and Cynthia fell in love. She converted to the Beatles, then after the Beatles to the Rolling Stones and after the Rolling Stones, the Dave Clark Five and after the Dave Clark Five to any other English groups with long hair, eventually branching out to all the other groups, including American ones. Then it was a matter of meeting them, invading their hotel rooms and 'making out'. Cynthia's diaries described every detail but to prevent her mother catching on, she used a special code: 'rig' for penis; 'plating' for oral sex; 'banking' for masturbation; and 'charva' for sexual intercourse.

Cynthia had told Frank how she'd first dreamed up her strange hobby. One day in art class, the teacher asked them to bring something to cast. It could be anything, a fork, a piece of celery, a half-eaten chunk of cheese, and Cynthia thought, *anything?* She made a mould of her hand and while she pressed down into the alginate, the dough-like mixture used by dentists to make moulds of gums and teeth, she realised an erect penis would make a damned good impression too and if she could get a model of a rock star's 'rig', what a star prize that would be. By this time, she'd met and made friends with most of the musicians who'd toured Chicago in 1967, but before she dared approach any of them, she must practise on someone else first.

A boy from school had played a willing guinea pig and after two attempts, Cynthia had produced a passable semblance to a penis, albeit a bent and shrivelled one. The process involved several stages. First, Dianne, Cynthia's friend, must stiffen up the rig using her hand, mouth or both and when the rig was almost ready, she must signal to Cynthia to quickly mix the alginate powder with water – not too dried-out to prevent penetration and not too wet to cause the walls of the mould to collapse after withdrawal. Speed was essential because the alginate mixture would set within fifty seconds. In the beginning, Cynthia tried piling the paste around the rig but it fell apart on to the boy's stomach, so she progressed to holding a vase horizontally so the boy, careful not to rub against the sides of the vase, could thrust his penis into it. Essentially, he must remain hard for a full minute while the mould set – not an easy task as anyone who's had a dental mould would know, it feels cold and clammy. Once the boy had withdrawn his rig, Cynthia made a reverse mould with liquid plaster, pouring it into the indentation and leaving it to harden. Soon a replica of the penis or something like it would emerge.

After a series of hits and misses during which their schoolboy friend showed impressive patience, the two girls brought their art to a good-enough standard, the best ones revealing details like veins and sometimes parts of the balls, too.

Now they were ready for the real thing – rock stars. Cynthia explained to Frank her approach. Not believing herself to be especially attractive or pretty, and hiding her well-proportioned but overweight body under loose t-shirts and jeans, she grabbed the boys' attention by walking up to her target at the concert or in the hotel lobby and asking directly, 'How's your rig?' It evoked a universal response – smirks and sniggers accompanied by, 'Come up to room 2701 in ten minutes.'

The diaries outlined page after page of erotic detail, detail that Cynthia could never have imagined that we, a bunch of strangers two thousand miles away, would guffaw over. While Mutt's dogs and cats nuzzled at our feet, we laughed aloud at Cynthia's description of Jimi Hendrix's casting – an almost catastrophic event. She described his manhood as so large that she needed a broader, longer vase. When it came time to withdraw, however, he could not pull his penis out. Whereas others in the same situation had panicked, terrified that Cynthia had damaged the most sacred part of their body, Jimi had remained calm. Dianne thought his pubic hairs held him fast because she'd failed to smear sufficient Vaseline on them, but Cynthia believed Jimi's enjoyment of the tight enclosure in which he was trapped prevented him for a full fifteen minutes to soften sufficiently to slip out. Undeterred by this near mishap, Noel Redding and Mitch Mitchell lined up to have their own models made.

Sometimes, after the casting was complete, sexual intercourse would take place, but more often than not, the procedure exhausted everyone's ardour.

Frank probed for more. He wanted to know if they operated as a pair when it came to reap rewards for their labour, or did they take turns? Did Cynthia sit on the side of the room and wait for Dianne to get done?

Cynthia explained they invariably gathered an audience as word spread among the group. Sometimes one of the boys would start 'banking' himself. Sometimes, rock stars welcomed the girls into their beds; other times they dismissed them. Whichever way it went, Cynthia recounted with astonishing honesty the pleasures as well as rejections she and Dianne suffered at the hands of those chauvinistic musicians.

Best of all were her brilliant drawings in the diaries, drawings that illustrated not only the successful castings, but the disasters too, the little faces dismayed at the bent, forlorn results.

Not all rock stars agreed to be cast, including Frank, so I thought it unfair of him to express disappointment that, in six months, she'd produced a mere seven casts. He'd expected a whole stack of them and encouraged her to boost her output.

Cynthia told Frank about her father, who was separated from her mother, and how he liked to tell her dirty jokes. Frank wanted to know if her father had any desire for Cynthia's own young blood and she acknowledged that she'd once caught him stealing a glance at her tits. Frank asked what he would think if she offered to cast him, a suggestion that left Cynthia aghast. She thought he'd be really angry – that he would think it obscene behaviour for a girl, to which Frank remarked wryly, 'Especially my daughter.' Dianne, Cynthia's friend, thought her father would kill her if he knew about her plaster-casting activities. Frank responded with his often-made remark, 'Well, I think that if anyone were to see either of you on the street, they would never suspect what bizarre madness lurks, except for that little suitcase and the brown paper bag.'

While in New York, Frank had met two other groupies, fourteen years old. A 'groupie', one of them had explained, was more than just a fan who merely worshipped the stars from afar – a groupie must not only meet the groups but must make out with them as well. But whereas Cynthia made her diary her confidant, these girls gained most of their prestige from going home and recounting their escapades to their friends in minute detail. Frank wanted to know how many points they would give kissing and hugging compared with fucking, and suggested a figure of thirty percent of a fuck. Not used to reducing their lovemaking to statistics, the girls hesitated but decided, in the end, on forty percent.

They told Frank how they would rub away against the sinks in the ladies' room at the Garrick Theatre after watching the Mothers onstage. He pressed for more details, wanting them to describe the process. Did they take their clothes off, for example? But the girls explained that their layers of clothing helped the stimulation. One of them once tried to remove a tap from the sink in order to push it inside herself, but she couldn't get it off and had to stop because other groupies walked into the toilets and they didn't want to lose face in front of them. Masturbating over a pop star carried no value compared with fucking one.

Frank played the interview with the New York girls to Cynthia who, in turn, was shocked by the girls' frankness. He told Cynthia that just as she felt under-developed after hearing about what fourteen-year-olds were up to, so there were girls of twenty-five who didn't know what Cynthia knew. Frank seemed to think it was valid to pass on this knowledge, if told in their own words, from one group of girls to the other. Frank seemed convinced that because of the sixties sexual revolution, an explosion of interest in girls' sexual behaviour would follow and a market for their journals would soon open up. Secretly I felt disappointed in Frank. What could I learn from this grubby and tacky stuff?

Everyone else thought the diaries were great. Mutt, after careful scrutiny, thought we should publish and be damned, which meant I had my work cut out for me for the next few months. In that respect I was pleased, but certainly I would not write home to mother about this particular task.

At the log cabin, the GTOs were waiting, wanting to show Frank their songs, but Cynthia Plaster Caster had become his new fixation. He showed them her diaries and the GTOs also balked at their frankness. Anxious to bring them together, Frank telephoned Cynthia and passed the receiver in turn to Christine, Lucy, Mercy and Pamela.

Without beating about the bush, Christine said, 'We heard excerpts from your diary tonight and it's really, really wonderfully written but – I don't want to sound like a mother – it's just that someday maybe you'll meet someone who'll really object to that and you'll be madly in love with him and I just think it would be nice if you would be a little more discreet.'

As I listened to Christine chastising Cynthia without fear of sounding prudish or prim, I wondered why I couldn't express my disapproval in the same free way. There was something refreshing about their uninhibited voices, their willingness to express whatever came into their heads. All the American girls I'd met – Gail, PamZ, and the GTOs, as well as Cynthia in her diaries and the girls in New York – all of them had this wonderfully free voice and I wanted it too. 'True to yourself' was the mantra in my family, which in effect meant, stay the same. I envied these girls' ability to adapt. I had thought they were irrelevant, inconsequential, the dregs of society. But now, as they'd seeped into my consciousness, in comparison with their spontaneous, unbridled flair, I felt rigid, taut, and unmoveable.

Lucy, with her New York Puerto Rican accent, spoke equally candidly. 'This is Miss Lucy. I don't have much to say except that I'm really proud of your journals and the plaster-casting stuff. That's really er, um, wow! They're very thorough and I got the message. What more can I say? When did you start this plaster-casting business anyway?'

'We started chasing groups about two and a half years ago, but we never made a cast until this February.'

'Boy, it must have been fun.'

'Yeah, it was.'

'You know who would love to have a cast made? Jeff Beck. He is such a *pervert!* He's fantastic for that sort of thing.'

'How's his rig?'

'His rig? Oh, his rig is big.' Lucy gave one of her low laughs like a dramatic drill. 'Rig, huh? I never thought of calling it that. It's a good name. I mean I've never heard tell of rig for balls or joint, you know.'

'We've heard 'em called Hamptons.'

'Hamptons? God, where do you pick up these names?'

Lucy's very short attention span kicked in at this point, her eyes glazed over and she handed the phone to Mercy.

Mercy wanted to talk about Brian Jones, who Cynthia said was bisexual, but Mercy, who loved him, would have none of it. 'Brian Jones is *not* bisexual,' Mercy insisted. 'I know because I'm a friend of Mick Jagger and I've just spent a week with Brian Jones and he has about four kids. I mean, he might be slightly bisexual, but he's not directly bisexual. Mick's bisexual, and Keith is, but Brian Jones isn't.'

For all her matter-of-fact worldliness, I found Mercy's ingenuous persistence to get the facts exactly right about her favourite rock star quite touching. I warmed to her as I had begun to do with all of the girls. Frank had been so clever to see within them a humanity that I had dismissed in the beginning as purely vulgar. This was better than university, this was learning about real life.

Finally, Frank handed the phone to Pamela, perhaps the most pretty of the girls with her golden locks, heart-shaped face, blue eyes and full lips which she painted vivid red. She and Cynthia clicked immediately sharing their experiences, particularly about Noel Redding, who both of them had plated and been plated by, and agreed was the best. They could have gone on and on but Frank rescued the phone.

'You must come out to LA,' he told Cynthia, 'and bring your little trophies with you.'

At that time, Cynthia kept the seven casts hidden from her mother in a shoebox at the bottom of her wardrobe, but Frank wanted her to bring a suitcase-full.

Frank must have felt the heat because he took off his t-shirt and sat hairy-chested by his desk while the girls encircled his feet, itching for him to read the lyrics they'd struggled for the past ten days to write. He sat, one leg crossed over the other, a smouldering cigarette poised in his fingers, and slowly read through each of the handwritten pages. The girls, with arms linked, sat motionless. Occasionally Frank would chuckle and the girls would stretch, trying to see which lyric amused him. Finally, at the end, he handed them back and said, 'They are all *inspiring*,' which evoked a palpable sigh of relief from the girls.

'So, what you should do now is write the melodies for the lyrics.'

Mercy said she'd already done hers and began to sing 'Shock Treatment', but her howling voice rasped even on my damaged ears. Undeterred, Frank said, 'Maybe I'll ask a couple of the guys to help you. Maybe Don or Ian. I'll give you one week. We'll meet here again next Monday, okay?' and he padded off upstairs.

After he'd gone, the girls gossiped about why Frank revelled in Cynthia so much.

Sandra said, 'I think it's sexual,' but Mercy would have none of it. 'Frank goes where others fear to tread.'

Normally reticent to speak up and fingering a fold in her skirt, Sparkie said, 'I think Sandra's right. It is all about sex with Frank.'

Was that true? Earlier in the day in the kitchen, out of the blue I'd found myself alone with Frank. He'd said no word, but had pulled me gently and without passion into his arms and I had wrapped my arms around his body, too. Normally we girls got bear hugs that cracked our ribs but this fond embrace surprised me. He'd tied his hair back, but his long sideburn tickled my cheek. I wondered what had brought this on – last night his little knock on the door, and now this. Had he missed me during his fifteen days away? I hardly dared believe it. Perhaps he realised I did not want to work at the office away from him and this was his way of reassuring me. I leaned back to search his face and found a little smile with no sexual intent at all. He coaxed a stray strand of hair from my face, 'That's to say, nice to see ya.' There was a soft tenderness in his voice.

I heard footsteps approaching and pulled from his arms. 'I know. I still can't believe I'm here.'

He turned to search in the fridge.

I said, 'So you want me to type those incredible diaries? What will you think of next?'

'The next thing is to get her over here. You won't believe it when you meet her.'

And it was true. Cynthia turned out to be a shy, inhibited girl, the least likely person you could imagine to be the illustrious Chicago Plaster Caster.

31

I began the first week at the office full of optimism and vigour, determined to prove my worth to Frank. But when I arrived at nine-thirty on Monday morning in Ian's car, Donna, the accounts girl, sat in reception like a queen on her throne and welcomed me in as if *I* was the newcomer, as if *I* was the underling. She had a heart-shaped face, grey-brown eyes and thick, brown hair waving to her shoulders. She exuded that poise and self-confidence that all American girls seemed to possess. Where did it come from? Adoring parents? 'Honey, you're wunnerful, the best.' Compare that with my family, my brothers in particular: 'Who's Miss Hoity-Toity? Want to be a journalist? Forget it!'

The morning passed in a haze while everyone, under Rick's guidance, settled in. He hovered by Donna's desk admiring her pearl ring and teasing her until she almost choked from giggling. So that was the end of my first possible boyfriend in America.

I brought in Frank's Uher tape recorder to type Cynthia's interview, but it had no headphones and I thought visitors might get the wrong idea if they heard Frank's deep voice, 'How does one steal a glance at their daughter's tits?' So I closed Neil Reshen's door and set myself up behind his gigantic desk.

After an easy day, I returned to the log cabin and, in line with my new duties, descended the stairs to the basement. Low voices, punctuated by squeals of laughter and 'You didn't!' and 'What did you do then?' floated up to greet me. Inside the vault, a bare light-bulb lit the pine-panelled walls, where the GTOs had notched up more fave-rave names, 'Rodney Bingenheimer,' 'Arthur Brown,' 'Jeff Beck.'

'Want to see?' I asked, and held aloft their fantastic photographs taken at the zoo. There they were, natural models folded around each other in perfect silhouettes. Even I swelled with pride as they competed with each other about who looked the worst. 'My ass looks huge,' wailed Cinderella, and Mercy jibed, 'Gard, is my nose that big?'

The vault, always cold and spooky like a dungeon, made me shiver, so I hastily returned to my room, where Pamela's fourteen hardback diaries with their metal clasps lay higgledy-piggledy on my desk like crustaceans waiting to be shelled. I began to type, but when Frank returned from the studio just after midnight, I joined him, Motorhead and Dick Barber in the living room. Despite the late hour, he dictated a long list of things to discuss with Neil Reshen. That done, he talked almost lustily about his hopes for Bizarre Records and I wanted to stay longer, but I'd been up since seven and now, twenty hours later, my eyelids drooped and my shoulders sagged. As it was, I slept through the alarm until Herbie telephoned. Conscience-stricken, I raced over to the black tower on Wilshire Boulevard.

On the way, news on the car radio reported that the Russians had invaded Czechoslovakia although they had not declared war. Czechoslovakia! Europe! A distant continent floating in a mist. Like everyone else I'd met in Laurel Canyon, I found myself losing interest in the other side of the world. And why *should* anyone in California be interested in Czechoslovakia? I doubt they even knew where it was. To be fair, if you'd asked me to draw Arkansas on a map of the United States where would I put it? For all I knew, it backed onto Canada.

At the office, Neil Reshen swept through like a tornado, his darting eyes worked over me, missing nothing and giving me goose-bumps. A fat cigar clenched between his teeth, he grasped issues before the sentence was finished, barked orders that made us all jump, including the wonderfully quiet and laidback Grant Gibbs. When Neil entered the office, even the walls seemed to shake.

He pulled me into his room and shut the door.

'Here's what we're gonna do. You get one hundred dollars every Friday, cash in hand,' he said in his quick rat-a-tat delivery. 'Royalties, you understand, for your song.'

Good, I thought, because if they'd officially included me in personnel I would have felt compelled to work at the office. This way I could be a free agent.

He moved behind his huge desk. 'Another thing,' he said, his eyes boring into mine. 'I'm looking for an apartment in Los Angeles.'

'That'll be nice,' I said lamely.

'Now what I propose is this. If you find me the right place, something classy, not big, I'm offering you the apartment, rent-free.'

Stunned, I could hardly believe his words. Was he being exceptionally kind, or was this part of a seduction routine?

He knocked the ash from his big, fat cigar into the ashtray. 'In return, you keep the place tidy, clean sheets when I arrive, fridge and freezer stocked with basics, know what I mean?'

It sounded like a good deal – just the sort of beautiful home I was looking for – expensive, sophisticated, in a well-heeled part of town. 'Are you talking about two bedrooms?'

'Have you seen the price of real estate in Los Angeles? I'm here two nights a month, come on.'

'Well, um – '

'You just move out for two nights – or you stay. It's up to you. No sweat.'

No sweat? Wherever I moved in the office, his eyes followed me like a hungry dog and when he finished speaking, they continued to search my face as if caressing it. I wilted like a flower under too much heat.

'Okay, see what you can do,' he said and abruptly switched subjects. 'So what's going on out there?'

'What do you mean?'

'Between Donna and lover-boy?'

'You mean Rick? I don't know. I think they just like each other.'

'Do you think if I fire Rick, Donna would leave too?'

'Oh! Well – '

'Find out, okay? Let me know by tomorrow,' and with that he placed his arm round my shoulders and guided me back into reception, already onto his next task.

I waited until Rick went out on a delivery before conferring with Donna. We both agreed Neil was a horror of the first order, a devastatingly attractive horror at that. But she would not sacrifice herself for Rick. She needed the job too much.

In the evening in my room, I typed more of Pamela's diaries. She joined me and read them aloud, tracing her place with her long, red-painted nail. Of all the GTOs, Pamela was the most professional. Already taking speech, drama and dance at the California Repertory Company, during the day she worked alongside Sparkie at a candy store to pay her way and still lived at home with her long-suffering mother. I really had to admire her energy and drive, and with her beautiful, angelic face and blonde tresses, she would surely succeed.

She told me she had a crush on Ian but knew there was no hope, not with Ruth in the background. 'You know there's one thing that I really find moche about him. He uses the word "boss". "This is boss, that's boss." You must have noticed, Pauline. He says it all the time and no one says boss anymore.'

Of course not. Why use old-fashioned 'boss' when cool words like *moche*, *groovy*, *gross*, *spiffy*, *hung up*, or *bad vibes*, would do?

And you know what else?'

'No.'

'Don't tell, Frank, will you?'

I shook my head.

'I want my diaries published alone. Now Frank says they'll be dunked in with Cynthia's. I'm secretly upset about that.'

Little did she know what a blockbuster of a book she would write ten years later, the incredibly candid description of her experiences with pop stars, *I'm with the Band,* a book that would become a bestseller.

Although wretchedly tired, we kept going until three-thirty when Frank invited us to watch a film by Tim Dawe, another cranky find of Frank's, but for once, I made a sane decision, declined the offer and crawled into bed, too tired to take my clothes off.

On Wednesday, directly after we'd congratulated Rick on his twenty-fourth birthday (we'd bought him a cake with one candle and sung 'Happy Birthday'), Neil called Rick into his office and fired him. Naturally, Rick stormed out and who could blame him? Later, after everyone else had left, Neil grabbed my arm and said, 'Herbie, Suzie and I are going out to dinner. Would you like to join us?' Out of loyalty to Rick, I should have said no, but how would Rick benefit if I refused? He was gone now.

We dined at the luxuriously red-carpeted La Rue on Sunset and slid into a gold leather semi-circle booth under huge chandeliers. Waiters in uniform brought daiquiris. I felt ill-at-ease without Frank's reassuring presence or my shorthand book to hold onto.

Neil exuded power even as he stomped his fork into a sorbet and exchanged jokes and stories about New York with Herbie and Suzie. Every so often, he would burn his eyes into mine and I struggled to keep my cool, blinking fast at the antiqued mirrors on the far wall.

Then, Herbie and Suzie moved onto another engagement and Neil slid round the booth to my side. He leaned his heavy shoulders forward on his elbows, lightly tapped my dangling earring with the back of his perfectly manicured fingernail and said, quietly, 'So, Pauline, what turns you on?'

Flushed, I said, 'Oh, goodness, what an odd question,' and fumbled for a cigarette. Within seconds, he'd flicked his solid-gold Dunhill lighter and as I bent to draw on the flame, he cupped my hand in his.

'Okay, I'll go first,' he said, 'I'll tell you what turns me on.'

He lit one of his smaller cigars, took a deep drag and waved away the smoke. 'My girlfriend has very long, very strong fingernails, *very* long, *very* strong. She paints them with dark red varnish. When we make love, she claws hard into my back. Sometimes she draws blood. I like that. I have scars.'

I could see myself locked in his apartment, the air conditioning for some inexplicable reason broken down, and Neil peeling off his shirt, while I'd be forced to admire his wounds.

'It's lucky you've found something you both enjoy,' I said feebly.

'We do. Now it's your turn.'

He was so close, I could smell his cologne, something expensive. If I wanted to keep him interested, I must keep my reserve and remain cool. I tried to laugh, but managed only a silly, forced giggle. 'I'm not going to be drawn, Neil, I really am not.'

'All right, another time,' he said, his eyes drifting carelessly around my face as he snapped his fingers for the waiter to bring the bill.

Relieved, I said, 'Did you know Frank is showing a film to everyone at the theatre tonight?'

'I did,' he said. 'I'll be there.'

After Neil brought me to the house, I quickly shampooed my hair and then joined a whole crowd of us at the Lindy Theatre to watch Frank's footage from the Whisky a Go-Go gala. With good sound but poorly lit and grainy, it made no difference to Frank. Unfazed, he planned to sell it to television. His sureness and faith in his ability to succeed never failed to amaze me.

Once again, three hours after midnight, Frank, Herbie and Neil held another meeting in my room. As I scribbled down the gist of Neil's monologue, it occurred to me that he and I *could* carry out a clandestine affair. I felt sure that Neil would be discreet but then, what was the good? How could I, a girl with little experience in the art of love, hold the interest of a sophisticated New Yorker like Neil Reshen? What if I lived in his apartment and one day he turned on his bullying tactics, where would I be then? And when the inevitable break-up came, most likely sooner rather than later, then what would I do? But why was I worrying about the end of an affair that so far had progressed no further than a delicate dab at my earring? My thoughts rambled on in this way while Frank, Herbie and Neil discussed high finance and, though I scribbled it all down, I took not one word into my conscious brain.

After the meeting, we adjourned to the living room where Motorhead was already seated on the back of the sofa, his bare feet tucked between the cushions, languidly strumming a few chords on one of Frank's guitars. When we appeared he put down the guitar and lay on the couch, his sombrero tipped to cover his face. As I shovelled his feet up so I could sit down, Gail appeared through the square arch and sat by Frank's chair at his feet. Unbothered by their presence, Frank dictated notes on the meeting. When he'd finished, he said, 'Okay, Pauline, what's really been going on between Neil and Herbie?'

Actually, I had seen nothing conspiratorial but I had to rustle up something. 'Neil's very harsh on Grant. Grant keeps trying to persuade Neil that we should promote other tracks from the albums, not just the singles, but Neil won't stand still to listen so Grant keeps trailing round the office behind him until Neil slams the door in his face.'

It wasn't much but it seemed to satisfy Frank. I also told him about the accountant who rented the office down the hall.

'He wears a white pinstripe suit, the brightest red open-neck shirt, white shoes and a baseball cap. Can you imagine the reaction in the City of London if an accountant turned up to work dressed like that? They're still wearing bowler hats!'

'Yeah,' Frank said, 'and what you really need to know is he'll be stoked up to the eyeballs with stuff he's shoved up his nose.' He pushed at his nose with his thumb and sniffed. 'These guys are out of their heads and they're making decisions on people's behalf, bad decisions that affect their livelihood. But *he* can afford it, no problem, he's an accountant, he'll get away with it and you're the victim, y'know? It pisses me off. And it's not just accountants,' he went on, now fully in his stride, 'it's the same in the legal profession, in government, in medicine, across the whole spectrum of society in the United States.'

Why Frank thought it necessary to convince me I was not sure, but by this time it was nearly five-thirty and, unable to stop yawning and with my eyes streaming, I ventured, 'I'm finding it quite hard working all day and then again at night. I'm supposed to be at the office before ten.'

'Better get to bed, then,' was his cold response. Sometimes, he could be very unsympathetic.

Thursday, still determined to do well, I set the alarm for eight, woke up on time but wretchedly tired, showered in slow motion, pulled on a dress and left it cock-eyed, ate breakfast in a dream and began to act drunk, stumbling over chairs and dropping tapes. Even at the traffic lights, I sat comatose as they changed from red to green, green to red while people behind me honked in anger.

On the corner of Fairfax and Beverly, Phyllis, the new girl, waited patiently. She had slightly frizzed, tied-back hair, a gently hooked nose and clear, arched eyes. She made it clear from the start she would not allow Neil Reshen to bully her. They were both from New York and argued from the moment they met.

'Get me a club sandwich downstairs, Phyllis.'

'I'm not buying that crap. I'll go to the deli. It's further but – '

'Did I ask you to go to the deli? Get it from downstairs.'

'If you ask politely.'

When he flung open his door and bellowed, 'Call Fritz Oppenheimer in New York,' she retorted, 'Call? Why call? He can hear you from here.'

I marvelled at her temerity. Why didn't I have the same gumption? When Neil charged into the office, I felt I wanted to duck to avoid the grenade waiting to explode. Not until he flew over the clouds to the East Coast did my heart beat at an even pace.

Then Ian telephoned from the log cabin. For three weeks he'd been in New York with Ruth and I couldn't wait to see his chiselled face again. When I got back, the last ever Mothers rehearsal at the log cabin was underway but I refused to descend to the basement, feeling suddenly shy. Why was this latest separation any different from the others? Perhaps my tired state muddled my brain.

When finally he burst into my room, embarrassed mutterings about what time he'd arrived and the strange weather we were having passed between us, and it was not until we sat across the table at Cyrano's that he lifted my chin, looked deep into my eyes and said, 'The only thing I missed while I was in New York was you, Pauline.' I blushed and didn't know whether to laugh or cry.

We drove to see his new apartment, a one-room studio with bathroom.

He said, 'You can stay here if you want, till you find your own place. It could work. The Mothers are on tour for six weeks soon and I'll be in New York in between. You wouldn't have to pay rent, so you'd save money.'

'Well, what would I do if Ruth comes?'

He shrugged. 'We'll work it out.'

So now I had three offers of free accommodation and all apparently unconditional: Ian, a musician, in love with someone else; Neil Reshen, a hot-rod businessman not used to hearing the word 'no'; and Mutt, a lawyer who lived in a miniature zoo. Whom should I choose? I would have to talk it over with wise heads at the log cabin.

In the kitchen, David Gilmour and Richard Wright of the Pink Floyd were flirtatiously enticing Cinderella, Pamela and Sparkie into the night. Christine, true to her self-image, remained at the sink doggedly scrubbing a saucepan with a brush, a striped linen dishtowel tied round her waist. Because Ian had taken his car, I was not expected at the office the next day, Friday, so I idled away the hours with Christine until daylight assured a long sleep and lie in.

Imagine my disappointment when Ian, mysteriously ill, banged on my door late morning, interrupting my dreams, and almost ordered me to take him to the doctors. Grumbling at losing my first chance of a rest, I dropped him off at the surgery before collecting Christine, Cinderella and Mercy for their first rehearsal at the Lindy Opera House, their new venue. Gail, after being their biggest fan and friend, now sank to yelling, 'They are taking advantage of my hospitality and I'm fucking sick of it.' So Herbie had arranged for the girls to use a small room upstairs at the Lindy Theatre and trusted me with the key.

Once I'd set them off practising their dance routine, I dawdled back to collect Ian from the doctors, where he waved a prescription for antibiotics under my nose as if I'd accused him of malingering. The temperature rose to ninety-eight degrees and I faded fast, trailing after Ian through his shopping spree for supplies for his apartment. Then I dropped him off and returned to the Lindy, climbing the stairs so wearily that my feet felt glued to the steps.

The girls were straddled across the floor like Cleopatra's maidens and clearly up to malarkey, but my tired brain was too shattered to care. I could sleep on my feet. A wooden trestle in the corner, nine inches wide and three feet long, looked inviting. I stretched along it like a cat and closed my eyes. Soft air, warm as bath water, drifted in the open window as I lost track of the girls' squawking and spun into blurry dreams.

I slept deeply until Christine's bony fingers prodded my bare arm.

Dressed in her filmy paraphernalia, she looked like a fairy godmother. 'Pauline, I have something for you,' she said. On her palm, she held out two tiny red pills. 'Here, take these.'

Unable to believe I'd slept on a narrow wooden trestle without falling off, I gingerly pulled myself up. 'What are they?'

'They'll help you stay awake, you'll see.'

In my dazed stupor, I gulped them down, breathed in deeply and coaxed the girls, squabbling and shrieking, down to Ian's car.

Within an hour, inexplicably, a feverish energy took over and I found myself hurtling forward as if propelled by an engine, my brain speeding three moves ahead. I chased to the office where two tapes magically transcribed themselves and a backlog of filing fell obligingly into folders and drawers. At the log cabin, replies to fan letters raced through my typewriter, two long letters to England wrote themselves, my hair shampooed and dried in a whirlwind and clothes flew to the launderette unaided. Like a triple speeded-up film, I scrubbed the bathroom and cleaned my room just as dawn broke over the hills. Brilliant. A work-rate like this and I could run Bizarre Incorporated.

Thrilled with my stamina and all because of two, or was it three, little red pills, I fell into the kitchen, radiating happiness. At my news, Gail spluttered, 'Uppers? Are you crazy? Do you know what they'll do to your body, let alone your mind? Take a nap if you need to, but don't ever swallow coloured pills.' The vehemence in her voice echoed all the way back to my mother.

Within the hour the band left for Seattle but I had no knowledge of it. I passed out on my bed, fully clothed, and slept through the whole kerfuffle.

32

The era of the log cabin was almost over, though my head refused to believe it. No more bombardments day and night from untold visitors, no more rock stars wandering in, no more wonderful jam sessions. And only this past week, we'd had fun when Frank wanted everyone in the house photographed and we'd tumbled about on the sofa-bed while Calvin dove this way and that, light-bulbs flashing. And on Thursday night, Wild Man Fischer had shouted out his lyrics, prancing around the floor until four o'clock in the morning, and Calvin had taken movies of us all. And what about late-night film shows, family nights and gossiping in the kitchen until daybreak? And never again would I sit on my step and watch Frank composing his music. All of these things I would miss.

But such disorder could not continue forever and we needed to move on. Now that I knew Frank wanted me to complete the diaries and look after the GTOs, I felt secure about my future. It wouldn't be so bad to work and live away from him – but where *would* I live?

I'd not tried hard to find a flat for Neil. The more I'd thought about it the more I realised its impossibility. What would I do with all my stuff whenever he showed up? And where would I stay? The option to hang around and share his bedroom was out of the question.

I thought Ian's set-up equally precarious, with a one-room studio flat where Ruth might show up any moment. I could not bring myself to think of it. The only sensible way forward was to accept Mutt's offer – my own room in a house on Woodrow Wilson Drive half a mile along from Frank and Gail's house, and a swimming pool – it could not get much better. Three days before we moved, I telephoned him. He sounded so delighted; I couldn't imagine why I'd hesitated.

The woman who owned Frank and Gail's new house invited us to visit her so, with Frank on tour, Gail, Moon, Kansas and I drove up to the top of Laurel Canyon, turned right into Woodrow Wilson Drive, which runs along the top of the Hollywood Hills, and parked on the slope in front of the garage. A thick row of exotic flowering bushes and vines hid the house. But when I walked through the wooden gate, I was surprised to see an English, mock-Tudor house, complete with shutters and sloping lawn, set up on a hill. No one would imagine that Frank Zappa lived there.

All day we sat on the beautiful patio around their enormous pool at the back, hidden on all sides by more trees and shrubbery. A gentle breeze softly brushed my skin as I rested on the luxurious lounger and closed my eyes. Sounds of softly piped music and Gail and Moon splashing in the blue water grew fainter. Here was the life I'd imagined all those months earlier when I'd arrived in Hollywood, and I thought grimly that things had come to a pretty pass when PamZ, who had schemed to knife Gail in her back, should be the one they chose to move to this beautiful place. It was all I could do to stand her triumphalism, especially when we returned to the log cabin and found her panting with the latest hot news from Chicago.

While Hubert Humphrey and Eugene McCarthy slogged it out for the Democratic candidacy, a demonstration against the Vietnam War had turned to violence.

'The motherfuckers laced barbed wire over their jeeps and drove through the crowd. Can you believe that? The guy said it was like Russian tanks in the streets of Prague!'

This led my friends in the kitchen into their usual uproar and indignation about the 'fucked-up' state of their fascist country.

'Tell that to the Romanians,' said a suited, middle-aged Romanian who came to the house and heard their rants. 'Let them live in Romania and face a firing squad for opening their mouths,' he rued to me quietly.

And so, on Friday, 6 September 1968, the dreaded day arrived. I borrowed Ian's car and, after dropping him and Frank at *The Joey Bishop Show,* drove onto the office. In the bank on the ground floor, I opened an account and deposited $550. It was tricky because I had no social security number. The teller eyed me suspiciously and counselled her colleagues. Trying to set my face in an unconcerned fashion, I told them I earned royalties for my songs. Well, this was Hollywood. It could happen.

Back at the house, I carried on answering fan mail until they literally took the desk from under my nose, though why I bothered I wasn't sure. Tomorrow United Mutations would be out of my hands and Gail would take over. I pictured letters floating away in the wind or sinking below the surface in the pool.

Eventually, Ian and Frank returned from *The Joey Bishop Show*, Frank having missed all the upheaval. Ian kept calling, 'Come on, come on,' annoyed that I'd still not packed.

Indeed, I dragged my feet so slowly, I finally found myself alone in that enormous wooden building, though Gail would be back later for a check. As I hastily gathered up my last box of belongings, I glanced around that forlorn room that seemed to be willing me not to leave. There was my antiqued desk I'd slaved over so lovingly; there was the rug, its pink and blue flowers still glowing from where I'd scrubbed them clean; even the white walls on which I'd toiled so hard and long seemed to cry out, 'Don't go, don't go.' As I pulled the door closed behind me, I hoped its new occupants would not harm, demolish or vandalise it all over again.

I passed through the living room, empty and desolate, while the two wild cats that Gail had left behind skipped and hopped at my feet. I'd asked Mutt if I could bring them with me but he refused.

'They've lived wild before,' he said, 'they can do it again.'

I carried some leftover milk and ham to entice the pair out the screen door. They ran beside me, eagerly, trustingly and buried their noses in the bowl. When I slid into the seat beside Ian, they didn't even look up.

Through the back window, I watched the log cabin widen out like a reverse zoom, and as the car swung round the bend, the sun lowered behind the hill, casting the house in shadow.

PART THREE

33

In September 1968, the Mothers of Invention left for a five-week European tour and while they were gone, I plunged into mothering the GTOs – those wacky girls who never ceased to amaze, amuse and surprise me.

Frank had been right and I had been wrong. Whereas before I had seen a dishevelled, immoral bunch, now when they swore like troopers, fell into squabbles with each other, or confessed that they were too stoned to work, I would shake my head and smile indulgently.

I learned that, just as Christine had said so long ago in her interview, they were not nymphomaniacs as their lifestyle and skimpy, see-through clothes seemed to imply. Pamela and Sparkie, at nineteen, were still virgins (though that would soon change); Christine led a life of sexual abstinence; Lucy had a camp boyfriend, who dressed like Beau Brummel; while Cinderella still hung out with Tiny Tim, who did not believe in sex before marriage. Even Mercy, for all her flamboyance and eyes like a raccoon, did not attempt to attract boys.

Only Sandra, who looked twelve years old with her small, cameo face, showed any sexual appetite. She and Calvin cavorted in the tree-house, proof of which was her daily nausea and a burgeoning tummy on which the other girls painted their designs for public view – a happy face or a black star to match Lucy's on her cheek.

Mercy, whose real name was Judy, told me that after running away from juvenile hall in San Francisco, she had found her way to LA.

I asked her, 'If you don't work, how do you survive?'

'How do I survive? I steal. Food, clothes. I go into a store and when I come out, I'm wearing four different outfits.'

I balked at her honesty and, in a perverse way, at Cinderella's too. She admitted, 'I'm a chronic liar.' She said she was seventeen, but in reality she could have been any age. She'd say, 'Erm, let's see, I'm engaged to Tiny. Oh, and I'm pregnant. I don't want to get an abortion because it may be my only chance to have a kid but I don't want to have a kid yet.' Tiny was a declared virgin but no matter, Cinderella tossed the details around without concern for contradictions.

The future of my job now lay with those girls and I put all my efforts into their care. They were wild and unruly as colts, and their guile, cunning and high-strung energy kept me forever on my toes. The diaries, which Frank hoped the publishers would accept in place of his political book, made up the other chunk of my workload.

Frank realised the girls needed financial support and agreed to pay them each thirty-five dollars a week. So every Friday I cashed a cheque and counted out the notes into each of their outstretched hands. Not sufficient to pay rent, it was then my job to find the three girls who were homeless – Christine, Cinderella and Mercy – somewhere to live.

We traipsed across Hollywood, but doors slammed in our faces as soon as proprietors saw their outrageous clothes, hair and make-up. Finally, Herbie suggested the Landmark Hotel, a two-storey trail of apartments amongst trees on Fountain Avenue just off Hollywood Boulevard, a retreat for many rock stars. Janis Joplin passed her last moments there two years later from an overdose of heroin. Even so, the woman at the desk remained unconvinced until I confirmed I would personally deliver a cheque each week from Bizarre Records.

I was becoming increasingly bold about my troupe of girls and one night I even coerced our way into the Factory, the most elite nightclub in Hollywood. The girls put on their best regalia and looked extraordinary. In the dark, black leather and chrome interior, heads swivelled through 180 degrees. Though Janis Joplin screamed from the sound system, you could hear the swish of whispers, 'Who are they?'

Sammy Davis, Jr and Peter Lawford sat in a large booth with three beautiful women and I tried to tell my girls to be cool but they were already jumping out of their seats. Sammy Davis sent over a blonde, svelte woman, early twenties, dressed in a curvaceous black suit. 'Are you girls professionals?' she asked.

'We are, we are, we're the GTOs,' they babbled. 'We're with Frank Zappa, we're making an album. We write our own songs. We're playing at the Shrine. You must come and see us.'

When the blonde returned to Sammy Davis's table, the girls waved across the dimly jewelled room, and Sammy waved back.

Unable to sit still, the girls got up to perform their wacky dancing while I remained in the booth tapping in time to the music and beaming. My girls in their rags outshone the perfectly groomed women in their silks, satins and priceless gems.

A short while later Sammy Davis made a special detour to pass our table. 'I'm honoured to meet you all,' he said, a big cheesy grin creasing his face. As he shook hands with each girl in turn, diamonds flashed from his fingers. 'I think you're fantastic,' Sparkie cooed.

Well, after that, the manager almost bowed at my feet while I discussed membership for the girls and with some grandeur, shrilled, 'Send the bill to Bizarre Incorporated.'

The encounter uplifted the girls and at the next rehearsal they got down to serious work, pummelling together lyrics with amazing speed, lyrics based on their own lives or people they knew. Christine wrote about being a television baby and that her mother was a tube, and her father a knob. *'When I'm sad, my horizontal dips and my vertical skips. But when I'm glad, my brightness metre shines brightest.'*

Imposing human attributes onto inanimate objects reflected her separateness. When the girls hugged and kissed each other, she alone remained aloof, her staring, blue eyes and china-doll face rarely showing emotion.

Other lyrics touched on the perils of hitchhiking, pubescent love, soul brothers, Captain Beefheart and groupie life. But despite the flow of lyrics, the melodies would not come.

They roped in Nicky Hopkins, pianist with the Jeff Beck Group, to help, and when I returned to collect them three hours later, they gave me a premiere performance of Cinderella's song, 'Eureka Springs Garbage Lady' through its long verse and chorus: *'She creeps down the lane as sane as you make her. Rake held proudly in her hand.'*

Although off-key, it sounded surprisingly good. How could I have criticised them? Here they were showing burgeoning talent and impressive effort.

The day after the Mothers returned from Europe, Frank climbed the stairs at the Lindy to hear their progress. After he had bear-hugged each one in turn, they stood before him, straight-backed like a school choir and, because they couldn't harmonise, sang in unison as flat and discordant as a scratched tin plate.

Astonishingly, Frank nodded and applauded, surely more for encouragement than appreciation of their talent because he told them, 'You've got a hell of a lot more work to do before I can even think of taking you into the studio.' Instead, he booked them to play as a support act for the Mothers at the Shrine on 5 December.

Six weeks of frantic, nightmarish rehearsals began. Piling eels into a basket would have been easier than controlling their bursts of tears, temper tantrums and flare-ups. The noise was deafening and they wore me to shreds. Outclassed and out-manoeuvred, I fought back, badgered, cajoled and threatened. 'You've been here twenty minutes, come on, let's get started,' or 'Why not dance in unison, that's what other groups do.' To get them to sing without musical backing was difficult, to dance at the same time, a nightmare. 'Okay, let's start again from the beginning.' I would not allow them to finish until they'd got through without a mistake. I even conducted time with my pencil, one-two-three-four. On good days, I could send them into merry peals of laughter, on bad days, they treated me like their worst schoolmistress.

I also tried hard to encourage decorum, although on that point, Frank was my worst enemy. 'If you must giggle till you can't stand up, try not to wee on the carpet,' I pleaded. When I complained, 'For heaven's sake, Mercy, it is not appropriate to pick your nose in public,' Frank solemnly rejoined, 'Mercy, you pick your nose if you want to,' and then elaborated by adding other filthy things she could do with the snot.

'Do you realise, Frank,' I retaliated, 'it will take me weeks of nagging to get Mercy to stop picking her nose again?' but he merely whacked his knee, his mouth hanging open in a silent guffaw.

Lucy, the most rebellious and untameable of the GTOs, refused to cooperate. She had known Frank in New York, a familiarity that gave her an edge, a willingness to treat his plans and ideas with aloof casualness. She seemed to resent the girls' success and complained that they'd sold out. 'It's getting too fucking commercial,' she would say. She refused to write lyrics and groaned, 'I am not a songwriter. It's Frank's way of belittling us.' Belittling! To be given the chance of actually becoming a pop star? She became morose and difficult to talk to, turning up late to rehearsals, if at all. Well, of course, she was the fiery one, unpredictable, and this was just one of her stages, the other girls told me. Yet, even on her rare appearances, she refused to sing, complaining, 'I'm bored.'

Sandra, with her pint of milk by her side (which was 'for the baby, not for me, 'cos I hate milk'), wailed 'Don't you know Frank's goodwill is at stake, Lucy?'

'Gard, get the diapers out,' Lucy cried scornfully.

Frank, aware Lucy needed pulling into line, joined us one night and said sternly, 'If you don't want to do this, Lucy, then you can leave. No one is stopping you.'

She stood up, bent her voluptuous Puerto Rican body into a reverse s-shape and said, 'You're right. No one's stopping me, so fuck it,' and with the ease of a flamenco dancer, flounced out.

In the stunned silence, we watched Frank's face take on a cold, hard look. I knew what the girls were thinking. Lucy's contribution had been minimal, her presence an irritant more than a help. Yes, things would probably be better without her. Frank seemed to think so, too.

On 5 December, a night I thought would never arrive, I stood anxiously on the side of the stage at the Shrine Exposition Hall, as wound up as if they were my own daughters. Hours and hours and weeks and weeks of struggle and torment had left me shattered and drained. The audience, bored and fidgety after Wild Man Fischer's wearisome set, increased my paranoia. Then on went the girls, who flung themselves into their quirky dance routine with such flourish, passion and ingenuousness, I could have hugged them all. Mercy, despite her bulk, swayed to the music like a showgirl while the others stomped, shook, gyrated, whirled and twirled around her. They looked fabulous in their colourful, outlandish outfits on which they'd worked so diligently, and when they came to sing 'Eureka Springs Garbage Lady', they got all the words right. When Jimmy Carl Black said in my ear, 'Who cares if they're flat and can't carry a tune in a bucket,' I didn't mind – the whoops and cheers said it all.

Back at Frank's house, PamZ lauded me with praise. 'They pulled together really well, Pauline, and it was because of you.'

'Well, not really.'

'Yes, it *was*. You've coached them. You've worked with them a long time and you gave them that oomph. When they got on the stage – that was *your* baby. That was one tremendous performance.'

Always embarrassed by anyone's praise, I protested, 'I did work hard with them, but they took no notice.'

'You're wrong. They *did*. They're *your* girls. They never would have made it without you. You've turned them into something really amazing.'

PamZ and I hardly saw each other these days but I appreciated her loyal words, knowing she rarely dished out compliments to anyone, let alone the GTOs. I also felt guilt about misgivings I'd held toward her, but then again, I'd been a good friend to her, too.

What did Frank think, the one person whose praise I most wanted to hear? Once again, I had to read it indirectly. After the show, he told the girls, 'Okay, you guys, I think you're ready for the studio.' *That* was the extent of his praise.

There followed a round of rushed rehearsals so that when, a week later, Jimmy Carl Black, Roy Estrada and Ian plodded through the back-up for Pamela's 'I'm in Love with the Ooo-Ooo Man', which Davy Jones had miraculously pulled into shape, they were ready to record. They sounded like, well, a group of girl singers, Pamela leading the fray with confidence while Frank bounced along, tapping the tambourine. So far so good.

Then, during Cinderella's 'Eureka Springs Garbage Lady', Jeff Beck, Nicky Hopkins and Rod Stewart loped in, all beads, brightly coloured velvet jackets and the tightest of pants, a sight that thrilled the girls. Frank immediately roped in Jeff to play guitar riffs while the girls wailed the words. Cinderella sulked because Frank chose Christine to sing the lead. With her thin, tuneless voice, she stood staring blankly before her without movement or expression, sang to the end and then stopped as if she really had no idea what the song was about, only that Frank had asked her to sing it.

Mercy complained when on her song, 'Shock Treatment', Ian alone pounded the piano. 'God, Frank, here we have one of the best guitar players in the world and you're sticking him on Cinderella's song?'

'So, what do you wanna do? Stick him on your song?'

'My song's as good as hers.'

They ran through it again, this time Jeff adding some extra phrases while Mercy made a vain attempt to mimic Janis Joplin. '*Shock treatment, oh let me go-oh.*' You had to wonder at Frank's sanity.

Then Rod Stewart, a newcomer who'd quietly lounged in the background and whom everyone had ignored, stepped up, bent into the microphone, upped the rhythm and began rasping, 'Please, please, *please*, let me go, let me go, please, please, let me go, let me, let me, let me go.' The studio erupted. Wow! Maybe they would make something out of this record after all. No one had heard Rod sing before and the girls were stunned. 'Oh, my God, listen to this guy!' Suddenly, it was, 'Rod, come and sit by me.' 'Rod can we come by your house?' Somehow, he and Jeff had metamorphosed into gallant gentlemen, displaying courtesy and perfect manners toward the girls. So I, in turn, began to greet the two pop stars with gracious respect.

Sometime during the evening, Mercy had a moment of inspiration for the title of the album, 'How about *Permanent Damage*?' Frank liked the suggestion, a good metaphor for the girls' own experiences.

Over several other sessions, Frank brought in Lowell George. He had a chubby body, unlike the other hollow-stomached rock stars, but flaunted the same look with dark, shoulder-length hair and a full beard. He had recently joined the Mothers and slotted right in, popular with girls and guys alike. He produced two of the best tracks on *Permanent Damage*, composing sing-along, catchy melodies. To Sandra's 'Circular Circulation', he speeded up the backing vocals and added his own harmony. To Mercy's song, 'I Have a Paintbrush in My Hand to Colour a Triangle', about her love for Brian Jones, Lowell added a bouncy, tap-along instrumental with some great guitar licks. His talent was unmistakeable and I found him most attractive – but for his girlfriend.

The girls' reputation was spreading quietly through Hollywood, so when I took Christine and Mercy to a photo shoot for *Rolling Stone* magazine and we bumped into George Harrison, he didn't flee as he'd done on a previous occasion.

I had just parked the car in the parking lot when he and Patti Boyd emerged from the building. This time I ran over and grabbed him, 'Have you heard of the GTOs?'

'I've heard rumours,' he replied with his Liverpool accent, which in America sounded quaint. 'Come and meet them,' I ordered.

Over her large breasts, Mercy had swathed chiffon and framed them with fur and glitter; they protruded like two giant papaya. Her gold velvet skirt, cut to the thigh, was held together with a low-slung leather belt. She wore bangles to the elbow, a colourful pirate's scarf wound round her head, and her eyes were circled in black rings like jumbo tires. Christine's tulle headdress formed a halo as wide as her shoulders, her silk top was cut low over her bony chest with one sleeve missing, and her leather skirt was hitched up high with satin and pearls. She wore one trouser leg, the other clothed in pink tights, one boot and one shoe. They preened and posed, almost curtseying.

Well, after all, it *was* like meeting a prince. Patti Boyd looked dazzled while George kept squinting as if the sun blinded his eyes. I told him with brazen confidence, 'You'll be hearing a lot more about the GTOs in future,' and they nodded, apparently convinced.

As he and Patti started out of the parking lot they nearly crashed into Pamela's jalopy, the sudden jolt almost throwing out Sparkie, Cinderella and Sandra. George stopped his car to let them through and waved. Well, that made their day.

At the photo shoot, they couldn't stop talking about George. 'Was he holding her hand?' 'Did he say hi or did he say hello?' Amid the tumult of noise, the photographer looked shell-shocked.

Mercy fancied herself as the Mae West of the group – endowed with the body if not the wit – while Christine was more taciturn. 'We want to spread our philosophy.'

Frank told *Rolling Stone* about the GTOs, 'I think pop music has done more for oral intercourse than anything else that ever happened, and vice versa. And it's good for the girls. Eventually most of them are going to get married to regular workers, office workers, factory workers, just regular guys. These guys are lucky to be getting girls like these, girls who have attained some level of sexual adventurousness. These guys will be happier, they'll do their jobs better, and the economy will reflect it. Everybody will be happier.'

There it was again, the idea that the political and economic wellbeing of a country relied on the sexual satisfaction of its people.

When the *Rolling Stone* issue came out in February, a huge photograph of Mercy graced the front page and seven photographs of the girls splashed across the centre spread. Not bad considering they were unknowns three months before. In the article, they described the girls' appearance at the Shrine: 'It was beautifully choreographed,' they wrote, but gave no mention of my name.

34

In December, Gail threw a party for my birthday, a sign of our growing friendship. I had half hoped to break out of the Zappa fold once I'd moved to Mutt's house, to seek new horizons in Hollywood, but I found it as hard to get out of that tight-knit circle as any interloper might struggle to find a way in. I was so enclosed that when Robert, a friend's brother from England, made a one-day stopover in October, I found I did not know that the Olympic Games in Mexico City had already started, that Jackie Kennedy's wedding to Aristotle Onassis was imminent, and that Apollo 7 with three astronauts onboard was orbiting Earth. He also told me that the road tax in England had gone up to £25 a year, the bank rate had risen to eight percent and petrol was an exorbitant seven shillings a gallon. Evidently, I needed to start reading newspapers and watching TV.

Meantime, my life went on just as it had at the log cabin. I would arrive at the office late afternoon or evening to type either the diaries or Frank's film script, *Uncle Meat* (of which I'd already typed about ten versions), work until two or three in the morning and then drive over to Frank's house in my rented Volkswagen hatchback. I would give Frank the typed pages to skim through and sometimes take dictation, maybe a few letters, advertising copy or new lyrics. Then I would climb the stairs and join Gail and anyone else who hung out at the house, often staying until five or six in the morning, falling into bed eventually at daylight. If they needed me at the office, I would simply miss any sleep and struggle on. Then, in the evening, I'd give Frank the lowdown on events at the office and catch up by staying in bed the following day. Donna grumbled about my irregular hours but I relied on Frank's full-hearted support to defend me against Neil Reshen, whose brusque and arrogant ways made it clear he thought my services superfluous.

Gail was easygoing and happy in her new home and welcomed me each night like one of her own. I would sit in her pretty but cluttered kitchen, cocooned and secure, nestled in my regular spot in the corner by the table. Her house had turned from the home of a talented composer into another hippy pad with a new family: Carl, Frank's quiet and reserved younger brother; Squidget, Gail's sixteen-year-old brother newly arrived from Hawaii; Janet, Gail's friend, who had replaced Christine as Moon's nanny; Kansas who had set himself up in the pool house; and PamZ who held out in the small guest house, a mystery that I'd given up trying to solve. They crashed wherever they could and inevitably, squabbles erupted. Thank goodness they'd booted me out.

Frank would let the muddle go on over his head while he buried himself in his basement. In fact, it was not a basement at all but the ground floor at the front of the house. Here, in this enormous room with its patterned shutters overlooking the lawn, and dissected by wooden pillars, he carried on just as he had at the log cabin. Surrounded by his favourite things – thousands of records and a growing tape archive stored in the built-in cupboards along the back wall, two five-foot speakers either side of his desk, his rocking chair, a black sofa, and everywhere a tangle of guitars and other musical instruments. Here he listened to music, edited his films, gave interviews, greeted various artists and musicians or held work sessions with Herbie or Calvin or me. Indeed, he rarely lifted his head above the parapet save to slump into bed or search for food in the kitchen.

And it was into the basement that we all crammed for my birthday party. The living room and dining room were not furnished yet, although they'd painted the beautiful panelled walls and shutters bright orange; in the kitchen and staircase it was all bright pink, and in Frank's basement, everywhere purple. With royal blue carpet throughout, I thought it gauche and wanted to say so; after all, Frank never failed to condemn other people's choices. 'I like it,' I lied.

I say 'party', but Frank didn't enjoy parties, so we sat watching films of the Mothers in Europe. While Frank threaded the film through the 16mm projector, Motorhead, Dick, Don Preston and Calvin wrestled for a place on the black sofa, making their usual lewd comments while Roy Estrada and Bunk Gardner straddled the arms at each end. Art Tripp squashed into a saggy armchair with Adrienne, his wife, on his lap.

Their good humour belied the bad temper and bickering that had marred the Mothers' tour in Europe. In October, Ian had telephoned.

'Frank's been mean and nasty since the tour started and it's getting worse.'

'Oh, dear.'

'He hates the way the band sounds and instead of being constructive or at least grown-up about it, he simply mopes around, and if he says anything, it's so critical and so cutting that everybody's feeling low. At Hamburg he got very bad so I got him in the hall and said I thought his hyper-critical attitude wasn't constructive and brought everyone down. I told him he'd have to expect it to take time to correct some of the mistakes people are making. I reminded him how he said the band would never play "Brown Shoes".'

'So what did he say?'

'He reacted like a child. He shuffled his feet and said, "I'll stuff socks in my mouth." I got really pissed off at this but didn't carry it further as we had another show to do. I hope he gets a bit better from now on. I'll try to talk to him again, this time for more than thirty seconds. The music hasn't been that bad. In fact, it has been very good a lot of the time.'

'What are the critics saying?'

'I haven't heard, but all the concerts have been quite full or sold out.'

Then later, from Munich, he phoned again. 'The concert last night went fairly well. I had to speak up during rehearsal to Frank for being a bit nasty to Don. He stopped so I guess it had a good effect temporarily. He's still in a funny mood, though – I can't quite describe it. We'll see what happens.'

Although, here in the basement, animosity between Frank and the Mothers had evaporated and the air, instead, crackled with humour and jokes, a clear demarcation between the guys and Frank held fast. The Mothers, very touchy-feely with each other and constantly play-wrestling and kidding around, never, *ever* touched Frank. Though he would join in their jokes and laugh at their horseplay, he never jostled physically with any of them. Even onstage, he would stand alone, isolated. Only at photographic sessions did he allow some closeness, some proximity. With all us girls, of course, it was different. He could hug us to eternity.

The live-ins – Kansas, Carl and Janet – nudged into spaces across the floor, while Squidget carried Moon on his shoulders, ready to whisk her out should she make a fuss. Captain Beefheart, flanked by the enormous five-foot-high speakers and dressed in his ragged sheepskin coat, stood at the back by Frank's desk and chatted to a normal-looking Arthur Brown, who was decked out in jeans and sweatshirt.

I knelt on the floor, careful not to touch knees with Ian despite our earlier romantic birthday dinner at the Mexican El Coyote restaurant. Well, *romantic* if you ignored Ruth's spirit hovering overhead. I had written home: 'I adore Frank, and am extremely fond of Ian; everyone believes I'm in love with Ian. Ian is still in love with Ruth, Ruth is infatuated with Frank – Ian knows.'

Frank's enthusiasm spilled over as we watched the grainy footage of the Royal Festival Hall concert. Everyone laughed at Roy Estrada dressed up as the Pope with aluminium-pointed breasts, and Don Preston gulping down foaming liquid and attacking Ian at the grand piano. Long-faced at first, I eventually broke into giggles when Roy, with serious concentration, sang in his high soprano voice. Still, you could sense the audience at the Festival Hall growing impatient until Frank gave the signal; they dropped the farce and got on with their wonderful music.

During a break, when Frank changed one of the reels on the projector, applause erupted when Gail came down the stairs bearing a surprise birthday cake decorated with my name and, as she placed it on the desk, my newfound friends bellowed out a perfectly harmonised version of 'Happy Birthday'.

Touched by all this attention and flushed, I bent low over the cake to blow out the candles. My hair, now quite long, fell like a curtain shielding my face. 'Make a wish, make a wish,' they called and I blew hard but the candles would not go out. Then I heard screams and shouts. My hair was alight and flames flared round my head. Something splashed all over me. On reflex, Kansas had thrown his beer and drenched my head so I gasped for breath amid a sickening smell of scorched hair as charred pieces fell to the floor. Shocked, I also felt foolish, but once everyone realised I was safe, many ribald quips flew sharp and fast about my new hairstyle while Calvin, grinning, inspected its ragged ends.

But that embarrassment was nothing compared to the humiliation Frank had in store for me a short while later. Always one to enjoy a prank, he pulled me, spluttering and protesting, over his knee. He lifted my dress to reveal my orange tights. I wriggled in shame but it was too late. Everyone who clambered around could see I wore no knickers, a missing feature of my wardrobe I normally did not advertise, but knickers formed a ridge and spoiled the line of my dress and now my secret was out. Despite my kicks and struggles, my nose scraping the floor, my legs flailing in the air, Frank held me down fast and spanked my bottom hard. The crowd cheered and chanted down the numbers while Frank continued his smacks to the bitter end. Blushes, guffaws, whoops and applause.

'I will never forgive you, Frank,' I protested as I struggled to my feet, my face bright red, and although I pulled down my dress, it would not reach much below my buttocks. I realised then that I must definitely stop shortening my skirts (which at my last reckoning were eight and a half inches above the top of my knee bone and six and a half inches below my thigh bone). But you could not prick Frank's conscience or repress his wicked, silent guffaws.

Gail, too, beamed as she cut small squares of pink and white sponge cake decorated with white icing before Janet handed them around on napkins. They gave me a bottle of scotch and I shared it out, pouring it into a mishmash of glasses and cups. I got quite merry. I wrote home: 'I had a really nice birthday.'

35

From then on, Christmas beckoned and I racked my brain about what to buy Frank and Gail. Much easier were presents for my sisters, brothers and their children in Washington and England (though there was an embargo on parcels at all English ports, so the gifts sat in my room for over a month). Then Gail told me that my newfound friends in LA had bought me presents and, in panic, I raced around shops as rich and bright as Aladdin's cave to buy leather wallets for them, too.

I asked Mutt, who was Jewish, if I could buy a Christmas tree and string it with lights, a small token of gratitude for living at his place rent-free. His children clapped with joy at the fairy on the top waving her magic wand. When I'd moved into his house, I'd written in my diary: 'I could sleep on the carpet in my room, it's such luxury. A new era. I need time to myself to relax, to read and write.'

The plan didn't work out like that, though I did settle in easily at his Spanish-style ranch. When I'd unpacked, I'd placed my long, heavy hairpiece in the bottom of the wardrobe, never to be worn again. Artifice, I'd learned, was not part of Laurel Canyon's lifestyle. Since then I'd let my hair hang in natural waves to my shoulders. Indeed, I hardly even backcombed it but, thanks to the candles on my birthday cake, it was still a ragged mess and I wore it tied in a chignon.

Mutt gave me a beautiful gold, musical jewellery-box, really pretty. I bought him a saucepan. Embarrassed that my gift did not match his sweet offering, I tried to make amends on Christmas Eve by offering to shorten his new drapes. Seven inches too long, they hung ceiling to floor along the patio windows overlooking the pool. When Mutt's friends arrived and downed daiquiris before leaving for a party further up the winding road, I sat perched on my stool like Cinderella, trying to convince myself I didn't mind. My big day would be Christmas Day.

With parcels balanced precariously in my arms, I arrived at Frank and Gail's in the early evening. Moon spotted me and dropped to her knees, scuttling between the grown-ups' legs. She took hold of my ankle boots and hauled herself to a standing position, tipped her head back and nearly fell over. I squatted down so she could help me push my presents under the giant tree, a tree so big Gail could lay underneath it when she retrieved them later.

Already the house smelled different, spicier and more festive. Gail, in unusual hostess mode, poured me a glass of mulled wine. Despite the tangled hair and no make-up, she looked pretty in a dress with tiny flowers and short, puffed sleeves. I made a beeline for Dick Barber, pleased to see him again. Our paths rarely crossed these days because he lived an hour's drive away in Pomona. His gentle eyes looked at me from under sandy lashes as he grumbled about the endless groupies on tour who hustled the Mothers.

'They offer the guys dope, just march up and shove it in their hands.'

'Oh lord, I hope Frank doesn't know.'

Dick shook his head – one advantage of staying in separate hotels. 'But my God, those girls, they try everything – bribe the security guards, climb the fire escapes. And in the mornings, the guys are stoned out of their minds, late for rehearsals and who gets the blame? Me!'

I walked through the living room to get Frank from the basement and Moon, who'd developed her walking skills, tried to run after me but fell flat on her tummy, picked herself up and ran back to the kitchen. When he reluctantly appeared, she toddled over squeaking, 'Fwank!' He and Gail had not only taught her *his* name, but Gail's too. We found it very odd that Moon wouldn't say 'mom' and 'dad', particularly later when she could speak in sentences and would bossily tell us, 'Fwank work, no go down,' or 'Gail sleep.' It served to emphasise her distance from them, as if her relationship were no different from anyone else's.

Frank whisked her up and sank into their new acquisition, a purple leather armchair placed by the redbrick fireplace, on which was balanced a framed cartoon of Herbie. Frank propped Moon on his lap as if she were a shield protecting him from the fun about to unfold.

I manoeuvred on the floor among the others – Gail, Kansas, Janet, Carl, Calvin, Dick, Squidget, PamZ, and two girls I hardly knew, Anna and Tracy. Gail acted as 'Santa', collecting the gifts from under the tree, and we tore off the paper amid much oohing and aahing. Frank and Gail gave me a calendar with a photograph of a nude man on each page. They also gave me a pair of false eyelashes and red panties that I held aloft. I say 'panties', but they were not joined at the crotch. I pulled an appropriately haughty expression while

Frank's eyebrows went up and down. Still, an improvement on the two rats in a cage they presented to Anna and Tracy.

Totally flummoxed as to what to buy Frank and Gail, I wrote them a poem each, written in my best decorative writing. I told them how much they meant to me and although the one for Frank rolled more naturally from my pen. I ended them both with the line, 'It's love.'

Gail looked embarrassed but Frank ordered me to stand up and gave me an affectionate hug. 'Just what I always wanted,' he said, and I blushed.

Calvin had bound a brightly coloured scarf in brown paper and string. He handed it across with a nonchalant air as if to say, 'I'm not really giving you this.' From Dick I unwrapped a pretty Mexican glass box for jewellery and some candy; and finally from Kansas, an apron inscribed with an 'olde worlde' English poster offering a £500 reward, all very touching as I had no idea they cared. How I'd developed the art of making friends with men was a mystery, but firm friends they were. Ian, forever in New York with Ruth, had left his gift – an electric alarm clock with a ring loud enough to wake a corpse.

By the time Moon peeped from under mountains of wrapping paper, the meal was ready. On the stove in the kitchen, Gail had laid out a surprising feast. We found pans with vegetables, mincemeat, stewed fruits, mashed potato and, from the platter, slices off the enormous turkey.

We allowed Frank to go first and once he'd gathered his plateful, a surprisingly large amount, he squeezed through the rest of us with a few quips, crossed the living room and disappeared into the basement to eat alone, probably stabbing at editing buttons working on the Mothers' film while shovelling in mouthfuls without even noticing how delicious it was.

To be honest, the atmosphere relaxed once he'd left. It was not that one could not laugh and joke in his presence – everyone loved to make him laugh that big hearty, out-loud laugh – it was more that, if I joked with Kansas or Dick or Calvin, you sensed his unease, his dislike of being sidelined or excluded.

Soon we'd exhausted the food and Moon, who'd fallen asleep in front of the fireplace, woke up cranky when the cat accidentally fell on her. Dick called out, 'That's our cue! Time to go!' They all heaved themselves to their feet and departed at once for the Troubadour, leaving behind a cacophony of torn gift-wrapping and dirty plates.

With no interest in folk music, I chose not to join them, and Gail, clearly exhausted, slouched off to bed. Janet, who saw her role not as a maid but a guardian for Moon, refused to help so, left on my own, I scoured and cleaned, washed and dried everything by hand. Though I did it for Gail, in the back of my mind I hoped Frank might come up and appreciate my efforts. But, although it took more than two hours, he remained hidden in the basement.

36

I began 1969 full of optimism and wrote home: 'I am perfectly happy. I love being here and have the strongest feeling that this is where I'm supposed to be. I find Frank fascinating and I adore him. He is extremely humble, unassuming, very compassionate (which I love the most), exceptionally talented and intelligent. He has shortcomings – is extravagant with money, will never have enough, spends it all on more and more expensive sound equipment and now elaborate technology for his films. Most people treat him like a god. I try not to. It is very hard to let oneself go with him. He never lets go.'

In a way, I felt some empathy with Frank. I too resisted shows of emotion, fearing that once allowed loose, anger or sadness, say, would rush out of control. Yet, within a few days of the New Year, Frank and I would let rip with a stream of vitriol that surprised us both.

The GTOs had an audition at *Turn On*, a follow-up TV show to *Laugh-In*. As I bundled Cinderella, Christine and Mercy into the back of my car, they chatted with their usual bawdiness, most of which I ignored. When we stopped at a red light, I glanced in my rear-view mirror and caught Cinderella holding something to her nose and sniffing a great deal.

'What's that you've got?' I called out

'Oh, nothing,' she replied blithely.

'No, really, what is it?'

Her forehead puckered in an abstracted frown, she said, 'Smelling salts – for my cold. I have a cold.'

'*Smelling salts!* I thought they went out with my grandmother.'

The girls convulsed into giggles and I let the matter drop while I concentrated on the heavy traffic in the five lanes of Ventura Freeway.

At NBC, the uniformed commissioner followed them through the doors, not convinced he should let them in. I gave the receptionist at the desk a knowing smile – yes, they are weird, aren't they?

Directed into a small private room off a long corridor, the girls sat primly on one of two red sofas. There were flowers on the wooden coffee table and bottles of water and glasses with ice to the side. Nervously, I paced around. Pamela should have brought Sandra and Sparkie by now. Cinderella began pushing at her nose and sniffing.

Concerned, I said, 'Cinderella, why not take your smelling salts again before you go on. You don't want to be sniffing in front of the cameras.'

There was a noticeable stop in the room as if waiting for a camera to flash. Cinderella's cat face, sharp and knowing, smiled. 'It's okay, Pauline, I'm fine.'

After a long wait, I stood on the side of the set and watched those loopy girls prepare for their audition. It gave me time to reflect on how immersed I'd become in this new life, so different from anything I'd known in England. No longer on the outside looking in – I *was* in. This was where I belonged now, not in colourless Twickenham or hanging on the fringes of swinging London. And for that, I had Frank to thank. Yet why he had brought me to California I had never understood. It did seem odd. He could have chosen any one of numerous girls who would have fitted in much more smoothly, understood him more clearly, and conducted what little work he handed out just as expertly. Why, only last week he'd asked me to buy a cringe-making birthday card for Calvin, 'the gooiest, yuckiest you can find'. I wasn't sure what he meant – a flower-fronted card with sentimental words? A girl dressed in pink? When I went to look, I could not find anything suitable and brought back a card with a modern design, almost tasteful, the words 'Happy Birthday' in bright colours on the front, the inside left blank. 'Will this one do?' I asked sheepishly. After a quick look, he thanked me and said he'd have to think up some spiffy words for the inside. On impulse, I quickly wrote in my notebook that I carried with me, never knowing when he might throw out dictation, 'You are the best, you are the most, without your good work, I am lost.'

'Would this do as cringe-making words?' I asked showing him the scribble.

He snorted a laugh. No, not quite, but I was off the hook. He thanked me as he always did and I scooted away wishing I was more worldly, more 'cool'.

Certainly, he never offered an explanation as to why he'd brought me to California and I was too nervous to ask, lest the question might prick the bubble, nix the magic that bound us. In the end, I decided my straightness, Englishness, complete oppositeness of everyone else around him appealed to his sense of the absurd. When I raised the issue with Herbie one time, he'd said, 'Frank didn't want anybody who was involved with or connected with anyone in the business. He didn't want a groupie and it's hard to find girls who are not groupies.' And when I asked PamZ the same question, she said, 'He's not exactly surrounded by a lot of intelligent women,' another compliment which I greatly appreciated.

A year had passed since I'd left England for a two-week vacation and eight months since my arrival in California. Frank and Gail (who was newly pregnant) said I had changed and, superficially, it was true.

I had altered my hairstyle – draped round my face like curtains and tied at the nape of the neck. Mutt had grumbled I looked like a hippy but hippies had scraggy hair, mine was neat and tidy. And though I retained my English accent, 'Christian name' and 'surname' had become 'first name' and 'last name'. I relinquished 'at all' for 'adawl'. The letter 'zed' had become 'zee', and I used the words 'hang-ups' 'bizarre' and 'weird'. It sounded wrong for me to say 'uptight', 'outta sight' or 'flipped out'. My one swear word remained 'schizzle'. 'Bloody' never passed my lips and the word 'fuck' no longer made me flinch – I could even utter it myself if I quoted someone else.

I had stopped translating dollars into pounds to understand the value of things. For example, I used to think a cheeseburger, which cost eighty-five cents, seven shillings in English money, was an astronomical sum, but now eighty-five cents seemed reasonable. In London, my friend Pat was earning £3 a day for freelance secretarial work. With an exchange rate at $2.40 to the pound, I reckoned she earned $36.00 a week. It made my $100 seem huge.

External changes aside, I could also feel within me a growing self-assurance. I noticed that every single letter I received from England, be it from family or friends, ended with an apology – *sorry for this muddle*, or *I'm on the bus so sorry it's a scribble*, or *sorry this is so short but hubbie's just come in. Sorry, sorry, sorry.* And it was not just English people. Letters from Dick and Ian while on tour ended in the same way, *sorry about the tatty paper.* In my own letters, I no longer apologised. Perhaps I'd picked it up from Frank.

The audition was passing in minor chaos, the girls not only singing 'Eureka Springs Garbage Lady' out of tune, but getting the words wrong as well. The producers ushered us out with unseemly haste. I was upset, not only for the girls but for myself. I'd so looked forward to peeking behind the scenes of a real television show.

An hour after the girls had climbed out of my car at the Landmark Hotel, Gail telephoned. 'Pauline, get your butt over here. Frank wants to see you.'

'What, now?'

'Now.'

The abrupt tone of her voice surprised me. Surely he wasn't blaming me for the GTOs failing their audition? I hurriedly parked my gear-shift Volkswagen on the slope outside their house.

'He's not happy, Pauline,' Gail said as I passed through the kitchen.

'Why?'

'Just a warning, that's all.'

I felt a little notch of dread in my stomach but as I walked through the living room Moon, who lay curled up naked with the cat on the floor, scrambled up, dragging her blanket. She realised I was about to visit her father and ran ahead, delighted at any chance to sneak into the forbidden basement. She slid backwards down the stairs on her tummy shrieking, 'No, no, no,' when I tried to help. Her little voice alerted Frank, who jumped up from his desk, deftly wrapped her in the blanket and whisked her upside down while she screeched and giggled deliriously. He laid her on the floor, swaddled like Moses, where she lay miraculously prone, staring up at the wooden rafters and the tangle of guitars towering around her like sentinels. She rolled toward an album Frank had put on the floor, but he snatched it up.

Dressed in a white jumper and denim dungarees, his hair tied back to reveal his long sideburns, I thought how handsome he could be, but when he turned my way his smile changed, his face hardened and his dark eyes snapped fire. 'What the fuck were you thinking, Pauline?' he said with deadly quietness.

'I'm sorry?'

He dabbed a finger at me. 'You know my position on drugs.'

'Certainly I do.'

'So why are you telling Cinderella to stick cocaine up her nose? IN THE FUCKING TV STUDIO?'

He didn't actually shout, but the words cracked like a whip and made my knees go weak. I had never seen him so angry.

I frowned. 'Well, no,' I protested. 'That's not true,' and then the seriousness of the situation struck home. 'Oh, my goodness, it was *cocaine?*'

'What the fuck else did you think it was?'

'Who told you? Cinderella?' but as I said her name, I immediately abandoned the thought. Cinderella would never have owned up, especially not to Frank. I tried again. 'I saw Cinderella sniffing something in the back of my car. I asked her what it was and she said it was smelling salts and I believed her. Silly me, *I believed her.*'

We stood glaring at each other. All at once, I saw my predicament and turned on him swiftly, hot words almost spitting from my lips. 'Do you honestly think, Frank, I am stupid enough to tell Cinderella to sniff a drug in front of people in a television studio? Have you worked with me all this time not to understand that I would never do such a thing, something that I know is abhorrent to you?

He raised his hand. 'Christine said – '

'Christine?' I shrieked. So it was Christine! Oh, she must have gloried in telling him, she probably wanted PamZ to take over, someone equally heavily into drugs.

'Christine said that the girls did not believe you did not know it was cocaine. They did not believe you could be so naive.' He flipped the album onto the desk and fell back into his chair.

I stared at him beseechingly, unsure how to respond to this charge, worse than the first, a slur on my character. Appalled that I'd allowed a group of girls to make a fool of me, girls whom I secretly believed to be foolish themselves, I wondered if Frank would ever trust me not to be hoodwinked again.

My nerves jangling, I moved a pile of papers from an upright chair close to his rocker and sat down. 'I'm sorry, Frank. Okay, tell me off for being foolish but do not suggest – *ever* – that I would connive behind your back.'

He remained unmoved, his face steely cold. On the floor, Moon twisted like a caterpillar to get a better view of us, her little face confused.

'I am astonished, Frank, that you would actually believe the GTOs over me, girls who lie and steal.' With a deep sense of injustice and dragging remnants of dignity about me, I added, 'Why is my head on the block for something the GTOs have done?'

'I need to know this stuff,' he said. He bent down and scooped Moon into a bundle, ready to carry her to the kitchen.

'I think,' he said, stopping briefly to let me go first up the internal stairs, 'the logical next step for you is to contact the girls and try to straighten this thing out.'

His words were tinged with disdain and his eyes distant and cold. Feeling disgraced and fighting back the tears, I raced through the house, passed Gail without a word and stumbled down the steps. But when I got through the gate, my car was not on the slope where I'd left it. My eyes swept around, and there, across the street through a flattened fence, I could see my car balanced on the edge of a swimming pool, one rear wheel dipped perilously into the blue water. No one from the house was in sight, so I was forced to go round the side of the very grand house and knock on their front door.

A maid answered and when I explained, she ushered me into a large room where a Japanese family sat on the floor at a round table eating a meal. Six pairs of oval eyes turned toward me.

'I'm so sorry, but my car's in your pool. I'm going to have to get someone to pull it out.'

'In the pool?' they cried, and crowded to look through the window.

The eldest man, whom I presumed to be the patriarch, remained inexplicably passive and calm. He said, 'We will take care of it. We will bring your car back. We will finish our meal first.'

Of course, I understood, they must finish their meal first.

They bowed and, like a robot, I bowed too. 'So sorry, so sorry,' I said, hands praying and backing out.

Within an hour, they had returned my car, the fence was propped up and the family, resisting intrusion into their lives, insisted they would pay. Their polite, kind response contrasted with Frank and Gail's – they were furious. I must be the most stupid, silliest girl, they implied, and my confidence slumped, my self-esteem fell to its lowest ebb.

When I collected Christine, Mercy and Cinderella the next afternoon for an interview with *Time* magazine, Christine's long lashes veiled her blue eyes and her button mouth hardened. 'You're lucky Frank believed you,' she said. The loaded feeling in my throat prevented me from saying anything.

An uneasy truce ensued not only between me and the girls but also between me and Frank. He maintained a cool distance during our next two meetings, passing me hand-scrawled notes and barely looking my way.

But then, a week or so later, the police raided the Landmark Hotel. In the apartment shared by Christine, Mercy and Cinderella, they found syringes, heroin and cocaine, some of it stashed down the toilet. Handcuffed and locked in jail until their parents bailed them out, they soon learned that Frank had cancelled their contract, stopped any further work on the album and banished them to the wilderness.

A feeling of smug satisfaction enveloped me, but only for a moment because then I realised that a huge chunk of my own job had vanished and my own future looked decidedly bleak.

A few weeks later, I ran into Mercy in Hollywood. Over a cup of coffee, she told me, 'You remember that one time at the Lindy Opera House when we were in the toilet? It was Christine, Cinderella and me, and you were looking for us?'

'You mean that time you were all squashed in together?'

'Right, right. You were telling us to hurry up and I called out, "It's okay, Pauline, we'll be right there," and you yelled back, "Well *do* it," and marched out.'

'There were so many times, but go on.'

'Well, we were all shooting drugs in the bathroom.'

'At rehearsal? Are you saying you were injecting needles at rehearsal?'

'Right, right. We were shooting up. It was speed.'

'*Oh – my – God!*'

'You didn't have a clue,' Mercy said with a wave of her hand. 'It went right over your head.'

It made me realise I hadn't changed that much after all. The message was clear – stop being a 'dumb fuck' and *get your act together*.

37

Part of 'getting my act together' was to acquire a green card. If I wasn't a criminal, I was getting damn-near close to it, working illegally in America. During a tricky meeting with Immigration in October, when they'd wanted to know how I was supporting myself during a nine-month holiday, I'd stretched the truth and told them I'd just arrived in California and that my parents sent money from Washington DC where they were also on holiday. The authorities accepted the story and granted a new visitor's visa until 31 December 1968, but if I wanted to stay longer I needed to apply for an official green card.

Early in January a letter arrived asking me to attend a medical and interview, the venue seventy miles away. I set out on a day of appalling wind, rain and floods severe enough to upturn trucks and caravans. The radio warned people not to go out, but I dared not miss my appointment. I drove through lashings of water that flung themselves at the windscreen and, despite the wipers working at full speed, I could not see the front of the car. Gusts of wind almost swung my Volkswagen into a ditch and I should've turned back. If I ended up dead what use would my visa be then? And was I even sure I wanted it? I thought of my dear father, who'd supported eleven children against the odds and was unhappy that yet another of his daughters might emigrate to America. When I finally arrived an hour late, my stressed-out state rather displaced the nerves I felt about the interview. For the medical a small, heavy-set man with a slight wheeze, asked me if I'd had any operations or suffered from heart disease or asthma, and when I told him no, he stamped and signed the form and handed me a copy with a bored wave. The interview was equally absurd. In a bare room with a desk and light shining on my face, two middle-aged men in suits, and a woman in a tight-fitting red dress, asked me to stand, raise my right arm and swear that everything I said was the truth. The questions were short and simple, requiring yes or no answers, aside from my name, age, address, sisters' occupations and details about Mutt. As he had urged me to say, I told them I'd sold my car to another sister in England for $1,500 and now lived off the proceeds – well, it was partly true. And that was it! They said my green card would arrive in the post. I had driven seventy miles in atrocious conditions for that!

The torrential rains continued in California for eight more days and nights. Laurel Canyon Boulevard raced with water and was closed for a week. The tree around which we'd climbed to reach Calvin's apartment at the log cabin fell down, taking my office wall with it, while the basement filled up with water. How grateful we were that we'd moved out. Flood controls were inadequate and more than a hundred people lost their lives. Property damage, state-wide, totalled more than $213 million.

****

'Come and have your photograph taken,' Frank called as I stepped through the gate and found him on the front lawn, surrounded by the Mothers. It was such a surprise to see them there, not only because they rarely visited Frank's house, but because they were lounging on the lush green grass, now dried out by the sun.

The Mothers were bunched together, wry and full of humour, posing for photographs for their forthcoming album *Uncle Meat*. They were well into their bawdy camaraderie, the more absurd the better, encouraged and egged on by Frank. Into this tangle I stepped, holding aloft the glass of beer they thrust generously into my hand. Never mind that I was unprepared and wearing the shortest of skirts, Ed Caraeff, familiar with their zany quips, bent low over his camera and kept clicking, like a machine gun.

Once that was done, the Mothers lingered, easy and relaxed, strolling between Frank's basement, the kitchen and the garden. One of the sad things about stopping work with the GTOs was that I'd lost contact with these men, no longer sharing jokes at the Carnation on Wilshire after rehearsals. I wouldn't have counted them as close friends but they were, to my mind, a special bunch and, with the smoothest of ease, I rejoined their playful repartee.

Frank, though, had already withdrawn from the glorious sunshine into his darkened basement and invited everyone to watch footage of the Mothers he'd taken in the Vienna Woods, film which most of them had not seen and which Frank would incorporate into his next movie, *Uncle Meat*. There they were full of zany antics, play-fighting among the trees, clearly on one of their 'good' days.

The Mothers of Invention were now a business as much as a band. Frank and Herbie owned both the management and record companies and as such had complete power over the group. If any of the band failed to show up for rehearsal, they must present a doctor's letter or have wages docked. Yet, while Frank's lifestyle and expenditure soared, the Mothers still languished on a wage of $250 a week, and this despite their tours selling out everywhere. Their reputation as *the* most innovative, trendsetting group on the circuit had grown, their form of rock theatre appealing to more and more audiences. Journalists began to acknowledge Frank as a unique figure in the music scene, a composer and songwriter who pushed the boundaries of what was musically acceptable. In every country the Mothers played, journalists wrote longer and more insightful pieces. I could picture their surprise when they began their questions and got answers not from a weirdo but from a quiet, serious, intelligent, stand-no-nonsense type of guy.

While I waited for my visa, the months rolled by. In March, they released the soundtrack of the movie, *Uncle Meat*, the first Mothers of Invention album on Bizarre. I thought it a masterpiece. Stunned by its brilliant combination of studio and live performances, some of it recorded as far back as 1967, I marvelled at Art's and Ruth's delicate xylophone, piccolos and intricate percussion, the rich mixture of the instruments, Ray Collins's beautiful voice and Ian's stunning saxophone. The critics quietly raved and it sold well, reaching Number 43 in the *Billboard* charts, a much better result than *Cruising with Ruben and the Jets* (the Mothers' doo-wop album I'd derided at the log cabin), which had been released back in November 1969 and reached a disappointing Number 110. Even worse, *Lumpy Gravy*, which came out a month later, lasted a disastrous one week in the charts at 159 and disappeared. Frank had compiled it in the studio from recordings dating as far back as 1966. Damned by critics and fans alike for being neither rock nor classical music nor a follow-on from the Mothers' previous albums, it was something else, something very new. Frank, always gung-ho about his own work, told me it was his favourite record to date and that it would take time for people to catch on.

But time was not on Frank's side. At Bizarre Incorporated, with little income through the fall of 1969, salaries still had to be paid. Grumbles and in-fighting had sprung up. Publicity and promotions manager Grant Gibbs had blamed Herbie, Herbie had blamed Neil and Neil had blamed Grant. No one had blamed Frank or, at any rate, not within my ear-shot. Then Neil had sacked Grant, a sad day because Grant and I had developed a real rapport, and soon afterwards they asked Phyllis to leave. She returned to New York and found a job as personal manager for the Soft Machine. Only Donna remained, and these days Neil's lusty eyes followed her round the office.

Neil was by now my arch enemy. When Frank and the Mothers went on a tour of the East Coast through most of February and into March, Herbie joined them and Neil Reshen took over at the office. He brushed past ignoring my presence or choked me with cigar smoke. Tinged with indignation and in need of moral support, every few days I wrote detailed letters to Frank. He never wrote back but occasionally he would telephone with encouragement. I sorely needed it.

Neil's bullying ways contrasted markedly with Frank's disarming modesty. When Frank came to the office one evening, rather than ask me to go down seventeen floors to bring back coffee for us both while he made a business call, *he* went for the coffee and *I* made the call. For those kind acts which singled Frank out as special, I put every effort into my work to please him. I wrote home: 'Frank is just twenty-eight years old, but he is so revered; you would think he was forty-eight.'

For the rest of March, I saw very little of Frank because he was locked in Whitney Studios in Glendale producing and editing Captain Beefheart's *Trout Mask Replica.*

In April, Bizarre released their first non-Mothers production, *An Evening with Wild Man Fischer*, not surprisingly to crushing reviews. His mildly amusing two-hour rant at the log cabin as he stalked the room with his excruciating howls was one thing, but who would want Wild Man puncturing their eardrums in their homes?

Never mind. Frank, who seemed to have sidelined his composing hours to those on the road, had moved on to the next few projects. He founded a new label, Straight Records, to produce the 'weird' albums! First off the press was Alice Cooper's *Pretties for You*, though Frank quickly lost interest, passing the production onto Ian. A similar thing happened with Tim Dawe's *Penrod*. New people were hired, new offices acquired and new antagonisms developed. Although I showed up every day, I tried to stay out of the commotion, quietly doing my own thing.

My own thing, all this time, had whittled down to resuming work on United Mutations (because, as I'd expected, a backlog had built up in Frank's dining room, Gail and PamZ having reneged on their promise to do it 'by the pool') and trundling through Pamela and Cynthia's diaries, more than five hundred pages long and still not finished. As it was too late to present them to a publisher in place of his own political book, Frank had paid back his advance, probably with a deep sigh of relief.

In June, like a double-edged sword, my green card arrived. Although jubilant to at last be a legitimate worker, I could not chase up to Frank and Gail's to celebrate with champagne because Frank was on tour, nor could I tell Neil or Herbie or Mutt because they would be obliged to put me on the official payroll and I knew they would not want to pay me $140 a week, the sum I would need to cover taxation and social security payments and retain one hundred dollars in my hand. So I kept quiet, secure in the knowledge that whatever happened at Bizarre, my future lay in America.

38

To my great relief, in July Frank got over his angst and asked me to call Pamela and Sparkie back into the studio at Sunset Sound to finish recording *Permanent Damage*. Once again, my job felt secure, or at least that's what I mistakenly and foolishly thought.

Bizarre had already invested a large sum of money in the girls' album, so finishing it was a rational move. Pamela and Sparkie were close friends and considered themselves the Lennon-McCartney of the GTOs, a slight inflation of their egos since neither could write music. And since there was no time to find others to compose, chant they must. They stood holding hands while Frank, in a jovial mood, coached them on timing and pitch, flourishing his baton wildly and making them giggle so they would have to start again.

These last four songs continued the theme of their lives: 'Wouldn't it be Sad if There Were No Cones', a clever lyric about soul brothers with quaffed hair who hung around the Whisky a Go-Go to pick-up girls. More mundane were 'Who's Jim Sox?' about showers and dyke gym teachers at high school; 'The Moche Monster Review', which described the grotesque advances made to the girls when they hitch-hiked; and, finally, 'Love on an Eleven-Year Old Level', about a schoolboy who looked like Brian Jones.

Meanwhile, Sandra had retired after giving birth to Raven, a baby girl, on 5 July, and shortly afterwards Sparkie flounced out too. She was disillusioned with the showbiz razzmatazz that fascinated the other girls as they fought like cats over who could bed the loftiest rock stars. So, with Pamela and the return of 'the three terrors', as I called them – Mercy, Cinderella and Christine (who Frank grudgingly forgave) – there were now just four GTOs. Less flamboyant, less argumentative and more willing to follow my instructions, we stumbled through interviews and photographic sessions in preparation for the release of their album. Once again my life became manically busy and worries that Neil Reshen wanted to fire me faded.

There was a moment of euphoria when, on 20 July, Neil Armstrong and his fellow astronauts dropped gently onto the moon. Frank and Gail, now heavily pregnant, trailed along Woodrow Wilson Drive to Mutt's house to watch the momentous occasion on our eighteen-inch black and white TV. I closed the drapes to sharpen the screen, set between rows of aquaria, the fish prodding at the glass inquisitively. As Apollo 11 touched down after four days of travel, Mutt exclaimed, 'Fantastic! Brilliant! Can you believe it? Are they really on the moon?'

Frank, equally animated, waxed lyrical. 'This operation has put thousands of people to work,' he said, nodding his head with approval. 'It will make the country feel good about itself.'

At last, here was Frank enthusiastic about something American. He even looked and sounded proud to *be* an American.

Journalists often got the impression from Frank's songs that he was anti-American, but he learned very quickly to put them straight. 'I'm proud to be an American. I think America is the best place in the world. Unfortunately, that's not saying too much because other places in the world are pretty messed up too. I just wish things were better here because, if America was in good shape, then perhaps the influence that we used to exert on other places in the world would be more of a positive influence.'

The astronauts would not step on the moon for several hours, so Frank and Gail went home to watch the historic event on their tiny twelve-inch screen.

The thrill I felt at entertaining Frank and Gail at Mutt's house was short-lived because, within days, my life took a perilous turn.

From New York came a letter from Phyllis. Her job with the Soft Machine had fallen through and she'd taken a crash course in film editing. Frank had invited her over to work on the *Uncle Meat* footage, work that I myself coveted. They spent hours together in the studio which gave them a connection, but I felt no threat: she and I had become firm friends, hanging out together.

Sharon Tate's brutal murder in Cielo Drive, a similarly secluded street to Woodrow Wilson Drive less than five miles away, brought all socialising to a halt for a while. The murderers had suspended the eight-months-pregnant Sharon in a noose from a rafter and stabbed her to death. They had tied her friend Jay Sebring, an internationally known hairdresser, to the other end of the rope, shot and stabbed him. Two other friends – the heiress to the Folger coffee fortune, Abigail Folger, and her boyfriend – tried to flee but were caught, stabbed and shot. In the driveway, the police found an eighteen-year-old boy dead in his car. The murderers had smeared the word 'pig' in blood on the back door.

The next night, a supermarket executive and his wife, a dress-shop owner, not famous, not celebrities, had been similarly slaughtered in their home, the word 'pig' again daubed on the door. If anything, this second murder frightened me more. The murderers could target *anyone*, not just celebrities. Until that day, people had left their doors unlocked but now you heard, 'Did I lock the car?' 'Bolt the latch, would you?' It brought an end to the hitchhiker conveyor belt. No one wanted to offer rides because who knew where the maniacs would strike next?

Frank and the Mothers had been on tour, but when he returned he lost no time in turning his perimeter into a fortress, replacing the wooden gate with a steel one and an intercom to the kitchen. Mutt did nothing. Though there were no street lights and no other houses in sight or earshot on our lonely section of Woodrow Wilson Drive, he said the ducks, whose quacks could be heard half a mile away, were our protection, and so they were. (If the four almost wild dogs – an Alsatian, Dalmatian and two Labradors – didn't get to them first.)

So anxiety was already high when, on this particular evening, I sat chatting to Gail in their living room. They'd furnished it with a large wooden and chintz sofa, another sofa like a railway bench in a dog-tooth fabric, easy chairs and a large oil painting by Ed Beardsley on the wall. We'd moved from the kitchen because a giant potato spider, six inches across and green, had scooted in. Aware of how terrified I was of spiders, Gail had swiftly dropped a large bowl over it to act as a cage, but that was not enough distance for me and I insisted we adjourn to the living room, where Gail now played colouring with Moon on the floor, crayons scattered around, while I remained firmly, feet up, on the sofa.

At some point during that languid evening, Gail said casually, 'You know, Pauline? I think Phyllis is angling after your job.'

Suddenly, the fresh, green foliage of the potted plants turned sickly and the sun Moon had drawn, so bright a moment ago, faded and dulled. Phyllis was my friend, so at first I would not believe it. Yet Gail did not tend to make things up and in a flash, I realised it all made sense. How often had I found Frank and Phyllis in the basement together, Frank erupting in laughter at some rejoinder from Phyllis? Pretty, witty and clever, she could type and took no nonsense from Neil Reshen, a characteristic I knew Frank found compelling.

Realising that Phyllis might actually succeed with her plan, a notch of dread began twisting in my stomach. With Frank far away in Ontario, it felt as though he'd abandoned me. Had he abandoned me? I had a sudden urge to get out, but an abrupt departure would arouse Gail's suspicions. While I sat and admired Moon's drawings and gossiped some more with Gail, an idea, coldly and logically, began to form in my mind. By the time I'd escaped, feigning a headache, and had driven along Woodrow Wilson Drive to Mutt's house, I'd worked out the plan in detail.

No one must know. I would call in sick at the office, take a cab to the airport, buy my ticket and be over the clouds before anyone realised. Next, I would capitalise on the surprise factor. What other secretary would fly three thousand miles and spend over three weeks' salary for a quiet word with her boss? And wouldn't my very presence remind him how remote he'd become, how impossible it was to speak to him privately? I pictured the whole scene, saw the sympathetic look in his eyes when he learned how anxious I was; heard his reassuring words that Phyllis, phooey Phyllis, was truly an afterthought and that I, Pauline, played the central role in his working life. *I like you working for me.* Hadn't I felt it in his warm embrace? Yes, all I had to do was present myself to him in Ottawa and we would renew our close bond. As I lay in bed, the three cats settled warm and heavy on my feet, the idea that had flickered on the cold ride home grew into a flame that made my heart pump. A reckless excitement made me want to laugh aloud. Not beaten yet, I thought exultantly.

But the next morning as I soared over the clouds, my confidence plummeted. Suppose Frank saw my trip as audacious, even arrogant, supposing he turned me down, swept me aside and confirmed that he planned to give me notice – what would I do then? I pictured a groupie snuggling into his neck and Frank's vacant look. A lot of deep breathing and clutching at my breast did nothing to calm my nerves.

Late afternoon on a clear, warm day, I caught the bus into Ottawa, my first trip to Canada, but my mind was too addled to notice what kind of buildings flashed by. At the hotel, I could find no trace of Frank or the Mothers. Not only that, there were no free rooms in the hotel.

Two hours dragged by as I nibbled crumb after crumb of Black Forest gateau and the knot in my stomach tightened until I felt sick.

And then all at once there they were, marching across the lobby like a posse of cowboys, Frank at their helm, his yellow socks at odds with his red tapered trousers, pink t-shirt and brown lace-up shoes. Though he'd tied his hair back, it hung tousled round his narrow face. I stood up, my heart beating extra fast, and walked quickly to greet them. At the lifts, amid much confusion, delight and astonishment, I laughed almost deliriously. 'What are *you* doing here?' I said with my rehearsed line.

As Ian gave me an affectionate kiss on the cheek, I could sense their minds bristling over so in order to clarify things immediately, I blurted out, 'Frank, I never get a chance to talk to you on your own in Hollywood, so I've had to come all this way. I hope you're suitably impressed?'

With bemused speculation, his eyes swept over my sleeveless brown mini-dress with its low-slung white belt and strappy sandals.

'She's after a raise, Frank.'

'She's going back to England.'

The lift doors opened and I squashed in with them, their laughter and jokes building up quickly and bordering on lewd. When we came to Frank's floor, he held the door with his hand and said to me, 'Come up to my room at ten o'clock, okay?' which elicited more bawdy jibes. I had hoped he would invite me to dinner but I reasoned he must have work to do. Trapped in the lift, I went up to a higher floor with Ian.

Once he'd taken a shower and I'd tried all the TV channels, Ian told me they'd been to the CJOH TV studio to record a television programme and I told him about my fears for my job. He reassured me that my trip was not a foolish endeavour, but my stomach remained twisted and tight.

Over dinner, the Mothers' light-hearted grumbles about not playing at Woodstock, a concert that had been going on for the past three days in New York, wafted in and out of my consciousness while I worried how to approach Frank and, more importantly, how he would respond. Gradually, though, the Mothers' jesting and humour was too much to resist, so that by the time I knocked on Frank's door and he welcomed me in, I breezed past, almost cheery. And when he padded around in his surprisingly small room clearing his music papers into a neat pile on his desk, placed a cushion on the chair for me to sit on, poured me coffee, placed an ashtray on the bedside table, threw himself on top of the blue and green patterned bedspread and nestled into the pillows with a glow in his eyes I'd never seen before, I braced myself and burst into some inane chatter until I finally stopped and said, 'I suppose I'd better tell you why I'm here?'

'I figure you haven't travelled across America for a cup of tea.'

I'd had hours and hours to rehearse my story, but could remember none of it. 'It's Neil Reshen. I know I've told you before but I'm having such a difficult time with him at the office. I get the impression, or at least, I *know* he wants to fire me. He thinks the diaries are a waste of time, a dead end.' (I knew that would raise Frank's hackles.)

'Neil can be an asshole sometimes and you should know this, he's just as creepy as all the other guys who take care of the money.'

'Yes, but does he have the authority to sack me?'

'Well, first of all, Neil works for me, so he does what I tell him.'

'Exactly, that's why I need to know your thinking on this.'

'I haven't told him to fire you.'

'Will you?'

'No.'

Oh! Everything was all right then. My job was safe.

'You mean you came three thousand miles to ask me this?'

'Well, yes. Recently it's been impossible to find you alone. It's not the sort of thing I can discuss in front of other people.'

'We'll see what we can do about that. Come 'ere,' he said, patting the space on the bed beside him, a faintly humorous smile in his eyes.

'Well, no, there's something else.' The delicate issue of Phyllis was trickier but, fearing my courage would fail me, I blurted out, 'I've heard rumours that Phyllis is after my job.' There. I'd said it and, now that the words were out of my mouth, I no longer believed them.

The smile faded. 'First I've heard of it,' he said.

'So, so – it's not true?'

'Is this what you've been worrying about? Par-leen, come on now.'

'It's just that there's no one else I want to work for. And I get so nervous when I don't see you.'

'Where are you staying tonight?' he asked casually.

'Ian's offered to let me sleep in his room. He said he'd sleep on the sofa. I guess it's a return token for all the times he slept on the floor in my room.'

'There's room here if you want.' He patted the space beside him once again.

'Well, no, Frank, I can't.'

'Why not?'

'Well, for starters, it's not proper. I'm your secretary.' I could see he was not convinced. 'And there's Gail.'

'I notice you two spend hours in the kitchen,' he said a little sourly. 'What the hell do you find to talk about?'

'Mostly, we put the world to right.'

'I could not do it,' he said. 'I could not waste my life in endless chit-chat.'

'I think Gail gets lonely, y'know?'

'Well, in two weeks she'll have another munchkin. She'll have more than enough to keep her occupied. Don't worry about Gail. Rest here awhile.' Once again, he patted the space beside him.

I pictured myself, fully clothed, joining him on his bed just as Calvin crashed on mine for many nights. I figured this was a Californian thing and not carnal at all. In any case, I'd missed Frank's warmth and fondness. I needed that reassurance.

I settled beside him and said, 'So am I to assume that I should not be worried by Phyllis? That there is no possibility of her taking my job?'

He put his arm round my shoulders and squeezed. 'Stop worrying. Phyllis is not going to take your job.'

With his words, all tension melted away and I sat comfortably while Frank related more stories from the road, the air warm and soothing. Occasionally he would give one of his hearty laughs and I would giggle too in perfect harmony. How foolish I'd been to believe Frank would even consider firing me. Wasn't it obvious that we had a special rapport? Then he took my chin in his hand, turned my head to face him and kissed me on the lips.

I could see the graininess of his skin and my mind was flying in every direction. This was wrong, all wrong, not the way I had planned it at all. Then I felt his hand begin sliding up the inside of my leg. On reflex, I pushed away. 'Frank – Frank – this is impossible, you know that.'

'What's the matter?' he said, 'Don't you want nookie?'

'Well, no,' I muttered.

When I had climbed on the bed, I had sought affection, that was what I expected, that was what I honestly meant, but now I saw that my action had implied something more, that by climbing on his bed I had signalled a direct 'come on'. If I'd been embarrassed all that time ago in New York, I was doubly, trebly, oodles of times more embarrassed now. At least then, his hand had remained in proper positions, *outside* my clothes. Foolishly, I had believed I was somehow exempt from his lustful needs, that he understood any illicit liaison between us was impossible, would never happen. Appalled at my own naivety, I wriggled free and scrambled to my feet, pretending I thought it was a joke, but when I turned to face him again, malice danced in his eyes. Why hadn't I realised that Frank, ever a sexual predator, would take his chance? Hot-eyed and dizzy, I adjusted my dress. 'I really ought to be going.'

I hoped Frank might come to his senses, jump up and make some gesture of contrition. Instead, he leaned back on the pillow, his face dark and unreadable.

Humiliated and with renewed fears about my job, I grabbed my handbag and muttered some lame goodbye. 'I'll see you in the morning, okay?' As I glanced back, something flickered behind his eyes, but he said nothing.

I raced along Ian's corridor so swiftly that when I reached his door, I thought I might faint. I clutched the handle and took great gasps of air to calm my thumping heart. Wasn't I the biggest dolt ever? 'I'm as bad as a groupie,' I thought. What would Ian think? And the Mothers? Oh, they'd think everything.

When I told Ian the tale, he regarded me with veiled and impassive eyes. He said, 'I thought you might not come back,' which outraged me. For the first time since I'd known him, an unhappy awkwardness rose up between us. But, like a gentleman, he lay on the sofa while I, emotionally exhausted but too wound up to sleep, tucked myself into his bed. Momentarily, I cringed. What had my job sunk to? I had come to see Frank as his employee and been welcomed as a . . . it was not to be borne. With a different man, would a proper businesslike meeting have taken place? What would have happened, I wondered, now that it was too late, if I had *not* come to Ottawa and had allowed fate to take its course? Would I still be riding high in Frank's estimation, or would I very soon be on a plane home to England? What change had my flit to Ottawa brought about? Very little, I now realised. In fact, I had no doubt made it worse – because what would I say to Gail, my good friend? We'd been to see *Easy Rider* together, gasped in horror at the film *The Freaks* at a private viewing, we'd shopped and on occasion eaten out tête-à-tête. Would she assume something untoward had occurred with her husband when no such thought seemed to have entered her head before? Was it because she was heavily pregnant, the baby due imminently, that Frank had stepped out of line? Did all men who expected a baby lust after other women, any woman? The worrying, nagging thoughts would not go away and hours passed before I slept.

The next morning, when Ian and I climbed on to the Mothers' coach for the trip to the airport, Frank sat beside an empty seat. 'Good morning, Frank,' I called, slightly too airily but, as if to ensure that I would not sit beside him, he leapt up and clambered to the back of the coach. It felt like a plastic shield had dropped between us. What a fool! What had I expected, a paean of thanks?

The next day, back in the leafy surrounds of Laurel Canyon, Frank dropped his bombshell and broke up the Mothers of Invention for good.

39

Everyone had been writing from England concerned that I would never find a boyfriend because I seemed so infatuated with Frank. I couldn't have cared less. I was having a great time and had made some very good friends. I wasn't interested in finding a boyfriend because my work, which I loved, was back on form. To my great relief and a little surprise, Frank had become more attentive since our return from Ottawa, answering my phone calls immediately and calling me to his basement at least twice a week for personal sessions. Evidently, he had chosen to ignore our little contretemps.

As for Gail, no word passed her lips. When I raced through the kitchen, she barely looked up, too engrossed with her new baby, Ian Donald Calvin Euclid Zappa (known as Dweezil), vigorously shaking his bottle or smothering his cupid face with bubbly kisses.

It would be three months before she would challenge me head on.

So August rolled into September and Mutt, in a wild and happy mood, invited over two hundred guests to a barbecue party. Just when I least expected it, romance entered my life, and with an Oscar-winner to boot.

Luckily, the mountains, normally hidden by smog, emerged against a blue sky, their folds brightened by the sun into multi-shades of green so beautiful it explained why people used to rave about California.

Lolla, one of Mutt's voluptuous girlfriends, with jet black hair and an hour-glass figure, prepared the extras; specially-made corn bread, potato salad, ham and cold chicken and, for pudding, blueberry cheesecakes, and fruit salad laced with marshmallows dipped in mayonnaise – delicious.

Thankfully, Mutt had turned out to be the best landlord, though sometimes I wondered why; I'd had so many mishaps. I'd put the bathroom carpet in the washing machine and gone to work, returning ten hours later to find it hopping around the laundry room in agony, or so it sounded. I'd struggled and shoved but could not push it back into position. The next day I'd found it safely in its corner. Mutt made no comment, and even when I broke one of his precious cups, one of a set of twelve, he uttered no word of reproach. We seemed to be in a conspiracy of silence, neither wanting to upset the other lest the fragile peace between us should break.

On occasion, when he did get grumpy, I would pile on the flattery, teasing him about his girlfriends, and he would break into the sauciest of grins. He saw himself as a Casanova and, judging by the stream of blondes, brunettes and redheads, black, Indian and Asian, tall, short, shapely and slim, it was true. Each one wanted a wedding ring on her finger, which seemed strange because most of them were his clients from divorce cases.

Once they had quizzed me about *my* presence in the house they, in turn, used me to divulge Mutt's feelings about them, seemingly unaware of each other. Yet Mutt was depressed. He wanted to get married but could not find one among them who fitted the bill. I hoped he would not find her soon, realising a permanent mistress would kick me out.

Sometimes friends, as opposed to girlfriends, would crash on Mutt's sofa in the formal living room, friends like Linda Ronstadt of the Stone Ponies. She and I would sit at the counter in the kitchen and, over long cups of coffee, gossip. I could not understand how she had so little confidence, not only in her musical talent but in her beauty. Stunningly pretty, with a heart-shaped face, pert little nose and eyes like Natalie Wood's, I was sure men must fall at her feet, but she'd suffered as many heartbreaks as any other downtrodden woman. If someone as beautiful and talented as Linda had trouble finding a man, what chance was there for me?

She came to the party in pedal pushers and a t-shirt and joined the throng of guests who spilled from the kitchen onto the patio and up the hillside. It felt like the whole of the music industry was crammed into our home. Even Frank and Gail with Moon and Dweezil made an appearance.

Ian had been gone for two months and had finally, finally married Ruth, and Calvin, who was my new friend these days, came to the party with a girlfriend. Hungry for company of my own and light-headed from the wine and sunshine, I almost danced into the arms of Zal Yanovsky – tall, dark and handsome – who'd left the Lovin' Spoonful in 1968 to pursue a solo career. When he offered to pour beer into my glass I said, 'Just a touch,' and he said, 'Where would you like the touch?' and we were off on a round of teasing and counter teasing which sent me bubbling with laughter. I found his drooping moustache, shoulder-length hair and heavy fringe extremely attractive and could not believe my luck. We sat on the brick steps and I told him I had to sit on his left because I had an ear infection and couldn't hear on one side. He put his arm round my shoulders and whispered into my neck, 'There's no stereo effect with you, that's for sure.' I felt easy and relaxed and snuggled into his suede jacket, teasing him cheekily about his blue and yellow striped trousers. Sadly, before any romance could get off the ground, he was leaving for a recording session in New York that very hour, and would be gone for six weeks. He kissed me goodbye and I felt flushed with desire. His penetrating eyes showed me he felt the same and he promised to phone from New York. I was thrilled that at last I would break out of my tight-knit 'family' circle.

The barbecue had by now reached its peak, the air full of laughter and talk of record sales and contracts and who was divorcing whom. Mutt brought the baby goat out of its pen to many oohs and aahs. The ducks quacked and the four dogs scurried to find shade round the side of the house. Mutt had hired waitresses who walked through carrying aloft trays of drinks, offering tall glasses of beer to men in tattered jeans and t-shirts and girls in long skirts.

I took Moon's hand, a little cream puff of a hand, and led her up the hill to show her the different colours of Mutt's prize ducks. So preoccupied were we, I failed to notice Mutt bring up a fair-haired man. 'Pauline, this is Fred Wolf. Fred, this is Pauline, Frank Zappa's secretary.' We shook hands but he was shorter than me and not particularly handsome, and my head was so full of Zal that I hardly gave him a glance. He therefore surprised me by lingering rather than returning with Mutt and Moon to the guests below.

Fred wore a green seaman's cap over his short, fair, curly hair, a striped green and cream t-shirt and cream jeans. As we watched the ducks washing in the newly-cleaned pond, I got into full bloom. 'I used to be terrified of the animals,' I gushed, 'especially the goats because they're always breaking out of their pen.'

'*That* little thing?'

'No really, it's still got horns and it bucks and jumps. One time they both got out. I tore up the road and screamed and shouted like a rodeo hand before I got them back in their pen. And then the animal people came over and gave me notice about the dogs, because they roam all over the hillside and it turns out it's against the law to have more than three dogs without a kennel licence so I had to deal with that as well.'

Fred moved to squat on a boulder and I dropped down beside him, aware I should allow him a moment to speak, but he seemed content to chew on a piece of grass. 'One day, Nova, our Labrador, she's only a puppy but incredibly strong, she slaughtered three of Mutt's prize rabbits and dropped them at my feet in the kitchen, all torn and shredded. I nearly threw up. Calvin dumped them in the trash but I made him take them out and dig a proper grave, which, in fact, is just by you.' I pointed to Fred's feet and he leapt up. 'I thought Mutt would go ballistic because they were a special rare breed, but when he came home he was fantastic. He knows Nova is semi-wild. I think Mutt was patient because he had such a good time with his children.'

Fred squinted down at me. 'Mutt likes to have a good time.'

'He thinks it's easy, but look, Nova had seven puppies two days before he went away and he was gone for five weeks. They peed everywhere in the kitchen, and we've got four ducks, three rabbits, three pigeons, four dogs, four cats and two snapping turtles, without the goats and all the fish in the house and the special cacti and precious plants. In the rainy season, this whole slope is a sea of mud and I slip and slide trying to open the rabbit hutches, floundering around like a clown on a rotating ball. And the smell! The ducks do their poo in the pond, and who has to empty it once a week? I do! I live here rent-free but really I earn my keep.'

'So you live here with Mutt. Isn't that a little odd?'

'Everyone thinks that, but it's not. No.'

Though used to hairy moustaches, Fred sported an almost full beard that normally I hated, especially fair ones, but on Fred it served to enhance the gleam in his pale eyes. I saw now that he *was* handsome in a devilish, captivating sort of way, and he kept me amused with his sharp, cynical remarks about the long-haired music folk milling below us on the patio, their laughter and talk rising in the late afternoon air, pleasant, carefree sounds. We could see Frank sitting on the wall at the bottom of the steps, his kilometres of hair brushed out in its wildest look.

Fred said, 'Why are you working for a man who looks like Jesus Christ?' the first of many derisory comments Fred would make about Frank. I found it refreshing. Everyone in my circle complained about Frank's ways, but no one overtly criticised who he was. Fred, though, had no interest in paying homage to Frank.

He told me that he and his partner, Jimmy Murakami, made animated advertisements for television. Then, in 1968, he'd won an Oscar for his short film *The Box*, a witty story about patrons in a bar trying to guess the contents of a box brought in by an old bearded man. Later, Fred and Jimmy went on to produce the phenomenally successful *Teenage Mutant Ninja Turtles* series for television. So, after waiting nearly two years for a boyfriend, I now found myself courted by a film producer, rich and celebrated in Hollywood. Bingo!

I chatted on about the cartoons I'd enjoyed, but that was one of many mistakes. 'They are not cartoons, Pauline,' he chided with a little sarcasm. 'They are works of art, paintings that move and tell their own story.' He frequently admonished me in this way but in the beginning, I held my own. In fact, in the beginning I treated him with nonchalance while I waited for Zal Yanovsky to return, but by the time he did, it was too late. Fred's persistent phone calls, trips to his studio and meals by the sea had won me over.

He wasn't romantic in the conventional sense – he didn't send flowers but instead paid a dentist to fill my front tooth. Well, it saved me a lot of money and I felt he was being kind.

If Fred did not rate Frank's image, I would soon learn that he rated his music even less. Just as well he hadn't seen his films, I thought, shambolic, all over the place, whilst Fred's animation was masterfully crafted and controlled. In a peculiar way, their creative styles were complete opposites from the way they lived their lives. Frank spent his days confined in his basement producing films full of chaos and anarchy, while Fred would often let fly with more than a drink or two, rarely turning down an invitation to a party, yet *his* films were highly structured and restrained. I felt ambivalence towards Frank: emotionally he had me hooked, but I didn't like his films and quite a lot of his songs, so that Fred's irreverence was a relief in a way. I learned about Harry Nilsson, a close drinking friend who Fred thought was supreme. 'Could Frank sing, "Everybody's Talkin'"?' he asked.

'Well, no but – '

'And what about Leonard Cohen?'

Sitting on the balcony of his house in Malibu where we spent many happy weekends, we played 'Suzanne' and 'So Long, Marianne' repeatedly. Later, in Frank's basement, I told Frank I'd bought all three of Leonard Cohen's albums. He chided, 'Why do you want to listen to nonsensical love songs, Pauline? Are you in love?'

I felt embarrassed, but Fred Wolf had status in Hollywood and if Fred was prepared to say he listened to Leonard Cohen, why shouldn't I? In any case, how did Frank know what Leonard Cohen's music sounded like? If Frank was not at the studio recording, he was in the basement composing or editing films. As far as I knew, he never listened to the radio and I was sure there was no Leonard Cohen record in his collection. That meant that when Frank was on the road, he must have trawled through radio stations and watched TV. It was the only explanation.

I felt strong enough to stand my ground. 'What's wrong with love songs?'

'"Let's make love"? What kind of tomfool says shit like that in the real world? You ought to be able to say "let's go fuck" but you gotta say "let's make love" to sell a song.'

We'd had different versions of this discussion several times but I felt emboldened by Fred. 'Are you saying you don't believe in love?'

'I believe in love, but not phoney, bullshit love. It makes me feel sick. A mother can love her child; a child can love its father. That's different from love lyrics. I detest them. If you're a kid and you hear them, you go through life looking for something that *will never exist for you.* You go through life feeling that you've been cheated out of something because of some dumb fucking love song.'

'I don't.'

'Maybe you're the exception,' he said a little sarcastically, and turned to the music sheets spread around his desk, an indication I was wasting his time and he must get back to work.

I felt uneasy. When I listened again, I realised Leonard Cohen's songs *could* be heard as sentimental tosh. Poetry and words of gush and goo glossed over the love-you-and-leave-you story. Frank was right. Women, and even men, were stupid to fall for it. Not that I heard any words of love from Fred. He was too caustic, too biting, but I didn't notice at first.

The next two months were a whirl of romance as we whizzed along Sunset Boulevard to the Pacific Ocean. The invigorating wind blew through my hair and I sang, 'They'll never believe me, they'll never believe me,' while Fred aped agony, covering his ears. He drove his roll-top convertible Porsche sedately in response to my fear of speed, which was just as well because sometimes he drank more scotch than was wise. Whenever we passed another roll-top Porsche, Fred would flash his lights in their direction and they would flash back a signal to say, 'Hello you other hot-shot, whoever you are.'

We would sit on the veranda of his beach-front house at Malibu, sipping whisky and breathing in the salt-sea air while couples in matching strides paraded by the water's edge leaving their footprints in the sand. I looked out for film stars – after all, didn't they all live in Malibu? But again, I searched in vain. In a restaurant, Fred had introduced me to Stan Freberg, the top comedian. Did that count?

One balmy night, as the sun slipped beyond the horizon on the Pacific Ocean, Fred asked me to make coffee for two of his friends, casually dressed, forty-something filmmakers. They rattled off private jokes that excluded me and I tried to arrange my face to show indifference, but when I poured the boiling water into four mugs and some of it splashed from the saucepan onto the work top, leaving puddles of brown liquid, Fred snorted, 'Are you going to wipe that up?'

I glanced at him, taken aback by his harsh tone.

'If I left a mess like that, you know what my mother would do?'

'No.'

'She'd give me a wallop,' he said, adding with a scowl, 'Let's just leave it at that.'

Why didn't I answer back? Why didn't I rebuke?

Feeling like a naughty child, I quickly wiped clean the few droplets on the marble worktop but right there, the course of our relationship crystallised.

We stumbled on in the same vein: me always seeming to blunder from one mini faux-pas to another while Fred corrected me with increasing sarcasm – 'You have to take that monstrous Tretchikoff print down from your wall, Pauline' – so that whereas in the beginning my self-esteem had soared when he'd zeroed in on me at Mutt's party and wanted to hear my life story and, naturally, how I'd met Frank, very soon my inability to counter these criticisms with any retorts of my own left me feeling close to worthless. While I suffered terrible pangs of love-sickness, Fred's interest withered away. I telephoned Calvin hoping for words of comfort but he wallowed in his own pit of misery, penniless and without work, and was no help. So, like an injured ferret that burrows underground, I sought to boost my self-esteem and scurried to the basement to find Frank.

40

In November 1969, I typed the last page of *The Groupie Papers*, the last page of nine hundred pages. Who would publish them? When I proudly handed the tome to Frank, I felt ambivalence: happy that the task was over, but worried because – what work would he have for me now? He'd been busy for the past two months composing the film score for *200 Motels,* his next movie, the GTOs were in the midst of a lull, so all that was left was the fan club, United Mutations.

I took the opportunity, green card in hand, to take my long-promised holiday in England. There my friends greeted me like a mini-celebrity, laying on parties and candle-lit dinners. Apparently, working for Frank Zappa gave me an aura, a dazzle I'd hitherto not possessed. While my friends married and had babies, commuted each day to humdrum jobs, I lived in the heart of Laurel Canyon, the most happening rock'n'roll caveat in the world. Wasn't that glamour for you? I thought it was, yet after the initial euphoria had worn off, my friends' true feelings began to emerge. Pat, the proud mother of Polly, her first baby, said, 'It wouldn't suit me to travel so much. I need roots, I need to be settled,' a veiled attempt to re-set the balance.

At my parents' house, I found the non-stop prattle of my visiting siblings overwhelming. I'd spent so much time with Calvin, when sometimes neither of us would speak for hours, that this bluster and noise felt like a raging battle. I listened in wonder to their passionate arguments which, in the old days before I'd absconded to America, I would have barged into with vigour. Now I sat in silence, stunned while they screamed at each other across a room the size of a matchbox yet stuffed with four armchairs, two straight-back chairs, a fold-down dining table, sideboard and huge boxed television.

My mother, father, Pat, Carole, Peter and Doreen battled over recent legislation to give eighteen- to twenty-year-olds the vote.

'Teenagers are still children,' Doreen shouted, as if across a football pitch, 'some of them are still at school. What do they know about the world?'

'What are you talking about?' Peter shouted back, his words reverberating between the walls. 'Most eighteen, twenty-year-olds are out working, paying taxes, they've got a right to say how their money's spent, same as the rest of us.'

'Yes, but they're not interested in politics. All they want is to enjoy themselves. I bet most of them won't even bother.'

'That's not the point . . .' and so it went on, everyone yelling one on top of the other.

Eventually, Doreen said, 'What do you think, Pauline? You're sitting there so quiet.'

I replied, 'Why do you want my opinion? You've got six different ones already?'

It sent a silence through the room and, too late, I regretted my sullenness, but I couldn't take it back.

Outside, cold weather set in abruptly with a killing frost and I pined not only for Frank and Gail's swimming pool, where I'd basked in sunshine only the weekend before, but also for the leafy winding lanes of Laurel Canyon with their individual houses hidden behind a multitude of lush shrubbery. Compare that with this 1930s suburban sprawl around London, semi-detached houses in barren, treeless streets that sapped ambition and dulled the spirit. Eager to get back, yet worried what fate might await me, I boarded the plane after a three-week stay promising my family that I would get out and socialise: there would be no sewing curtains this Christmas.

At the airport in LA, Calvin, thumbs hooked into a wide leather belt slung low on his narrow hips, greeted me with a little smile and said, 'I missed you.' Still, I was shocked when I saw the length of his crinkled hair, freshly washed and flowing; it reached his shoulder blades, longer than mine. In England, if a man wore his hair to his shoulders, they considered it shocking. For the past year even Frank had pulled his hair into a band, and more recently had scraped his fringe off his forehead too. At twenty-nine, did he feel too old for the hippy image? Or maybe it carried too much weight now that they'd arrested Charles Manson for the heinous Sharon Tate murders? Manson had shoulder-length hair and a moustache, an image that until now had granted access through unlocked doors and offers of couches to crash on. He had connections to the music business and had been searching unsuccessfully for a record deal with Terry Melcher, a record producer, the previous tenant of Sharon Tate's house and the apparent target of the murders. How easily Manson rather than Wild Man could have crossed Frank's path, and how lucky we were that Manson had missed us. If one of the music industry's own could torture and murder others, who else might be lurking in the shadows? Who now could you trust? But here was Calvin, still brandishing the hippy look and looking gorgeous with it.

It was Thursday morning and there was not much traffic on the road but still Calvin drove slowly, one arm resting on the hot metal frame of the open window, the tip of his fingers guiding the wheel to change lanes. Normally, I would tut and nag about his untidy car but today I was so pleased to be back, even the empty cans of Ronald's dog food, tangles of newspapers and empty packets of Pall Malls seemed somehow touching, like forgotten toys found in a garage.

I prattled on about how girls in England were wearing waistcoats and pinafore dresses, knitwear suits and maxi coats. Calvin listened to the end before asking casually, 'Listen, can you lend me ten dollars?'

He was constantly broke despite the fact that, other than *Freak Out!*, he'd designed all of Frank's album covers to date (*Absolutely Free*, *We're Only in It for the Money*, *Lumpy Gravy*, *Cruising with Ruben and the Jets*, *Mothermania*, *Uncle Meat*, *Hot Rats*, and most recently *Burnt Weenie Sandwich*), and although he was looked upon as a surrogate son by Frank and Gail, it had not been enough to save him from Herbie's hatchet. No longer on the payroll and therefore free to seek commissions elsewhere, he hustled work, but hustling was not Calvin's strong point, so the habit of borrowing money from me that had started at the log cabin became constant.

'Calvin, I've been back five minutes.'

'Oh, well. Ronald is running low on food.'

I sighed. What was the use? Still, it meant I could barter, push for the latest gossip, something he would normally refuse to do. 'What's been going on? Anything exciting?'

'You wanna hear Frank's latest crazy idea?'

'Yes please, tell me.'

'Cynthia Plaster Caster, right?'

'Yes.'

'He wants to cast her models into bronze and then he's going to put them on show in LA.' He let out a little smirk and swung the car round the bends to Frank's house.

Surprisingly, we found Frank alone in the kitchen. He held a frankfurter with a fork over the gas ring flame but laid it down carefully on a plate to give me a warm bear hug. He said gleefully, 'I have a new job for you, Pauline.'

That was a relief.

'I plan on recasting Cynthia's casts into bronze,' he said, and watched for my reaction.

'So Calvin told me – for an exhibition – but surely you can't.'

'Why not?' Frank never saw obstacles to his ideas.

'Well, won't they protest? Jimi Hendrix? Anthony Newley? It's not as if they're dead.'

'If anyone seriously objects we'll take them out, but I don't think there'll be a problem.'

Hmm. I bet if Cynthia had cast Frank, and someone else had wanted to display *his* private parts publicly, he'd have gone ballistic. I tried again. 'The police might not approve.'

'Why? Have you seen any of Michael Angelo's work? I don't see any fig leaves covering the statue of David's tiddly winkle.'

Yes, very amusing.

'I want you to find some sculptors and get a few quotes.'

Good, I liked these kinds of tasks, tasks that would take me out of the office and away from Herbie's dragon-like breath.

It took several phone calls before I found a sculptor who worked in bronze and, without telling him my request, arranged a visit. Next, I contacted Cynthia. She'd arrived in LA earlier in the year, loaded with her plaster casts. Frank had set her up in a small apartment on Grace Street so that she could expand her stock from the crowd of rock stars who hung around Laurel Canyon. Indeed, it had been part of my job to chauffeur her around Hollywood, but for the most part Pamela took on the role, adopting her like a long-lost sister.

Cynthia surprised everyone. So shy! How could that be? A pretty, fresh-faced girl, infamous for moulding the most intimate parts of boys' anatomies, she stood in Gail's kitchen with lowered lashes, nervously tugging her t-shirt to hide her ample bosom, a bosom that most girls would have flaunted. Boys often said, 'If you could lose some of that fat, you'd be really cute.' But how unfair! She *was* overweight but perfectly proportioned. Modest, quiet, a small lisp adding to her timid charm, she seemed perplexed by everyone's attention. Frank said she was an artist, but she felt her casting was so effortless and fun, she didn't think of it as art.

Her 'babies', as she called them, lay wrapped in separate shoeboxes in her closet. Lovingly, she carried each one to the table as if they might break. There they all were in their wilting glory, bent over, limp, some detailed with veins, others more like door knockers, mere blobs, and then there was Jimi Hendrix, a veritable Venus de Milo.

We chose Noel Redding's, despite it looking more like a worm peeking out of the ground. I wrapped it in a brown paper bag and placed it beside me on the car seat. Cynthia waved a sad goodbye as if sending one of her kiddies to school for the first time. I hoped a burly policeman would not flag me down and demand an explanation.

The address led me to the other side of downtown Los Angeles, a dusty, boarded-up street. The sculptor's studio was slotted between a 'Get It On' porn shop on one side and 'Madame Trudy – Love Problems Solved' on the other. Opposite, a group of black men dressed in bright colours stood outside a billiard hall. They nudged each other when they saw me and sniggered, but how much more they would have sniggered if they'd seen my secret hoard.

A bell jingled when I pushed the door into the cluttered studio which smelt of raw wood. Among a muddle of plaster sculptures, a woman in a calico smock with her hair knotted on top of her head was arranging carved wooden animals on a table. I approached her across creaky floorboards as a man who looked like Einstein – with a bush of grey, wiry hair – appeared from the back of the shop.

Mortified, I unwrapped the pure white droopy penis from the paper and placed it on the table. 'I'm not sure if you've done anything like this before. It's not a bust exactly.'

They picked it up rather calmly, I thought, and passed it from one to the other, scrutinised its bent-over shape and inspected the veins from every angle, all the while babbling in Spanish while I stood aside trying to appear nonchalant. 'I have eighteen others, some larger, some smaller. I would say this is about average size.'

'Some of your conquests?' he asked.

'No. Of course not.'

'Pleased to know that. Specimen like this, not good,' he chuckled.

They asked me how I'd come by the casts. Self-consciously and pink-faced, I related Cynthia's role and technique. They simply nodded and babbled though I understood not one word.

Anxious to get out of there, I quickly explained that we wanted them displayed on individual wooden stands with the name engraved on each one. I gave him Herbie's name and address and he promised to send a quotation.

Because Cynthia's apartment had been burgled, Herbie took possession of the bronze versions once they were made. But the exhibition did not take place until 2000 (at Threadwaxing Space in New York). Somehow a quarrel over ownership had erupted and a bitter court case ensued when Cynthia sued Herbie for the return of her 'babies'. The judge awarded Cynthia both the originals and bronze models, but she retrieved only the bronze versions because Herbie testified that he did not know where the originals had gone.

41

From the moment I returned from Canada through to the beginning of 1970, Gail had used Dweezil as a decoy to avoid asking the salient question: 'Why did you travel three thousand miles to see my husband?' Whenever I passed through the kitchen, she would whisk Dweezil into the air and I would make the necessary cooing sounds before quickly making an excuse to find Frank downstairs. For months, we'd scarcely exchanged a word. Even at Christmas when, at four o'clock in the morning, a full moon peeping through gaps in the hills, Calvin and I had driven along to Frank and Gail's house to exchange our gifts (Calvin had already given me a page-a-day-diary to encourage me, he said, to start writing again), the atmosphere was very low-key and Gail and I hardly spoke. Still, she and Frank gave me a beautiful cream leather handbag, a real surprise, and for each of them, I'd wrapped a silver ashtray inscribed with their names.

The coolness between us had led me to arrange Christmas dinner with Calvin at my house rather than eat at the Zappas. We sat on the floor around Mutt's low Japanese table and, with two of our friends, had munched through a variety of macrobiotic dishes, basically rice and vegetables which I'd moved round my mouth trying to pretend it was the roast turkey and trimmings I could have enjoyed at Gail's.

So it was not surprising when, a few days after Frank went on tour, Gail telephoned my house. 'Is Calvin there?'

'No, he's not. I don't think he'll be here today. He's got his own car going.'

'Okay, well, if you see him, ask him to give me a call?'

'I will.'

'I hear he's round your place quite a lot.'

'When he wants something, Gail.'

'Oh, it's like that?'

'How else did you think it was?'

'Nothing.' And the phone went down. How odd, I thought, and then forgot about it.

The following day, she phoned again, this time at the office, a second call in a week, all bright and cheery, as if we'd been talking every day. 'If you're looking for Calvin, he's not here.'

'No, it's *you* I want. You'll never believe this.'

'You're pregnant.'

'No-ah!'

'What?'

'I'm writing a book.'

'A book!'

'Yeah. About Frank and the groupies he's slept with. Frank suggested you help me.'

I felt a rush of adrenaline at this news – Frank still believed I could be a writer! It also meant my job would be safe for the next few months. 'Thank you, I'd love to.'

'I have to check them out first. Interview them all.'

'Great. When do you start?'

'Tomorrow.'

Tomorrow! 'Goodness, you're moving fast.'

'And I thought I'd start with you. Interview *you*.'

'Me! Why me? *I* haven't slept with Frank.'

Donna looked up from her desk trying to hide a grin.

'That's not what Frank told me, Pauline. Listen, I'm bringing Frank to the office tomorrow afternoon. Maybe we can have coffee and talk some more?'

I knocked the receiver over trying to rest it on the hook, clambered into the ladies' room to gather my thoughts, dropped the lid down and sat on the toilet. I had known Gail for twenty months and not once, in all that time, had she challenged or asked me about my relationship with Frank. We'd spent endless hours gossiping about everyone else's love lives, who'd slept with whom, and she'd never shown the slightest concern or inkling that she thought Frank and I – well, it was too awful to contemplate. And what exactly had Frank said? And why now?

I dreaded our conversation. What would she ask?

The rest of the day passed in a blur and I felt a headache coming on. No wonder Gail had become so remote since I'd returned from Ottawa. She believed I'd had sex with her husband! Then again, perhaps she wasn't even referring to Ottawa. Perhaps she was referring to New York, or even London?

To my relief, Linda Ronstadt called in and invited me to the Troubadour, where Tim Hardin, stoned, fell off the stage while trying to perform. Though a big star and popular, Linda, like Frank and the Mothers, carried no sense of her own celebrity, and introduced me to everyone who was anyone and for a few heady hours my troubled, irksome worries faded away.

In the morning, I took special care with my appearance and put on a demure mini-dress, cream and white striped with long sleeves and a dainty collar. When Gail arrived at the office, she gave me a little smile. She wore a loose t-shirt and jeans.

We adjourned to the sterile coffee shop on the ground floor, where I slid into a red-leather booth and Gail surprised me by sliding to my side. After we'd ordered coffee and I'd asked after Moon and Dweezil, we got onto the business proper.

'So you want me to co-write this book?'

'That's what Frank said but, no. What I would like you to do is be a kind of sounding board and collaborator? Maybe give me some guidance?'

Her lashes fluttered slowly from heavy-lidded eyes, but I dreaded what would come next, so I plunged in. 'Frank's happy about you writing this, is he?'

'Happy? He suggested it.'

'And he's told you about all the groupies he's slept with? Given you names?'

'Not yet.'

'And you don't mind? That he's sleeping with other women?'

'What can I do about it? I'm pragmatic. He's a rock star for fuck's sake.'

'But why is that an excuse?'

'It comes with the furniture. The only thing guys on the road think about is getting their rocks off. And girls who marry musicians and then sue for divorce the minute they find out the guy's fucked some groupie – they're insane. What do they expect? They know the score. Get *real*.' She scorned Jimmy Carl Black, who phoned his wife religiously every day. 'What's the point? Before he even puts the phone down, he's balling some chick.'

I had to admire Gail's resilience.

'When he's on the road, I try not to think about it.'

She snatched up her pack of cigarettes from the table, tapped one out and held it in her pursed lips while lighting it from a book of matches. She inhaled deeply and let the smoke filter out through her nose.

'But what I *do* find hard to deal with is when it's at the house.'

'At the house? I've not seen anyone there.'

She lowered her lids a fraction of an inch. 'Francesca was.'

'Francesca!' Astonished, I remembered how people said Francesca could be Frank's sister with her long, thin face, slightly hooked nose, dark eyes and cascades of black hair. I'd seen her in the kitchen talking to Moon with her strong Italian accent. 'I wondered about her,' I said. 'She just sort of suddenly appeared.'

Gail lowered her voice. 'Frank wanted her to move in permanently. Some kind of communal threesome. God!' she said, rolling her eyes, 'the things Frank puts me through.'

Bewildered that Gail wanted to tell me these intimate goings-on in her married life, baring her soul like I was her therapist, I nevertheless prodded, eager to know more. 'What did Francesca think about it?'

'She's so in love with him, she *drools*.'

'I thought Calvin told me she'd moved out.'

'She has. I don't know what happened exactly, but this one night they were gonna fuck for the first time, and I'm fluffing around getting sheets and blankets and pillows to make up a bed in the basement for Christ's sake and the next thing I know she's back up and she says she's gonna leave.'

'What happened?'

Gail flicked at her wild, backcombed hair and shrugged, her scrubbed face delicately flushed.

'So you don't know.'

'No. And I didn't ask. She doesn't come to the house now.'

I applauded Gail's sixth sense, her ability to handle Frank. By going along with the plan, indeed encouraging it with her willingness to prepare the love nest, she'd taken away the risqué, sinful element. I was speculating. What did I know?

'So Francesca's crossed off the list,' I said.

'Yeah, but you're not.'

'Gail, I – '

She tapped at the side of her full cup of coffee while I called the waitress for more. 'Okay, Pauline. Let's hear it.'

'Did Frank really tell you I slept with him?'

'That's what he said.'

'Well, he's lying.'

She stared at me, a steady, unblinking stare. I stared back just as firmly. 'Ask Ian. He'll tell you. I spent the night in Ian's room.'

'Yes, but you had sex with Frank first.'

'We did not!'

'That's not what Frank said.'

Was she bluffing? Why would Frank tell Gail he'd been having sex with me? Why would he do that? Had she asked him and he'd called his fumbling, *having sex*. Or, could they have lain in bed together and he just drolly told her the truth and she didn't believe him completely – knowing Frank and his lustful needs – and now she was pushing, trying to wrangle for the truth? She was clever and canny. Yes, I reckoned she was bluffing.

'Look, he made a pass. He wanted me to have sex with him, but I didn't. What is Frank up to telling you this? Why is he doing it?'

She continued stirring her coffee and it seemed she would never get around to taking a sip.

'Okay.' I lowered my voice – well, the café was full and there were people in the next booth. 'He put his hand up my skirt and – '

'He gave you a hand job,' she said flatly, as if bored.

I leaned in closely, whispering. 'He *tried*. Gail, this is so embarrassing.'

Her pupils danced, searching mine. She believed me. I could see she believed me.

'You're bluffing, aren't you,' I said. 'Frank didn't tell you anything, did he?'

She smiled a broad, goofy smile and shook her head.

I squinted as hard as I could. *'Gail!'*

From then on, to my great relief, we became firm friends again.

42

Nineteen-seventy had started in the most miserable way. On New Year's
Eve, Mutt had thrown a big party with its usual assortment of music
producers, musicians, singers, lawyers and accountants and to my
utter dismay, Fred Wolf had walked in with a woman on his arm. From a
distance, she'd looked like a schoolgirl with her hair in bunches and white
bobby socks, but close up, she was much older. Fred, slightly drunk, wore the
arrogant, looking-for-a-fight expression that I knew meant trouble, but when
he threw sarcastic comments Mitzi's way, she threw them right back. They
seemed so at ease, like a married couple, I could have puked.

Exasperated and miserable, I'd slouched off to my room to lie comatose on
my bed. Ten minutes before midnight, Calvin telephoned, waking me up and
insisting I should not sleep through the New Year. Always pleased to hear
from him, on that particular night, I grumbled, 'Oh, *Calvin!*' From his slightly
slurred words, I could tell he'd been knocking back the whisky too. I told him
about Fred but he was useless in consoling me as he was just as miserable
himself, his own situation and work equally perilous.

As for me, I had a new task. It had come about when I'd persuaded Frank
that Cynthia and Pamela's diaries, all nine hundred pages of them, needed
editing. 'At the moment it takes forever to get to the hot poop.'

'Hot poop?' he'd mimicked.

I'd giggled. When things went well, it was easy to laugh with Frank.

'If you cut out Pamela's school years,' I'd suggested, 'and start with her groupie
days when she's sixteen, *that* will eliminate four hundred pages immediately.
Then, if the material is arranged by subject rather than chronological order,
so that everything about Noel Redding, for example, is brought together, not
only from their diaries but their letters and telephone calls, it would be easier

to follow and more interesting.' Then, I'd added as nonchalantly as I could, 'I'd like to do the work myself since I know the material better than anyone.'

Deep in thought and gently rocking in his chair, Frank had considered the suggestion. Finally he'd asked, 'Do you think you can complete it by the end of January?'

'Yes of course, even if I have to lose sleep for two months.'

Like no one else I knew, he was always ready to listen to suggestions and ideas with an open mind. Who else would pay *me*, a total ingénue, to edit and compile a book?

So, when the office closed at Christmas for two weeks, I had taken the typewriter to Mutt's house and worked all day and into the night at the desk Mutt had given me, cutting with scissors and pasting with glue, very often with Calvin lying like a corpse, on my single bed by my side.

He often crashed there if his car broke down, which happened frequently. Even if he borrowed my car, I would often need it in the morning and we both knew he would never get back in time from the shack he rented in Silver Lake, a bohemian area some twenty miles up the highway. Instead he would lie fully clothed, flat on his back on top of the covers, his arms crossed over his chest, fast asleep even though my typewriter clattered inches from his head. Then, when I'd finished for the night, I'd climb over him, squeeze under the sheet and blanket and feel the cats rearrange themselves around my feet. Often I would read and in the morning would wake up, squashed, the book, John Updike's *Couples*, still in my hand propped between the wall and my nose.

In return for the ease with which he borrowed my car, Calvin cooked many of my meals and fed the animals. The arrangement suited us well.

One evening, Gail made a surprise visit to Mutt's house to show me her remarkably good synopsis and breakdown for the book. She'd put on a vintage dress and her sandals that wrapped round her legs. Bizarrely, she kept asking me questions about Calvin, who was cooking my dinner in the kitchen. It was most odd.

She lowered her voice. 'Have you seen how long he takes to get ready? What woman would put up with that?'

Gossip still lingered that Gail was in love with Calvin and for the first time, I began to wonder. Calvin had always been her closest confidant. Maybe she thought I threatened her powers now that he almost lived at my house. Could this explain her sudden intrusion into my life?

When the office opened again, I would often stay late, typing non-stop for twelve hours until Calvin picked me up and brought me home.

On this particular night, it was after midnight but despite feeling tired and unwell, I washed my hair. While I was setting it in curls fixed in place with metal Kirby grips, Janet telephoned.

'Hi, Pauline. Listen, are you sleeping with Calvin?'

'What?'

'Well, see, I'm back on him again, and I just need to know.'

'Janet, Calvin uses this place as a crash-pad. Honestly, he stays here, he sleeps on my bed, but it's purely platonic. I love him to death, but it's more like a brother and sister thing, you know?'

'Oh!' she said, sounding pleased, and put the phone down.

Because Mutt was away, I said to Calvin, 'If you'd like to sleep in Ewan's room, I can change the bedclothes before Mutt comes back. He'll never know.'

We were in the kitchen and Calvin, dressed in a pale blue t-shirt and jeans, more holes than fabric, rested his lean frame against the counter, folded his arms and stared down at one shoe. You had to wait while he thought about these things. 'Or do you want to go back to Janet? She seems keen.'

He looked up at me with soft, unreadable eyes and said, 'No, that's okay.'

Well, all right, whatever.

So imagine my surprise when I wiggled my way down under the bedclothes in the narrow space between Calvin and the wall. Instead of remaining in the 'dead' position as he usually did, he turned towards me and, with a little smile, rested his arm across my shoulders. I was so astonished; I yanked my head back and several of the metal Kirby grips fell from my hair onto the pillow. I searched his eyes for an explanation – I knew he wouldn't explain verbally – and, for a moment, I suppose the world stood still. Then I giggled too, snuggled into his arms, and surrendered.

No one could have been more astonished than me. I just didn't think it would happen. Whereas with Ian, I'd constantly dwelled on the fact that one day we might end up in bed together, with Calvin, it hadn't crossed my mind. It had become such a mundane process sleeping in the same bed, Calvin with his clothes on and on top of the covers. He had so many women running after him – indeed, he seemed to have sex with every woman he met, so there was no room for me and it had been the very, very last thing I'd thought about. We had known each other for twenty-two months, not counting the time we met in London in August 1967, and I wondered why things hadn't developed earlier. Somewhere in the back of my mind, Gail's shadow hovered.

Mutt was away and so it seemed natural for Calvin to move in. He brought Ronald, his dog, his clothes, toothbrush and lots of artwork, and for a month until Mutt's return I lived in wonder that for the first time in my life I had a boyfriend, someone with whom I felt totally at ease, never having to worry about smudged make-up or hairs growing on my legs. I loved him dearly.

We rarely socialised because I was too busy, though sometimes we ate out with Dee, Herbie's new bookkeeper, at Ben Frank's or Canter's Deli. I tried to adjust my pace to Calvin's. One morning, on our way to see Frank, he refused to give up his breakfast and ate his corn flakes going along in the car. When we went to see Tiny Tim at the Troubadour, we missed the show while Calvin shaved, showered, washed his hair and selected which ragged t-shirt and torn jeans he should wear. It was worth it. He looked gorgeous and I was proud and happy.

He had often complained that Frank had an easy life because he had Gail to look after him. Now I took over that role for Calvin. He finished his design and drawing for the Fugs' album cover, *Golden Filth* – a collection of dustbins and spilled rubbish that could have come from outside his house – it showed immense flair and talent. He was paid $300, money he desperately needed to pay for the studio he'd rented in an abandoned dentist's clinic above a hotdog shop on Melrose. If only he could get more commissions.

His father, a handsome Clark Gable lookalike, visited from Philadelphia. A bit of a gambler, he took us out to dinner and to the trotting races and I lost on every race. If Calvin's father speculated on me as a daughter-in-law, I doubt if he bothered to ask. Calvin was no more talkative with his father than he was with anyone else.

Meanwhile, almost physically ill, I pounded at the typewriter for ten and twelve hours at a stretch, pummelling *The Groupie Papers* into shape, and I was proud when I'd reduced the nine hundred pages to three hundred and fifty in two months. On 2 February 1970, exhausted, I handed the edited version to Herbie and he, in turn, handed them to the Free Press in Los Angeles. The verdict was very good and publication seemed inevitable. Jubilant, I not only looked forward to my next task, Gail's book; I luxuriated in my new romance. Nineteen-seventy had begun, after all, with me as happy as I could be.

43

After their return from Canada the previous year when Frank disbanded the Mothers, he had called everyone to his basement to round things up. The group had come in, subdued but not beaten: Frank had changed his mind before and perhaps they could make him do it again. Repressed testosterone seemed to rest in the guys' tense muscles as they found seats where they could – there were never enough to go around.

Looking gaunt and pulling one leg tightly over his knee, Frank had told them, 'I've been feeling for some time that I need more space to work on films and the albums. And if I'm doing that, I can't afford to pay you two hundred and fifty dollars a week while you lay around twiddling your thumbs. There've been times I've had to take out loans just to pay expenses.'

If the Mothers understood his reasons, etched into their faces were anger and bitterness – anger at the way Frank had disbanded the group without severance pay or any kind of 'thank you'; and bitterness at the timing, when their years of struggle and toil should have reaped rewards.

Jimmy Carl Black spoke for them all. 'We don't see why things are different now, man. You've worked on albums of your own before. It hasn't stopped us rehearsing. We just kept on going. We could do it again.'

Frank shook his head. 'Am I supposed to do this over and over again when it's not fun anymore?'

Mumbles and grumbles rippled round the room.

Frank offered them a carrot. 'If you will go out and join other groups and play different styles of music for a while, maybe later on we can all get back together when we'll have a lot of new ideas and new material.'

This was worth considering and some discussion followed, but no one wanted to give Frank a crumb of comfort to assuage his conscience – if any conscience he had – and when it became apparent that the plan was actually a cock-eyed idea and could never work, they collectively refused.

Frank's face hardened and he snapped, 'Hey, if that's your attitude, then that's it, it's over.'

So there it was – the end of the Mothers of Invention. No more playing great music, no more limelight. For five years, they'd laboured through thousands of hours of tense rehearsals and wonderful performances but now it seemed their close bond, as full of harmony and discord as any marriage, was about to be annulled; they were no longer loved and Frank was telling them, 'I'm leaving you and it's going to cost.'

The Mothers heaved up their jeans, sniffed and coughed and straggled off to the bathroom or to seek refreshments from the kitchen, a chance to privately whisper and express disgust. Was this the fate of all leaders of rock groups? If Mick Jagger wished to leave the Rolling Stones, would Bill Wyman, Charlie Watts and Keith Richards gang up on him?

Herbie called them back to go over the financial statement. Unwilling to sit down again, they stood awkwardly between the guitars, piano and wooden pillars while Herbie handed out papers that showed zero profits, even after they'd sold all the equipment. 'In fact,' Herbie said quietly, 'as you can see, there's a deficit of ten thousand dollars.'

At this news, angry protests fell over each other and I thought they might lynch Herbie, but he stood firmly, his arms folded. The news defied logic and none of them could believe it. Hadn't they been touring non-stop for months, sold out huge venues? Where had their profits gone, *their* earnings? The original plan – that they would all become rich and famous if they played Frank's music – had come to nothing.

Unperturbed, Herbie slapped the page with the back of his hand. The details were all there – salaries, hotels, per diems, extravagant equipment, staging and travel costs, they all added up to a sum far exceeding the income from concerts. 'And since Frank's been paying you from his publishing royalties,' he said matter-of-factly, 'each one of you owes him a share of that ten thousand dollars. Somehow you'll have to find a way to repay it.'

The guys stared in disbelief at Herbie and a silence fell on the room. No one questioned the figures. Instead, despair and hurt pride showed in their eyes. At last Jimmy found a voice. 'I don't know how you lose money when you're packing places and you're the headliner. Don't you get paid so much money for doing this shit?'

Frank's conscience may finally have pricked him. He'd cleared his throat and said, 'Why don't we forget about the ten grand? Let's just call it even.'

It took a moment for the guys to absorb his words but then, as if struck by a sudden bout of claustrophobia and almost as one, they crowded to the wooden door and pushed it open into the moonlight. Only two or three bothered to say goodbye.

And so, in October 1969, Bizarre/Straight had issued a press release: 'The Mothers of Invention, infamous and repulsive rocking teen combo, is not doing concerts any more . . .'

When Frank's first solo album, *Hot Rats*, reached Number 9 in the charts in England, the highest position of any of the albums so far, it seemed to justify Frank's decision to break up the band.

In March 1970, Frank invited a whole crowd of us to Todd-AO, a post-production facility, to see the latest version of his film, *Uncle Meat*, mostly stuff in the Vienna Woods and the Festival Hall. To tie it all together, he needed to interview each of the Mothers, but there lay the nub: the Mothers of Invention no longer existed.

Never one to allow obstacles to stand in his way and ever the optimist, Frank called the band together a second time and once again, they herded into the basement. If Frank noticed the hostility which hung thick and heavy in the room, he chose to ignore it.

'What I propose to do,' he told them, bringing his coffee to the rocking chair, 'is interview each of you in turn. Then I'll use those interviews to connect the various parts of the film we already have.'

'How much do we get paid?' Jimmy Carl Black demanded to know.

'You don't,' Frank said. 'No one's getting paid. It's already cost me twelve thousand dollars before we start.'

The general response was along the lines of, 'Well, fuck that.'

'You'll get food and expenses,' Frank said, trying for a compromise.

Jim, Bunk, Roy and Art sprang up, voices clashing, clearly furious that Frank was using them yet again just so he could swell his ever-growing fortune. Only Don Preston, Motorhead and Ray Collins remained and agreed to take part.

So the script of *Uncle Meat* had to be quickly rewritten and Frank dictated it over my shoulder directly into the typewriter. He'd already hired lights and equipment and bought film. The action began on 30 March in Frank's basement.

Haskell Wexler, a cinematographer who'd won an Oscar for *Who's Afraid of Virginia Wolf?*, had offered five days of his services – free. He'd made a film, *Medium Cool*, in 1968, a documentary for which he'd used Frank's songs 'Oh No' and 'Who Needs the Police Corps?' on the soundtrack. It covered the Democratic Convention in Chicago in that year. Haskell had used real actors to infiltrate the crowds and then filmed the response from the police and media. Frank loved it. Good gracious, a film he liked.

Aynsley Dunbar arrived from London to add teen appeal to Frank's new line-up. A devilishly handsome, Jack-the-lad rock'n'roll drummer, he would stay at Frank's house for ten months. Often I would find him at four in the morning waging water fights at the pool or goofing around in the kitchen.

I refused to play a part in the film because you never knew what crazy stuff Frank would ask you to do. He urged Phyllis to strip down for the shower scene, for example.

'What's the matter? Do you have an ugly body?'

'No, I have a great body. I just don't want to show it.'

'Why not? If you've got a great body, don't you want to share it with the world?'

'It's not that, I just don't want to do it.'

She won the argument and stood, fully clothed, in the shower with Don Preston (unclothed). Drenched, they proceeded to rub hamburgers over each other and gasped about getting hot. In another scene, Calvin wore a dustbin lid and tapped the cymbals with pliers, and Motorhead had angel's wings strapped on his back and played a stick of wood protruding from the zip in his jeans. They looked ridiculous and I decided I'd made the right choice.

There was no time to learn every bit of dialogue so, with the camera still rolling, most of the 'actors' referred to their scripts, ad-libbed or waited for Frank's prompts. Looking his most handsome, hair tied back, deep sideburns and a squiggly fringe, he padded around in dungarees giving out props: a rubber chicken whose rectum Ray stuffed items up; socks for Don to fantasise over; a doll's head for Motorhead and a large vibrator for Aynsley to attach to his belt and prance around a supermarket while Janet and Lucy beat him with a toilet brush. In the billiard hall scene, they tied Frank's younger brother, Carl, up with rope and then Don Preston lay on the pool table buried under a pile of billiard cues. Haskell, his heavy camera loaded on his shoulder, filmed congenially all week and patiently offered advice.

At best, arty, at worst, amateurish, it didn't matter to Frank that the week's filming followed no storyline nor made any logical sense. Apart from Phyllis's ad-lib when she asked with her broadest Brooklyn accent, 'You can't tell I'm from New York, huh?' I found the scenes more tacky than funny, but Frank was delighted. All it needed was his careful editing, he said.

Once filming finished, there followed another awkward period when Frank needed the Mothers a third time. For months, he'd planned a big orchestral concert of his film score *200 Motels* at the Pauley Pavilion, UCLA, a university stadium normally reserved for basketball and not noted for its acoustics. The organisers did not believe a classical film score could fill the stadium and insisted he include the Mothers of Invention.

Unfazed, Frank rustled together both Aynsley Dunbar and Billy Mundi (from an early incarnation of the Mothers) on drums, Ray Collins on vocals, Don Preston on keyboards, Ian Underwood on alto sax and Motorhead on baritone sax. The newest recruit, Jeff Simmons, a skinny boy, nineteen years old, played bass and vocals. Herbie had set up a few gigs in Chicago and New York for preparation, but noticeably absent were the original Mothers, Jimmy Carl Black, Bunk Gardner, Roy Estrada and Art Tripp.

In order for Frank to hear what his beloved dots would sound like played by the Los Angeles Orchestra conducted by Zubin Mehta, he happily fished out $7,000 to a team of copyists for the orchestra parts. But I felt disheartened with Frank. Only ten days earlier, the Kent State University massacre had occurred. At the end of four days of demonstrations and riots on campus, the National Guard had opened fire, killing two boys and two girls and injuring nine other students, one of them paralysed from the waist down. I had hoped Frank would write a song about it but he remained silent. When I dared to raise the issue, he said caustically, 'Other people are doing it. I don't need to fill that niche anymore.' Instead, at the Pauley concert, he parodied Jim Morrison's stage act. Motorhead appeared to 'beat his meat' with a copy of *Playboy* magazine rolled into a tube.

On 15 May, eleven thousand people sat through an extraordinary evening of modern classical music mixed in with the Mothers' instrumentals, songs, snorts, grunts and zany carryings-on. Later the entire ninety-six-piece orchestra stood up and walked into the audience playing whatever they chose and Frank, who was not allowed to tape it because of objections from the Musicians Union, lost the chance to objectively hear it except through bootleg copies made by zealous members of the audience.

The critics were damning, but others jumped to Frank's defence. 'When you have two separate audiences, classical and rock'n'roll, neither can be satisfied.' 'It's not easy to dabble in rock and classical, two opposing musical worlds, when both regard you as a traitor.' 'For Frank Zappa, there's no difference between a string quartet and a rock combo. High culture, low culture, it's all the same.' 'Zappa creates his own genre. His imagination knows no bounds.'

Frank himself was elated and thought it the most successful concert of the year, while I remained dazzled by his extraordinary ego and audacity to put on such an outlandish event. Sadly, I could not suppress the nostalgia I felt for the old Mothers of Invention. Frank would release two final Mothers' albums in February and August 1970, *Burnt Weenie Sandwich* and *Weasels Ripped My Flesh*, and there might be royalty cheques in the post but the guys knew from experience not to plan their futures on it. When their devoted fans wrote to express their anger and regret, I passed the letters on to Jimmy Carl Black.

44

One evening at the beginning of June 1970, while I was home alone brushing my hair, a knock at the front door brought surprising visitors. Frank and Gail, arms round each other and giggling like a pair of teenagers, stood there. 'Won't you invite us in?' Gail said, and stepped past me directly into the living room. They peeped into the two bedrooms and bathrooms on either side and glanced into the kitchen along the back. In the main bedroom, I pointed to a heavy axe hidden under the bed. 'Collin said it's to frighten away burglars.'

Frank rolled his eyes. 'Collin? Who is this nutter?' He dropped into the beige leather sofa and lifted his brown laced shoe gently onto the coffee table. Gail settled beside him.

Frank never visited anyone, which may explain why, notwithstanding his incredible memory, when I interviewed him in London eighteen years later, he recalled this scene in detail: that I wore my floor-length velvet house-coat zipped up through the front, that I had just washed my hair and, in the absence of a hairdryer, brushed it from root to end to get it dry. Perhaps my attire, lack of make-up and very feminine activity set Frank's eyebrows to rise up and down? 'Have we interrupted something here, Pauline?' he asked.

The little cottage they visited nestled at the bottom of Nichols Canyon, which ran down the hillside from Woodrow Wilson Drive. With a colour TV and no-need-to-defrost refrigerator, I'd moved up in the world, coming to this house courtesy of Fred Wolf, who'd moved out to live permanently in his Malibu home, where he was working on an animated feature for television called *The Point*.

'So things getting sticky with Mutt, huh?' Fred had said over the phone, his deep voice sounding warm and sympathetic.

'I don't know what's wrong,' I'd told him. 'We've got on so well for eighteen months and now suddenly – '

In truth, Mutt had returned from his trip to Europe a stranger, and Calvin had hastily returned to his own home. In his wake, Mutt had stormed and snarled like a hungry dingo. Now, instead of finding my every move a source of amusement and pleasure, he began to criticise and the more he criticised, the more nervous and cack-handed I became. I'd failed to collect Mutt's repaired record player on the specified day because Calvin had my car and so when Mutt brought home three Israelis who performed at the Lindy Opera House, he'd got 'pissed off' because he couldn't get his crackly office one to work, and I'd got the backlash of his tongue. Then he'd smashed up his car and asked me to chauffeur him to the doctor but I couldn't because Calvin had borrowed mine and kept us waiting for an hour. Later, while Calvin had cooked dinner, you could feel Mutt's temper smouldering as he crashed and banged around the kitchen.

'I want this house cleaned, *properly!*' he'd growled through my bedroom door.

'Mutt, do you know how hard it is cleaning up after four dogs and four cats? You get it pristine and then in they march with muddy paws. Why do none of the cleaning ladies ever come back a second time?'

'Well, get another one. I can afford it. I'm a rich man.'

And so I did, but when the woman arrived and wanted to be paid, Mutt said, 'It's your privilege. *You* pay her.'

So I took on the cleaning yet again, even going to the extreme of washing Mutt's bedroom windows and becoming bad tempered myself – the dirt wasn't *that* bad. Then Mutt flooded the laundry room trying to fix the washing machine and his temper flew again.

'Where are the towels?' he bellowed from his bathroom.

'What towels?'

'*My* towels. What have you done with them?'

'I haven't touched them.'

'Well, they're not here. They can't walk.'

'I don't use your towels,' I protested, and then I remembered they were at the laundromat, where I'd forgotten to collect them.

The inevitable showdown arrived. Mutt stood in my bathroom doorway and yelled. 'I asked you to buy *big* bags of dry food. Why do you ignore what I say?'

'I can't carry them. I brought an extra number of small ones. What's wrong with that?'

'They cost more, that's what.'

The contemptuous look in his face triggered the realisation that appeasement would get me nowhere and I snapped, 'If you're going to complain about every little thing, buy the damn bags yourself!' The shock of hearing my voice answer back upset me as much as suffering Mutt's anger. I went to bed dreading what he would complain about next, and every night I dutifully fed the animals.

'Where the hell is Tania's collar? What have you done with it?' Mutt yelled.

'I don't know.'

'It's been missing for days. Haven't you noticed?'

'Well, no. She often doesn't wear it.'

'It's not that Pauline. You just don't care anymore.'

'Of course I care. I feed them every day, don't I?'

'Your attitude's changed. You don't give a damn. This can't go on. You'll have to find somewhere else.'

'Why suddenly is everything not good enough?'

I burst into tears, a rare show of emotion, but I was so darned convinced of the injustice of it all. I must have looked pathetic because he said quietly, 'Take your time.'

Between my sniffles, I realised it was true. Devotion to Calvin had dominated my life, with everything fitting around his needs: my work, the animals, cleaning. At night, I'd sneaked him in because his presence seemed to fester the sore that troubled Mutt, or we withdrew to Calvin's house. I could have moved there if only he would clear the trash from the kitchen – stacks of old newspapers on the small wooden table, grungy saucepans piled in the sink, and thousands of cockroaches that slid behind the units when you switched on the light, their scratching feet sounding like a giant waterfall. He had no television so in the evenings we pasted his Blue Shield stamps into books, now sixteen in all. From the torn and coffee-stained catalogue, he exchanged them for a drill. Often he would lay on the couch, eyes closed, while I reminisced about the log cabin days. 'Calvin, are you listening?' but he was asleep.

Even PamZ, who had finally moved out of Frank's house for reasons unknown, surfaced from obscurity with offers to help me find a new house. We rarely saw each other these days and I was touched by her generosity and kindness. In the end, though, Fred Wolf had returned my call, and here I was in Nichols Canyon having rustled up coffee for Frank and Gail, chuffed that they'd honoured me with a visit.

I wanted to discuss the delicate subject of my salary. With $140 a month rent to pay and loans to Calvin, I was almost broke. But Frank had other things on his mind. He wanted to talk about the songs he planned to write for Mark Volman and Howard Kaylan, who'd recently joined the latest line-up of the Mothers. In a few days, they would leave for a hurried tour of Europe with Ian Underwood, Aynsley Dunbar, Jeff Simmons and George Duke, Frank's first proper tour for nearly a year.

He picked up my pink hairbrush and motioned that he would brush my hair. Slightly embarrassed, I glanced at Gail but she smiled encouragement so I sat on the armchair and he stood behind me and began to stroke my damp locks from scalp to end, sometimes yanking my head backwards. 'So, Pauline, tell about the weirdo who gets off on axes.'

'Collin? He's all right. He's a film cameraman.'

Gail asked, 'How old is he?'

'Twenty-five, though he looks much older and what a hypochondriac! Every day it's something different, hay-fever, back pain, acid stomach, headaches.' The jerks on my head made it difficult to speak smoothly. 'He thinks every tic and cough is a sign of cancer and he shovels down aspirins and tranquillisers.' I made no mention of his rakish friends, who every weekend snorted phials of coke until they dropped like dead flies on our living room floor.

With a little smile on his lips, Frank knelt beside me, placed his palm on the top of my head, bent it forward and began brushing from the nape of my neck through to the ends, forming a curtain over my face. Good lord, I could see egg stains splattered on the front of my dressing gown! I felt Frank's closeness was too intimate for my liking but could find no way to stop it until I reached up and said, 'It's almost dry now,' and Frank, having teased the parting on the wrong side, handed back my hairbrush.

Eighteen years later, at the Hyde Park Hotel in London, Frank gave me a lengthy interview. At the end of it, I said, 'Is there anything you would like to ask me?'

He'd pondered for a moment, then with a glint of mischief in his eye, said, 'Remember when we stopped by your house that one time? What were you doing in there with that hairbrush?'

'I beg your pardon!' I said. 'I was probably brushing my hair.'

'Whoooah, I don't know, Pauline.'

If anyone else had implied that there was a sexual motive behind the use of my hairbrush, I'm sure I would have curled my lip and walked out. But this was Frank. Since lust played a salient part in his life, he assumed it took centre stage in everyone else's. Of all the things he could have asked me, my activity with a hairbrush was the one he'd stored in his memory for eighteen years. But it was also touching because, although I was now married with a young son and he was forty-eight years old, here we were rekindling the way our relationship worked: he teasing me about my sex life and me defending my virtue.

****

While Frank and the new Mothers travelled through Europe that summer of 1970, English newspapers filled up with two main stories: Edward Heath had defied the polls and rolled into Number 10 Downing Street on 18 June, and hysteria about the World Cup in Mexico. In America, photographs of women marching in the streets dominated the headlines. They came charging off the front page, bra-less, chests thrust forward, fat, thin, short, tall, well-heeled and down-trodden, all with one resolve: to end men's oppression of women. 'Love me less, respect me more,' their banners railed. Of course, why hadn't I thought of it before? It was not *love* women needed from men, but *respect*. 'Equal pay for equal work.'

I bought Kate Millett's book, *Sexual Politics*, and devoured her argument in all three hundred pages. The patriarchal system that exists throughout the world, she said, maintains its hold by passing itself off as nature. The natural order of things is for men to dominate and for women to submit. Her book set out to deconstruct that view and argued that women must collectively rebel. Kate Millett, along with other visionaries, had opened the creaky door to women's liberation.

Convinced that Frank would applaud, I charged up to his house to discuss the issue as soon as he returned. Frank cared for the underdog. Well, women were underdogs and he would surely support their cause. I'd practised my arguments on Calvin but he couldn't see what all the fuss was about and simply grunted.

I found Frank seated on a stool in his white-tiled bathroom, submitting to Gail's scissors as she snipped great dollops of black curls and let them fall to the floor. Now his hair skimmed his shoulders and ears with only a heavy fringe to retain the shaggy look.

In a tart mood, he complained bitterly about audiences in Europe, audiences who had chanted for the *old* Mothers of Invention. And to make matters worse, the new Mothers had not performed well. Frank blamed their hasty formation and insufficient rehearsal time. He kept bouncing his head to emphasise his disgruntlement, movements which forced Gail to hold the scissors aloft until he stopped. Gradually though, as he talked about Mark and Howard's contribution, their great harmonising skills and willingness to step up and speak to the audience, he softened and his mood improved.

It gave me confidence to launch into my tale about women's liberation. Dressed in my denim hot-pant suit and knee-length black boots, I perched sideways on the edge of the bath to avoid touching Frank's knees. Under his steady, almost cross-eyed gaze, I stuttered through a summary of Kate Millett's book. 'She says love is a "grant" men bestow on women to retain power and that women should reject it. She says women don't need the promise of romantic love in order to offer sex because it puts women in perpetual subordination. That's more or less what *you* say, isn't it? But whereas you replace romantic love with lust, women's lib replaces it with *respect*, which makes sense, I think.'

'You mean if women turn themselves into inorgasmic people devoid of lust, they're going to be happier?'

Taken aback by his sour tone, I protested, 'But respect doesn't exclude lust, does it?'

'That's what it sounds like you're saying.'

'She says it better than I do. You should read her book.'

'From what you're telling me, it's not worth a diddly winkle.'

'I think it's brilliant. I've never thought about these things before.'

'Well, I don't have the time or the inclination.'

Disappointed, I glanced at Gail for support but her eyes focused on lopping off smaller and smaller curls and checking she'd balanced both sides correctly. I tried another tack. 'She says the first question anyone asks when you're born is, "Is it a boy or a girl?" And from that moment on you're delegated either to the dominant group with the boys or the inferior lot, the girls. And it stays that way for the rest of our lives. Ever since Eve appeared out of Adam's rib – '

'Yeah. And what a fairytale that is,' Frank said.

'Exactly – '

'That evil woman convinced the man to eat the apple, but the apple came from the tree of knowledge. You eat the apple, you're going to be as smart as God and we can't have that. So the punishment is if you're a woman, it's going to be running down your leg, and if you're a guy you're going to be in the salt mines for the rest of your life.'

'Exactly,' I agreed, not having understood at all, 'but it doesn't have to be that way.' The tap in the bath was dripping lightly. To give myself time to think I leaned over and turned it off hard. 'She agrees with you. The Adam and Eve story is nonsense. She says its conditioning that makes men and women different.'

'You really believe that?'

'She makes a good case. If you give dolls to boys and trains to girls, they'll grow up the same – girls will stop learning feminine tricks like pretending to be helpless, they'll cut the faints and tears and as a result they'll be all round better people.'

'Why do you want to turn yourself into a man?' He pushed the fringe from his face, almost knocking the scissors, but Gail reacted in time.

'I don't. That's absurd.'

'You think you'll be a better person if you put on a bowler hat and carry a briefcase? If you want to fuck a man, why not get a real one?'

'Frank, it's not about sex, it's about equality, giving power to minorities.'

Gail trimmed round the front now and stood between me and Frank. She said, 'How can you call women a minority? They're half the population.'

'Women are a minority because they have no power,' I said. 'Nixon's got three women in his government. That's hardly representative of half the population. It's the same with coloured people, they have no power either.'

For the first time since I'd known Frank and Gail, I felt I knew more about a subject than they did and PamZ's words floated into my mind. 'Frank has some very powerful insights and is very bright, but I think there are times when he masquerades as brighter than he actually is.' But then again, I reflected, that could apply to many people, including myself.

I ploughed on. 'At the moment a woman's role is reduced to the home and children, while men deal with everything else, that is the military, government, religion, judiciary, finance, everything. Women get their social class from their husband. Is that right?'

'Unless she's not married,' Gail said, stopping for a moment to rest her left hand firmly on Frank's shoulder.

'Well *her* case is even worse. Do you know that in an experiment they gave people an essay to read: those who thought the author was a man scored it twice as high as those who thought a woman wrote it? So you see,' I said, looking straight at Gail, '*all* women are seen as inferior. And what's bad is patriarchy sets women against each other, career women against housewives, older women against younger ones.'

'So what do you want in its place, a matriarchy?' Frank asked sourly. 'You want women in charge while men show up once a month with a piggy bank full of sperm? You'll end up with a society full of dykes.'

This was not going the way I'd expected, but I felt confident and looked him straight in the eye. 'Not dykes, Frank. The press have picked on the wrong stuff about hairy legs and armpits. It's about standing on your own two feet and you can't do that without money and power. Why should women be reflections of men, subservient to them?'

'Gail's not subservient to me.'

I could have said quite a lot about that but bit my lip.

Gail put the scissors down and ran her hands through Frank's hair, lifting and moulding it with her fingers. I blamed Aleister Crowley, whose book they'd recently acquired. Gail had started using words like *occult* and *mysticism* and *alchemy*. 'The tension between male and female,' Crowley claimed, 'is fundamental to existence and sexual magic.' He saw women's role as subjugated to men, a role that Gail seemed happy to accept, and Frank wholeheartedly concurred.

If I could vaguely understand Gail's interest in Crowley, I could not fathom

Frank's, a man who exuded rationality. Yet an interest in the 'otherness' of life stayed with him. Many years later, he explained his position. He told me about his youngest daughter, Diva. 'She's very peculiar. I think she's psychic. We have a fax machine at the house where you just write something and it goes through a satellite to another place on the planet, and we were in Berlin and I got two drawings via a fax from the house: one of 'em was a comparative map of China versus Germany. And the other one said, "Happy Birthday," and it wasn't my birthday. But it turns out that it was my bodyguard's birthday. I don't know how she could have known that but he was certainly amazed to see the drawings.'

'Are you suggesting she has some kind of extra-sensory perception?'

'Well, let me put it to you this way: I think that some of the things we experience as weird phenomena will one day be explained in the future by physics when we have the tools to give rational explanations to stuff that today is just too scary.'

While Gail snipped and tweaked his sideburns into a slimmer shape, Frank said, 'I think what we have here with the Women's Liberation Army is a modern version of penis envy.'

'Do you really think everything's about sex?'

'Just about. It's why guys join rock'n'roll bands. They don't do it because they love the music. They do it because they'll get plenty of action. Same with surfers and surfer girls, truck drivers, newspaper writers, gynaecologists, they all have their own little things they do to get laid. Same with these dykes, they want equality with men so it gives 'em an excuse to ball other women.'

'I don't know why you're going on about dykes, Frank. Women's liberation is nothing to do with sex. It's about women wanting the same money for doing the same job. Apparently, women earn half as much as men even when they're educated. You can't tell me *that's* right.'

'Women get paid the same in my band.'

I wanted to say, 'You don't have women in your band, period,' but as if reading my thoughts, Gail interjected, 'Frank's had women in his band.'

Brushing hairs from his nose with his thumb, Frank added, 'I don't have women in my band because there's a smaller pool to choose from and because they bring with them a whole lot of other baggage.'

It did seem odd. Ever since I'd known Frank, he'd encouraged *me* to expand my horizons, to write about my experiences; given *me* tasks that no other man would give a girl who had no experience, let alone pay her for them, so why did he raise barriers against the independence of all women?

Gail lifted the towel from Frank's shoulders and shook the hairs to the floor. 'I don't see how marriages can work when two people are working,' she said.

'Who's going to look after the children?'

'Some women,' Frank said, 'are born to be housewives,' and Gail echoed triumphantly, '*Exactly.*'

'Isn't that what, deep down, you want to do, Pauline?' Frank asked, one wry eyebrow raised. 'Get married, have little munchkins? Why don't you marry Calvin?'

'Look, we're getting off the point here.'

'I don't think we ever got to the point.' He stood up to inspect the result in the mirror and pulled at a few strands here and there. He gave Gail a nod of approval. She beamed.

A mass of curls like a giant wig covered the floor and, as Gail bent down to scoop them into a plastic bag, I said to Frank, 'May I have a lock of your hair?'

He plucked up a deep curl and held it between thumb and finger as if it was a dangly earring. 'Take a piece of my hair, Pauline,' he said wryly.

Gail giggled.

'Thank you kindly,' I said with equal parody.

Then I took the curl home and pasted it into my diary.

45

As the summer of 1970 ebbed into cooler temperatures, my work for Frank trickled away. I had gotten excited for a while when Frank wanted me to work at the publishers in New York to complete more edits on *The Groupie Papers*, but Herbie suggested I do it by telephone and then, like other projects, the plan was abandoned.

Frank said I could chaperone the GTOs on their planned tour of the States, but Herbie quashed that too. Their album, *Permanent Damage*, had sunk into oblivion. A few promotional photo sessions and interviews for magazines followed, but the tracks themselves, once heard, had served their own death knell. Television and radio had ignored our knocks on their doors, and so another big chunk of my job was lost.

I jumped at the chance to work with Calvin on setting up NT&B (Nifty, Tough & Bitchin), Frank's advertising agency, but in the end, Frank couldn't drum up financial backing. He tried to get Gail to start work on her book so I could help her but she said she was too busy looking after the children.

Frank grumbled, 'Are you telling me we employ a houseful of people and there's no one to help you with the kids?' Gail said, 'Not when I want them to,' and Frank said, 'Then kick ass,' which I thought was a joke because I'd never seen Frank kick anyone's ass, so Gail's proposed book remained a synopsis in the drawer.

Meanwhile, at Bizarre, things went from bad to dire. Frank's TV talk show (of which he would be the host), planned for February, never materialised, albums were not selling, Neil Reshen was getting five percent of nothing so it was not worth the airfare, and only Herbie and Dee, the new bookkeeper who'd replaced Donna, still worked there, while I ran around like the junior office help.

Much as I tried to pretend otherwise, even I could see that working full-time for Frank was no longer tenable, but I shrank from cutting the umbilical cord, so much of my self-esteem was bound up in his tranquil eyes and unflinching belief in my talents. Why, only last month Frank had told Joe Boyd, manager of the Incredible String Band, who in turn told my friend Oonagh in London, that he thought very highly of me. I grabbed at these small crumbs of praise since without them I had no idea if I was doing a good job or what was expected of me. If only he would say it to my face. Instead, I made do with his body language and kindly looks, which always filled me with assurance like a tonic warming my blood.

I could reappear in Twickenham like a sparrow with an injured wing, but that was inconceivable. What was there to do in London anyway? Resume teaching at the modelling school? And surely the dead-end secretarial work at Forum would be a defeat? Also, the thought of modelling again made me puke – a walking, glorified coat-hanger to be ogled at.

The solution came from Oonagh. She wrote: 'Would you like to work for Ronan?' Ronan O'Rahilly, her boss, had started a revolutionary TV channel in England playing music videos twenty-four hours a day. They would beam the signal from an aeroplane coasting over the UK. Could I beg or borrow video clips of their artists from record companies in LA, 16mm or 25mm films from one minute to one hour? If I could, they would pay me by the hour.

I thought this the perfect answer – a chance to do outside freelance work and still work for Frank on an hourly basis, too. When I announced this news to him, he looked relieved.

There was no big jamboree for my departure because, in the end, it was no departure at all. I still drove to Frank and Gail's house every day, either to take dictation, lounge by their pool or while away the early hours with Gail. In fact, I saw more of Frank than I did when on the payroll. The arrangement suited us all. But the record companies in LA loathed to hand over their tapes. They didn't believe a twenty-four-hour TV channel would ever get off the ground and I was forced to beg and cajole. Also, Caroline Television was very slow in paying my fees and I ran into debt. Frank and Gail loaned me $300 and my sisters sent regular top-ups. Fred Wolf came to my rescue too. He loaned me a car to save me paying for a rental. I say car, but it had no top, no sides and no back and I chugged around town like some old hippy, my hair blowing in the breeze.

Yet I was not unhappy. I had spent the first half of 1970 hanging out at Calvin's one-bedroom cabin set in its wild hillside, the yard filled with leftover car parts and unfinished building projects. Joined by our friends, Squidget or Midget, Gail's twin brothers, Jim from Philadelphia, and Casey, an overweight junkie who helped out at Frank and Gail's house, we idled away hours of fun time. I had left behind the dream of a glamorous, rich life. Somehow or another, over that long spring and summer, I had become a bohemian – that is to say, I had settled into the moneyless culture, learning to make do, to live on less, surviving on very little at all.

Sadly, and to my great regret, Calvin's house also became a Mecca for a horde of other females. As the summer moved into autumn, I never knew when I drove up who I would find seated in the kitchen waiting for Calvin to raise himself from his bed: Francesca (looking as if she'd stepped out of *Macbeth*, dressed in a black dress from chin to toes) might be there, or a girl called Pete (Frank's pet name for Lorraine Belcher, who was arrested with him during the Cucamonga raid), or a stream of others whose names I didn't know. In the beginning I fought them off despite the pain tearing my heart, but gradually I lost the battles and with each skirmish, the anguish became less. Calvin and I remained close. I loved him dearly.

Meanwhile, Janet had decided she'd had enough of looking after Moon and Dweezil and had escaped to London. Gail had hired and fired a series of nursemaids who failed to meet her exacting standards. As a result, she stopped hiring them altogether and I became her surrogate nanny and friend. With Dweezil bundled in her arms and Moon toddling at her side, she would drop by my house daily and if she missed a visit, we spoke on the telephone two or three times a day. When Frank travelled or worked all night in the studio she would ask me to stay, offering the guest house in the garden but, too afraid of spiders, I chose instead to crash on the floor in the small family room off the living room. Indeed, we were in such constant contact I felt she was more married to me than she was to Frank. Sometimes we would lounge on Gail's bed while she and I chewed over the latest deaths in 1970 – Jimi Hendrix drowning in his own vomit on 18 September, and two weeks later Janis Joplin overdosing on heroin at the Landmark Hotel.

Dweezil still slept in sizeable chunks but Moon, with whom I had a neat little relationship and for whom I'd developed a real fondness, would keep going all night. Gail always sided with her, no matter how foolish her desires or how outrageous her needs. She treated her little daughter as an adult, listening to her opinions with apparent seriousness and pretending to be guided by them. As a result, Moon interrupted whenever she pleased, contradicted and put Gail in her place, and Gail would simply laugh and praise her spirit. But I hadn't grown up with a father of eleven children for nothing.

'I'm going to tell the wall about you,' I told Moon.

'Can't.'

'Oh, yes, I can. You watch,' and I leaned over and spoke conspiratorially into the space between an old menu and a press cutting about Frank's concert in Cincinnati. 'You must not watch Moon anymore,' I told the wall. 'You must close your eyes and not watch her.'

Moon giggled.

'Shush, I'm listening to the wall. The wall says it's not watching Moon anymore. It's going to sleep.'

Moon looked quizzically at me, trying to work it out. She said, 'No like game,' and toddled off out into the garden. But later I caught her tapping the space on the wall. 'Wall?' she called. 'It's Moonie.'

All this while, I still lived at the dinky cottage on Nichols Canyon with the drug-crazed Collin, but one night he arrived home and muttered that he'd had a hard day at the office. I said, 'I'm sorry,' and he said, 'But doesn't that bother you that I've had a hard day at the office?' and when I spluttered. 'Well, yes, but . . .' he flew into a rage, tore into his room, dragged out the axe from under his bed and, with gritted teeth, whirled it round and round above his head in a frenzy, breathing heavily, eyes almost popping. I stood rooted, paralysed with terror that he would lose his grip and send the axe on a trajectory, decapitating me in its tracks, but to my relief, he slowed and chugged to a halt as if his batteries had run out, dropped the axe to the floor, collapsed on the couch and passed out.

Trembling, I scrambled up to Gail's house. 'Crash here tonight,' she said without hesitation and warned me to find somewhere else to live. Much to her chagrin, however, I began searching and found a flat in Westwood several miles from Hollywood. It created the separateness I needed to build a life outside Frank and Gail's influence. But when Fred's old wreck of a car broke down completely, Frank found the solution. He had just bought his parents a new Oldsmobile and offered me their old one. It seemed like every step I made to pull away, they pulled me back in. Now I had no excuse but to visit at every moment and to be honest it was easy to succumb. For the time being, I felt secure and cocooned in their fold. If life with the Zappas was a compulsion, then let the compulsion take its course.

46

I had been typing various versions of the script for *200 Motels* for over a year, and in November 1970 Frank submitted a ten-page treatment to United Artists. He convinced them that by using video tape instead of film, several cameras at once instead of one, he could shoot the film in a week. There was no disguising his pleasure when they agreed and put up $630,000.

Unusually, Frank became quite canny about cutting costs, and when he found he could hire the Royal Philharmonic for £1,000 a session, he arranged to move the entire shoot to England. It also meant that he and Gail could go over early and spend the holiday season there. There was a job for me, too – five weeks work on the production. Brilliant! Here was my chance to not only experience real filmmaking, something I wanted more than anything, but also once again I could work full-time for Frank.

I spent Christmas in the bosom of my family. My sister, Carole, who'd paid £300 for my Mini and fitted it with seat belts as per the new law, kindly loaned it back to me so I could whizz up to Notting Hill Gate, where Frank and Gail had set up home in a terraced Edwardian house with big draughty rooms on four floors.

At Pinewood Studios, Calvin slunk around, miserable. With Frank, he had designed weird and wonderful sets for their imaginary town, Centreville: along Main Street, a newt farm, a colonics parlour, a bank, a meat market and a motel. There was also a psychedelic night club, Electric Circus Factory, and a bar called Redneck Eats. On the wall at the end of Main Street, they painted a huge 747 to depict an airport while at the other end, barbed wire and a guard tower represented a concentration camp. Stylised and unreal, it looked terrific, but Calvin had not incorporated sufficient space in each set for a film crew so Leo Austin, the art director, took charge and overrode a great deal of Calvin's work.

I, too, suffered disappointment when Frank gave me no official role on the production, but on the other hand, as his personal assistant, I saw at close range his remarkable ability to cope with disasters which lesser mortals might have stamped, shouted and raged about but which Frank dealt with in a calm, pragmatic manner, never losing his cool. Jeff Simmons, who played the leading role, quit the first day of rehearsals, a major disaster to most directors, but Frank simply asked, 'Who else can we get?' And when Wilfrid Brambell – who'd played Paul's grandfather in the Beatles' film *A Hard Day's Night* and who probably thought he was in for a similar project – agreed, he suffered nine days of rehearsals before he, too, walked out on the first day of the shoot.

Though clearly furious, Frank remained stoical and sat around with the band trying to figure out who would replace the replacement. Then Martin Lickert, Ringo's chauffeur, walked in and there were whoops and applause as everyone cried, 'You!' A carbon copy of Jeff, young and thin with long, tapered hair, he read the script, sounded good and just by chance, also played bass. A new star was possibly born.

Jimmy Carl Black played Lonesome Cowboy Burt and Don Preston resumed his *Uncle Meat* role as the mad scientist. Motorhead became a newt rancher and Dick Barber a vacuum cleaner. Mark and Howard played themselves.

Frank had scripted the lines to coincide with the music but, with insufficient time to learn their parts, the cast ad-libbed most of it. Theodore Bikel, the only professional actor, refused to say the word 'fuck' – another minor problem.

The story told of a rock'n'roll band on the road and how it drove them crazy. I'd become so used to scenes with vibrators that turned into machine guns or girls unable to climax that I no longer flinched, even when Howard whipped a groupie with a baby octopus or sprayed her with corn. She declared, 'The only thing that might make me come is if you tell me that you *love me*,' and Howard replied with one of the few witty lines, 'Wait a minute, that's going too far!'

Frank had hired Tony Palmer, an expert in shooting film with video tape, to direct the film. So, not surprisingly, Tony became miffed when Frank took total charge and Tony found himself sidelined to an assistant's role. You could find him in the back shrugging his shoulders and smirking. He later told a reporter it was the worst film he'd ever worked on.

While they rehearsed a scene at one part of the set, filming took place in two others. But as the week progressed, like everyone else, I became disillusioned with the under-rehearsed, rushed and badly acted scenes. Out of Frank's earshot, mutterings of discontent and criticism crackled round the back lot.

Throughout the film, the orchestra sat behind barbed wire in the concentration camp and played the entire score of *200 Motels*. Also imprisoned and dressed in warden uniforms were the lead soprano and choir, who sang 'tinselcock' repeatedly. The funniest moment occurred when Keith Moon, haphazardly dressed in a nun's habit, ducked and dove through the orchestra rows while Ringo Starr, dressed as Frank Zappa in his beard and wig, chased him. I thought it hilarious and could not stop laughing.

My eyes turned to Frank, who walked around naked but for a bead necklace over his hairy chest and jeans high on his waist. Always he issued orders, suggestions and ideas with the quietest, most reassuring voice. For his own part in the film, he sat at a desk supposedly writing the script before the camera zoomed through the window to the actual scene.

In the evenings, he withdrew to his house. I took my sister Carole to meet him again. They'd met after an Albert Hall concert when she'd taken him to Blazes nightclub in my Mini and got lost. Frank had asked her, 'Do you always burst into song like Pauline?' an observation he'd never commented on to me. He looked handsome in a ribbed, tight-fitting roll-neck sweater and jeans, his hair skimming his shoulders. While he lounged low in an armchair at one end of the long, narrow living room and played the day's orchestral tapes, Carole and I sat at the other end. But Carole, unaware of the rules, kept chatting to me until finally I whispered, 'Stop talking.' We sat silently listening to the music for half an hour until I sensed that Carole, and probably Frank, could stand it no longer.

When I took my friend Pat, head-turningly pretty, groomed and stylish, to visit the studio and house, Gail asked me, 'Why does she always wear red?' I said, 'Does she? I hadn't noticed,' but Gail knew and I knew that Pat had caught Frank's eye because once her red, high-heeled shoe and a perfectly shaped calf disappeared through the door, Frank snapped at Gail, 'Why don't you brush your hair for once?' and she skulked off looking everywhere and nowhere, concealing the hurt.

At the end of the week, after seven days of intense filming, Frank gave no farewell speech and, amid a mixture of euphoria and sadness, everyone slipped away like snakes into the long grass. Still, there was more work to be done and Frank remained in England to edit the film and prepare for his concert of *200 Motels* at the Albert Hall. Gail and the children stayed with him but my task was finished and I returned to California.

On 8 February, Gail telephoned from London with upsetting news. The Albert Hall, where the Mothers were due to play *200 Motels*, had cancelled that very morning. Four thousand fans who'd paid £2.2s for tickets would have their money returned.

Gail said the officials had looked at the content of the programme and found the lyrics obscene. 'Do you know what word they were complaining about?'

'No.'

'Crap!'

I laughed. 'It's got a different meaning in England.'

'Then some woman complained about the line, *"What kind of girl wears a brassiere to a pop festival?"* Can you believe that? It's insane. Frank is tearing his hair out. He agreed to take out every "fuck" and "bullshit" but stalled at "Penis Dimension".'

'Oh, well, no wonder.'

'And everyone still wants to be paid so Frank is going to have to find the money out of his own pocket. The London Philharmonic is over one hundred and forty people! Do you know how much that is going to cost?'

'Goodness, a lot.'

'Frank is gonna sue.'

I wondered why Frank would rather hand out money to lawyers than eat humble pie and meet the demands of the Albert Hall.

I had begun to feel that the Zappas had swallowed up my life and so, while they were still in England, I used the opportunity to loosen my ties and put down new roots. I contacted several women's organisations and planned to join their meetings; I visited an organisation for deaf and dumb children and agreed to help; I went to openings of art galleries and meetings about violence on television and its effect on children. I started to meet a new group of people, which made me busy and excited. Unlike my early impressions, when people in Laurel Canyon seemed to be a crowd of introverted soul-searchers lacking in passion, I now saw an intelligent, thoughtful group, socially aware. I began to buy books like *How to Find Your Inner Self* and *How to Win Friends and Influence People*, and I began to question the meaning of my life and what I wanted from it. Overall, Los Angeles was proving to be a great liberator.

In the middle of this, in March 1971, Frank, Gail and Calvin returned and somehow my new interests lost focus. Calvin immediately got down to animated work for *200 Motels* with Fred Wolf.

I eagerly raced over to Whitney Studios in Glendale to see Frank and Gail because yes, I had missed them.

Frank was working alone, deep into editing the soundtrack of *200 Motels* and Gail, who had the left the children in her younger brother Midget's care, had chauffeured Frank over and stayed to offer support. In a sour mood – what with the Albert Hall fiasco and now grumbles about United Artists – Frank complained, 'They gave us eleven days to edit which was bad enough, but then they took the used video tapes, erased them all and now they plan to sell them as "used stock". Hours of material I could have used elsewhere, they chewed up.' His hard expression conveyed anger, but somehow he subsumed it into a black hole, never raising his voice above a low drawl.

It was two o'clock in the morning and I bade them goodnight. When I reached my car and turned on the ignition, the engine would not catch despite my persistent attempts. I trudged back into the studio and asked Gail if she would help me push it, half hoping that Frank might leap from his chair and offer too, but he remained rooted to the monitor. So Gail and I, in a deserted street, huffed and puffed trying to move the car, but it would not budge. There was nothing for it but to phone the emergency services and disturb Frank again. When he saw me, his face turned icy, one of the few times he and I seemed out of harmony. He said to Gail, 'Why don't you give the kids a call? Check out what Midget's up to.' Suddenly he was a devoted husband. He seemed to imply that my predicament was my fault, especially if I'd wrecked his father's car, especially if it required Gail to go out into the street late at night, and especially if it interrupted his work on something as important as *200 Motels*.

47

The plan at the back of my mind when I'd come to Hollywood, insofar as I'd had a plan, had been to work for Frank Zappa for a while, then when I had met lots of film stars, I would leave Frank and work for a top actor or director. Through those connections, I would make a breakthrough and find a job with a writer. That was as far as the plan went, as far as it needed to go. But now I realised how naive a plan it had been. After eighteen months, the only film star I'd met fleetingly was Sammy Davis, Jr and the only Oscar-winner was Fred Wolf. In any case, my modus operandi had shifted. Actors and directors, I'd learned through magazines and gossip, were full of hot air and insufferably vain. The talented people in Hollywood were the writers. But it was no longer my ambition to work for one. I wanted to *be* that writer. Frank, with his endless faith in my abilities, had encouraged that ambition. I noted that the University of California ran a course on journalism and the idea began to grow in my mind that I could apply for their course. At last I could live out my dream, rise out of the secretarial trap and achieve equality with men. It would gratify all the aspirations that had unfolded in me in America, a place where anything was possible. Yes, you too could become President of the United States, or, if not the president, then a journalist at least. I would support myself by working part-time for Frank and I would be the first graduate in my family – a thrilling prospect.

When I told Frank of these plans, he turned sour. It was a hot night and he lay bare-chested, stretched out on a lounger next to mine. His hair was scraped back and he wore baggy cotton mauve trousers. Moon was paddling expertly on the li-lo and Gail stood waist-deep at our end with a wriggling, squealing Dweezil. As the still darkness of the warm night closed about us, Frank said, 'Why do you think a course in journalism will make you a better journalist? A long time ago we didn't have schools for journalists and yet they published magazines.'

Moon called out for Frank to watch her jump into the pool but he sent a cursory wave. 'You know what I think will happen if you go to UCLA? They'll turn you into a robot asking the same boring questions as everyone else.' He began pointing with his thumb to emphasise his point. 'Teachers in those places – their business is to breed a certain kind of student and at the end of it, if you conform to their stereotype, they'll give you a piece of paper with a star on it. If I were you, I wouldn't go near the place. Just write your own pieces and send them off.'

It was all right for Frank, he had an ego sufficient to blast him into space. I did not. I needed encouragement; I needed to share my progress with others. For once, I disregarded Frank's advice and decided to apply.

And then a strange thing happened.

I was driving down one of those streets which run like a beam of light for several miles through the Valley, flat scrubland on either side. Strong winds had blown away the smog and the Hollywood Hills, coloured mauve in the shadow of the sun, loomed ever closer. Then, all at once, those huge blocks of granite got up and jumped, in little hops, to the left. Not only that, but the road, which I knew travelled straight ahead, decided to bend like a hose and follow them. I thought I would pass out and slammed on the brakes, skidding to a halt on the verge. I looked around to see if anyone else was alarmed, but the cars sped past seemingly unconcerned. How could such a thing happen? How could solid rocks, half a mountain high, jump sideways? How could a road that I knew to travel straight ahead snake off in another direction? Were my eyes playing tricks? I blinked hard and slowly the hills and road slid back to their rightful position as if transported on a conveyor belt.

I sat clutching my head as blood thudded in my ears and I could barely breathe. Clearly, something was wrong. Should I get out and flag down a passing car and ask for help? But what would I say? 'The hills just moved. They did. They moved!' I imagined their response, 'That's nothing, man. I've seen them explode!' It was useless. I must somehow get home. I put the car into 'drive', gripped hard on the steering wheel and stared at the horizon, trying to paralyse it with my unblinking stare.

I told no one about my mishap, not wanting to sound like a hypochondriac. In any case, after a few days I began to believe that my imagination *had* played tricks. Perhaps it was the result of long hours and overwork? But then, a week later, as I sat in Du-Par's on Fairfax with Calvin and Dee (Herbie's bookkeeper), the wall at the far side of the restaurant suddenly lifted up and, in little hops, shifted twelve feet to the left. I grabbed the edge of the table to stop from falling off my chair and called out. This was no hallucination. This was real. Calvin and Dee, who'd been discussing how to share out the bill, looked up and saw my drained face.

'What's up?'

'The painting! Look!' but as I pointed to a picture of a clown, it returned to its rightful position as if pulled by string. I felt sick and thought I would throw up the steak pie we'd just scoffed. I could tell from Calvin and Dee's worried glances that they were concerned. I walked out of the restaurant on unsteady feet, more from shock than the symptoms that had subsided as quickly as they'd appeared. Dee said, 'You looked like you'd seen a ginormous spider.'

In the morning, I called my doctor for a complete check-up, a check-up I could ill afford. They found nothing wrong with my eyes or my body but pressed a letter in my hand for my ear specialist. It was marked 'extremely urgent'.

Despite my mother sending Sofradex eardrops – a steroid treatment for the chronic ear-infection and swollen glands I'd suffered since a bout of measles in childhood – repeated infections every time I sneezed or caught a cold had forced me to seek medical advice. By now I was familiar with the ear specialist's sumptuous waiting room and knew to pick the chintz sofa by the plate-glass window and grab the latest *Vogue* to flick through.

My specialist, a handsome man who wore rimless glasses, had already told me on my first visit that the infection had eaten away the three bells in my left ear, three bells that magnified sound into the inner ear. He'd peered through his metal, cone-shaped device and exclaimed, 'In thirty years I have not seen ears as bad as yours. You just don't see ears like this in America. Didn't they give you antibiotics?'

'No. They used to heat up steel hooks over a flame and scrape. I learned not to cry.'

He told me, 'In someone so young, it's very serious, and you should consider an operation to restore your hearing.' I had refused.

This time he led me through to a special room where I lay down on what looked like an operating table under a huge camera and gadgets. After a lengthy inspection probing deep into my left ear, he told me that the infection had permeated through the bone and was leaking into my brain, and this despite endless doses of antibiotics over the past year. 'It is essential we operate and cut out the diseased bone immediately. We will do what we call a mastoidectomy.'

The word 'mastoidectomy' had a peculiar poetical ring about it, which explained how I remembered it when telling Frank and Gail later.

My handsome doctor stared at me waiting for my response.

'I'll have to give it some thought.'

'*Give it some thought?*' he scoffed, screwing his face in disbelief. 'This is serious business, Miss Butcher, not a gym application.'

I'd heard so many stories about specialists drumming up business on false diagnosis, I felt sure this was salesmanship. I said, 'Well, I have some work to finish.'

'Miss Butcher,' he said with as much seriousness as he could intone, 'maybe you don't understand. This is the kind of problem you take care of *now*; you take care of it *yesterday,* not next week or next month. I can't state that too strongly. We're talking about possible meningitis, even brain damage. You cannot wait.'

Brain damage! *Brain damage!* Immediately I sat up straight, petrified. The vehemence in his voice, the way he peered directly into my eyes finally convinced me. I was ill! I felt weak and helpless. He gave me a double-dosed antibiotic injection, pressed a bottle of antibiotic pills in my hand, said I would be hospitalised for up to a week and sent me through to the nurse next door to discuss finances. Without finance, regardless of urgency, I would not get the operation.

There followed page after page of questions about my medical history, diet, job, where I lived, family and who could look after me after I left hospital. When I told the white-coated nurse that I had no money at all, she told me financial assistance would take weeks and was there someone who could lend me three thousand dollars, which would include the cost for the surgeon, anaesthetist, hospital stay and medication? She said I should convalesce for a month and probably not work for another two months.

I staggered out of their office in a state of shock; bewildered and now terrified I might have another attack that could damage my brain. I needed my mother, my dear mother whom I'd neglected with no letters for months. In a terrified state, my head swimming with the surgeon's words, 'meningitis and brain damage', I phoned home.

What happened next happened fast. I made hurried phone calls to family and friends as well as Frank because he was in Canada, chucked books, photographs and knick-knacks into boxes ready to store in Frank and Gail's garage along with the car they'd so generously handed me, and within minutes, it seemed, I was wrapping Gail, Moon and Dweezil in my arms and kissing them goodbye. As I climbed into Calvin's jalopy for the trip to the airport, I did not feel sad at all. In a flick of an eyelid I would be back.

48

In the morning when I awoke, for a drowsy moment, I was working for Frank again and the sun was bright in the lemon trees outside my window and the larks sang and the musty smell of cats slumbered at my feet. I was happy and carefree. Then I heard the screech of curtains round the bed and there was a startled moment when I realised, 'Why, I'm in hospital and I've left California behind.'

Trying to ignore the pain, the tubes down my throat and my tongue, thick and black, I concentrated my thoughts on Mick Jagger.

The day after I'd arrived in England, my friend Oonagh had telephoned telling me about a job in the South of France for the Rolling Stones. 'It's your type of thing, I think. Their secretary is leaving in September, can't take it much more, but I believe there's a flat involved and they aren't ungenerous with their pay. You might try for it. I'm sure with Frank's references you would get it standing on your head. Apparently, they daren't advertise for obvious reasons and they need someone used to freak scenes but also efficient. St Tropez should do you the world of good and enough money to pay back your debts.'

The timing could not have been worse. Mr Zwiefach, a Polish ear specialist close to retirement, had inspected my ears that morning. He'd used none of the hi-tech space-age equipment employed in America. Instead, he'd held up a finger and moved it slowly to my far left. 'Keep your head straight ahead and follow my finger with your eyes.' He'd repeated the procedure across my field of vision to the far right. After several goes of this quick inspection, he'd announced with grand authority, 'There's no threat of brain damage! If there were, the pupils in your eyes would dance about, but they don't.' As if to show his superior skills over the Americans, he'd found suspicious polyps in my throat that they'd missed. 'We must check those immediately.' I staggered out of the clinic in a state of shock. Throat cancer! By comparison with a death sentence, who could care less about a job with Mick Jagger? On the other hand, it would take my mind off the worry so, while I waited for a bed in hospital, I made the trip to the South of France. My brother said, 'If working for Frank Zappa gets you an invite to meet Mick Jagger, think what working for Mick Jagger might do.' True, true.

Mid-afternoon, in a mini-palace overlooking Cannes, Mick Jagger had shuffled into his exquisite library wearing a short maroon dressing gown which exposed his hairy legs. He had no idea what to ask me or how to run an interview and I'd kept saying, 'Why don't you tell me something about the job?' and he'd kept flapping the tassel of his dressing gown and staring down at his naval. He remembered me from the log cabin because, with a sly little grin, he said, 'Must have been somethin' working for Zappa. How the hell did that happen?'

'Well,' I began, but then I thought, *really!* Was I ever going to meet anyone who showed any interest in me beyond the fact that I worked for Frank Zappa? So all right, I could understand it with people outside the music scene, people who might be keen to hear about anyone who was famous, but Mick Jagger? A man as pivotal to the rock world as anyone could be and yet he, too, wanted to hear not about my expertise or my skills or how I could do his job. Oh, no, none of that, only the story about how I'd met an American icon. And I have to say that by this time these questions had begun to irritate. Surely there was more to me than Frank Zappa? Slightly offhand, I said, 'It was very interesting.'

'What did you do?'

'Well, I worked a lot with the GTOs – '

'Oh, no,' he said, interrupting. 'That's no good. That's not a qualification for this job.'

'What qualification would that be?'

'Well, a business brain for a start.'

Despite this faulty beginning, our easygoing chatter went on for an hour and I could see he warmed to me. He said, 'I've had a better chat with you than the other two girls. Do you know, one of them kept telling me how clever she was to get her boss's poodle on a plane! And the other one, well, forget it. She was shaking so much, I think if I'd raised my voice, well – I'm pretty even tempered but if I do lose it, the last thing I want is some bird blubbing on me.'

We shared the humour in the story, both smiling. Then, all at sea about how to finish the interview, he said, 'What shall we do now?' and I said, 'Why don't we sleep on it? See how we feel in the morning.' I realised that this was a disastrous tactic as soon as I'd opened my mouth but really, I did not want to commit. I might be dead in a week.

A few days after my operation I got a call from Jo, Mick's present secretary. Against the odds, she had agreed to stay on, so it felt like fair dues when my specialist, Mr Zwiefach, informed me that the operation had been a false alarm, the suspected tumour in my throat was not malignant. However, he said, I must stay in England for six months for follow-up checks on my throat as well as my ears.

A letter dated 20 September arrived from Gail full of love and concern. She told me that Frank had a new assignment that she thought I would enjoy and that it would give me something else to think about, other than my illness. She wrote that Noel Redding would be in touch with me shortly about his diaries, as he'd agreed for them to be included in *The Groupie Papers*. My job was to type them up. Gail also told me that David Walley's book on Frank was coming out in December, but she was sceptical about its content because he didn't know of my existence and hadn't interviewed any of the band.

After a card arrived from Noel Redding's mother, I took the train to Dymchurch to collect his diaries. The Kent scenery flashed by unnoticed as I sunk my nose, captivated, inside Eldridge Cleaver's book of letters, *Soul on Ice*. I soaked up the anger and violence that he'd acquired during his incarceration in prison so that by the time I alighted at the tiny Dymchurch Station I felt rage on behalf of all the black people in America. I stopped at the news kiosk to buy a newspaper and placed my handbag on the counter so I could retrieve my purse deep inside. The saleswoman asked me to take my bag off her magazines and when I continued searching, she leaned across and shoved it to the ground, cascading every bit and bob from my bag all over the ground. On reflex, I said, 'How dare you?' picked up a paperback and tossed it over her head. Her face drained of colour which egged me on, and while she stood paralysed with shock, I picked up another brand-new book and tossed it over my shoulder, then another and another, throwing them this way and that. With half her books littering the ground, and not quite sure what had come over me, I dumped the money for the paper on the counter, straightened myself tall, turned my back and stalked off.

On the journey home, I dipped into all four of Noel's diaries. To my dismay, none of the entries consisted of more than two, three or four words. 'Got up, ate cereal, read my book, van not ready.' Even when on a major tour with Jimi Hendrix, his entries grew no more expansive. 'Went to gig, went down a bomb, Hendrix did a moody, may have the clap.'

Seated in our sun-lounge that we converted into a temporary study, I slogged through page after page hoping that before Frank arrived, I would achieve some enlightenment regarding Noel's life – to no avail.

On 14 November 1971, Frank telephoned and I raced up to the Royal

Garden Hotel to meet him. By now, I understood why he sought my company. He did not socialise with the Mothers or any other musicians and certainly not rock stars. Herbie was not exactly a friend and there were no groupies in sight. I believe he felt I was one of the few people he could relax with. I'd shared his history for the past three years and knew his family well. I demanded no explanations or defence of his actions.

His suite was identical to the one where we'd met what seemed like aeons ago, only this time we were higher up and the view across London grander. I said, 'It's four years, three months, less one day since you came into my life.' He indicated a one-inch gap between his finger and thumb and said wryly, 'You were wearing white boots and a skirt about this small.' I laughed and told him how everyone was curious about how we'd met and he said gently, 'Well, better get writing.'

He lay back in the corner of the sofa while I plumped up the cushions at the other end. A few phone calls intruded but otherwise we were alone for nearly three hours. We drank whisky and coffee and gossiped about everyone back in LA. He told me that Jimmy Carl Black had made an album. 'I told him it was very commercial. That kind of pepped him up a bit,' Frank said with a chuckle. Calvin had apparently cut his hair. 'I've told him to start researching computer animation and 3-D images. I think that's where the future lies.'

The new 'Mothers' band with Howard Kaylan and Mark Volman as lead singers was doing well. Their second LP, *Fillmore East,* a live album released in June 1971, had reached Number 38 on the *Billboard* charts, their best success in the States yet. To my disappointment, this album and *200 Motels* marked the transition to more songs about groupies and sex. There was less about social issues, although 'Rudy Wants to Buy Yes a Drink', about a union boss, was an exception.

I told Frank about my trip to see the Rolling Stones. 'I met Bianca Jagger at Mick's house. She was nine months pregnant and had on a long white dress cut to the waist so her breasts hung out heavy and blue-veined. It was like she was some kind of reigning queen and I was her subject. Very regal. I went to Keith Richards's huge ramshackle mansion first, right on the Mediterranean at Cap Ferrat. Anita, his wife, kept complaining about him being away on long tours and how they never had a holiday together. She was really fed up. She wants them to tour anonymously in small clubs all over Europe.'

While I talked, Frank watched me closely, as he always did, his quiet calmness sending me rattling on. 'As a group, they appear to be quite wild. Their chauffeur told me stories. Apparently, one night they had dinner overlooking the Mediterranean and ended up pouring the soup and wine all over the floor and smashed every plate and glass. Another time, they went one better and threw the tables and chairs into the sea. The proprietor brought the bill and Mick Jagger apparently tore it in half and paid fifty percent.'

Always interested, always wanting to know more, I ploughed Frank with details, how broke the Rolling Stones had been, even recently, when they'd not even had enough money to pay their staff. Now the Stones used the Bank of England to take care of their earnings.

Frank asked me about Noel Redding's diaries.

'I find them boring,' I complained, and gave him a few examples.

'Well, impose your own treatment on them. Put yourself as a character into the book and write it from the first person.'

I shook my head in wonder at Frank's perpetual urging me onwards and upwards, loving him too for his unending faith in my wish to be a writer. 'If you find it difficult, then write it like your letters that you write to me, even write the whole thing as if it's a letter.' He went on in this encouraging vein for quite some time and I could have hugged him. No other person inspired me as he did. I wanted to dash home and start immediately, but he was in a talkative, amiable mood and on those occasions, I found him the best company in the world.

He told me about Noel Redding's visit to his house and how they'd jammed for a while but, owing to technical difficulties, Frank had only captured one song on tape. 'Noel's just signed with Atlantic Records,' Frank said, now leaning forward and animated. 'He played me some of their efforts but I told him he wasn't ready to record.'

'What did he say to that?'

'He ignored it,' Frank said with a shrug. 'But his exit was kind of spectacular. He disappeared into the midnight air and emerged by the garage at the bottom of our steps with a broken arm. So now, he can't even rehearse. He kept telling me he's not interested in suing. I told him, "I didn't ask if you would."' Frank looked at me, incredulous, and I shook my head with empathetic disbelief. 'His doctor told him if he'd been drunk he probably wouldn't have hurt himself!'

Light-hearted banter seemed to flow easily between us. I flung off my heels and curled my legs beneath my maxi-dress. He gave me a copy of *Billy the Mountain*, his latest film script, to take home to read, the story of a mountain that gets a royalty cheque for all the postcards sold with his image. I asked, 'Do you remember when you wrote the very first outline of this? Gail and I were lying on the bed with Moon and Dweezil and you brought a handwritten sheet and Gail read it aloud and you kept stopping her to add minute details?'

Frank nodded, a little smile peeping from under his moustache. I didn't mention how mystified I'd been when he'd screwed up his nose with an 'euwwoo' to describe fluids oozing from Ethell, Billy's wife, a tree growing out of Billy's shoulder, and Frank's wide-eyed wonderment when Gail described the tree taking off into the sky. He'd waved his arms in ballet fashion to illustrate the roots trailing into the clouds like the tentacles of a jellyfish. When Frank had returned to the basement, I'd expressed misgivings to Gail, but she'd said it was a fairytale for children. Now, in London, I read the latest version and had the sense to admire it. He told me it was quite changed from the earlier versions and gave me a long account of the new storyline, vividly acting it out with facial expressions and gestures.

Finally, we talked about *200 Motels*. Frank was in London for the premiere. He said it had received favourable reviews in America but since Frank always praised his own work, I relied on Calvin, who wrote to say the film was 'selling like hotcakes in LA and Boston and has broken box-office records'. Frank gave me a copy of the script to take home and tickets for the premiere.

'I've had a good time,' he said giving me the fondest of hugs. 'Come by in a couple of days. There's someone I want you to meet. She's a filmmaker. I think you'll like her.'

Another letter arrived from Gail, who was thrilled that I would figure prominently in the diaries. She told me I was the letter-writer in the family and must keep on writing to her because Frank provided only skeletal information 'with all your amusing approach left out'.

Well, he wouldn't tell her everything. How could he?

49

'Come and meet Karen Sperling,' Frank called as I entered his hotel suite. A young, dark-haired woman with natural beauty came forward and shook my hand. She wore embroidered jeans, with a low-slung belt and a maroon silk top. Frank leaned on the back of the armchair and pulled her to him, trapping her between his legs and wrapping his arms around her incredibly slim waist.

'You're a filmmaker?' I ventured.

While Frank kept nuzzling into the nape of her neck she told me how she'd written, directed and starred in her film, *Make a Face*. 'It's excellent,' Frank said. His praise galled me more than her mere presence. It indicated how much he liked her. She radiated health, like women do when they're in love, full of smiles and blooming, but I found their silly, romantic smooching insufferable and left after half an hour.

At the premiere the next day at the London Pavilion, Piccadilly Circus, I leaned back in the luxurious seats and found my senses assaulted by weird special effects, rapid cuts, flashing screens and double exposures intermixed with clear, sharp, vibrantly coloured scenes. Crude, funny and far-out, the film conjured up life on the road, and Keith Moon as the nun, once again, made me laugh aloud. Who else but Frank would include newts dancing from the concentration camp and a clever animation sequence of the hero's acid trip in the motel room? Brilliant editing had somehow transformed the seven days of chaotic filming into a coherent storyline. And all the while, the London Philharmonic Orchestra sat behind barbed wire and played the pulsating, throbbing, maniacal score. Mark and Howard gave an impressive stab at Frank's songs about their obsession to get laid and penis dimensions, and the whole film vividly evoked how touring with a rock'n'roll band *will* drive you crazy.

Symbols in the film I recognised: the vacuum cleaner spouting white liquid evoked his mother's incessant vacuuming; the magic lamp and foaming liquids, his teenage experiments with explosives; and from Catholicism, the devil played by Theodore Bikel, who induced the characters to do things against their will. Frank's talent seemed to be a bottomless pit full of ingenuity, invention and originality. As far as I could see, the film had no precedence other than a brief nod to *2001: A Space Odyssey.* I loved all of it, but then I was biased.

Frank and the Mothers left the next day for a mad dash around Europe, seventeen cities in twenty days, the sort of tour that drives you crazy. Frank encouraged me to meet up with Karen while he was gone and I thought, 'Uh-oh, here I go again, everybody's friend.' She invited me to the screening of her own film at the National Film Theatre. It told the story of a wealthy girl, Nina, played by Karen, who lived alone in her lavish, high-ceilinged apartment in the Dakota building on Central Park, the building where John Lennon would be murdered nine years later, and the apartment where Karen actually lived. The film followed her reclusive life with her dog, her art, her radio, television and many imagined terrors. For an hour and a half her face dominated the screen save for her psychiatrist and a menacing leather-jacketed figure who kept appearing in the elevator and outside her door – only to disappear when she tried to show him to anyone else.

Unlike *200 Motels*, which displayed sharp, clear colours, raucous songs and fast editing, Karen's film took the conventional, moody and sensual path; shot with dark, fuzzy colours and long, languid shots. The two films, though both fantasies, could not have been more different. In Karen's film, she exhibited sexuality by lounging in the nude with her dog, a scene that no doubt got Frank hopping in his seat, while Frank conveyed sex in his film through girls dancing topless coupled with smutty dialogue. Ringo Starr spoke the lines, 'He wants me to fuck the girl with the harp. He wants me to stuff the magic lamp up her reproductive orifice,' followed by the most sinister, devilish laugh.

Karen was just as convinced of her film's excellence as Frank was of *200 Motels*. She said, 'We are both very gifted, visually and artistically.' I wrote in my diary: 'Karen talks incessantly of Frank, compares herself on the same level as him and thinks she and he could be like John and Yoko doing everything together. She is not as brilliant as Frank but thinks she is.'

Clearly, if you wanted to succeed, you must exude total confidence in your work. This I lacked, and I had no idea how I could ever acquire it.

Karen's friends, all equally young, rich and cavalier, made an attractive and alluring bunch and I found myself seduced. Did Karen's upper-class New York stock attract Frank as much as her artistic talent? In every respect, he'd moved socially upwards.

Following Frank's instructions, I loaned her my copy of *The Groupie Papers*. Perhaps she could adapt them to film. I pictured Karen trying to control the GTOs, but a different image crowded my mind: Karen, like Shirley Temple, tied to the stake while *my* girls pranced around the burning pyre whooping in the manner of Red Indians.

Once again, Frank's praises reached me, not from his own lips, but from a third party. 'Frank speaks very highly of you,' she said. Why was he always telling other people?

Karen quizzed me about Gail and it was all very tricky, yet I allowed it to happen. At night, I dreamed I was drowning and huge waves enveloped us all.

The band returned to London in a bedraggled state four days early. During their gig in Montreux on 4 December, a fire had broken out in the auditorium. Apparently, Frank had shown impressive nerve in the face of serious danger, urging the audience to remain calm and to leave the building in an orderly fashion. It was not a trivial fire and had quickly gutted the building, taking with it the Mothers' very costly equipment (an event that Deep Purple chronicled on their album *Smoke on the Water*). Even though they would have to hire instruments, the Mothers voted to continue the tour rather than abandon it, the most ill-fated decision Frank ever made.

He invited me to join him and Karen for an Italian meal. Also at the table were Dick Barber, Herbie and his wife, Suzie, and two friends of Karen's. By this stage, I'd become somewhat enchanted by the sophisticated, stylish Karen and began to think that she might permanently replace Gail. But then, at dinner, I saw the first hint that Frank found her non-stop attention cloying. While she possessively hugged his shoulders and continued to rap on about the films she and Frank would make together and the music they were going to record, he hardly responded. Instead, he spent most of the meal talking across the table to me. Even now, he found me alluring and I again felt that old love and affection. Yet I had to remind myself that although I was sure I had some rare, deep understanding that drew Frank and I inexorably together, I also knew that everyone else who had dealings with Frank felt the same way, felt that they too had some special link with him.

While we dallied through that pleasant evening, none of us could have imagined the personal disaster about to befall Frank. I had tickets for the final show on Saturday night at the Rainbow Theatre, but late Friday, news came on the radio that a madman had knocked Frank from the stage into the orchestra pit ten feet below, knocking him unconscious. Later Herbie told me Frank was in hospital and awake and added, with sick humour, 'Karen's at his bedside, but don't worry, Gail's on her way.'

When I went up to see him at the Weymouth Street Clinic, just off

Harley Street, he lay on his back, arm in a sling, one leg in the air in a cast. His head was bandaged like a mummy. You couldn't see his hair or his moustache, just his dark, sunken eyes and lips where they had cut a hole in the bandage. Because the doctors suspected concussion, they refused to give him painkillers, so that when the nurses came to adjust his position he cried out and cursed. Occasionally we'd help him light a cigarette with his one good hand, and I lit up, too. An anti-smoking commercial came on the black and white television. 'Another government conspiracy to prevent people enjoying themselves,' he croaked. Had the pain sent him slightly delirious? In protest, I stubbed out my own.

Trevor Charles Howell, the twenty-four-year-old labourer who had pushed Frank off the stage, had apparently become jealous of his girlfriend's lust for Frank. Did Frank think he should go to jail? After all, had he not told me two years earlier that no one should go to jail? But somehow, seeing Frank in agony was not the moment to challenge him. His bitter comments suggested that the worst kind of jail would not be adequate punishment for Mr Howell. 'Give him hell,' he croaked.

My heart hardened and I thought him a very poor patient indeed. I'd watched my father suffer agonies in silence and became irritated by Frank's lack of heroism. I should not have stayed two hours.

By my next visit, Gail had arrived and the doctors had given Frank painkillers, both events likely contributors to his resumed good humour. Herbie had described the charade he'd conducted to smuggle Karen in and out of Frank's room in between Gail's visits, but I imagine Karen soon got the message that Gail was number one. I never saw Karen again.

By Christmas, Frank had improved. They had removed the bandages from his head, and he and Gail appeared to be enjoying a honeymoon period. For Christmas, they gave me a vibrator and chuckled when I pulled my well-practised face of mock disgust.

On one of my visits in January, Frank was alone save for his new bodyguard, a large black man who sat bulging out of a chair in the corner. The bodyguard popped open a bottle of champagne and we shared it with Frank's nurse. Frank's arm had been let out of its sling and we drank to celebrate that he would play the guitar again. His leg, though, with its multiple fractures, would prevent him from walking for a year.

Propped up on pillows, he placidly watched TV. At a football match between Celtic and Rangers in Glasgow, a stampede in an overcrowded stairwell had crushed sixty-six people to death, the ghastly scenes plunging our room into stunned silence. It placed Frank's own calamity into perspective. The Open University began broadcasting that day and, given Frank's attitude toward university education, he surprised me. 'I think it's a good idea to help educate the masses.' When I told him that Herb's bookkeeper, Dee, had bought a colour TV, he surprised me again when he said, 'Maybe we'll buy one when I get back.' The accident had surely mellowed him. Peace and tranquillity filled the room and I had never known him to be so sweet. He asked how I was getting on with my book and when I told him I was finding it very hard, he said something to the effect of, 'Never stop until your "good" becomes better and your "better" becomes the best.' I never tired of lapping up his encouragement and told him I would bring the finished product back with me to LA in March or April. When I left, he held on to my hand as if he didn't want to let go.

I wrote in my diary: 'His affection I can feel. Our rapport has the same feeling to it as when we first met.'

Gail came in about eleven o'clock. She almost cried when I left, wrapped her arms round my neck and clung on. I believed we would be friends forever.

On 7 January, Frank and Gail left England, Frank in a wheelchair. I promised to follow as soon as the doctor gave me the all-clear. They waved goodbye like the happiest married couple.

50

My yearning to return to the shady glens of Laurel Canyon intensified when Mutt arrived in London with his new wife, Lyisha. Our squabbles forgotten, we gossiped across the table at the Ivy restaurant about our mutual friends, Gail, Calvin and the GTOs, all of whom kept writing, imploring me to go back. Pamela was writing about her groupie experiences. She wrote: 'You're about the only person who could help me get it together. So efficient, Pauline!' No one in England gave me such praise, and I made plans for a flight in April 1972.

Gail sent me the last batch of money for work on Noel Redding's diaries, but to finance my own writing I took up temporary secretarial work. I was lucky and worked for a lovely, young, red-haired doctor at an old-fashioned pharmaceutical company. On the first day, they sent me home to exchange my trousers for a skirt. Even the eating arrangements proved a shock: one canteen for the executives, another for the clericals, and a tacky place for manual workers.

Then, in May, another frightening thing happened – the office walls lifted up and made little hops to my far left. I grabbed the desk, petrified I would keel over, my brain damaged. I immediately telephoned Mr Zwiefach. Without hesitation, he rushed me to West Middlesex Hospital. My family paid for a private room with a telephone but it was a very poor imitation of Frank's sumptuous accommodation in Weymouth Street. It had no television or radio, bare green distempered walls, old furniture of the cheapest kind, linoleum just about clean, no towels by the sink and six flies buzzing in front of the open window.

When I opened my eyes after the operation, there was pain in my ear and the room rumbled with dull voices, distant as though in some far off place. Six images of a man in a white coat loomed, each image splayed on top of the other like a seriously out-of-focus photograph, and I cried out. After more muttering, the doctor leant close to my face and shouted, 'We're going to loosen the packing. It's pressing on the brain.'

Recuperation was slow – masses of running blood, twenty pills and two injections a day – it took two months before they killed off the infection. I continued to feel unwell and anxious. The doctor stuffed me with tranquillisers while I worried that if I did not return to America by August (one year since I'd arrived in England), I would lose my work permit. But Mr Zwiefach warned that I must stay under his care to ensure there were no leftover problems. In any case, I could hardly hear anything. In August, I wrote to the American Embassy and asked for an extension on my green card. To my surprise, they agreed. I could stay until April 1973.

Convalescing at home, I read books by Betty Friedan and Germaine Greer and articles in newspapers about women's rights. I learned that in working-class families, wives did not know how much their husbands earned and had no control over their weekly allowance. An ex-boyfriend told me, 'Women are so much better at being women. Why do they want to work in a man's world? I think it's taking the competitive instinct too far. Women have too much already.'

My childhood girlfriend, after years of secretarial work, had enrolled to study law at night school to become a lawyer. Women everywhere were breaking out. What was I doing? Closeted in my parents' house, the volume full up, I watched Open University programmes. They reignited my desire for a university education, an ambition I knew not to raise with Frank.

He arrived with Gail in September and sat in the corner of his hotel room, surrounded by strangers. As I approached, I saw his lips move and I said, 'Are you whispering?' and he said, 'No,' and I said, 'I knew this would happen, I can't hear you.' He spoke again, louder, but it was not natural for him to raise his voice. I said, 'I'm sorry, I just can't hear you,' and tears stung my eyes. He stood up and in front of everyone gave me a warm hug. 'Better now?' he asked with an affectionate smile and, feeling shy and embarrassed, I nodded. Gail smiled too, proud that her husband, as so often, had gauged the situation perfectly. Relieved, I reflected that our relationship had more to do with rapport than verbal communication.

After everyone else had gone, we moved to sit adjacent to each other so I could not only hear him properly but also lip-read – although his thick, black moustache made this difficult. Like two old fogies, we exchanged illness stories. 'Being confined to a wheelchair for nearly a year drove me insane,' Frank said, 'but the important thing is to use the energy from a negative event to drive you someplace else,' a gentle dig to pull myself together.

The doctors had urged me to get a hearing aid and when I told Frank, he said simply, 'I have to get my ears tested. I think I may need one of those.' I could have hugged him. In all our time together, I'd never heard him say an inappropriate word.

Even before my operation, my poor hearing had led me into silly situations. One time, when the plumber had called at the log cabin to mend the leak in my bedroom ceiling, he'd asked to look at Frank and Gail's bathroom. I had bounced up the stairs and knocked. It was mid-morning and Gail's faint voice had called out, 'Come in,' but when I'd opened the door, I saw Frank and Gail on the bed, naked. Gail, sitting with her back to me, turned and stared, her face aghast. '*Pauline.* I said, *don't* come in.'

At the hotel, Frank was pouring more coffee and I was still struggling to catch his quiet drawl. I said, 'I wrote an impassioned piece pleading for hearing aids to be designed like jewellery but every magazine I sent it to turned it down.'

'So? Send off another one. Just keep doing it. Don't be discouraged by failure. People who are afraid of failure are people who think themselves so great, they can't fail.'

I knew by now he did not direct his faith to me alone – members of his band received the same encouragement, and let's not forget his extraordinary formation and uplifting of the GTOs and Cynthia Plaster Caster. I'd absorbed his teaching: aim for the top and if you miss, grab something on the way down – anything is better than lounging at the bottom, never having tried.

After his accident, Frank had disbanded the Mothers headed by Mark Volman and Howard Kaylan. Now, a year later, he was on tour with a new combination, the Grand Wazoo. It included a twenty-piece electric symphony orchestra with six reed, six brass, two concert percussionists, synthesisers and an electric cello, and here they were playing at the Oval Cricket Ground. Gone were the comedy routines and songs about sex. In their place were driving instrumentals that tested the rock'n'roll audience. Journalists in broadsheet papers wrote intellectual pieces about the paradox, the juxtaposition, the anomaly of Frank's music, so diverse and unusual in rock'n'roll. 'Unique in music, Zappa goes places no one else will go,' they wrote. His name no longer evoked a maniacal weirdo but a serious-minded, intelligent, twentieth-century composer. The *Guardian* newspaper printed a large photograph of Frank and Gail, another indication that a wider world acknowledged his talent. There they stood in the middle of the cricket ground, Frank in his floor-length coat and Gail in a black cape and Doc Marten boots, a more striking couple would be hard to find.

I had not been backstage at a concert for months and found I knew only

Ian and Ruth, from whom I felt oddly estranged. Unexpectedly, Tony Duran, the slide guitarist, a very handsome Mexican, put his hands commandingly around my neck, looked hard into my eyes and ran off a eulogy about their beauty and what ends he would go to in order to employ me as *his* secretary. I brushed him aside rather rudely and he skulked away. When I expressed remorse to Jay, the road manager, he said, 'Don't feel sorry for Tony. He scores every night, each night a different chick. All the other guys in the band are jealous. They keep trying to score but they don't make it. Only Tony scores so don't feel sorry for him.'

Two hours later, one of the girls, Lixie – a groupie who knew many guys in bands, including Tony Duran – arrived. Jay said, 'I feel sorry for her. Last night she was with Tony, the night before with Fred and tonight she's with Jim.' He shook his head despondently. I jumped to her defence and surprised myself. 'Why do you feel sorry for her? She's doing the same as Tony. Every night he's with a different chick and you say he *scores*. Yo ho for Tony. But Lixie, you feel sorry for. Why? How do you know she isn't having a good time, too? Why is she spoken of in derogatory terms?'

Later in the evening, I found Frank alone behind a curtain at the back, strumming his guitar and in a sombre mood. Rehearsals had not gone well, the acoustics were dire and the whole show was running hours late because Herbie refused to let them go onstage without cash payment out front. So when I told Frank about Tony and Lixie, two little anecdotes that at one time might have grabbed his attention, he merely shrugged and looked bored, totally uninterested in the double standard. 'I don't know. I don't think that way, that's all I know about it.'

And yet, on a later European tour, Gail telephoned from the Royal Garden Hotel, inviting me to join her for dinner.

'Is Frank with you?'

'No.'

We ate in her room, steak and chips, followed by apple pie and ice-cream. Not until we started coffee did she tell me the reason for her sudden flit to London. Frank, it seemed, wanted an Australian girl to join them under their sheets and Gail had rebelled. If she felt heartache, she chose not to show it. 'It's tough to watch when he walks around with a fucking hard-on this big.' She spread her hands wide apart.

Frank's infidelities were, of course, not news to me, but with this episode I felt shame. How could I reconcile the two sides of Frank: on the one hand, the man I knew – the brilliant composer, kind, generous, thoughtful, inspiring, and so admirable, and yet, on the other, a man who abused his wife's feelings and wishes? I kept my disappointment to myself. Even in her low state, I knew

Gail would not tolerate negative comments about her husband from anyone. In any case, Gail saw herself as the real powerhouse in Frank's life, the lynchpin that held the family together – as indeed she was. 'I'm on the payroll just like everybody else around here,' she would say.

As the waiter wheeled the empty table from the room, the phone rang. When I heard Frank's voice on the line, I made a discreet exit to the bathroom. Frank wanted her to fly back to him and he would agree to all her demands. While she considered her options, she brushed a rolling tear aside. I never did find out what she chose.

A week later, Gail telephoned and left a message with my mother. 'My dear friend, Pauline,' she said. 'Thank you for your ears. I think the reason why you have hearing difficulties is that you haven't been using your ears – you listen with your heart. Will be in touch.'

Years later, I interviewed Frank in London and challenged him on this very point. He was staying at the Hyde Park Hotel and made a lonely figure in that immense, dour sitting-room decorated in dull, muted colours, and although the central heating was on the air felt cool. It was 17 April 1988, a few weeks before he disbanded the very last Mothers of Invention over a contentious issue and five years before he died of prostate cancer at the age of fifty-three.

He'd survived twenty years in the music business and produced fifty albums – an extraordinary compilation of social commentary, satire, doo-wop, jazz and progressive orchestrations, several of the albums reaching the top half of the American charts. He'd received six Grammy nominations, a Grammy for *Jazz from Hell* and another for Best Rock Instrumental Performance on *Sofa*. All the while, no one had played his records on the radio and yet over twenty years, he'd sold enough records to make him a rich man. In Europe and across America they both reviled and revered him. Even John Lennon, when he visited Frank, had been deferential. 'I may be popular, but he is the real thing.'

Now, here in the gloomy light, he seemed thinner than when I'd last seen him, the cheeks sagging from his narrow cheekbones, the hawk-bridged nose sharper. I noticed, more than before, that although his voice resonated with the same deep, quiet drawl that always commanded anyone's attention, now he broke every phrase with little coughs.

We sat on the sofa together, me fiddling with my Uher tape recorder, Frank squinting – the blue haze from his ever-present Winston wafting across the room. Since I'd given up the habit, I found it an irritant but I knew not to comment, knew that asking him not to smoke would be like begging a bee not to buzz.

Instead, I plucked up courage and said, 'Why is it that you grant yourself the right to a girl in every port whereas Gail is not allowed to flick an eyelash at any man?'

He'd looked at me oddly. Inscrutable. I could not tell if he was amused or annoyed. I don't think anyone had ever asked him that question before and indeed, he gave me the impression he'd not even seriously considered the point himself. I could see his mind ticking over as he bobbed his head this way and that, took a drag on his Winston, inhaled deeply, stubbed it out, took another and lit it before answering.

He said, 'Gail is my wife. We've been married for twenty-three years and we like each other. She takes care of me and the kids and the business. There is no one else I trust the way I trust Gail. She is good at what she does and although it distresses her sometimes, the amount of time I spend on the road and where my mind gets when I'm working a lot, she can still understand the value of it and her role in it. When I look around and I see marriages where the wives fuck guys other than their spouse, the marriages tend not to survive. It may seem unfair to say that, but it's true. I've seen it and Gail knows it too. She enjoys looking after the kids and I provide her with a nice lifestyle to go with it. That's our deal and that's why our marriage works. We're best friends.'

Here was proof that Gail's canny, feminine guile had worked. No matter how many other women appeared on the scene or how close they got to Frank, she'd hung in there and, one by one, they'd slid away.

I said, 'But what about sex? Surely that's important in a marriage? How do you have sex with your best friend?'

'Well, when you think about it, sex is very silly.'

He paused, brushing his fingers backwards through his hair, now wiry and streaked with grey. Did I hear correctly? 'When you get right down to it, when you look at it for what it is, at what's really going on, sex is just fucking silly.'

Astonished, I could but stare. Here was a man who, almost from the moment we'd met, had blasted on about 'lust', how lust was a major component in his life, the best form of exercise and all of that, the man who had admonished me for intellectualising sexual behaviour, scolded me for rationalising too much, and yet here he was reducing sex to something as absurd as a penguin's waddle. I had so many arguments against it; I was struck speechless.

At the beginning of the interview, Frank had seemed weary, the fire behind his dark eyes faded and the energy that had propelled him through forty-four concerts across America and Europe in the last seventy-six days momentarily gone, but by the time I'd turned off the tape recorder, some of his old wicked teasing and fun had returned. He told me, 'They were an unusual bunch of questions. No one has asked those sorts of questions before. You make a good interviewer.' Right to the end, he never failed to make me feel good about myself. Perhaps my questions stimulated his mind because when he returned to the States a month later, he dictated his autobiography, *The Real Frank Zappa Book*, in which he wrote a full chapter about Gail. After years of cynical comments about romantic love, he wrote simply, 'I met Gail and I fell in love.'

****

While I waited for my ear to heal, I had time to reflect on my hurried return to England, a trip unbidden and unwanted which had severed my life from America. More than one year had passed and I found it difficult to feel again that other bohemian person in Hollywood, a person who had experienced high self-esteem through closeness with Frank Zappa. Now, with this lengthy separation, questions began to niggle: why should association with someone famous, even infamous in some people's eyes, make me more worthy? Without Frank Zappa, I was surely the same person with the same qualities and quirks. If I did not go back to California or never spoke to Frank again, I would not disappear, people would still like me, perhaps even love me. I began to mention Frank's name less and less. When I met someone new, I mentioned his name not at all.

Once upon a time, before I went to Hollywood, I believed education was the road to enlightenment and success. Frank Zappa had overshadowed that view and in Hollywood it was glamour that had mattered – enter life with the beautiful people and you will attain everything you desire. Yet glamour had eluded me and women's lib had redirected my route. Now, back in England, I seemed to have come full circle. I learned that I could apply to study for a degree at Cambridge University. All I needed was three A-levels. I reckoned that if I studied economics, sociology and mathematics in the evenings over one year and worked during the day, I could do it. Cambridge would be more prestigious than UCLA, and Cambridge would give me status not reflected by Frank. But it was a gamble. If I remained in England, I would lose my American work permit. Worse still, there was no guarantee that, even with the best grades, Cambridge would accept me.

There was a clear-cut choice – return to the chaotic lifestyle in Hollywood, disciple to Frank, friend to Gail and surrogate mother to their children, or I could be brave and take a different route toward a university in England. The excited and naive girl with her notebook and pen who had arrived in Hollywood had, somewhere on the winding road through those four years, slipped away, and in her place stood a woman whose future, I hoped, lay in independence and the grey steeples of Cambridge.

Another card arrived from Gail: 'Everyone wants to know when you're coming – am I your agent? Love you to death, my dear! Love from the Munchettes too! Sincerely and embarrassedly, Gail.'

Resisting the gravitational pull from the West Coast, I began to fill in the form. Halfway through, I hesitated. Should I include the three years I worked in Hollywood? Did it matter? Would intellectuals be impressed? Would they even know Frank's name? What if by some quirk, the Cambridge scholar was nerdy enough to recognise the leader of the Mothers of Invention, would such a mention ensure me an interview? On the other hand, if faced with the inevitable question, 'How did you come to work for Frank Zappa?' the question that now irritated rather than thrilled, would I flunk the interview with my offhand reply? I scribbled through his name until it was illegible.

It had been my good fortune to meet Frank Zappa on that fateful day in August 1967 and I had reaped all the benefits and goodness from that union, its own education of sorts. Now it was time to fly from him just as I'd flown from my own family five years earlier. No longer content to be a bit-part player in someone else's drama, I wanted to be the heroine in my own show, plough my own furrow, stir my own waves and paint the future with my own brush. Yes, today was the last day I would bask in the reflected glory of Frank Zappa. From now on, I would chart my own.

PICTURE CREDITS

We would like to thank the following for supplying photographs: Warner/Reprise; Syndication; Melody Maker; Calvin Schenkel; Pauline Butcher Collection; Art Tripp; Art Tripp; Calvin Schenkel; Calvin Schenkel; Calvin Schenkel; Calvin Schenkel; Art Tripp; Rolling Stone; Ed Caraeff; Cynthia Plaster Caster; Cynthia Plaster Caster; Cynthia Plaster Caster; Joel Axelrad; Pamela Zarubica; Pauline Butcher Collection; Pauline Butcher Collection; Pauline Butcher Collection; Art Tripp; Warner/Reprise; Ed Caraeff; Ed Caraeff; Pauline Butcher Collection; Pauline Butcher Collection; Pauline Butcher Collection; Pauline Butcher Collection; Brenda Cohen; Ed Caraeff; Pauline Butcher Collection; London Evening News; Pauline Butcher Collection; DiscReet/Herb Cohen Management; Barrie Wentzell; Pauline Butcher Collection; Pauline Butcher Collection.